BEFORE SEATTLE ROCKED

BEFORE
SEATTLE
ROCKED

A City and Its Music

KURT E. ARMBRUSTER

. . .

UNIVERSITY OF WASHINGTON PRESS
Seattle & London

Before Seattle Rocked: A City and Its Music is published with the assistance of a grant from the Naomi B. Pascal Editor's Endowment, supported through the generosity of Janet and John Creighton, Patti Knowles, Mary McLellan Williams, and other donors.

This publication is also supported by a grant from the Musicians' Association of Seattle, Local 76–493, American Federation of Musicians, and by funding from the 4Culture Heritage Special Projects program.

UNIVERSITY OF WASHINGTON PRESS
P.O. Box 50096, Seattle, WA 98145, U.S.A.
www.washington.edu/uwpress

LIBRARY OF CONGRESS CATALOGING-IN-PUBLICATION DATA
Armbruster, Kurt E.
Before Seattle rocked : a city and its music / Kurt E. Armbruster.
   p. cm.
Includes bibliographical references and index.
ISBN 978-0-295-99113-9 (pbk. : alk. paper) — ISBN 978-0-295-80100-1 (ebook)
1. Music—Washington (State)—Seattle—History and criticism.
2. Music—Social aspects—Washington (State)—Seattle.
3. Musicians—Washington (State)—Seattle—Biography.
4. Popular music—Washington (State)—Seattle—History and criticism.
5. Popular music—Social aspects—Washington (State)—Seattle.
I. Title.
ML200.8.S43A43 2011
780.9797'772—dc22   2011005005

The paper used in this publication is acid-free and 90 percent recycled from at least 50 percent post-consumer waste. It meets the minimum requirements of American National Standard for Information Sciences—Permanence of Paper for Printed Library Materials, ANSI Z39.48–1984.

FRONTISPIECE PHOTO: The Jackie Souders Orchestra at the Olympic Hotel in 1955.
   Courtesy of Dick Rose
PAGE 7: Drawing by the author

To Ed "Tuba Man" McMichael (1955–2008),
a working musician

For Cedar

He that dances should always pay the fiddler.

—Abraham Lincoln

Contents

Acknowledgments

I WANT TO THANK Taylor Bowie Jr., Pete Leinonen, and the anonymous reviewers whose corrections and suggestions made this a better
book; my editors at University of Washington Press, Lorri Hagman
and Kerrie Maynes, for their encouragement and patient guidance; Warren Johnson, Monica Schley, Motter Snell, and the executive board of
the Musicians' Association of Seattle, Local 76–493, American Federation of Musicians, for their solid support; and Al Smith Jr. and Alexandra
Smith for granting access to Al Smith Sr.'s wonderful 1940s images. Most
of all, my warmest appreciation goes to all who lent their perspectives and
memories to this project: Chai Ahrenius, Douglas Q. Barnett, Overton
Berry, Norm Bobrow, Stan Boreson, Hugh Bruen, Harley Brumbaugh,
Tamara Burdette, Pamela Casella, Michael Crusoe, Marty Dahlgren,
Stuart Dempster, Don Firth, Burke Garrett, Dick Giger, Howard Gilbert,
Don Glenn, Scott Goff, Ed Gross, Bonnie Guitar, Gary Hammon, Bob
Hill, Mike Hobi, Dave Holden, Grace Holden, Jack Hungerford, Warren
Johnson, Stan Keen, Sally King, Milt Kleeb, Jim Knapp, Ed Lee, Pete
Leinonen, Rev. Samuel McKinney, Joni Metcalf, Lucy Mitchell, Johnny
Moton, Craig Nim, Ronald Phillips, Edward "Andy" Piatt, Ronnie Pierce,
Nick Potebnya, James Rasmussen, Jack Roberts, Dick Rose, Richard Sand-
erson, Monica Schley, Gerard Schwarz, Peter and Ellen Seibert, Ron
Simon, Don Smith, William O. Smith, Floyd Standifer Jr., Alice Stuart,
Jay Thomas, Walt Wagner, Jim Wilke, Phil and Vivian Williams, and Rev.
Patrinell Staten Wright. You made our world a joyful place!

BEFORE SEATTLE ROCKED

Everything was confusion. A vast space . . . a cat's cradle of arching girders . . . perfume and cigarette smoke . . . the hum of three thousand voices. Then everything went black. A blue-white spear lanced the darkness and lit up fifteen men in white coats, and out of chaos came a sound of indescribable sweetness. The audience fell silent and settled happily into their seats. Colored lights blazed, skaters twirled, but my eyes kept drifting back to the men in the white coats. I pointed to them. "The musicians," my mother said. I was hooked: The skating was good—but the music was better!

■ ■ ■

Introduction

OR GENERATIONS the men in white coats—and the women in black dresses—were the very definition of "musician." Music for these practitioners was not necessarily fun or artistically fulfilling. It was work. In theater pits and dance halls, taverns and opera houses, ballrooms and skating rinks, making music was a *job*. For much of the twentieth century, most of Seattle's working musicians belonged to the union—specifically, the Musicians' Association of Seattle, Local 76 of the American Federation of Musicians. The union dictated wage scales, work rules, and how many performers must be hired at the various classes of venues. Failure to obey the rules meant fines or expulsion. Venues deemed "unfair" by the union were boycotted, and support from sympathetic union brotherhoods—bartenders, stagehands, teamsters—made those boycotts effective.

Working Seattle musicians acquired professional standing through simple cultural evolution. By the late nineteenth century, as society grew steadily more affluent and more artistically sensitive, music became a valuable commodity, and its practitioners came to recognize that they formed a distinct professional entity as worthy of substantive remuneration as their brothers in mine and factory. During the heyday of professional music in Seattle, it was by no means unusual for a well-placed union musician to make a living plying his or her craft. Of his six-night-a-week job at the Seattle Town and Country Club, trumpeter Don Smith exclaimed, "That job paid an actual, honest-to-goodness living wage. I bought a house, made my car payments, and paid for the delivery of our first child on that one paycheck."[1]

Seattle is a music town, and for many, that means rock and roll. The "Northwest sound" of the region's early rock bands is universally acknowledged, and the fact that their city succored in her bosom Ray Charles, Jimi Hendrix, and Kurt Cobain fills Seattleites with proprietary pride. Fifty years of rock, however, were preceded by more than a hundred years of music that was equally exciting to its listeners and important to the community's evolution. More centuries of continuous native music preceded that.

Seattle's early industrial development made a vibrant musical life inevitable. Logging and coal mining created a strong demand for a large male labor force, and that labor force demanded food, shelter, and entertainment—lots of it. The latter was by no means subsidiary, and a hallmark of old Seattle was a lusty culture of saloons and sporting houses. To the young man lonely and hungry for both stimulation and a morale boost, music was at least as essential as beer and sex, and echoes of the cornet and the piano sustained the city's workforce through its long, bone-wearying days in mill and shipyard. As people worked harder and more newcomers showed up, Seattle demanded bigger, fancier gathering places—and music to fill them. In the wake of railroad and gold-rush booms came hotels, restaurants, theaters, and legions of musicians.

From the day of its birth, Seattle craved connection to the outside world. The early settlers assumed that this connection would come in the form of railroads and steamships, but it was another, subtler sort of connective tissue that took root first: music. Popular songbooks gave the first white settlers reassuring ties to their old homes; classical music encapsulated their children's aspirations to gentility and cosmopolitanism; jazz gave African Americans a vehicle of affirmation and economic advancement; ethnic music eased the transition of émigrés from homeland to "melting pot"; and, before whites ever lived on Elliott Bay, song and drums connected native peoples with neighboring groups and the spirit world.

There is a growing belief that music predates human speech and is one of the foundation stones of human civilization. Why, then, have we looked down on it for so long? The Puritans enjoyed singing and even dancing on occasion, but music was something to be indulged in sparingly, and chiefly in the service of God. Tunes that roused the sensual impulses filled us with uneasiness, even hostility. Music was a diversion, an idle use of precious time, and certainly not a proper pursuit for a serious man. Said one early American to his son who had asked for a fiddle: "Be assured that if you be not excellent at [music], it's worth nothing at all. And if you be excellent, it will take up so much of your time that you will be worth little else." Whatever enthusiasm young America felt toward music seldom extended to its makers, for in western civilization, musicians had long been marginalized. In seventeenth-century England, itinerant "masterless" musicians were routinely flogged and thrown into prison. "I would rather see you in a hearse," the father of composer W. C. Handy told his son, "than hear that you had become a musician." When Seattle bandleader Jack Hungerford snagged a prestigious job at Parker's Ballroom in 1952, he did so under an assumed name for fear that his day-job boss would fire him: "There was a general feeling then that musicians were just no good."[2]

Against this headwind, musicians trod a social and economic minefield in their attempts to professionalize their craft. Generations of saloon keepers and society matrons have considered music chiefly as something to be obtained as cheaply as possible. Keeping the music playing in Seattle has been the stuff of high drama: paying off the cops, massaging the liquor board, stroking city authorities, battling "reform" politicians. For decades the symphony was a snake pit of Byzantine intrigue, the musicians' union a farrago of feud and factionalism. As radio and music education became universal, amateur and school musicians flooded the market, eager to play for peanuts and displace working professionals. Then came rock and roll, and a Great Divide in our attitudes toward and expectations of music. Hordes of guitar-toting kids turned a profession into a hobby, and the exploiters' dream came true: free music! With the rock revolution, the American musician has become a beggar.

It is not this book's aim to denigrate rock and roll. In my fifties, I still dig the joyful anger of punk and play in a rock band. I do not dig, however, our cultural delusions that trivialize music and its makers. I heartily condemn the exploiters who will find money aplenty for interior decorators, for advertising, and for lawyers, but who, when the time comes to pay the musicians, discover they've left the checkbook at home. As far as Seattle rock and roll goes, it is an oft-told tale that will never lack a forum. These pages belong to the white coats.

This chronicle *is* an attempt to honor the musicians who have labored throughout one American city's existence to maintain and renew this essential connective tissue of human existence. Our cultural disdain for the musical profession may explain its conspicuous absence from Seattle's historical record. Seattle in the late Victorian era loved to boast of being the "commercial entrepot" of Puget Sound; consequently, the urban hagiography is dominated by railroads and factories, thrift and industry, the Great Seattle Fire, and the Klondike Gold Rush. But Seattle was also the entertainment entrepot, and, more precisely the *musical* entrepot. The city's first historians ignored this reality; town elder Arthur A. Denny had no use for music, and early-day chroniclers held him in high esteem, leading popular historian Bill Speidel to claim that "ninety-nine percent" of the first standard histories of Seattle were written under the direct or indirect influence of Seattle's pioneer Sobersides. And so the record is largely a dry and sober one. As folk musician Phil Williams says, "Nobody ever wrote about what people did for *fun*."[3]

Arthur Denny may have eschewed music, but his kin craved it. David Denny sang as he sawed timber, his children tootled mail-order cornets, and most of their neighbors quickly developed a ravenous appetite for all things musical. There were no fewer holidays, weddings, parades, circuses, or concerts in Seattle than in thousands of other American cities of the nineteenth and early twentieth centuries. Yet these activities, indispensable even in a hardscrabble frontier outpost, might as well have been conducted in pantomime for all the mention given the one ingredient without which they would have passed in leaden silence. This oversight certainly does not equate to any paucity of musical activity in the Queen City of Puget Sound. Late Victorian Seattle enjoyed a gloriously raucous music scene, the twenties roared with a brash new sound, and even the Depression-haunted thirties demanded plenty of musicians to keep spirits up. The 1950s brought the decline of big bands and the rise of another radical new music, yet there remained lots of work for the average musician. Even into the sixties and beyond, the men in the white coats were playing up a storm. It's time we lent an ear.

Telling the stories of working musicians and rediscovering the forgotten music of Seattle's first century furnished the primary inspiration for this book, whose title might imply that it ends abruptly with the birth of rock and roll. But history doesn't like clean breaks; rock and roll did not sweep America into a new age overnight (some might say it was not until the British Invasion of the mid-sixties that rock was truly here to stay), and while the kids were sorting things out, too many significant developments in "traditional" music were taking place for me to overlook. I therefore, and in good conscience, close this narrative in 1979. Any examination of the vast social phenomenon of music can be but a narrow prism in a million-faceted gem; here, I have attempted to represent a broad cross-section of music, with an emphasis on professional genres. The seventy-five individuals I was privileged to interview are a tiny fraction of those who have given Seattle her voice, and space did not permit including even all of these. To those who don't find their favored artists and musical styles in these pages, and to those who were omitted, my regrets.

■ ■ ■

The river wound like a snake to the big water. The rising sun burned through the morning mist. Along the shore, close in to a looming bluff, stood the cedar houses of a village. One day a great bridge would cross the river near this spot. But on this day no one knew of such things. Smoke was beginning to rise from the dwellings; the women were starting the home fires, and as they knelt to the task of food preparation, they sang softly: Thank you, Salmon, for your nourishment. And while you're at it, keep your bones out of my boy's throat, um-mm. Out by the river's edge, a young man inspected a canoe, eagerly anticipating the day's fishing trip. He too sang, loudly and boldly: Sun! Warm my bones and let your light show me the best fishing place! When a kingfisher rattled past, it too received greeting: Good morning, Fisher! Give me a piece of your skill at catching fish! And while you're at it, make them big ones, too!

■ ■ ■

Chapter 1

Song of the Duwamish

OR THOUSANDS OF YEARS many different groups of human beings have lived beside the great inland sea of the Pacific Northwest called by some Whulge and by others Puget Sound. Among them are those whose home grounds lie along the Duwamish River and in the hills surrounding Elliott Bay. To its native people, the Duwamish River is not simply a river but a chain of significant places. A bend might also be the home of mischievous spirits; a boulder the place where a man dropped his canoe paddle, causing him to lose a day's fishing and his friends to laugh at him. Falling Ground, Place of Sliced Things, Fingers Pulled: such names remind us that the Duwamish and its hills and beaches are a living place for its native people.

The land that became Seattle was dotted with villages: Little Crossing-Over Place—*Tsehalalitch*—on the lagoon just south of the site of present-day Pioneer Square; Place of the Entering and Emerging People, on Salmon Bay; and one of the largest, Herring's House, or Muddy, near the mouth of the Duwamish at the foot of the eastern bluffs of West Seattle. Here were half a dozen longhouse dwellings and a large dance house for communal gatherings, of which there were many. Portions of this village remained in use until it burned in a mysterious fire in 1893. The names of these places were often given to the Duwamish Indian groups who lived in them.

"We had fifteen to twenty-five villages, each one associated with a clan," Duwamish musician James Rasmussen told me.

The concept of "tribe" didn't really fit on Puget Sound. There were loosely affiliated tribes, some of that based on trade, but mostly these affiliations were a white man's imposition. That made signing treaties easier. Traditionally, villages would intermarry to strengthen ties and trade. We were a very stratified society, with everything from serfs to royalty and everyone in between, including slaves. Mostly, it was a trading culture, and [Seattle namesake] Sealth became an important person because he worked to foster trade.

The Duwamish was a land rich in good things and spirit energy: things that remain in the river, and in the city that rose at its mouth. "The entire city is a palimpsest," said Coll Thrush, "a text erased only partially and then written over again. It is a landscape of places changed by power, of Indian places transformed into urban ones, and sometimes back again. Seattle's past is rich with theses kinds of crossings."[1]

The nearest word to "music" in most Native American languages is "song" or "singing." Historically, song was as common to the Duwamish people as breathing, and not a frivolous amusement separate from workaday "reality." Duwamish music is music with a purpose, not an artistic medium in the European sense. Songs are sung to the spirits, to offer praise and thanksgiving, or to ask for favor and protection. Virtually any occasion is occasion for song: harvest time, before and after fishing and trading expeditions, at weddings and births and burials, at the sickbed, during games, and at meetings of different tribal groups and families. Sacred songs are composed by individuals, by groups, and sometimes by professionals who are rewarded for their talent. A man would sing when hunting a deer or walking in the woods in communion with spirit powers. A woman would sing as she sewed cedar mats or dried fish, instilling in her work the power to give her family strength and wisdom. Meetings with neighboring groups—potlatches and powwows—are enlivened by singing, drumming, and dancing. Duwamish music offers connections with ancestors and with other times and worlds; elders sing to prophesy forthcoming events and to keep the memories of important events in the life of the group.

One day, North Wind blew hard, and his breath threw out
    a great fall of ice.

The ice stopped up the river and kept it from flowing.
Salmon could not enter, nor could they pass out into the water
    or return to lay their eggs.
The People began to go hungry, and so they sang a special song to
North Wind's grandmother, Storm Wind, to entreat her to melt
    North Wind's ice.
They sang also to North Wind's wife, Mountain Beaver, and so
    Mountain Beaver and Storm Wind together overcame North Wind,
    And they melted his ice!
The salmon could once more pass into the river, and
    The People could once again eat and live.[2]

Puget Sound Salish people have no written language. Songs are transmitted orally and are shared among family members and between friendly tribal groups. A song might be only a passing chant to accompany a single experience, but even so, songs are considered the valuable property of an individual, family, or tribe and are not to be used lightly or to be casually appropriated by outsiders. An individual might be considered especially adept in the creation of songs or in the leading of dances and be given professional status. European bel canto is foreign to Native American song tradition; instead, Duwamish singers use subtle gradations of throat and mouth tone, glottal stops, and nonverbal chants called "vocables." A principal vocal line might be joined by two or more accompanying lines sung in unison and in octaves. Some songs center on key recitation tones within pentatonic scales, others have no tonal center at all. Some move along in a steady rhythm, others break into spirited syncopation. Drums accompany voices to add to the power of a narrative or to project spirit voices, and dancing is an integral part of traditional Puget Sound Salish music making.

Far from fading into oblivion as a "dying race" after the white settlement of Seattle, the Duwamish Indians remained an active part of a biracial community. They toiled alongside whites in Yesler's Mill, helped put up commercial buildings, and worked as domestic servants. A large Duwamish contingent took part in the 1883 celebration welcoming railroad baron Henry Villard, baking salmon, singing, and beating drums, and one newcomer pronounced the town "more Indian than white . . . along the beach stretched the shanties with the inevitable canoes. . . . Every [night] the singing and pounding in the shanties was

A Duwamish woman weaves baskets at Tsehalalitch—Little Crossing-Over Place—on the Elliott Bay tideflats in 1900. University of Washington Libraries, Special Collections NA 1500

the mighty orison." Another noted that singing seemed to peak in the warm months: "The frogs have begun to sing in the marsh, and the Indians in their camps. How well their voices chime together! All the bright autumn days we used to listen to the Indians at sunset; but after that, we heard no sound of them for several months. They sympathize too much with Nature to sing in the winter." Seattle's growth as the commercial center of Puget Sound also drew Native Americans from throughout the region in search of work and convivial gathering with their old friends and neighbors. The central waterfront was lined with Indian houses and camps, and the ancient "sing gambles" of the bone game meant nearly continuous music making. "For days at a time the racket of their board drums and monotonous chanting . . . made the nights hideous," recalled Clarence Bagley. Ceremonial lodges remained standing along the bay into the 1890s, and on a summer night along Front Street, the mingled strains of brass bands, saloon pianos, and native song produced music that was uniquely Seattle's.[3]

A century later, James Rasmussen was making Duwamish music in traditional and nontraditional ways. In 1987 he formed an orchestra, the Jazz Police, that performs big-band music reflecting many cultures. Noteworthy in its repertoire is Rasmussen's epic, *Tribute to Angeline*, which mixes European and native idioms in a colorful, sometimes sardonic, but ultimately optimistic brew. Of Duwamish music he said,

First, I think I would say, don't try to "understand it in your soul." Instead, look for stories—stories that can be connected in a string. There is no such thing as a Duwamish "songbook" coming down through history. A song is very much an individual thing: personal property, to be shared or not, depending on the occasion and the individual or family. Mostly it's about family, and things that are passed down within a family. There are songs about everything: paddle songs, songs to ask permission to come ashore, welcome songs, cooking songs, carving songs, weaving songs, basket making songs. One of the most important types of music was gambling music. A *lot* of money was spent at the sing-gambles! Those things would go on for days. Each side has its dancer—the gambler. He has bones hidden in his hand: you bet on which hand is holding the bones, or how many he's holding. He'll dance for twenty minutes or more, while the group sings behind him, then the gambler opens his hands and yells *"AH!"* Our music is song; I know of no native flutes in the Duwamish culture. We use hand drums—individual drums, as opposed to the Plains Indians, who have several people playing one drum. Our hand drums are made of cedar, with cowhide or deerskin heads, and played with beaters. Each player makes his own drum, and creates personal designs on the head.

I asked James about music in the Duwamish continuum. He replied,

Thinking of life of one hundred and fifty years ago when Seattle was founded, or beyond, it's true that Duwamish and white concepts are light-years apart. Linear time does have meaning for us Duwamish people, but it's a meaning that relates to this region as our home. This is our "Garden of Eden"! So the songs we sing now are still part of that time, and they relate back to that time, even as they express our thoughts today. In a sense, the "new" ways are still the "old" ways. I had an epiphany when I discovered the music of Jim Pepper, the Native American songwriter. I was always taught that songs were sacred, special things, and never mixed in with other kinds of outside music. But Jim mixed traditional and nontraditional native music, and jazz, rock, and folk. It's kind of like you don't have permission to do it, until you see somebody else do it! Like contemporary native art today: it's still traditional, because it's part of The World. But it uses new forms, like glass sculpture.

Rasmussen has performed starkly nontraditional music for native listeners, with gratifying results:

Tribute to Angeline was inspired by Jim Pepper, and it's not an easy thing to perform. It calls for a jazz band, native drummers and singers, a bagpiper, and a percussionist who can swing an axe. That's part of the story—the clearing of the land. I mixed up Indian songs with hymns, the "Golden Potlatch March," and jazz. Yeah, it clashes! When we performed it at the University of Washington, a lot of native people came, and they liked it. The Duwamish tribal membership has always been very supportive. I recently played flugelhorn and keyboards with Preston Singletary's Little Big Band. He's a native glass artist and bass player, and he mixes native music with funk. The coastal native tribes get into a lot of pattern-drumming, and it fits perfectly with funk. We have syncopation, too, you know! We went to Alaska and got a terrific reception. We set up in a big gym and began with a Raven dance. All the families entered in a slow procession, wearing their bead jackets—walking backward, to show off the backs of their jackets—and all of them singing the same song. Different from what you'd hear down here. I cried like a baby! Then we played, and I was just a *little* apprehensive about how we'd go over. I mean, there were a lot of older natives there, and here we are doing pattern drumming with a funk bass and keyboard. But they actually got up and danced.

In the late nineteenth century, the people of the Duwamish and their songs entered a long twilight. The Duwamish were banned from owning property within the city limits and their children forcibly placed in Indian schools and compelled to adopt white ways while industry took possession of the Duwamish River. The King County census of 1900 counted only twenty-two Native American residents. The Duwamish people faded into urban legend, their memory revived briefly in the boosterism of civic Potlatches and Chief Seattle Days (in 1936 Sealth's image was appropriated for the city seal), then just as quickly forgotten. By the 1950s, said Rasmussen,

> there was almost no music at all, at least in public. That was the genera-
> tion that had come out of the Indian schools, where they were taught that
> all Indian things were bad. So they were afraid to practice the traditional
> customs. My grandfather and grandmother recognized that it was to their
> advantage not to have anyone know you were Indian—my grandfather
> was beaten up because of it. Then in the sixties it began to change. It
> was suddenly okay to be Indian! You had the Boldt Decision that upheld
> native fishing treaties, and a new kind of legalistic approach to Native
> American rights. These things brought a sense of economic indepen-
> dence to some of the tribes, and we began to be proud of our culture
> again. After that, we started having drum circles and sings. Now the
> Duwamish drum school meets every Saturday.[4]

In the early twenty-first century, Duwamish people are making music in traditional forms and in ways such as James Rasmussen's. They play drums at special gatherings and sing prayers to their dead on the banks of their home river. Native American music has had little influence on the European music of white society, and to non-Indians it remains an enigma—implacable, impenetrable. That is, sufficient unto itself and its makers. For the Duwamish people, music is one part of their culture that has remained whole and inviolable.

Richard Crawford states,

> After long contact with Europeans, much of it violently destructive of
> native custom, is it still possible today to find Indian musical traditions
> that are practiced as they were two or even three centuries ago? For histo-
> rians, no clear answer exists. But for many natives, the question is unim-
> portant. As they see it, they are still making the music that was passed on
> to them by parents and elders, who in turn learned it from generations
> before them—and they sing, play, and dance for the same reasons. They
> are engaged in preservation not of historically significant old songs but of
> a legacy that connects them to the past and to nature, from which they
> continue to gain physical and spiritual sustenance.

James Rasmussen directs the Jazz Police in 2007.
Photo by Kurt E. Armbruster.

Skagit elder Vi Hilbert put it thus: "All the spiritually powerful songs that have ever been sung by our ancestors are out there, in the universe. They come drifting down to us."[5]

■　■　■

The big side-wheeler thrashed into the bay like an angry duck. White parasols floated above the railing, handkerchiefs fluttered along the pier, and the old North Pacific *was giddy with another Sunday excursion. As the whistle echoed off the hills, a brass band struck up on the top deck. Soaring over the euphonium and clarinet of "The Mulligan Guard" was the clarion wail of a cornet: Tom Brown was cutting loose! The young blades and their girls smiled, edging closer to the band. Others had the same idea: a Duwamish canoe cleaved the calm waters, strong hands urging their sleek craft alongside the churning ship. Young Tom's way with the silver horn was well known in many quarters, and as he ripped off a high C, the men in the boat raised a lusty chant—Ayyy-AH! Tom Brown drew a bead on the boatmen and saluted them with a long, brazen blast. With a fading chord, the* North Pacific *foamed into the bright spring afternoon.*

■ ■ ■

Chapter 2

Gaslight Serenade

HE AGELESS RHYTHMS of Puget Sound native culture were broken on November 13, 1851, when twenty-four men, women, and children from the Midwest landed on a spit of land at the entrance to Elliott Bay. One of the newcomers, David Denny, gave the new settlement the optimistic name New York (the Duwamish people called the place Smaquamox). Less than a year later, most of the settlers abandoned the exposed spit for a more protected location across the bay to the east. They called their new home Seattle in honor of the Duwamish elder Sealth who had been kind to them, but the idea of New York never died. Possessed by urban visions, the settlers dug in for the long haul to prosperity.

Life was rough. Throughout its first decade, Seattle's white population barely topped one hundred souls. The pioneers were for the most part a sober, orderly lot whose priorities in life were shelter, food, and business. Men dug wells, pulled stumps, built houses, and opened dry goods stores. Women carded wool, planted gardens, picked berries, made clothes, cleaned, and raised children. What the settlers could not produce themselves—vegetables grown in kitchen gardens, soap rendered from animal fat—had to be shipped in. Staples were expensive: flour cost fourteen dollars a barrel, butter seventy-five. Mail service was at the whim of unscheduled sailing ships, sometimes only once a month. Stamps and paper money were practically unknown; people paid in gold coin or bartered.

The settlers brought with them a new kind of music, less organic than that of the Duwamish, less spontaneous, less an intrinsic part of daily life. For white society, making music was a formal thing, to be done on instruments appropriate to specific styles and occasions, in specified places. Whether for religious ritual, amusement, or mental "improvement," music was generally an event *apart* from everyday life, to be indulged in after the day's work was done. Many still considered music frivolous and morally suspect, and Seattle founder Arthur Denny was the archetypal Puritan holdover. By 1851, though, Puritan influence was fading, and among Seattle's first white music makers were members of Denny's own family. Arthur's brother, David, and cousin, Tom Mercer, sang as they cleared land, and Sarah Mercer hummed "Wrestling Jacob" while drawing sap for the family's sugar. David's young niece, Emily, and her cousins passed the evenings singing tunes from the latest songbooks. David and Louisa Denny's children were among the first to play mail-order musical instruments: cornets for the boys, a flute for Anna.

In 1852 Henry Yesler fired up his sawmill, setting the economic, demographic, and cultural tone that would define nineteenth-century Seattle: a foundation of extractive industry, performed by a male workforce that demanded abundant entertainment. They found it first in the mill cookhouse, and Emily Denny looked back on many "happy hours, jolly nights, strange encounters, and wild scenes" in the small frame room where mill workers and visiting sailors belted out "Ho! Westward Ho!" and "There's a Good Time Coming" and played along on fiddles, concertinas, and banjos. In 1853 Seattle first celebrated Independence Day with speeches, picnicking, and, in the words of J. Willis Sayre, "a dance that kept all the pioneers busy until late at night." That summer, future Puyallup town founder Ezra Meeker walked the dusty streets listening to fiddles, flutes, and reed organs wafting from the parlors of Seattle's little frame houses. Despite the harshness of everyday life and the lingering residue of Puritanism, Seattle was born a music-loving town.[1]

The Indian wars of 1855–56 dampened settlement and business activity, but by the end of the decade Seattle was gaining a reputation as the region's commercial and amusement center. Sometime around 1860, Fraser River gold miners and Hudson's Bay Company employees were singing "Seattle Illahee":

There'll be mowitch [venison]
And Klootchman [Indian women] by the way
When we 'rive at Seattle Illahee [country]
Row, boys, row!

Let's travel to the place they call Seattle
That's the place to have a spree!

In the summer of 1861 San Francisco saloon owner John Pennell got
wind of the doings up north and built a saloon-brothel-dance hall on the
sawdust tailings of Yesler's Mill that he named Illahee. Illahee (Chinook
for "place" or "home") was the prototype of a Seattle institution, the box
house, that would long play a commanding role in the city's entertainment
life. And the band, which Pennell had imported from San Francisco, was
composed of the precursors of generations of Seattle professional musicians:
an accordionist, a fiddler, and a drummer. The women of the Illahee were
said to have "had a powerful imaginative effect on the whole male population of the Puget Sound country." But the music—lively, well-executed, and
the first to be accessible (to men) every night of the week—must have had an
equally strong impact. With Indian hostesses on their arms, Illahee rounders
cavorted to "Little Brown Jug," "Champagne Charlie," and "Bourbon Bob."
The Illahee's reputation spread, doing its part alongside lumber and coal to
make Seattle the hub of western Washington Territory.[2]

More sober residents made their music at home or in church. Methodist minister Reverend David Blaine and his wife Catherine arrived in 1853
and two years later built their "white church" at Second and Cherry. An
anonymous donor contributed one hundred dollars to the building fund,
and, as the fifties ended, a steady trickle of newcomers lent an atmosphere
of cautious optimism. "There are enough good singers here," averred
Blaine, "if they would only take hold." This suggests a certain ambivalence
toward public music making, at least among the more inhibited, but those
who did take hold found solace in "The Old Rugged Cross" and "The
Wayfaring Stranger." If and when Blaine's congregation received keyboard
accompaniment is not known, but when the Methodist Protestant "brown
church" opened a decade later, a reed organ was on hand. With keyboard
support, voices grew strong and confident, and a solid vocal tradition did
indeed take hold.[3]

THE ALL-CONQUERING PIANO

Seattle was born into a nation in musical upheaval. In 1825 Rossini's *The
Barber of Seville* made its New York debut, making opera a major influence
in the American musical world. Touring choral groups carried bel canto

to every corner of the United States (what Gilded Age mining town did not have its "opera house," even if the proffered fare was not exactly along classic lines?). The first large wave of European emigration in the 1840s, including legions of German and Italian musicians eager to share their sophisticated instrumental prowess and theoretical knowledge, began transforming America's social landscape. The musicians found jobs and eager acolytes in new institutions—the Handel and Haydn Society (1815), Lowell Mason's Boston Academy of Music (1833), and the American Music Association (1856)—that reflected music's growing importance in American society. As if to counter the European incursions, minstrel shows hit the road late in the 1840s, spreading an intoxicating brew of sentimental song and African American inflection (even though early minstrel companies were mostly whites wearing blackface makeup). Pocket "songsters" flooded the land by the millions, offering a common musical language of hymns, old ballads, and instant folk songs—"Sweet Betsy from Pike," "Listen to the Mockingbird," "Old Folks at Home"—that mined a peculiarly American vein of longing and nostalgia. The tortured emotions of the Civil War found release in song, and thousands of young fighting men plumbed their latent musicality playing in regimental bands.

The eye of the musical maelstrom was the piano. The modern American piano was born in the 1850s, and New York manufacturers Knabe, Chickering, and Steinway placed the instruments in parlors across the country with advertising that appealed to middle-class yearnings for self-improvement. Pianos and their equally new and all-pervasive ally, the parlor song, made the American home an engine of cultural progress and the piano as much an agent of Manifest Destiny as steam locomotives and Winchester rifles. As the stolid uprights marched westward, the *Atlantic Monthly* declared, "Almost every couple that sets up housekeeping on a respectable scale considers a piano only less indispensable than a kitchen range."[4]

Seattle was not long getting its first piano. Four years after the town's founding, Charles Plummer opened a general store, secured a territorial liquor license, and appended to the store a "bowling saloon," which, according to one account, contained two pool tables and a piano. Seattle's saloon culture was born, and by 1862 the first president of the University of Washington was lamenting the town's "extremely backward condition . . . drunkenness, licentiousness, profanity . . . eleven drinking establishments, and one bawdy house." It is doubtful that the patrons of these watering holes conducted their jollification in silence, particularly when a

In the heart of the tenderloin, a quiet Commercial Street in the early 1880s. Come sundown, Seattleites in search of refined music will visit the Squire Opera House in the stately Brunswick Hotel at right, while others will jollify to saloon pianos. Author's collection

proven means of upping the ante among competing saloons was to provide entertainment. In the barrooms of the frontier West this meant pianos. At the end of the fifties Plummer built Plummer's Hall, also known as Snoqualmie Hall, at Commercial and Main. The hall was described by one as having a bowling alley in the cellar; a bar, billiard tables, and piano on the main floor; and a meeting hall upstairs. Temperance advocates warbling "Come Sign the Pledge" in the hall clashed in delicious counterpoint with rough voices bellowing "Wait for the Wagon" in the tavern below.[5]

Something more genteel was called for, and Henry Yesler responded with the first of two frame buildings that would serve as community center and concert hall until the 1880s. His civic-mindedness did not extend to providing a keyboard, however, so the Emerson piano owned by Pumphrey & Young's emporium was hefted over as occasion demanded. The names of the men at the keyboards are unknown, but they were the first resident professional musicians in the new city and the forebears of a long and illustrious procession of Seattle pianists. The profane element had no monopoly on the ivories; within a year of the University of Washington's dedication in December 1861, the little college was offering piano instruction by Virginia Calhoun. Twenty-four lessons and "use of the instrument" were valued at a hefty twenty dollars. From an open window of the prim white university hall, the notes of the piano floated over the little city, spreading a mantle of gentility.

REVOLUTION IN BRASS

George Frye was peeved. Not over the stinking, muddy streets or the incessant rain or the fact that the guys at the mill spent most of their free time drinking. This was to be expected in the New World, after all, and Seattle was the newest of the new. But to have no music—this was intolerable. The out-of-tune saloon pianos? Torture! The parlor, the church? Boring! Frye sighed and rammed another log into the saw. In the eight years since leaving Germany, he had enjoyed the hard work and the camaraderie at Yesler's Mill. But he hadn't played a note on his cornet since coming to Seattle, and now it was 1861. Now it was time for real music! At lunch in the cookhouse, he took his pipe from his mouth and turned to his mates: In Germany, every town has its band. Why don't we form a *Seattle* band? The jovial, full-bearded "Dutchman" was popular (he served as the town's first Santa Claus), his enthusiasm infectious, and within weeks a dozen men were eagerly unwrapping shiny new instruments fresh off the boat from San Francisco. The Smith brothers—Al, Lee, and Lew—joined Frye on E-flat alto "peckhorns," William Meydenbauer played counterpoint on baritone, and Tom Russell covered the bass with his stately E-flat tuba.

One of thousands forming across the country, the Seattle Brass Band tapped into local and national sentiments. The 1860s were far from easy times; businesses struggled and cash was tight. And yet hammers pounded incessantly, and every day new faces appeared on the boardwalks. The Elephant Store was soon followed by furniture shops, factories, and more saloons. Coal was discovered in the foothills east of town, and in the summer of 1864 President Lincoln signed the charter for the Northern Pacific Railroad, which announced it would lay rails to Puget Sound. Few doubted that Seattle would be the western terminus, and the hammers went double time. On October 25 telegraph wires reached Elliott Bay, and by the end of the decade Seattle was being touted as the Future Queen City of the Pacific. Standing in the mud of Front Street blasting "Tramp!

Tramp! Tramp!" the Seattle Brass Band was the perfect voice of the community's frenzied aspirations. At the same time, the Civil War was being fought, and even on Puget Sound patriotic fervor was running high. Local sentiment strongly favored the North, children strung up effigies of Jefferson Davis, and martial airs monopolized the latest songsters. At the University of Washington's first commencement exercises in 1864, Frye's boys serenaded the graduates with "The Battle Cry of Freedom," letting the remote settlement thousands of miles from the battlefields feel that it was part of the epic struggle for the Union.

Lacking woodwinds, the little group of "raincatcher" saxhorns lacked the depth of the modern concert band (one may yet hear their mellow sonorities in the Salvation Army bands that sometimes appear at Christmas). What Frye's band and its successors had plenty of was enthusiasm, and they offered mill workers and draymen the revelation that inspiring ensemble music could be made with reasonable ease by the average person. Rehearsals (leavened with hearty Seattle lager) gave men whose lives were dominated by grinding physical labor social and artistic satisfaction, and in doing so gave music something it had not fully possessed in America: acceptance as not simply a masculine pursuit but a *manly* one. A boy carrying a violin case may have been fair game for neighborhood toughs, but the same boy playing a cornet was now a figure of glamour, to be emulated and possibly bettered in musical competition. Their strong martial associations, enhanced by fetching, quasimilitary uniforms, made brass bands emblems of order, patriotism, and refinement. Moreover, the *Light Cavalry Overture* and "Wood-up Quickstep" prepared millions of American ears for the weightier fare of Brahms and Wagner.

The boys in the Seattle Brass Band were gratified to discover that horns and uniforms won them the attention of young women. They also discovered that brass instruments are easy to play badly. At evening rehearsals, horns clashed in embarrassing discords, unison passages were garbled, and differences in interpretation perhaps found occasional resolution through fisticuffs. Still, everyone agreed that a brass band was much to the city's credit, and the press drew a veil of discreet silence over fractured harmonies. A newspaper editor, after all, had to live in his community, and plate glass windows did not come cheap (when the *Seattle Post-Intelligencer* ventured a mild critique of the Methodist choir, an anonymous reader invited the editor to "keep your hands off"). Still, George Frye knew a clam when he heard it, and sent out a call for help. The call was first answered by

Albert Eggers, a trained musician who had led theater orchestras in Portland and who gave the band a few pointers before skipping out for Olympia. Following him was Professor Charles E. Bray. One of the new class of professional musician-educators fanning out across the country, Bray was born in Philadelphia in 1844. His family joined the canvas caravans to California, where he studied cornet, violin, theory, and harmony in Stockton. Moving to Portland, he built up the City Band and New Market Theater orchestra, then got Frye's telegram and headed for Puget Sound. On Independence Day 1870 the revitalized Seattle Brass Band showed what a little fine-tuning could do, and a reporter later recalled, "The improvement of the band under his tuition was a revelation to the citizens, many of whom took to the study of music at once. And talent so long dormant in the breasts of many blossomed out into promising life."[6]

HOEDOWN

If cornets were all the rage, the violin (more properly, the fiddle) had long since established itself as the universal American musical instrument. Small but durable, and the perfect mirror of the human heart, the fiddle braced up settlers everywhere. Recognizing music as a morale booster, Lewis and Clark hired two St. Louis fiddlers before making their epic journey. The utility of this foresight quickly proved itself, and the music was enthusiastically received by Native Americans, who might otherwise have accorded the explorers a different reception. In the 1840s the fiddle took to the Oregon Trail, carrying "The Arkansas Traveler" to the Pacific Northwest.

Seattle's pioneer fiddlers—Jake Blake, Mart Lewis, and Charles Testman—enlivened late sixties socials with "Brother Jonathan" and "The Jenny Lind Polka." The first dance bands often consisted of a single fiddler, joined occasionally by a mandolin, banjo, cornet, or piano. The sound was light, melody dominated, and the relentless oompah of plucked bass and guitar taken so much for granted by later generations was not yet common (though by 1870 at least one resident string bassist was adding heft to Saturday-night hoedowns). The guitar was heard more often in the parlor than in public, and would not emerge as a significant rhythm instrument until well after the turn of the century. No matter; a good bowman held both the profane and the genteel in his hands and could lay down plenty of rhythm along with sweet melody. Outside Yesler's Hall, the rain beat down and the forest loomed close. But inside, ladies served fried chicken, boots thudded on thin plank floors, oil lamps smoked, and to fiddle accompaniment the people of old Seattle laughed and talked of the future. "What fine times were had at the dances there!" reminisced Charles Bray. "Everybody went. Exclusiveness was unknown. Everybody knew everybody, and sociability reigned supreme."[7]

The big blowout was Independence Day, which brought all of Seattle together in a picnic, street parade, and grand ball. Inspired by the great New York Peace Jubilee concerts of bandmaster Patrick Sarsfield Gilmore (one of America's first pop stars and composer of "When Johnny Comes Marching Home"), Seattle threw her own "grand monster musical jubilee" on July 4, 1872, in Yesler's Pavilion. Carl and Otto Vieuxtemps directed a chorus of as many as 300 (a number perhaps slightly inflated) and the Seattle String Band—violinists J. W. Scott and I. Palmer, string bassist C. Palmer, and cornetist C. E. Moore—who also played the evening ball. The concert was a milestone, for it was organized by the Women's Musical Society, a prototype of the clubs that would establish classical music in Seattle. And it convinced Reverend Blaine's reluctant choristers that singing could be fun! The following year, Seattle choral tradition was born with Josiah Settle's Philharmonic and Choral Society. The society was one of hundreds across the country that were propagating music not merely as entertainment but also as moral edification. Its aim was therefore nothing less than to "consolidate the musical talent of Seattle into a single organization, elevate the standard of music and culture, and cultivate the science of melody." While the Philharmonic and Choral Society fell somewhat short of fulfilling all of its goals, it did bring men and women together to make music, something brass bands and box houses did not, and it was the first brick in the lofty edifice of genteel Seattle music.[8]

As Seattle's cultural tone and income rose, so did opportunities for musicians. William Streit's Seattle Brass and String Band (Streit on fiddle, George Finn on cornet, and Mrs. Kuykendall on piano) made its bid for musical supremacy, offering "reasonable terms" of engagement. The band's July 4, 1876, debut elicited only cursory comment in the press—not a good sign—but the group was good enough to snag extended gigs at the Dolly Varden Saloon and at Guttenberg's North Pacific Beer Garden. They met competition in the form of Professor Brotherhood's Quadrille Orchestra, a trio of fiddle, cornet, and bass viol that was hailed as "music of very superior quality." The quadrille, otherwise known as the square dance, required sturdy fiddling and iron-lunged, nimble-tongued callers:

Swing that gent with your right hand 'round, partner by left with
    left hand 'round
Bird hop out and crow hop in, seven hands up and around again![9]

Brotherhood and his partner Charles G. Steinweg opened a dance academy and gave notice that they could furnish music for any occasion, making them possibly the town's first music contractors. There was plenty of
work for them, for by the late seventies Seattle was kicking up her heels very
smartly indeed. Waltzing and polkaing were now favorite recreations of the
youthful, and a near-continuous round of soirees, balls, hops, and masquer-
ades kept the lights bright and the feet pounding at Yesler's Pavilion.

BOOMTOWN

The 1880s were a time of excitement in a land that sensed it was entering
an era of limitless possibilities, and no American city made more of it than
Seattle. The decade began with a bang when gold was discovered on the
Skagit River, and crescendoed to a boom when yet another German émi-
gré, New York financier Henry Villard, threw his millions into Puget Sound
enterprise. In one stroke of the pen, Seattle became a strategic center in
an industrial and transportation empire, and hundreds of men piled off
ships to make shoes, candy, tinware, furniture, and rope, providing a diverse
industrial base that ensured Seattle's prominence. Horse-drawn streetcars
appeared, along with a telephone exchange, gas and electric lights, and
the long-awaited railroad connection to the outside world. Town lots sold
for between twenty-five and fifty dollars, and a four-room house could be
built on credit for a thousand dollars. And built, they were; by 1888, ten
mills going full blast could not meet the demand for lumber. Working this
transformation was a flood of newcomers, and before the eighties were over,
the thirty-five hundred souls who called Seattle home in 1880 were joined
by six thousand more, and the child city passed into feverish adolescence.
    A large percentage of the newcomers were educated, middle-class pro-
fessionals and business owners, mostly from the Midwest, mostly American born, of northern European descent, and affluent enough to make
the cross-country journey and establish themselves in a new city. This
relatively homogeneous diaspora would provide a ready audience for an
increasingly diverse and sophisticated music culture. But the influx had
another component: less affluent, wage-earning single men who would

give Seattle the largest transient population in the country and hold the male-female ratio at two-to-one until well after 1900. These would also sustain Seattle's rough-and-ready political culture, saloons, and musicians for decades to come.

Henry Villard drove the last spike on the Northern Pacific Railroad in September 1883, then rode his private car to Puget Sound, prompting the biggest bash yet seen on Elliott Bay. The Pacific Cornet Band, the Queen City Band, and the Carbonado Cornet Band vied to outblow each other on "Garry Owen," and even after the party ended, the festive mood lingered. The tinny wail of the cornet was nearly as pervasive as the steamboat whistles, and any excuse at all—a wedding, a funeral, a store opening, a new fire engine—was good enough for a parade and a band. Political campaigns were especially exciting, and brass bands and home-brewed beer emboldened street toughs to bellow doggerel calculated to invite fisticuffs. During the 1884 campaign for territorial representative, partisans of Thomas Brents lashed opponent Thomas Burke:

Brents is a bully man, Burke is a fool!
Brents rides a white horse, Burke rides a mule!

Young working men blew their wages in the raffish box house descendents of John Pennell's Illahee. Typical was the Maison Dore Garden, a jimcrack, red plush tinderbox of operatic pretensions (at least in dim light) containing a small theater ringed with "cribs"—boxes that could be discreetly curtained for privacy. Crinolined chorines spieled "Only Friends and Nothing More" on a postcard-size stage and plied the male clientele with spirituous refreshment and other services, while in the cramped orchestra pit a cornet, a fiddle, and a piano rapped out "Oh, Ain't I Got the Blues." The latest songs were available in flexible theater band arrangements, so even the smallest orchestras could sound modestly professional, the task of reading made easier by the gaslight that began to supplant the smoking paraffin lamps late in the seventies. The work was sweaty, the hours long, the pay low, and pit players were always at risk of being beaned by cigar butts. Moreover, musicians were obliged to lure customers by playing on ballyhoo out front. Still, the box houses were not only the most glamorous thing in town, they offered that most valuable of frontier commodities, feminine companionship. Many a young musician met either his downfall or his bride-to-be in the box houses of old Seattle.

Newly accoutered in snappy uniforms, the Queen City Band was one of
the stars at the celebration honoring visiting railroad magnate Henry Villard on September 14, 1883. Lacking woodwinds, the group is typical of
post–Civil War town bands. Museum of History and Industry 6289

It was the mushrooming middle class, however, that fostered a new form
of variety entertainment aimed not just at men but at women and children
as well. From the sixties on, Seattle families were entertained by a lengthening procession of itinerant thespians, phrenologists, spiritualists, temperance lecturers, and, most popularly, musical acts: Swiss bell ringers; the
singing and dancing Pixley Sisters, Annie, Lucy, and Minnie, who were
regular visitors for more than twenty years; Mr. Benjamin and his musical glasses; and the Alleghenians, a mixed quartet who tugged heartstrings
with their homely renditions of "Sleeping, I Dreamed Love" and "Far From
My Own Native Mountains." Theater was entering a new golden age, and
melodrama—*Ten Nights in a Bar-Room*, *Rip Van Winkle*, *East Lynne*—
came accompanied by hummable new hits such as Michael Balfe's "Then
You'll Remember Me." Opera, too, was sweeping the land, and Seattle got
her first taste in December 1876, when the five-member English Grand and
Comique Opera Company regaled Yesler's Pavilion with Flotow's *Martha*,
Donizetti's *Daughter of the Regiment*, and Offenbach's *The Grand Duchess*

(apparently predating its "official" 1887 New York premiere). This was not precisely the grandest of opera; these itinerant troupes typically numbered fewer than ten people, most carried only a piano player, and costumes were often ratty and props nil. Still, the performances inspired many a budding musician to sing or take up an instrument. (No doubt some of that inspiration was negative: "Nuts, I can play better than that!" is among any era's most potent calls to artistic achievement.) Governor Watson Squire opened the town's first opera house in 1879, in time to present one of the favorites of the age, Gounod's *Faust*. But it was old brass band hand George Frye (now making a tidy fortune in construction and real estate) who really made Seattle feel she'd arrived when in 1884 he built his $100,000 "New York–class" opera house with seating for over a thousand, a stupendous crystal glass gas chandelier, and a retractable dance floor. Planquette's operetta *The Chimes of Normandy* (Les Cloches de Corneille) opened the palace, while outside an Italian organ grinder—complete with monkey—cranked out selections from Balfe's *The Bohemian Girl*.

Theaters and box houses offered a welcome escape from gritty reality and a connection to a world of glamour and romance. If three-piece orchestras sounded a mite thin, they nevertheless offered the illusion of Continental chic, and Offenbach played by one fiddle or fifty was still Offenbach. Their faces glowing in the gaslight, young couples snuggled into plush seats, imagining themselves to be in Paris but proud to be in Seattle. "It would be safe to wager that there is more in the way of public amusements in Seattle than any other town or city in the United States, in proportion to population," crowed the *Post-Intelligencer* in 1884. "The public performances of the past three months have averaged at least twenty a week. . . . Seattle is certainly a generous patron of the showman, and has got a name among them that draws them in increasing numbers within her hospitable precincts." Across the country, raw young cities such as Seattle were melody-mad, and *Century* magazine gushed, "The progress which the American people show in every branch of music is remarkable."[10]

But raw Seattle still was. The air was heavy with coal smoke, the unpaved streets were vile quagmires much of the year, and downtown reeked of horse manure. Thieves and cutpurses owned the night, and the few police deputies were often ill inclined to poke their noses into trouble. Gangs of "plug-uglies" roamed the streets, taunting dandies, ladies, and Chinese. Down on old Tsehalalitch, the scabrous tideflat tenderloin (known variously as the Lava Beds or Whitechapel) was considered as tough as San Francisco's infamous Barbary Coast and would hold that reputation into the twentieth century. All this was abetted by a political culture that favored a wide-open town policy. Pro forma obeisance was paid to reformers who banged tambourines for temperance and honest government, but for two decades more Seattle politics would remain at the service of box houses, beer, and brass bands. As long as men outnumbered women, it was only good business.

SOJOURNERS

There were *no* women in Chinatown. Lured by promises of railroad and agricultural work, Chinese laborers began arriving on Puget Sound during the late 1860s, and Seattle's first Chinatown grew up around the Wa Chong Company Store at Third and Washington. After long days grubbing railroad grades, men from Toishan province in southern China relaxed in backroom parlors, smoking and playing games. Among them, a few played softly on fiddles and flutes as the dominos clicked.

Early in the 1880s, either local interests or an itinerant entrepreneur opened a Chinese theater. A nickel bought admission to the mysterious world of Cantonese opera, a kaleidoscope of drama and acrobatics depicting historical events: *The Defeated Revenge* and *The 8 Genii Offering Congratulations to the High Ruler Yuk-Hwang on His Birthday*. Actors worked on a bare stage, and on the floor to one side sat a small orchestra composed of Chinese fiddle (*erhu*), lute (*pipa*), reed flute (*sona*), zither (*sanhisen* and *guchin*), temple blocks, cymbals, and gongs. A conductor directed the music to reflect the mood of the action onstage, beating time with wood blocks or leading the orchestra with his instrument. Westerners listened with slack-jawed incomprehension, appalled to see that some of the musicians worked barefoot, and those living nearby cursed the "unendurable noise" coming through the windows in the evening. The city threatened action when the theater remained open on the Sabbath, and management told City Hall that they would continue to work on Sundays as long as the neighboring white saloons did likewise. And anyway, the performances were "religious concerts." The next step was to hale the theater owners into court, but the city council couldn't seem to find out exactly who they were. In 1884 a recession hit, and the Chinese were a convenient target. Mobs of angry whites drove most of Seattle's Chinese out of town, and their music disappeared with them.

In Confucian culture music has been traditionally regarded as an essential element of a harmonious life. Nonetheless, Chinese culture also shared with America a strong ambivalence toward music and musicians; this, together with the fact that many Chinese laborers in America considered themselves "sojourners," in the States only long enough to amass a respectable sum of money before returning home, had the effect, as author Ronald Riddle noted, of perpetuating a "generational discontinuity which has kept America's Chinese music in a corner by itself throughout most of its history." That "corner" remained backroom gambling parlors, funerals, and, most notably, Chinese New Year, which for most of Seattle's history has been one of few opportunities Chinese musicians have had to play in public. Evanescent though it may have been, Chinese music in Seattle was no less sustaining than the uptown theater to the indispensable men who built railroads and established businesses that helped Seattle grow. Like a rare orchid, the magnificent music of China faded. In time, it would bloom once more.[11]

MUSIC GOES PRO

The eighties boom was only momentarily interrupted on June 6, 1889, when the Great Seattle Fire swept away sixty-four acres of the business district, including Frye's Opera House and all the other theaters, clearing the ground for a more substantial city to be built of brick. Carpenters and mechanics flocked in, suppliers were swamped, and warehouses were piled to the rafters with building materials. Electric streetcars began running the same year, and the news that a second transcontinental railroad was on the way induced a fresh wave of excitement. Two years after the fire, Seattle's population had grown by 60 percent, surpassing 43,000. Accompanying the new boom was another kind of incidental music: a sonic nimbus of steam whistles from locomotives, mills, factories, and swarms of vessels that hooted, moaned, and cried all through the day and night, waxing and waning but—until the demise of steam in the 1950s—never ceasing completely. The whistle chorus annoyed many, but others accepted the wheezy diapason as the sound of progress—a symphony in steam.[12]

The 1890s were a decade of gaiety, depression, and unprecedented brilliance in popular music. Rising to the demands of a growing theater industry, a new breed of Broadway songsmith churned out some of America's most enduring melodies: "Ta-Ra-Ra-Boom-De-Ay," "The Band Played

On," and the anthem of the decade, Charles K. Harris's "After the Ball." As if eager to embrace the coming glory, Seattle's theaters and saloons rebounded quickly after the fire. Ex–New York hoofer John Cort, who during the eighties organized one of the first national circuits for variety entertainment (just then beginning to be called by the very continental sobriquet "vaudeville"), arrived in Seattle and opened his Standard Theater just in time to see it burn to the ground. Undaunted, Cort first set up in a large tent, then leased the old Turnverein Hall as the Seattle Opera House. Across the street, John Considine opened the People's Theater, and the race was on. Musicales, minstrels, and melodramas drew people by the carriage load, and by the late nineties Seattle was considered one of the West's top theater towns.

With such riches of entertainment now commonplace, audiences grew more discriminating, and musicianship of a higher order than ever was required to accompany the constantly changing kaleidoscope of acts. A working musician had to be able to "cut" any music placed before him, and sometimes double on more than one instrument. The ruckus on Puget Sound was national news, enticing scores of seasoned instrumentalists aboard Seattle-bound Pullmans. "It is surprising how many really fine musicians found their way to the city," said historian Harvey Jewell. "Many of the local musicians were far above the average of young growing cities, having come from recent residences abroad or from the East." Among the newcomers was Portland theater entrepreneur J. F. Cordray, who took over the year-old Madison Street Theater in December 1890, staffed it with an ear-popping twelve-piece orchestra, and brought old brass band tutor Charles Bray back to conduct. Making the old, thin sound passé, Cordray's band had *two* of everything: cornets, violins, clarinets, and deliciously slippery trombones, all briskly propelled by a snappy snare drum and stout bass viol. Leading in regal dignity with his violin, Bray was the archetype of the fiddling conductor who commanded Seattle theater pits until the Great Depression.[13]

As Charles Bray elevated the theater orchestra, so did another professionalize the raucous brass band fraternity and become Seattle's first musical celebrity. Born in Lansing, Iowa, in 1860, Theodore H. Wagner picked up the cornet as a young boy, and at the age of sixteen joined the town band. His German-born parents encouraged him—even sent him to a conservatory in France. Back in America, Wagner settled in St. Paul and was star soloist in the Western Band. The road beckoned, however, and in 1888 he joined a touring theatrical company. On June 7 of the following year—

the day after the fire—he arrived in Seattle with his wife and baby. Sitting in with the First Regiment Band of the Washington National Guard, Wagner demonstrated his natural leadership ability and was handed the baton. The twenty-man ensemble made a modest public debut in Denny's cow pasture, but better venues soon followed.

Wagner's timing was perfect, for the great touring bands of Patrick Sarsfield Gilmore, Alessandro Liberati, and John Philip Sousa were taking the wind ensemble to its nineteenth-century apogee. The American public had been steadily warming to classical music, and by 1880 brass bands were tackling the *William Tell* Overture and excerpts from *Faust*, material that demanded more depth and shading than brass alone could provide. The cornet began to share its lead role with massed clarinets, and flutes and bassoons added subtlety. Wagner bought as many of the latest arrangements as he could afford, and by 1893 his band was the best in the Northwest, taking honors at regional competitions and headlining at downtown theaters. European classics such as Meyerbeer's "Torchlight Dance" and Gounod's "Funeral March of a Marionette" dominated his programs, but Wagner obliged fashion with marches and cakewalks. His services being in demand for a growing number of civic and social events, Wagner's ranks swelled with musicians drawn by the genial bandmaster, who was a musical perfectionist yet always patient and encouraging with young players. Some hailed Wagner as the "Sousa of Seattle," but to Wagner's boys, the elderly, thirty-something bandleader was simply "Dad."

Streetcar lines reached Lake Washington early in the 1890s, and thousands flocked to new resorts at Madison and Leschi beaches. On radiant summer evenings, Wagner and his men serenaded the throngs in the Leschi gazebo and from the floating band shell at Madison Park. Couples spooned to "In the Gloaming," and weary laborers thrilled when Dad himself led the cornets in a rousing romp through "The Washington Grays." Things got really wild when both Leschi bandstands were occupied, one by Dad and the other by his deadly rival, the band of J. F. Langer and Alfred Lueben. And when that happened, the boys knew they were in for it! Clarinet players clamped on their stoutest reeds and brass men took a deep breath (and perhaps a discrete nip of fortification) and then let loose blasts that sent geese flying. As the bands did their best to outblow each other, they were cheered or razzed by gleeful partisans. The young star of the bandstand was cornet king Thomas Brown, who could be found belting out "Down Went McGinty" with a saloon band one night and fronting

Langer and Lueben's band the next with a solo turn on "Annie Laurie." Seattle music had truly entered a new era; "Those who followed music as a profession had a hard time to make a living by it," declared a reporter, "but now Seattle is a city in the full sense of the word, and its people appreciate and patronize a good musical entertainment, as well as those who seek to develop talent and train it in the right direction."[14]

Then—panic. Even as Seattle cheered her coming of age, the nation was hammered by the worst depression in two decades. Factories closed, building stopped, unemployment soared, and Seattleites joked grimly that the whereabouts of every twenty-dollar gold piece in town was common knowledge. For musicians, the Panic of 1893 was a disaster; saloons fired bands, theaters went dark, and the lucrative excursion business evaporated. The city council only rubbed salt into the wound when it banned the sale of liquor in theaters, closing the box houses for good. Seattle nightlife fell into a three-year funk, and with no welfare or unemployment insurance, many a musician found himself on a track gang or city street crew. By the summer of 1896 hard times began easing. Brick office buildings began sprouting, Ralph Hopkins drove the first automobile down Second Avenue, and in August the old festive mood was rekindled when the Great Northern Railway and Nippon Yusen Kaisha steamship line inaugurated the modern era of Far East trade. On August 31, the *Miike Maru* steamed in from Yokohama to waving handkerchiefs and Wagner's Band playing the "Miike Maru March." Dad featured the rousing anthem at the first city parks concerts at Pioneer Place, and on Saturday evenings at the *Post-Intelligencer* corner at Second and Cherry. In these early multimedia displays, marches accompanied magic lantern images projected on a screen, while young blades and belles tapped their toes and savored the feeling that they lived in one of America's most exciting cities. And when gold was found in the Klondike the next year, they were sure of it.

UNION MUSIC IS BEST

Music in Seattle was becoming professionalized and, thanks to Bray and Wagner, musicians enjoyed unprecedented community stature. It was a trend unfolding across the nation; during the 1880s the American labor movement launched its push toward the eight-hour day, improved working conditions, and higher wages that would create the American middle class. As the nation boomed, musicians found themselves in the same position as skilled workers in scores of other trades, facing rising demand minus any corresponding increase in compensation or control over working conditions. For Seattle musicians, remuneration had always been a sometime thing, and fiddlers and brass bands customarily passed the hat (though by one account Mart Lewis and Charles Testman were paid a very respectable ten dollars apiece for playing the Calico Ball of 1870). Dad Wagner chuckled ruefully that his boys were accustomed to "playing all night for a keg of beer."[15]

Riding the wave of American unionism, the American Federation of Musicians (AFM) was founded in 1886 with the aim of rallying musicians as a craft organization under the umbrella of Samuel Gompers's American Federation of Labor. The first order of business was to define just what a "musician" was—not unreasonable, given society's long-standing ambivalence toward the profession. The AFM took the position that music was a *craft*, like machining or pipe fitting. But many musicians preferred to think of themselves as *artists*, and they broke off from the AFM "shoemakers" to form the National League of Musicians (NLM). (The AFM scorned the defectors as "silk hats.") Then, however, NLM chapters splintered off from the national organization, and the AFM gained ground. By 1895 the AFM had emerged victorious under the strong hand of President Owen Miller, a militant and popular fighter for his union's interests. Late in the 1880s the Musicians' Mutual Protection Union (MMPU) was chartered as an AFM affiliate. The West Coast chapter took root in San Francisco, and in the autumn of 1889 Charles Bray, John Cross, Orville Snyder, and Theodore Wagner petitioned San Francisco for a Seattle chapter. On November 7, 1890, the Seattle branch of the MMPU, Chapter 30, was born; elections were held among some 120 members, and, after a factional battle between Wagner's boys and Bray's "uptown gang," V. K. Tout was named president.

Fittingly enough, Chapter 30 went into business on the second floor of the Our House Saloon, collecting annual dues of $10 and setting wage scales: $0.50 an hour for tavern jobs, $20 a week (six to nine performances) for theater work, $2.50 for "casuals" (dances, receptions, lodge functions) until midnight and $1 an hour overtime thereafter. One of the union's first acts was to launch a campaign against the "competitive encroachments" of military units such as the Bremerton Navy Shipyard band, which caused much union teeth-gnashing by playing at ship launchings and other celebrations. The union marshaled the rank and file in a letter-writing campaign to their congressional representatives, but the success of this effort may be reckoned by the fact that the union was waging the same battle almost a hundred years later.[16]

More immediate threats loomed. In the depression of 1893, the MMPU's hopes of enforcing a uniform price list were dashed as its membership faced the choice of working under scale, passing the hat, or not working at all. In February 1894 the union suspended its price list and threw its members on the open market, "the profession of musician in the face of the times, being in a measure a luxury and not an actual necessity to the public." Union deserters organized the Rialto Orchestra to get work at any price, and one of their first gigs was in a new venue born of hard times, Wilson's Dime-a-Dance, at Fourth and Pike. Patrons pitched dimes into a hat, and the proceeds were divided among the band at the end of the evening. Hat-passing proved difficult to overcome, even when times got better. "Once these dances were well-established," said Dad Wagner, "it was a hard problem to do away with them, and it took years to raise the price to twenty-five cents." When Chapter 30 wore out its welcome at the Our House Saloon, Wagner came to the rescue with rent-free space in the First Regiment Field Armory, where union members could hang together in an environment of mutual solidarity: "Often in the afternoons," a Wagner veteran recalled, "one could find the boys gathered about a cozy fire enjoying Dad's hospitality." Things hit bottom in 1896, when only sixty-nine members remained on the union books and brotherhood activity was virtually suspended. The next year, however, the Klondike Gold Rush brought a new boom, and as saloons, restaurants, and dance halls hired every musician they could find, the union was back in business with a vengeance. On March 1, 1898, the Seattle MMPU was reborn as the Musicians' Association of Seattle, Local 76 of the American Federation of Musicians.[17]

HOT TIMES

As Klondike fever raged, musicians found their gold in downtown Seattle, now the hottest spot on the West Coast. And the hottest times were had on the Lava Beds south of Yesler Way, the "deadline" that by general agreement quarantined tenderloin horrors from respectable uptown society. The tangled warren of saloons south of the line—Old Kentucky, Occidental, Star—was the living room for thousands of single working men, and the musical heart of saloon culture was a hard-pounding fraternity of pianists: Joseph Wagner, Charles Constantine, and dozens more unsung heroes of the Lava Bed trenches. The old Seattle piano players no doubt varied widely in competence and style; thousands of ivory ticklers were floating around the country in the nineties, and to keep a gig, make good tips, and not invite ridicule (or worse), it behooved a self-respecting keyboardist to take his proficiency seriously. Sheet music was common musical currency, and pianists had to be able to read in order to keep up with the latest song hits. The concept of tuning was little appreciated by most saloon owners (a piano was a piano), so wise keyboard men left their finer sensibilities at the swinging door (countless TV westerns have captured the sound perfectly). Enduring endless hours, pitiful instruments, and rowdy company, saloon pianists had to have fingers of steel, nerves of iron, and the fortitude to live on beer, peanuts, and cigar smoke.

To outdraw the competition, saloon owners sometimes splurged on full bands. In October 1891 pianist Joe Wagner was joined at the Old Kentucky by R. R. Mitchell on violin, L. C. Mecklenberg on cornet, and H. P. Hamilton on trombone. This classic Seattle saloon band would have served up the sentimental ("Sweet Rosie O'Grady," "Hearts and Flowers") and the rollicking ("There Is a Tavern in the Town," "Who Threw the Overalls in Mrs. Murphy's Chowder?"). Bands often played from tiny balconies; space and budgets were tight, so string basses were a rarity, while the drum kit was a thing of the future. The latest songs from New York required reading music, and orchestrations for small ensembles were inexpensive and written so as to be playable by groups of three to ten pieces. Extended, free-form improvisation was unknown, but seasoned musicians knew their harmonies and variations and easily "faked" familiar tunes. Instruments traded melody, countermelody, secondary strains, and refrains, and the addition of vocals, by either musician or audience participation, kept the beer flowing.

With saloons lined up cheek-by-jowl along Front Street, it became a point of honor among house musicians to out-play, out-finesse, and just plain out-blow their rivals. The *Post-Intelligencer* offered this rare taste of tenderloin nightlife in the last days of the nineteenth century:

It is at about 8 o'clock in the evening . . . the players of the brass band on the west side of the avenue file out from behind the swinging doors of some cool and darkened beer saloon and, removing their coats, hats, and collars, prepare for the fray. . . . the big bass drum . . . emits a thunderous boom as of a distant cannon shot, and the battle is on. . . . the strident brass instruments take up the carnage. An admiring crowd quickly gath-

Hot times: A newspaper artist made this rare and evocative portrait of
tenderloin nightlife in the summer of 1899. Instead of the more customary brass, the ballyhoo band is made up of a harp, a fiddle, and a flute.
"Little Jimmy" cavorts at lower left. From the *Seattle Post-Intelligencer*,
July 30, 1899, by permission of Hearst Communications, Inc.

ers. Night after night, it is there to applaud its favorite selections and to
encourage the performers by its presence. The selection is ended and the
leader of the orchestra, lowering his cornet from his ruddy countenance,
streaming with the sweat of zealous toil, bows low to the motley crowd
surrounding him and his brave supporters. In the meantime, however,
the champions of the opposition have . . . taken their stations on a high
platform built off the entrance of the rival theater. . . . the leader is armed
with a violin, which he handles with the same daredevil grace and ease
that a plowman does a six-shooter. . . . Another dark-faced young man,
with a melancholy cast of countenance, strums a huge harp, and the

third of the challenged musicians defiantly pipes away through a husky clarinet. . . . they strike up a lugubrious melody that seems to strike the fancy even of the most critical. . . . A stalwart young fellow with lungs of leather adds his voice to the efforts of the instruments: "She stole nine thousand and six hundred," he bellows forth in the deepest of baritones, "Say babe, I know we will be happy after a while." . . . The crowd applauds madly. . . . Suddenly around the block is heard the discordant blare of an untutored brass band and the voices of men and women upraised in a popular street melody. . . . It is the Salvation Army. Fifty-strong, the uniformed "soldiers of the Lord" swing into the street in front of the theater and march toward their Yesler Way barracks, flags flying, torches smoking. . . . Discord rends the air and the crowd cheers. The Salvationists are out-pointed two-to-one in the contest, but on they march . . . leaving the theater band to finish that enlivening melody, "There'll Be a Hot Time in the Old Town Tonight," with variations to hearken to. . . . "Little Jimmy" throws himself into the breach . . . and, throwing both hands back over his shoulders, begins a cakewalk on the pavement before the string band. The musicians strike up a lively air, "At a Georgia Camp Meeting."[18]

How far did those variations go? "Since the main requirement of the performers' trade was to support dancers by maintaining a regular flow of rhythm," explained author Richard Crawford, "one imagines that, like dance musicians of other eras, some exercised their imagination by decorating, embellishing, and perhaps also varying tunes rather than simply repeating them verbatim." As early as 1819, Philadelphia bandleader Francis Johnson demonstrated a "remarkable taste in distorting a sentimental, simple, and beautiful song into a reel, jig, or country dance." Playing night after night in the right circumstances (circumstances that by the nineties were producing the first hints of jazz in New Orleans) would have induced jaded musicians to explore the nether limits of instruments and chord progressions. In the aim of divesting drinkers of dollars as well as keeping the job interesting, piano players developed individual signatures: catchy bass runs, florid tremolos, and rhythmic vamps that gave them time to reach for a beer or light a cigar. Granted that Seattle was not New Orleans, it is still likely that musicians took inspired liberties with "A Hot Time in the Old Town." To paraphrase Dickens: not jazz, but going to be.[19]

■   ■   ■

The setting sun was a crimson ball over Elliott Bay. Gulls and steam whistles shrieked in raucous counterpoint to the plodding of drays along First Avenue. Salt air wafted up from the harbor and mingled with the pungent stench of tarpaper and horse droppings. As he strode to work along the busy thoroughfare, Charles Constantine savored the evening and the lightness of his new pearl-gray spring suit. In a window he admired the sleek profile of his low-crowned porkpie hat. What would the gang at the Central say when they saw him in his dude duds? Constantine chuckled at the ribbing that doubtless awaited him—and at the secret admiration the laughter concealed. Yes, the boys loved him and his way of making the old upright ring like a brass band. Just now, though, Constantine was anxious, and not on account of his new clothes. No, tonight he had in his valise (and what self-respecting piano professor did not report to work without an elegant pigskin?) a new piece of music. For weeks he had been practicing the thing—it had a curious swing to it that took some getting used to. But it was all the rage in the East, and Constantine was determined to premiere it in Seattle. Yes, he smiled, his heartbeat quickening: this "Maple Leaf Rag" would set the gang on their ears!

■ ■ ■

Chapter 3

Music on the Make

S EATTLE IN THE EARLY YEARS of the twentieth century was a
city full of young Charles Constantines on the make. The Klondike Gold Rush was succeeded by more strikes in Nome, and the
gold kept coming, fueling astonishing growth. By 1900 Seattle was truly
the Queen City of Puget Sound, and in the following twenty years its
population would soar from 80,000 to over 300,000, a microcosm of the
national population boom fed by a flood of European immigrants. The
1900s were in every way a transformative decade, and as hills were lev-
eled and the city limits pushed to the horizon, reformers fought to clean
up vice and conservatives battled progressives over taxes, unions, school
levies, and control of utilities. Along with the smoke from a dozen steam
shovels, change hung in the air, exhilarating some and frightening others. Pulled and prodded by opposing forces was a dominant and increasingly self-aware middle class.

Music reflected our restlessness. Broadway songsmiths mined that
peculiarly American vein of nostalgia with "Let Me Call You Sweetheart,"
"Down by the Old Mill Stream," and "Waiting for the Robert E. Lee,"
while leading the charge into modern times was Scott Joplin's "Maple Leaf
Rag," published at the very beginning of 1900. Tin Pan Alley became a
household name as Victor Herbert, George M. Cohan, and Irving Berlin gave Americans a fresh look at their way of life. Cohan's blockbuster
musical *Little Johnny Jones* sold out the Seattle Theater in September
1907, sending audiences into the night with wings on their feet and heads

cleared for a new day. From the south came a strange and, to some, barbaric new music. And at last, Seattle got a symphony orchestra.

SEATTLE'S TIN PAN ALLEY

Three thousand miles west of Broadway, Seattle's own Tin Pan Alley was in full cry in 1910. Third Avenue was a happy cacophony of clanging trolley bells, sputtering motor cars, and jangling pianos echoing from dozens of music studios. The city boasted more musicians and music teachers than ever, and it was another mark of cosmopolitan arrival and of the new stature of the music business that folks in the know called the street Music Row.

As early as 1870 the Pioneer Book Store on Front Street was selling pianos and sheet music. The first Seattle song, "Seattle Illahee," was already old hat, but it was a much older tune from across the Atlantic that became the city's enduring anthem. "The Old Settler's Song" is believed to have begun its polyglot existence as a seventeenth-century Irish drinking song, "Old Rosin the Beau":

> When I'm dead and laid out on the counter, a voice you will hear
>   from below
> Singing, Some plain whiskey and water, to drink to old Rosin the beau.
> To drink to old Rosin the beau! To drink to old Rosin the beau
> Singing, Some plain whiskey and water, to drink to old Rosin the beau!

Published anonymously in Philadelphia in 1838, the song's homely melody and hearty flying in the face of mortality made it a surefire hit, and it worked its way west, becoming an anthem of westward expansion. In 1874 Seattle police court judge Francis Henry wrote new lyrics, and as "The Old Settler's Song" the tune became a barroom staple:

> And now that I'm used to the country, I think that if man ever found
>   A place to live happy and easy, that Eden is on Puget Sound.
> No longer the slave of ambition, I laugh at the world and its shams
>   As I think of my happy condition, surrounded by acres of clams.
> Surrounded by acres of clams! Surrounded by acres of clams
> I think of my happy condition, surrounded by acres of clams!

Midway through the twentieth century the ditty was unearthed by song "collectors," among them Seattle restaurateur Ivar Haglund, who brought it back to prominence as his radio theme song.[1]

After Francis Henry came Seattle's first professional composer, Charles Bray, who penned the "Queen City March" in 1888. He followed that with orchestral pieces (such as "Rhododendron Idyll" and "Marguerie Waltzes"), sentimental songs ("Spot and I"), one of the Northwest's few "coon" songs ("My Black Gal, She's a Cuckoo and a Honey," co-written with George Kidd), and an operetta (*The Maid of Milan*). As the new century accelerated, Music Row met the prevailing taste for atmospheric romances and jolly frolics with "Isle of Dreams" and "All Aboard for Luna Park," while Seattle raggers Warren Camp and Bernard Brin weighed in with "The Rag with No Name" and "Jitney Bus Rag." Boosting, boasting "Seattle songs" hit their peak in 1909, when the city held the Alaska-Yukon-Pacific Exposition and Music Row cranked out reams of clumsily titled forgettables: "I Will See You in Seattle, Celia Mine," "It's the Really Real Thing Is the A-Y-P," "A Nice Little Girl in Seattle I Know." The sheet music now makes a nice wall decoration, but in their day these tunes offered sure-fire local pride to a city forever in need of it.

King of Seattle's Tin Pan Alley was Harold Weeks, who arrived in time for the fair, attended Queen Anne High School and the University of Washington, and became one of the Northwest's most successful songwriters. The first of his forty-odd commercial tunes was "Mew Mew Rag" of 1910, published by a New York house when he was still a seventeen-year-old student. Weeks did his bit for the boosters with 1923's "Seattle Town," but struck gold conjuring more exotic locales with the likes of "Siren of a Southern Sea" and "My Kandy Girl in Old Ceylon." His biggest hit, "Hindustan" (1918, with Oliver Wallace), sold over one million copies and was published by Weeks's own Melody Shop label. Weeks opened the Melody Shop in 1917, and it was the first store in Seattle devoted exclusively to sheet music. Piano players and small bands ballyhooed its inventory in the big shop window, but the garrulous tunesmith was not above employing more ambitious tactics to promote his wares. One day he hired a boy to scatter copies of "Melancholy Moon" around town; the boy returned with a policeman and a summons for littering—"but it made another story in the papers, and we sold 15,000 more copies right away!" Another time Weeks hired a man with a powerful baritone voice to plug "My Honolulu Bride" from the top of Smith

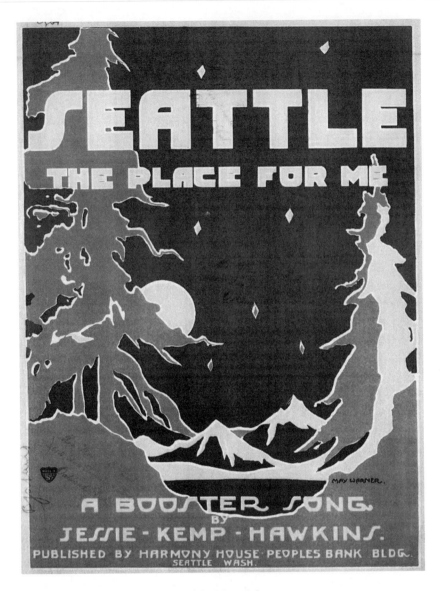

Sheet music cover. Property of the Music Library,
University of Washington Libraries, Ashford Collection

Tower. Using a megaphone, the singer was audible on the sidewalk forty-two stories below.[2]

Music Row was a happy meeting place for musicians and songwriters and their admirers, but Seattle songs and locally published sheet music were seldom big money-makers. (With national connections, Harold Weeks was an exception; he called his Melody Shop "a regular little mint.") Markets and distribution were limited; Seattle was too far from the arts epicenter, New York; and the phonograph (and later the radio) edged both sheet music and the piano from their long-held dominance. After World War II Music Row entered its long twilight, and by 1960 most of the music stores and studios had been supplanted by pawn shops and taverns. Now Benaroya Hall stands as a fitting replacement for, and memorial to, Seattle's Tin Pan Alley.

THAT SEATTLE RAG

Born during the 1880s in the sporting houses of the South and the Midwest, ragtime had its big debut at the 1893 Chicago World's Fair. Leroy Watkins and Blind Tom Wiggins took it to San Francisco's Barbary Coast, and when Klondike fever hit, raggers headed for Puget Sound. It was only after 1900, though, that ragtime's hip-shaking syncopations found acceptance in the pop music mainstream. Along with ragtime came the blues. Touring the Deep South at the very beginning of the 1900s, young bandleader William C. Handy was astonished to discover the hypnotic songs of black laborers in southern Mississippi. Working this "earth-born music" into new compositional forms, Handy wrote songs that changed the American musical landscape: "Beale Street Blues," "Memphis Blues," and "St. Louis Blues"—tunes that took their place in the foundation repertoire for the emerging style of syncopated dance music soon to become known as "jazz."

Seattle would not hear real jazz until late in the teens, but she still enjoyed plenty of hot music. The frothy nightlife of the Lava Beds roared unabated into the new century, breaking the Yesler Way deadline and surging northward up First Avenue in a jangling line of saloons and gaming houses. Bars came and went, but the formula remained the same: a sawdust-covered floor, free lunch, hearty Seattle-brewed beer, and an intrepid, cigar-chewing piano plonker. In 1902 Charles Wesley offered refined keyboard stylings at John Cort's Palm Garden, while Charles Constantine and Carl Weber broke up their arduous saloon runs by backing melodramas at the Madison and People's theaters. Over at the Good Fellows Grotto at Second and Yesler, Levi Worley led both the house orchestra and a grandly named six-piece ballyhoo band, the Seattle Military Band and Orchestra, which blared long and loud into the evening to entice customers. Leading small saloon bands were Fred and John Marotta, Fred Christensen, George de Luis, and many more young men whose successors would make Seattle famous for other kinds of music.

The tenderloin rang with ragtime by 1900, but it wasn't all prim renditions of "Maple Leaf Rag." The roots of classic ragtime are many: black string bands and the characteristic rhythms of claw-hammer banjo (which backed dancers doing shuffling "rags"), European military marches, and syncopated "jig piano." As ragtime emerged, so did a less refined relation, barrelhouse, or honky-tonk (later to be further stylized as boogie-woogie). Barrelhouse piano acquired further seasoning in Texas bordellos and western mining camps, and featured ragtime's heavy bass and right-hand rolls but in a simpler, cruder form with less-structured improvised variations. Volume and rhythm were favored over right-hand subtlety, and where Scott Joplin cautioned that classic rags should never be played fast, fast and furious was the hallmark of barrelhouse. Seattle's barroom ragtime was thus a hybrid of written and improvised piano, presented with wide variation and subject to the skill and inclinations of the man at the keyboard. In the saloons and bordellos of the Lava Beds, the polite tinkling of parlor piano may have sufficed early in the evening, but once things started heating up, a hard-drinking clientele would have demanded a thumping bass and a rocking melody, and never mind that the pianos were seldom in tune.

The music of saloon pianos and theater bands did more than entertain. It served as an essential adjunct to major components of the Seattle economy—gambling and prostitution—and was handmaiden to the city's wide-open political culture. The police payoff system became institutionalized at this time, and would persist into the 1960s as both regulator and facilitator of live music in shady—and even not-so-shady—places. As long as iniquity was contained south of the deadline, this was little cause for worry. In the early 1900s, though, vice began creeping uptown, and the Forces of Decency clamored for a cleanup. In 1902, despite strenuous Musicians' Association lobbying, the city enacted an ordinance requiring saloons to pay a ten-dollar license fee for each musician hired. The local and national mood grew increasingly sober, and in 1909 Seattle saloon life entered a long twilight with the passage of the infamous "blue law" banning alcohol sales on Sunday. Two years later, the election of reform mayor George Dilling sent pimps and gamblers scurrying for the city limits. Dilling was soon "dis-elected," however, and under Hiram Gill the doors swung open for a last, heady fling. Pouring from saloon doors came "My Gal Sal," the daring new dance tune "Ballin' the Jack," and Hughie Cannon's "Bill Bailey Won't You Please Come Home." Good times weren't restricted to the tenderloin. North of Salmon Bay, the mill town of Ballard boasted possibly more saloons per capita than any other city in the country, and along bar row popular songs and Norwegian ballads mingled with stomping pianos in the murky nights.[3]

UNION MILITANT

Battling stiff opposition from employers and the legal system, American unionism made big gains in the early 1900s. Among the most successful, on par with building trades and railroadmen's unions, was the American Federation of Musicians, which two decades after its formation boasted that 80 percent of American professional musicians were union members. Local 76 was among the strongest federation chapters, thanks to a political and economic climate that made Seattle more hospitable to unionism than many cities, and also to the adept leadership of Dad Wagner and his successors, Frank Rust and William A. Belard, men of strong business and diplomatic acumen. But the real mover was Local 76's jack-of-all-trades for nearly thirty years, William J. Douglas. A piano player who found his true talent as a labor organizer, Douglas joined the union in 1909 and made himself the scourge of nonunion employers and musicians, earning the nickname "Bulldog." The tireless Douglas delighted in showing up at venues with pad, pencil, and a sharp tongue no one wanted to tangle with. Taking turns as business agent, secretary, sergeant at arms, and managing editor of the union newsletter, Douglas kept the Musicians' Association in dogged pursuit of a good living for its members.[4]

Under this leadership Local 76 strengthened its hold on Seattle's musical life. Nonunion musicians and venues were pressured to join the fold; an examining committee auditioned applicants for sight reading and technical ability, and, once accepted, members were closely supervised. First-time rules violators were usually let off with a warning, but thereafter fines from fifty cents to fifty dollars were levied not only for such infractions as playing under scale and working in "unfair" establishments but for failing to attend union meetings, and even for patronizing nonunion cigar stands. Breaking in as accompanist at the Alaska Theater in 1909, young Grattan Guerin thought he would add spice to his piano licks with a tambourine and cymbal—that is, until Bill Douglas happened by one evening, found

A string orchestra helped make the Bismarck Café Seattle's poshest restaurant in the early 1900s. The young bandleader personifies the popular
image of the "longhair" musician. University of Washington Libraries,
Special Collections HES 227

the piano covered with percussion instruments, and pulled out his little
black book. Tut-tut, he chided: You're only being paid to play the piano!
Douglas's methods were resented by many, as were the bewildering array
of union do's and don'ts, which seemed to change daily. Union members
and officials constantly squabbled over rules and price lists, and bandleaders and sidemen were forever hauling each other before the board for trans-
gressions real or otherwise. People hiring musicians also chafed under the
rules, observing caustically that adhering to them did not guarantee good
music. "I notice that the union does not make any distinction between
good and bad musicians," complained a New York theater owner. "The
bad ones—and they are many—get just as much pay as the good ones."[5]

Especially loathed by theater operators were mandatory house minimums. As theaters adopted continuous show times in the early 1900s, musi-

cians found themselves working ten or more hours a day with scant breaks, seven days a week. Theaters were getting bigger, requiring orchestras to play harder. To ease the demands on players, Local 76 adopted the minimum-man rule in May 1910, informing the Pantages, Majestic, and Star theaters that their orchestras must henceforth number at least five musicians. The owners objected, but musicians commanded a sellers' market, and the owners had little choice but to knuckle under. By 1915 minimums were firmly established, with three musicians required in the smallest houses and five to eight in the larger ones. When business was good, house minimums were accepted as one of the costs of doing business, although owners continued to insist on their right to hire as many or as few musicians as they thought fit. When times were slack, however, venues complained that the union was squeezing them unfairly. For decades to come, the union would justify the minimum-man rule as a social investment vital to both the interests of working musicians and the public. It paid not only for immediate service but for the hours of practice and rehearsal time invested by musicians themselves, without which a professional musician "cannot maintain his ability as a member of his profession." Operators refused to see it that way, and in time the minimums policy, like its counterparts in the railroad and building trades, would be condemned as "featherbedding."[6]

WOMEN TAKE THE STAND

Saloon pianos carried the nineteenth century into the twentieth, and the tenderloin remained a man's world. Virtually overnight, however, the new century brought new faces to professional music—female faces. There had always been a few brave women in show business: In the 1860s and '70s the Pixley Sisters and two women's traveling circuses, Miss Jeal and Company and the Forrestelle Combination, were warmly received in Seattle, and soprano Lillian Nordica and violinist Maud Powell were stars of the concert stage. Otherwise, however, professional women musicians were few and generally considered novelties. Seattle's box house singers were hostesses first, musicians second, and their various other duties did not include playing in the tobacco-spitting male house orchestras. Nor were women welcome in legitimate theater bands. Only the piano, guitar, mandolin, and harp were considered instruments that a lady could suitably manipulate, and, in any case, the proper place for a woman musician was the parlor, with perhaps an occasional turn at the church social.

The telephone, the typewriter, and the growth of both the American economy and educational system changed all that. In 1890 some four million women worked outside the home; by 1910 it was twice as many. Clerical, educational, and medical fields clamored for female help, and so did music. Why did a resolutely male profession suddenly embrace women? New York restaurateurs of the 1880s found that women musicians had a remarkable stimulative effect on business, and a vogue for ladies orchestras worked its way west. In post–gold rush Seattle, restaurants and theaters multiplied furiously, begging for musicians—any musicians. Florence Partridge took the dare and in 1898 sat down at the piano at the Pike Street Theater, good-naturedly suffered the jibes of wisecracking males, and banked sixteen dollars a week for her trouble. Two years later, Minnie Glidden was named musical director at the Seattle Theater, a position she would hold for more than a decade.

In 1903 the American Federation of Musicians began accepting female members, and soon afterward women were working in a dozen downtown eateries: pianists Marie du Plessis Gower and Ethel Glidden at the Butler Café; pianist Mamie Shaver and violinist Bertha Lamotte at the Kaiser Keller; Marcella Lamotte and Ellie Campbell at the City Grill; and Zoe Peabody and her string band at Schelle's Grotto. Leading the culinary pack was the Bismarck Café, which opened in the spring of 1903 at First and Madison. Management engaged H. Bernhard Perboner, director of the Chicago Ladies' Symphony Orchestra, and he came west with ten women musicians whose elegant gowns and refined string music made the Bismarck Seattle's swankiest night spot. Local 76 complained about this "importation" of musicians, but Perboner's Ladies' Orchestra remained a popular attraction for several years.

Despite their new prominence on bandstands, women musicians continued to be seen as a novelty, and they continued to be barred from working in most orchestras alongside men. In 1918 a female flutist charged orchestra leader Franz Adelmann with discrimination in rejecting her for a café job. Adelmann told the Local 76 review board that there was little he could do—his men simply refused to work with a woman. Decades more would pass before mixed bands were generally accepted.

A CITY SINGS

There was one place where the sexes did make music together: choirs. Seattle has always loved to sing; the monster musical jubilee of Independence Day 1872 was an explosion of pent-up vocal impulses that begat Josiah Settle's Philharmonic and Choral Society of 1873 and Hodijan Hobache's Sing Verein Germania two years later. A far outpost of the German *Mannerchore* movement that began late in the eighteenth century (albeit open to both men and women), Germania brought new and old settlers the delights of Schubert's "Der Lindenbaum," Silcher's "Lorelei," and Bishop's "Home, Sweet Home"—even grumpy old Henry Yesler couldn't resist warbling "Old Grimes" at a church benefit. Singing sweethearts of the Gilded Age were Lizzie Bell and her sister Lillian, whose angelic sopranos were the high point of countless soirees. It was group singing, though, that became a Seattle hallmark, and Sing Verein Germania and its immediate successor, Sing Verein Arion, were the leading amateur art music ensembles of the late Victorian era.

The Teutonic accent of these choirs was no accident. From the 1860s into the 1900s, German immigrants were the most numerous ethnic group coming to Seattle. Among them, the Schwabacher brothers, Jacob Furth, Nathan Eckstein, and Bailey Gatzert were a potent presence in business, real estate, and finance. And it was in choirs that many of these kingpins met, sang, and changed the face of the city. "German and German-Jewish businessmen not only contributed to the economic growth of Seattle," noted the *Town Crier*, "but also to the city's social development, especially in respect to good music and food and friendly conviviality." After 1900, however, Scandinavia gave Seattle a distinct new inflection. When William Ballard incorporated his namesake town on the north shore of Salmon Bay in 1882, sawmills began chewing up the surrounding woods and fishing boats found the snug harbor a convenient base of operations. Old hands at these trades, Norwegian and Swedish men heard the news and flocked in by the thousands from the Midwest and from their native countries. Once settled in rooming houses, the newcomers repaired to saloons to enjoy Old Country talk and song. "The first two things they did when they formed a new community," said one observer, "was build a church and start a men's chorus. Then they built their home." The choruses were backed by solid tradition; born in Chicago during the 1850s, the Norwegian American choral movement became big business, sporting local and national *Sangerfests* and an umbrella organization, the United Scandinavian Singers of America. The tide reached Seattle in 1889 with the establishment of the *Nordmandenes Sangforening*, the Norwegian Male Chorus. Director Halvdan Rode led his ranks of black-suited men in rousing fishing songs and romances like "Olaf Trygvason" and "Serenade ved Strandredden." Norway was still under Swedish control, and the patriotic "Landkjenning" became a tearful and mandatory standby at Syttende Mai (Norwegian Constitution Day, May 17), Leif Erikson Day, Christmas, and fishermen's festivals.[7]

The Swedes did not take this lying down. In 1905, after years of feuding, the Swedish Glee Club and the Swedish Club Chorus decided to put aside their differences and counter Norsk effrontery with the Svea Male Chorus. "Vikingarne," "Angbatssang," and "Brollopsmarsch" rattled the rafters of the Swedish Club and won Svea honors in the competitions of the United Swedish Singers of the Pacific Coast. Svea and the Norwegian Male Chorus inspired a bevy of imitators and made Seattle a national center of northern European culture.

Though as many as half of the city's thirty male choruses since 1889 have been Scandinavian, other voices have been far from silent: the Ralston Glee Club, the Arion Male Chorus, and the Clef Club built a sturdy tradition of nonaffiliated vocal music during the teens and twenties. After that, choral groups of all kinds fell into decline. First-generation émigrés passed on, a new generation preferred dance music, and traditional activities passed from nostalgia for homeland to a more evanescent interest in "roots." World war, television, suburban exodus, and rising audience expectations dealt amateur choral groups heavy blows. Even so, Seattleites have never lost their love of singing, and through decades of changing musical fashion, Seattle Pro Musica, the Seattle Chamber Singers, the Total Experience Gospel Choir, and several incarnations of the Seattle Men's Chorus have kept the city's great vocal tradition alive and more diverse than ever.

DANCE CRAZY

Until the 1900s, dance in America bounced between the twin poles of ceremony and debauchery. Respectable society held its regimented waltzes and quadrilles in reserve for special occasions, while the unwashed enjoyed beery cavorting in saloons. Then ragtime burst forth, and in the teens its irresistible syncopations inspired a vogue for recreational dancing that swept the Western and much of the Eastern worlds. A bevy of "animal dances"—the Bunny Hug, the Turkey Trot, and, most importantly, the Fox Trot (actually named for originator Harry Fox)—were popularized by the touring dance team of Vernon and Irene Castle, and even staid John D. Rockefeller hired a private instructor to teach him the tango. The Victorian era was most assuredly over, and dancing the latest steps to the latest music made people of all walks feel "up to date." In Seattle, Lake Washington resorts—the Eagles, White City Ballroom, Laurel Shade—were the first pavilions dedicated primarily to dancing, later joined by restaurants such as the Puss 'n Boots Café, which advertised "after-theater dancing" (many of the new cafés sprang up around the theater district of lower Second and Third avenues). Framed by potted palms, small orchestras sawed away at "Temptation Rag" and couples did their best to Bunny Hug in hobble dresses and starched collars.

The growing hordes demanded more wiggle room, and music redoubled in the service of the dance. Seattle's ballroom era began in 1909 at the American Music Hall, and on the stand were the eight-piece bands of Fred Christensen, Paul Sternberg, and R. V. Knuppe, prototypical modern dance orchestras complete with string bass and drums. (In June 1914 the term "dance orchestra" first appeared in Local 76 records.) The full drum kit was another innovation driven by the rhythmic imperative of the foxtrot. Seattle was born to the sound of Duwamish drums, and these were echoed in 1858 when a Cape Verdean sailor named Manuel Lopes, the town's first African American resident and first barber, took a job at Yesler's cookhouse and began broadcasting the noon mealtime by walking Front Street beating his drum. Lopes and a fife player named Kelly were also a featured attraction of Independence Day parades for years afterward. Bass and snare drums propelled brass bands and entered the theater pit to accent vaudeville acts. The rise of ragtime demanded snappier rhythms from saloon and dance bands, and even as the American Music Hall opened its doors, the Ludwig brothers perfected the bass drum foot pedal, making possible the modern drum set. By the end of the decade, "trap" drums, with their accompanying contraption of cowbells, temple blocks, and cymbals, had become indispensable to dance music. Though melody continued to dominate the popular conception of music, heavy and mechanical rhythm took on a new importance it would never relinquish.

It was at the height of the dance craze in 1914 that the city's largest dance hall, the cavernous Hippodrome, opened at Fifth and University. Couples careened happily across the vast floor to the sprightly orchestras of Dad Wagner, Langer and Lueben, and Fred and John Marotta. If that wasn't enough, myriad dance clubs such as the Steppers, Evergreen, Crescent, and Minnewatha held weekly soirees in rented halls, to bands big and small. Long after it became widely accepted as a recreational activity, dancing remained suspect in the eyes of bluenoses and was continually subject to arbitrary intervention from authorities ever vigilant for lapses in public decorum. Lest things get out of hand, the police required dance halls to hire proctors. A Sunday evening fund-raising by the Ladies' Monteflore Society in November 1907 prompted complaints from neighbors; police were called, and the next day a ban on all Sunday dancing was announced. This was enforced on and off until 1909, when the Sunday blue laws were passed, making the ban official. The dancers would not be denied, however, and for the rest of the twentieth century the demands of fidgety feet would rule American popular music.

THE MIGHTY WURLITZER

Dance halls and cafés were new hotspots in a new century, but the center of musical activity remained the theater. Seattle's already busy theater life got busier in 1904, when Alexander Pantages arrived and opened the Crystal Theater, the first stone in a mighty national entertainment empire. The wily Greek met stiff opposition from old box house hands John Considine and John Cort, and the rivalry produced ever more opulent theaters and productions. Though the newspapers cheered the "New York–like" canyon effect of gleaming new skyscrapers such as 1913's Dexter Horton Building, it was the ever-grander showplaces—the Metropolitan, Orpheum, Winter Garden, Empress—that really made Seattleites feel that they were living in a city. With the profusion of first-rate houses came more touring talent, and by 1907 the city had taken its place alongside New York, Chicago, and San Francisco as a main pole in the great American vaudeville tent. On murky autumn evenings, glossy black motors drew up under the glowing marquees, while around back men in box-back coats scurried for the stage doors, fiddle cases under their arms. Dinner hour was done, and entertainment beckoned: saxophone duo Davey and Everson, comedienne Delia Stacey, and the Wolff brothers' acrobatic billiard table at the Pantages; soft-shoe dancers Creavy and Brown and tramp acrobat Charles Savan at the Coliseum; and George Smedley playing the lute, banjo, and harp-guitar at the Star. Vaudeville was an all-day event, customarily beginning at one on weekdays and as early as eleven on Saturday, and the accompanying jugglers, comedians, and singers netted an uptown theater musician eighteen dollars every six-day week.

Even as it hit its heyday, though, vaudeville met a new and ultimately triumphant competitor, motion pictures. Seattle went to the movies in 1901, when La Petite Nickelodeon opened on Pike Street, and in La Petite and its imitators the city's lusty legion of piano players—Charles Constantine, Carl Weber, Albert Klingbeil, George Olsen—found a handsome new source of income. Union "picture show" pianists got twenty-six dollars a week in 1908, and, if anything, the work was harder than in saloons. Planted on a hard bench in a stifling auditorium six hours a day, one eye on the screen and one eye on a cue sheet, the movie pianist earned every penny.

The piano served long and honorably as the lead instrument of Seattle theater music, but as the motion picture industry business grew and theaters grew larger, something more was needed to fill the space and attract new business. That something was the pipe organ, and the wizard of this new wonder of the musical world was Oliver G. Wallace. Born in London, Wallace (1887–1968) migrated to Seattle to begin his local career as pianist at James Clemmer's Dream Theater, which opened in 1908 at First and Cherry. In 1910 Clemmer replaced the piano with a $2,250 Estey pipe organ, the first theater organ in Seattle and possibly anywhere else. Two years later Clemmer went uptown and debuted his 1,200-seat Clemmer Theater, which boasted the last word in Wurlitzers. At Wallace's instigation, the instrument was loaded with special effects: barnyard animals, bird calls, train whistles, and automobile Klaxons. The debonair keyboardist pulled out all the stops in crafting a new musical idiom full of rapid mood swings, sly whimsy, and supple sensuality. Known up and down the West Coast as Wallace at the Wurlitzer, "Ollie" was perhaps the first Seattle musician to enjoy a wider reputation, a reputation that went national when he penned the hit songs "Gypsy Girl," "Indiana Moon," and "Hindustan."[8]

Giving Wallace a run for his money was Henry Murtagh, who came from Massachusetts in 1914 to take command of the gargantuan thirty-thousand-dollar Wurlitzer Hope-Jones Unit Orchestra at the new Liberty Theater ("Where the presentation of motion pictures has developed into a science"). This outgrowth of the church organ was designed to put symphonic sound in the hands of one player, and the Liberty was built specifically to showcase this trendsetting instrument—so complex and radically new that Murtagh was required to attend orientation sessions at the Hope-

Oliver Wallace takes charge of the new Estey pipe organ at the Dream
Theater in 1910. Museum of History and Industry SHS 9684

Jones Unit Orchestra School in New York. (Farny Wurlitzer himself called
the Liberty instrument the first major theater organ in the country and
credited it with making his company the leader in its field.)

For musicians in the teens, work was plentiful but hard, and none
worked harder than theater organists. The job of accompanying silent
movies—ten hours of flickering images a day—demanded nimble reflexes,
strong eyes, and iron posteriors. Very few films had written musical scores,
and the medium demanded feats of improvisation never before required of
"legit" musicians. Onscreen action shifted in a heartbeat, and woe betide

the organist who couldn't keep up. An eyeblink could be fatal; legendary among theater organ enthusiasts is the tale of the musician accompanying a scene of a shy young man calling on his sweetheart: The suitor approaches the door, extends his finger toward the doorbell, then suddenly changes his mind and walks away—leaving the hapless organist pressing the "doorbell" on his keyboard. It was stuff that kept audiences in stitches and coming back for more.

A GLORIOUS CACOPHONY

The greatest show Seattle had ever seen opened on June 1, 1909. Promoted by businessmen and *The Seattle Times* "to carry the message of progress and prosperity" and tout the city's Pacific Rim connections, the Alaska-Yukon-Pacific Exposition cost ten million dollars, some of which came from children's piggybanks. A few knockers grumbled at the expense, but most agreed that the sumptuous 250-acre aggregation of architectural wonders on the University of Washington campus was well worth the price and the hefty one-dollar admission fee. The fair was a masterpiece of planning that impressed the most jaded, and director general Ira Nadeau, entertainment committee spearhead J. C. Marmaduke, and director of ceremonies Josiah Collins labored ceaselessly to ensure that the fair would be a riot of spectacle, color, and, most of all, music.

Wagner's, naturally, was the official A-Y-P band, serenading the crowds in the towering white Nome Circle gazebo and racking up hundreds of miles marching the grounds. When Dad and his boys hove into view, delighted patrons tossed coins in appreciation. But the big stars were the world-famous symphonic bands of Frederick Innes, Alessandro Liberati, and Channing Ellery. Each was hired for five weeks, with the band judged to be the most popular to be held over for the duration. Who could pick one from such dazzling talent? "Paganini of the trombone," Innes was the fair's director of music, and his Orchestral Band of New York opened the proceedings with his specially composed official march, "Gloria Washington." Featured soloist was string bass virtuoso Vojta Kuchnyka, who astonished with his dexterity in his showpiece "Bohemia," and on Friday nights the band's all-Wagner programs packed the classically columned Temple of Music. Taking over in mid-July was the great cornet king Liberati, who had played with Patrick Sarsfield Gilmore and had fought for Italian independence alongside Garibaldi before fathering the modern concert band.

A portrait of Sealth adorns the drumhead of Wagner's Band, snapped at
the Forestry Pavilion of the Alaska-Yukon-Pacific Exposition in 1909. Dad
Wagner stands behind the drum, and to his right is new first clarinetist
Pietro Carrabba. Among the others are clarinetist Bill Osborn, whom
John Philip Sousa had once tried to hire and who would direct the
Edmonds High music program in the 1930s, and bass drummer Harry
Pelletier, first timpanist in the Seattle Symphony and a longtime Local
76 official. Now in its heyday, the Northwest's leading band includes
a large woodwind section and French horns, but no saxophones yet.
Museum of History and Industry SHS 17079

A picture of upright Italian grandeur, Liberati was in his sunset years but
could still drop jaws with his cornet artistry (though a toothache made him
set aside his horn for a week).

But the winner was Channing Ellery's eighty-five-man Royal Italian
Band. Even the rowdies were hushed into silence by director Taddeo di
Girolamo's "graceful, almost magical" interpretations, enhanced by guest
singers from the Metropolitan Opera. Hundreds were turned away from
the nighttime concerts in the Natural Amphitheater, where Girolamo
gave the first Seattle performances of Tchaikovsky's *1812 Overture* (billed

as "The Burning of Moscow" and complete with artillery) and Chopin's "Funeral March" (with special lighting effects). Ellery himself was in the audience for every concert, and on one occasion an admirer jocularly informed him that he was considering having him arrested: "You are breaking up my home life and I scarcely ever get anything to eat anymore. My wife and daughter have simply gone daffy over your music and . . . the house has become a mere dormitory, where we go and rest up for your next concert." Another remarked, "The Ellery band has become a live influence in the life of this city through the splendid and sincere quality of its work."[9]

All of these symphonic bands served a starchy diet of familiar old chestnuts. A typical concert by Wagner's band included selections from Gounod's *Faust*, "Dublin Daisies" by Wenrich, "La Paloma" by Missud, and that hoary brass band warhorse, von Suppe's *Poet and Peasant* Overture. There were few nods to contemporary American composers, except on American Music Day, September 25, which drew a music-hungry crowd to performances of short pieces by composers both local (Gerard Tonning, Louis Dimond, Mary Carr Moore, and Harry Girard) and national (Edward MacDowell, Arthur Farwell, and Dudley Buck) to the accompaniment of the Philippine Constabulary Band. Fittingly enough, the day ended with a Harvest Home Festival and Barbecue that drew hundreds ("traditional rural costume required") to the Washington State Pavilion, where a not-so-distant youth was relived by quadrilling to "Turkey in the Straw."

Under an administration sternly determined to quash any hint of rowdyism, ragtime was downplayed. Not completely, however: Innes got a big hand playing the *Merry Widow* waltz in four styles—those of Haydn, Verdi, Wagner, and ragtime—and Dad Wagner won over the rakes when he swung into the tune that was on everybody's lips that summer: "I Love, I Love, I Love My Wife, but Oh, You Kid!" Still, European classics were most people's idea of good music, and, as the applause of thousands testified, the chestnuts may have been old, but no one found them moldy. Hours ahead of performance time crowds poured into the Natural Amphitheater to once again savor excerpts from *Carmen* and *The Flying Dutchman*.

Seattle choristers had their finest hour at the fair. The SVEA Male Chorus took first prize against their Welsh and German rivals, and the Ralston Glee Club did Seattle proud against the Mormon Tabernacle and

Eisteddfod choirs. Every day featured a nation, state, lodge, or trade group (not to mention the Smith family, whose members came from around the world), along with a smorgasbord of music new to most ears: Greek fishing dances, French gypsy chants, Scottish bagpipes, and Japanese shamisens. On Norway Day, August 30, a Hardanger fiddler led a traditional wedding procession, and a host of choirs shouted the old songs to teary multitudes. Nostalgia welled up on August 21, when long-whiskered patriarchs from around the West gathered at Klondike Circle in what may have been Washington's first old-time fiddle contest. Seventy-five-year-old Captain D. A. Davis, a Civil War veteran who boasted of planting the Union flag on the Petersburg custom house, took first place with "The Arkansas Traveler" then danced a happy jig.

Native Americans and African Americans got short shrift. Small contingents of Nez Perce, Sioux, and Flathead tribes made brief appearances at the Wild West Show, and Tulalip Tribe member Vernie Cliff moistened eyes with a Cherokee ballad. A Seattle Day canoe race among Puget Sound and Canadian tribes was followed by singing and dancing on the Portage Bay waterfront. Black musicians could be heard playing cakewalks in Lacy's big brass band at the Dixieland exhibit but otherwise were virtually invisible. Fair management gave brief consideration to an "Afro-American Day," but nothing came of it, and Seattle's small black community had its moment of glory on October 15, when a cakewalk contest was held in the Washington State Pavilion. Under the bemused gaze of white bystanders, African American couples danced to the "coon shouts and ballads" of Ace Brooks, Alice Whittaker, King Rastus, Jesse Clipper, and John C. Payne, the "man with the double voice."

The Temple of Music made Seattle feel properly cultured, but the place everyone really wanted to go was the Pay Streak, the fabulous amusement strip *Variety* deemed superior to the Midway at the Chicago World's Fair. The Tickler, the Bug House, the Scenic Railway, and the Haunted Swing lured the kids, and their parents headed for the attractions packed cheek by jowl along the raucous avenue: the Chinese Village, the Japanese Theater, the Streets of Cairo, and the Spanish Theater. Spielers yelling *Step right up!* clashed with Turkish shawms, Muslim prayer calls, and a Chinese opera orchestra. The Hawaiian Glee Club, handpicked from the cream of island singers, showed off the "new Hawaii" accompanied by a quartet featuring Ernest Kaai's ukulele and Joe Kekuku's lap steel guitar. Ragtime was on tap in the Alaska Saloon until it was closed on

On the Pay Streak of the Alaska-Yukon-Pacific Exposition, a women's chorus is accompanied by a young man with a harp-guitar, an instrument that enjoyed a vogue in the early 1900s. University of Washington Libraries, Special Collections Nowell X 1688

suspicion of indecorous conduct, while the Streets of Cairo titillated, with belly dancers and a Turkish orchestra. Most popular of all was the Igorrote Village, an encampment of Philippine natives who lent the festivities a lusty background of song and drum. Lured by newspaper accounts of the scantily clad "dog-eating headhunters," sweltering, black-clad crowds forked over quarters and stood mesmerized by sounds they had previously been only dimly aware of, if at all. Predictably, many chuckled smugly at the "primitive noise." But others were enchanted by their first exposure to non-Western music.[10]

Doing the fair was an ordeal: a half-hour ride from downtown on a packed streetcar, jostling crowds at the most popular attractions, too few bathrooms, and stifling heat penetrating layers of linen and broadcloth. Many of the highlight concerts took place in the broiling sun of the Natural Amphitheater, where placards advised ladies to remove their hats so as not to block the view. Few were discouraged, however, and as the summer peaked, hordes of near-biblical proportions swarmed the grounds. Concert-goers often waited for hours to secure seats, but wait they did, and one of several high points came in early September when Ellery's Band and the Mormon Tabernacle Choir packed more than 20,000 into the amphitheater as the moon rose over Lake Washington. Despite the crush, polite gentility reigned—"The whole fraternity held his fist, the whole sorority held her tongue," a reporter marveled. The majority of locals attending were American-born whites of English, German, and Scandinavian ancestry, between fifteen and forty-five years old (nine years after the turn of the century, there were still one-and-a-half times as many male as female residents). Historian Richard C. Berner called them "a fresh middle class that had not yet developed a stake in sustaining the inequalities and iniquities that existed in the old cities of the east." That is, well-educated and open to new things. At the exposition they swarmed together amiably, littered the grounds with picnic wrappings, and couldn't get enough music. They requested the largo from Dvořák's *New World* Symphony, the sextet from *Lucia di Lammermoor*, and the *Peer Gynt* Suite. They listened intently to the Igorrotes and the Chinese orchestra. And how they loved it when Ellery struck up "The Whistler and His Dog"![11]

The Alaska-Yukon-Pacific Exposition surged to a climax on Seattle Day, September 6, when 118,000 souls jammed the grounds. Eight bands ensured that no one need suffer silence, continuous dancing was held in four pavilions, and the day of delirium was capped by a "grand mardi gras carnival" on the Pay Streak. For music and good, sweaty fun, Seattle Day was the granddaddy of the big outdoor festivals that the city would embrace decades later. On October 16, Wagner's band serenaded each of dozens of pavilions with "Taps" and as night fell led a 12,000-person conga line that burst into "Auld Lang Syne" beneath a shower of fireworks. Then the lights winked out.

Never had Seattle or the Pacific Northwest heard so much music, and in such head-spinning diversity. Not least among the fair's legacies—a new university concert hall, new international status, and a new lease on the old Seattle Spirit—was the echo of a glorious cacophony that left 3,700,000 pairs of ears ringing with a new sensitivity. As Innes and Ellery so stunningly demonstrated, classical music was indeed a manly and respectable pursuit, one that not just the elite but all people could

Sheet music cover. Property of the Music Library,
University of Washington Libraries, Ashford Collection

enjoy without embarrassment. It was a force that could bring otherwise
alien cultures together in harmony. And if the fair did not substantially
advance the general appreciation of non-Western music (a maturation
that would consume several more decades), it definitely increased aware-
ness of it.

THE OLD BANDMASTER

The Alaska-Yukon-Pacific Exposition lived on in Wagner's band. In a time of head-spinning change, Dad and his boys were a symbol of continuity and a bridge between eras. Its quality and longevity made the band not merely a source of civic pride but an important part of Seattle's sense of place in the world.

In the sunset years of the concert band, Wagner did encounter heavy competition: Ernest A. R. Meier, who in the teens was one of the first to play regular Sunday afternoon concerts in the ornate new band shell at Volunteer Park; Albert P. Adams, who started his Adams Band and Orchestra School on Music Row in 1915; and Charles La Gourgue, who came to Seattle from France in 1910 and founded the Music Conservatory of the Northwest, which he modeled on the fabled Paris Conservatory. La Gourgue's reminded many of the Ellery band (an unsuccessful effort was made after the fair to hire Ellery as Seattle's permanent town band), and like Ellery's, the La Gourgue band was considered the most refined of the group.

But it was Dad who remained closest to Seattle's heart, the incarnation of hometown pluck and pugnacity revered as "Seattle Spirit." In 1911 Wagner severed his ties with the national guard, and the First Regiment Band became Wagner's Band and Orchestra. By this time Dad had made himself the city's first big-time music contractor, supplying music for the Seattle Theater, the Opera House, and the Dreamland Dance Hall. Wagner sidemen were a hale and hearty lot, and had to be: A constant stream of concerts, parades, rallies, county fairs, inaugurations, dedications, convocations, and invocations demanded iron lungs and brass lips. Legend has it that on at least one Labor Day, Wagner marched his band down Second Avenue from Virginia Street to Yesler Way and back three times before the parade started, just to entertain the crowds. There were also statewide band competitions to be rehearsed for and traveled to, and Wagner invariably came home with first prize. For their services, Wagner sidemen earned a respectable $2.50 per daytime performance in 1910, and $3.50 at night. At full strength, the band rostered forty players, and many—among them snare drummer Harry Ingham (possibly the first to call Wagner "Dad"), baritone horn player George Carder, trumpeter Orville Snyder, and bass drummers Helmer Eggan and Harry Pelletier—stuck with him for decades. Musicians being musicians, they were not above on-the-job foolery. One warm afternoon at Volunteer Park, as cornetist Sam Price began a solo, the man behind him caught a fly, pulled its wings off, and dropped it on his head. Price appeared at the next concert in a toupee. On another Sunday, the bassoonist showed up drunk and flubbed his opening solo in the *William Tell* Overture. Wagner waved his baton at the first clarinet to take over, but the soused yet determined bassoonist puffed on, and the resulting duet had the audience howling with laughter.

A divide was crossed on April 26, 1914, when Wagner's Band celebrated its silver anniversary in a packed Moore Theater. The stage itself was packed with one hundred musicians, and when Wagner tapped his baton and they swung into "At a Georgia Camp Meeting," there was scarcely a dry eye in the house, Dad's included. If no one quite called it the end of an era, the nostalgia of the evening was lost on no one: "It was a grand old trip," sighed the *Seattle Post-Intelligencer*, "and took us past scenes that had faded from our memories long ago . . . when it was through it left us so deep in contemplation that for a moment we forgot to clap our hands." When Albert Nightingale's cornet sang out "When You and I Were Young, Maggie," all realized they were hearing the echo of a bygone day. Seattle had long used music as a connection to the rest of the world; now, music had become a bridge to the past. The old bandmaster played on, until illness compelled him to lay down his baton in 1926. Four years earlier he had successfully lobbied the city council to establish an annual fund for summer parks concerts, one of his proudest achievements, and in 1928 he was named president emeritus of Local 76, the only person ever to be so honored. Theodore Wagner died on March 19, 1933, but the concert band tradition he established in Seattle lived on in the park concerts enjoyed by thousands through the 1960s. "'Dad' Wagner is a man poor in worldly goods," reflected the union paper, "but rich as Croesus in memories of those whose lives were made happier for his having lived." On any totem pole representing old Seattle, Dad's face belongs near the top.[12]

NEW SOUND COMIN'

Kerry Mills's 1897 classic, "At a Georgia Camp Meeting," is an American music landmark. It was one of the turn-of-the-century's most popular tunes when Sousa's band recorded it in 1902, an event that hastened the mass acceptance of ragtime. A white composer's evocation of southern black society, the song stood with feet in two centuries and two cultures, and marked a coming-of-age of white America's growing affection for black America's music. Dad Wagner played the piece often in the early 1900s, making it one of Seattle's favorites and taking the city to the threshold of a new musical era.

Seattle was not a complete stranger to African American music. In 1864 the Taylor Brothers and the Excelsior Minstrels introduced Puget Sound to the inflections of black America, and the city heard gospel as early as 1884, when the Nashville Students stopped at Frye's Opera House. The crowd cheered the "plantation melodies and jubilee choruses" and whistled for encores. In 1900 Seattle's African American community numbered about 400 residents, many of whom had been lured from the South and the Midwest by the prospect of "free air"—the comparative lack of racial discrimination. The new state constitution of 1890 stipulated that nonwhites be accorded equal enjoyment of public accommodations, and in the booming late nineties African American entrepreneurs started businesses: Richard Roman's Blue Front Saloon, the Dove Dance Hall, the Minnehaha Saloon, and "Denver" Ed Smith's saloon, which, historian Esther Mumford has related, blacks and whites "of low economic standing frequented for drinks and to dance the quadrille in the dance hall in back." Square dances were leavened with Virginia reels, shuffles, and slow drags, while pianos and cornets spun out "The Spider and the Bed Bug Had a Good Time," "Bowery Buck," and Tom Turpin's "Harlem Rag." Black musicians were becoming a presence. "From the early nineties," said Mumford, "a few persons tried to make a living as singers, musicians, comedians, and actors. Some became fairly well-known around town." By 1901 there was also a Music Club serving the black community. Even so, African American Seattleites of the time did most of their music making at home, at church, and at picnics and other group functions.[13]

By 1910 the black population neared 2,300. Black bands were multiplying, too, exemplified by a mandolin-and-guitar ensemble in residence that year at the Milwaukee Bar. African American string bands had deep roots going back to the eighteenth century and were numerous throughout Appalachia, the Deep South, and the old Southwest. New Orleans had dozens at the turn of the century. String bands and ragtime were on hand at gambler-entrepreneur E. Russell "Noodles" Smith's Dumas Club, which opened on Jackson Street in 1912, just in time for a skinny New Orleans hustler named Jelly Roll Morton to drop in and give the sports a taste of his Creole keyboard creations. (Morton went east to Chicago and

In the teens the Wang Doodle Orchestra personified the black string
band tradition in Seattle. From left are Hughes, Ace Brooks, unknown,
Frank Waldron, and Coty Jones. Brooks sang in the cakewalk contest at
the Alaska-Yukon-Pacific Exposition, and Waldron gave up the trumpet
after losing his lip, but remained one of the most important saxophonists
in the history of Seattle music. Black Heritage Society of Washington
State, Inc., 2001.14.2.15.A

the big time, proclaimed himself the inventor of jazz, and in 1929 tipped
his straw hat to an old haunt when he recorded "Seattle Hunch.")

The Seattle string band was epitomized by the Wang Doodle Orchestra, a group of guitars and mandolins joined by pianists Archie Jackson and
Coty Jones, and cornetist/saxophonist Frank Waldron. Little is known of
the Wang Doodle string players, but they probably came from the South
or the Southwest and brought with them old songs and techniques. In an
era that considered the arts synonymous with white high society, "low"
music was ignored by the press, so we can only speculate on the repertoire of a black band in a period of musical transition. What is certain,
though, is that the Wang Doodle Orchestra found favor enough with

white audiences in the teens to make it one of the few black bands hired by downtown restaurants, which Local 76 declared off-limits to African American musicians. Winning this favor would have been a creative mix of ragtime, popular song, and "old-time" tunes calculated by hardworking African American musicians to please varying clienteles. They would have mixed familiars such as "At a Georgia Camp Meeting" and James Bland's "Hand Me Down My Walking Cane" with current hits like "Pretty Baby" and "Dardanella." With Waldron's horns singing out the bright melody, doubled by the mandolin and propelled by guitar chords, the band would have had a delicate yet infectious sound—they swung! Even as the Wang Doodle men reached Seattle, however, the southern black string band tradition was in decline, and it never took hold in the Pacific Northwest. It is unfortunate both that the Wang Doodle Orchestra was not recorded and that its subtle syncopations were soon drowned out by a new musical fashion.[14]

That fashion was a freewheeling extrapolation of ragtime just starting to be heard outside its native New Orleans. Seattle got its first taste in October 1914, when the Pantages Theater presented the Creole Orchestra. Early in the year, New Orleans bassist Bill Johnson judged that California had become a ripe market for his city's unique dance music, and headed west with a group that featured ace cornetist Freddie Keppard. They brought with them the Crescent City taste for embellishing melodies and filling in breaks between song sections with short improvised solos. The band also set the trend for what would become the standard jazz band, with a cornet-clarinet-trombone "front line" backed by a rhythm section. Not to be outdone by the horns, however, bass fiddler Johnson wowed everyone with his vigorous, four-beats-to-the-bar slapping technique, a radical departure from the customary two-beat bowing.

Impresario Alexander Pantages heard the band in Los Angeles, exclaimed, "I've got to have that music!" and signed them for a western tour that included Spokane, Seattle, and Tacoma. The word "jas," or "jass," was just beginning to seep into the popular vocabulary, and the Creole Orchestra was more properly a ragtime band, one that relied on old-time "coon" songs and minstrel-show antics (including buck-and-wing dancing and a live chicken) to put them across. Being part of a vaudeville act got them notice in newspapers otherwise tone deaf to black music. Still, the Creole Orchestra's dazzling execution and solo breaks amazed listeners. "This orchestra," exclaimed the *Post-Intelligencer*, "plays ragtime music that no one ever heard before, but they play it in such a manner that they have the audience marking time from its beginning to end. No one of the members appears to play the same piece, but as a whole, they turn out something that makes it hard to compel the feet to behave." The music of the Creole Orchestra might have been nothing more than a flash in a pan but for the fact that in early 1917 the Original Dixieland Jazz Band, a white group, released recordings of "Livery Stable Blues" and "Dixie Jass One-Step," and jazz was suddenly a household word. The new phenomenon prompted Seattle's African American newspaper to print this excerpt from *Literary Digest*:

> The music of contemporary savages taunts us with a lost art of rhythm. Modern sophistication has inhibited many native instincts and the mere fact that our conventional dignity usually forbids us to sway our bodies or to tap our feet when we hear effective music has deprived us of unsuspected pleasures. . . . of all moderns the jazz musicians and their auditors have the most rhythmic aggressiveness, for jazz is based on the savage musician's wonderful gift for progressive retarding and acceleration guided by his sense of "swing."[15]

Although the Wang Doodle Orchestra and several others were playing jazz-flavored music in the teens, it was on June 10, 1918, that pianist Lillian Smith led the first local group to bill itself as a jazz band in concert at Washington Hall. Smith's band played several dates during the next two years before lapsing into obscurity, and the names of the first Seattle jazz musicians remain largely unknown. One name still looms large in the history of Seattle's African American musical life: Powell Samuel Barnett. Barnett (1883–1971) started out as a child laborer in the coal mines at Roslyn, east of the Cascades; he learned to play the tuba and helped found a town band, and as a teen he became the band's manager. At one point, a company official tried to lock the band out of its rehearsal room, but Barnett stood up to the man and won everyone's respect, and for several years his band thrived.

At last, the barrel-chested, twenty-two-year-old Barnett had had his fill of mining and in 1906 moved to Seattle, working his way from street paver to sub-foreman in the city engineering department, no small feat for an African American at the time. In 1908 he picked up the morning paper and read that a band was forming to play at the Alaska-Yukon-Pacific

Exposition. "They don't want you," muttered his wife, "they want white people." Barnett replied, "Well, the ad doesn't say so, and they'll have to tell me." He got in the band, only to see it disintegrate in squabbling. But the Volunteers of America band needed a tuba player; yes, a friend told the bandleader, Barnett played a good tuba—but he was black. "It doesn't make any difference whether they're colored or not," replied the director. "If he can play, well and good." Barnett took the job and played in the Volunteers band for five years.[16]

Still, Barnett was eager to perform at Seattle's first world's fair: "We had a colored band here . . . what they might call a piece of a band . . . and I figured that if we could get a contract there, we could build it up and we'd have work all during the fair." Barnett approached the exposition music committee: Yes, a colored band would be acceptable, but only union music was being hired, so all members of Barnett's band would have to join Local 76. In an era when African Americans were treated with open hostility by the labor movement, Barnett's musicians refused: "[They] wouldn't have any part of the union, much to my regret," he lamented. "We tried every method we knew how, to get them to agree . . . but they wouldn't go for it." His world's fair dream dashed, Barnett remained determined to succeed as a musician in his own right, and in May 1913 he submitted his application to join Local 76. It was accepted, provided that he "waive the social rights of the headquarters"—in other words, not fraternize with white members. The potential inclusion of an African American in the membership of Local 76 troubled union officials, and they asked the St. Louis local how they handled the "color question." St. Louis's advice was to the point: Tell the blacks to form their own union. Despite this unequivocal counsel, Local 76 kicked Barnett's application around for a good year, then in May 1914 agreed to admit him. For the next forty-three years Powell Barnett was the sole African American member of the Musicians' Association of Seattle.[17]

Powell Barnett never stopped pressing black musicians to embrace unionism. With the concurrence of Local 76, he formed Local 458, the "colored union," in August 1918. The dual unions assumed an uneasy partnership that quickly deteriorated. Jazz was on the rise, and the growing stature of black musicians alarmed white musicians and union officials. Local 76 secretary Bill Douglas kept a sharp lookout for black bands working under scale and encroaching on the "forbidden territory" of downtown venues, and the "mother" local frequently threatened to disenfranchise the

Fourth from left, young Powell S. Barnett stands with the Mt. Zion Baptist Church Orchestra for a portrait in the twenties. During much of the twentieth century, churches afforded one of the few outlets for classically inclined African American musicians to practice their art. Courtesy of Douglas Q. Barnett

blacks. Having their own union failed to open doors for black musicians, and with very few exceptions they remained excluded from the theater and restaurant work of the musical mainstream. Not having to play to genteel white sensibilities, African American musicians continued to find their own voices, and in the process created a new musical community.

THE GENTEEL TRADITION

As much as old Seattle loved to kick up her heels, she always hankered for something higher-toned. Hoedown fiddlers Charles Testman and Mart Lewis were also violinists, and in 1868 they accompanied the newly formed Seattle Amateur Dramatic Club in performing excerpts from *Il Trovatore* and *La Sonnambula*. Two years later, George Frederick Root's popular cantata *Flower Queen* was given by a choir consisting of thirty women and one (very brave) man. Then came the great jubilee of 1872, touring opera companies, and a long succession of groups—the Women's Musical Society, the Philharmonic and Choral Society, the Orchestral and Choral Union, and the Mozart Orchestra—aiming to launch classical music in Seattle.

Obtaining that music did not happen overnight, either in Seattle or elsewhere. The New York Philharmonic was founded in 1842, the Boston Symphony not until 1881. In the post–Civil War years conductor Theodore Thomas took his private orchestra to the far corners of the United States, braving spitwads and catcalls to make Mendelssohn fans of ranchers, coal miners, and (perhaps most particularly) their wives. Some were not sure what to make of the "musical circus" (there were no acrobatic cornets, no busty chorines), but many more were forever changed by their first hearings of Bach, Beethoven, and Liszt. When skeptics questioned the ability of Americans to appreciate Wagner, the doughty maestro vowed to keep right on playing it until they *did* like it. It took a while; when Thomas was appointed director of the embryo Chicago Symphony in 1891, the press complained in best Babbitt fashion, "Why does Mr. Thomas play the soggy tunes of Bach, Brahms, and Bruckner? Has he never heard of Victor Herbert and Sousa?" Nevertheless, thanks to the lack of income tax and the moral persuasion of the Protestant "social gospel," America's aristocrats got out their checkbooks and endowed universities, libraries, and symphony orchestras. A few warned of elitism; "With this word Culture, or what it has come to represent," fumed Walt Whitman, "we find ourselves abruptly in close quarters with the enemy." Millions more saw nothing but good, however, and in 1908 the *Atlantic Monthly* proclaimed, "The musical activity of this country may be generally attributed to an altruistic purpose on the part of a minority to teach the great majority to find pleasure and comfort in the divine art."[18]

The thirty-to-one ratio in the *Flower Queen* concert was a graphic demonstration that, in America and in Seattle, late nineteenth- to early twentieth-century art music was a largely female phenomenon (although most major classical artists continued to be male). And the women were not to be denied. On March 20, 1891, the lights in Mrs. George Bacon's parlor burned bright as a select company enjoyed a performance with guitar, mandolin, and bandura. Then the ladies got down to business and began drawing up bylaws for a new musical association: All members would be required to be musicians, to audition, and to perform for the group; ticket receipts from monthly concerts would pay to bring in famous artists. First and foremost, this would be "an association of women"—the Ladies Musical Club. Ironically, among its first major undertakings was to form the all-male Seattle Quartette Club, the city's first string quartet, just in time to play at the Chicago World's Fair of 1893. The quartet returned home in triumph, bearing a Diploma of Good Performance from fair musical director Theodore Thomas himself.

The Ladies Musical Club stood shoulder to shoulder with clubs across the country—in Buffalo, Cincinnati, Cleveland, and Minneapolis—in transforming America's artistic and social life. Stepping into roles scarcely imaginable a few years earlier, women now worked as impresarios, fundraisers, artist's agents, and ensemble managers. Said one commentator,

> The annual expenditure of the American public for music in various
> forms in this second decade of the twentieth century amounts to no less
> than $600,000,000. To anyone who has observed the part that woman
> has been playing in the last five years in the musical progress of the
> nation, such statistics were to be expected. Woman's influence and persis-
> tency, accompanied by no little display of public spirit, have operated to
> solve the greater problems in the musical world.

Female domination of art music well into the twentieth century may have perpetuated its image as effete and "long hair." Certainly, it was elite, affluent, and narrow in artistic breadth (during the first fifty years, virtually all Ladies Musical Club active members were either pianists or vocalists). Nonetheless, the movement was enormously effective in developing artists, ensembles, and an audience for classical music. By 1910 the club boasted over three hundred members (sixty-seven of them male "associates") and was holding recitals that, for most of the year, were often the city's only classical events. Executive secretary Rosa Gottstein began a distinguished career as Seattle's first woman concert promoter, bringing in violinist Fritz Kreisler, contralto Marian Anderson, and Walter Damrosch and the New York Philharmonic.[19]

On the evening of December 29, 1903, Harry West and a twenty-four-piece orchestra convened in Christensen's Hall and gave Seattle its first performance of Beethoven's Fifth Symphony. West had directed numerous

West Coast orchestras since the nineties, was a founding member of the Seattle Quartette Club, and by 1903 had made enough friends in the small classical music community to pull together a symphonic ensemble. "The great audience was charmed," said a *Post-Intelligencer* reviewer; "the least musical man in it felt that he had got his money's worth, and then some." Within two years attendance prompted the West symphony to move to John Cort's 2,200-seat Grand Opera House at Third and Cherry. Rehearsals were held in the decrepit old territorial university building uptown on Denny's knoll, so musicians were obliged to trudge several blocks to and from performances lugging instruments and chairs.[20]

Able as Harry West was, he soon discovered that the business of running a symphony orchestra is beyond the abilities of one man, and he bailed out for easier work as musical director at the new Moore Theater. Still, his performances galvanized those who dreamed of establishing a permanent symphony orchestra, and in the fall of 1906 the Ladies Musical Club chartered the Seattle Choral Symphony Society, pledging a stake of $40,000. This they assembled in short order, thanks in large part to Mrs. E. C. Hughes, who put the arm on her friends, marched into the symphony office, and extracted $26,000 cash from her handbag. James Hamilton Howe was retained as musical director, and almost at once he and the ladies had a falling-out. The dissident faction launched a rival organization, the Seattle Symphony Orchestra Association, canvassed European talent, and hired Michael Kegrize to conduct at an annual salary of $5,000, a considerable sum for a musician at a time when many business executives earned less than half of that. A pianist, Kegrize had studied in Berlin and Leipzig, composed several piano and children's pieces, and came highly recommended by his mentor, conductor Carl Reinecke.

If the ladies thought that Professor Howe would roll over, they were mistaken. He had most of Seattle's symphony-ready musicians under contract and intended to hold them to it. Howe called a rehearsal of Handel's *Messiah* on the same day that Kegrize scheduled his own practice, and the newcomer was obliged to cool his heels while most of the musicians honored their contract with Howe. Partisans traded verbal brickbats ("Kegrize a leader? Pah!"), and the Kegrize faction won out. On November 18, 1907, the maestro and his forty-six-member Seattle Symphony Orchestra made their debut at the Grand Opera House. The highlight of the evening was Cesar Franck's *Symphonic Variations* featuring pianist Louis van Ogle, and if the orchestra was virtually all male, the audience was dominated by women (several of the

Fronted by Michael Kegrize, the new Seattle Symphony poses at the
Moore Theater in 1907. The orchestra is thin on strings, and harpist
Alexandra Marquardt intrudes upon the otherwise all-male fraternity.
University of Washington Libraries, Special Collections UW 21031

husbands had loaned their dress suits to the musicians, giving them a handy
excuse to escape to the cardroom of the Rainier Club). The drama attending
the birth of the Seattle Symphony would be repeated many times over during its history, but born the orchestra was. Only Portland's, formed in 1896,
predated Seattle's on the West Coast. Not everyone agreed that such an article was an essential component of a modern city: "Symphony orchestras are
expensive luxuries," lectured the *Seattle Times*. "Not more than one or two
in the entire United States are anywhere near self-supporting, and nearly all
depend for existence on certain public-spirited citizens." The Seattle Symphony would prove to be no exception to this rule.[21]

Problem number one was payroll—the planned eight-week symphony
season was far too short to sustain high-caliber musicians. Second, Seattle

had no decent concert hall. The Grand Opera House had opened in 1900, followed by the Moore, the Orpheum, and the Metropolitan. These were primarily vaudeville houses, however, and as fast as they opened they were booked with more profitable touring shows, leaving the symphony to scuffle from Armory to Arena, Hippodrome to First Presbyterian Church, and Opera House (which burned in 1917) to Meany Hall. None was entirely suitable. In 1914 music mavens formed the Seattle Federation of Musical Clubs and presented a wish list to government and business: money for parks concerts in a new city charter; a downtown music studio building; the "improvement" of music in theaters and restaurants; and a concert hall. Most of these goals were eventually attained, but the hall took the longest to complete, and the continuing absence of such a facility would bedevil the symphony and inhibit the growth of the performing arts in Seattle for decades.

Further stymieing symphonic growth was the fact that the acts that stole the orchestra's halls also stole its audience. In 1907 the symphony was nose to nose with Primrose's Minstrels, several itinerant drama companies, and continuous vaudeville. The congestion only got worse, prompting one critic to complain of the "plethora of attractions . . . uneven and dangerously piled-up schedules, throat-cutting, conflicting dates, and other features which spell disaster for certain ventures and profit for none." Now, too, there were movies that competed with *everybody*. Though many did have at least a passing taste for classical music, a substantial portion of the theater-going public discovered that genteel sounds could be enjoyed hand in hand with comedians, dancing girls, and a snappy action picture, all for a shiny silver quarter.[22]

Still, the future looked good. The Alaska-Yukon-Pacific Exposition brought money and new cultural expectations, and the Seattle Symphony Orchestra—now eighty-strong—did its hometown proud in weekly "promenade" concerts in the magnificent Forestry Hall. The concert bands of Ellery and Innes put local musicians on their mettle and raised performance standards and audience sophistication, and when the fair ended, the symphony found itself with new friends and new prominence in the community. All the same, Michael Kegrize decided to move on, and turned the orchestra over to Henry Hadley. Schooled in Boston and Vienna, and a resident of New York, Hadley (1871–1939) was perhaps the first American conductor to attain international recognition. He came with a luminous resume and a long list of compositions to his credit: songs, concert pieces, cantatas, and operas—*Safie, Azora,* and *The Garden of Allah*—and four symphonies, of which his last, *North, East, South, West,* was perhaps best known. (A later critic lauded the piece as "exceedingly interesting, and probably . . . the greatest American symphonic work that has yet been produced.") A December 1910 program reflected the lingering nineteenth-century habit of mixing light and heavy fare: guest soloist Emilio de Gorgoza singing Hadley's "The Rose Awaits the Dew-Drop" and "Thou Are So Like a Flower," and Tchaikovsky's Fourth Symphony. Newspapers gave it all solid marks and repeated the oft-uttered hope that Seattle's day as a cultural center had at last dawned. A year later, though, the economy slumped, so did ticket sales, and Henry Hadley went south to take charge of the new San Francisco Symphony.[23]

Luckily, Hadley had appointed as concertmaster a man ideally suited to pull the symphony through its next phase. Violinist John Spargur had worked with Victor Herbert and had served as assistant conductor for Walter Damrosch's New York Philharmonic before taking the directorship of the Cincinnati Orchestra. By 1905 he had succumbed to the call of the West and landed in Seattle just in time to relieve Harry West as bandleader at the Rathskeller Café. Well-seasoned with musical and people skills, Spargur had bigger things in mind, and when Hadley departed, Spargur befriended the Musicians' Association, reconstituted the orchestra as the Seattle Philharmonic, and plunged into a new season. Like Theodore Thomas, Spargur wanted symphonic music to be accessible to middle-class Americans, and in early 1912 he inaugurated "pop" and children's concerts. A February performance at the new Metropolitan Theater included, by request, two movements from Edward MacDowell's popular *Indian Suite* (the whole of which had made its local debut the previous week), selections from Verdi's *Aida,* "Dream Light" (a song by Seattle composer and vocalist Drucilla Percival), and Franz von Suppe's inevitable *Poet and Peasant* Overture. In January 1916 the great violin virtuoso Maud Powell awed a capacity crowd at the Metropolitan with Henryk Wieniaweski's Second Violin Concerto and Percy Grainger's "Molly on the Shore," and the Philharmonic gave Seattle premieres of Jan Sibelius's *Swan of Tuonela* and Tchaikovsky's Sixth Symphony. Clearly, John Spargur was doing something right.

The Seattle Philharmonic lasted five seasons, thanks largely to the support of banker James Hoge, Bon Marché department store manager Broussais Beck, and *Seattle Times* publisher Joseph Blethen (whom Spargur seems to have convinced that at least his symphony was something more than an expensive luxury). In 1917 Hoge took the presidency of the Symphony Society and changed the orchestra's name back to Seattle Symphony. Despite this help, the slog continued hard. Among Spargur's biggest headaches was keeping good players; complaining frequently that these were in short supply, Spargur received permission from Local 76 to "import" no fewer than thirteen musicians for the 1918 season—among them a bassoon, a French horn, and violins. Nor was rehearsal time ever enough. Still, the 1919 season began with ticket sales brisk enough to prompt a move from the Moore Theater to Meany Hall, and Seattle's classical music lovers had every reason to believe that theirs was an orchestra for the ages.

Opera took its own place in the new gentility. From the time the English Grand and Comique Opera Company trod the Squire Opera House boards in 1876, Seattle had always loved lyric drama. But it was a long and tortured engagement; professional grand opera is enormously expensive to produce, heavily dependent on a relatively small pool of lead voices, and until well into the twentieth century only New York could afford its own opera company (even Chicago's Grand Opera Company of 1910 lasted only three years). Lesser municipalities had to be content with touring contingents from the Metropolitan, or with Fortune Gallo's San Carlo Opera Company (also from New York), which for decades served as a peripatetic surrogate for hometown opera.

The market for opera grew in the early the twentieth century, as the first wax recordings brought Enrico Caruso into American homes. In 1907 *Seattle Times* scion Joseph Blethen and composer Harry Girard wrote a comic opera, *The Alaskan*, which premiered in New York to mixed reviews. At the Moore Theater in December, however, it was received as a refreshingly new kind of opera about real people, not the remote fantasy figures of European tradition (the team of Alaskan huskies didn't hurt, either). Seattle seemed to be well positioned to become an opera center, boasting many of the finest musicians west of the Mississippi: violinists Moritz and Leopold Rosen, and Josef Waldman; pianists Dent Mowrey, Louis Dimond, and Silvio Risegari; choristers Fred Zimmerman and Claude Madden; and tenor Theodore Karle. Karle's rival, H. Evan Williams, received an uproarious ovation at the Alaska-Yukon-Pacific Exposition and enthused that Seattle audiences had a greater appreciation of opera than any of their eastern counterparts.

Mary Carr Moore hoped he was right. Born into a musical Memphis family, Moore (1873–1957) began her music education at seven and wrote a one-act opera, *The Oracle*. She and her husband were treading water in San Francisco when relatives suggested that the wide-awake city on Elliott Bay offered abundant opportunities. In 1900 the Moores headed north, and Mary settled into teaching piano and voice in the cacophonous confines of the Holyoke Building, Seattle's turn-of-the-century music headquarters. In the afternoons between students and at nights after her three children were asleep, she spent four years writing and orchestrating her own opera, and in the spring of 1912 unveiled *Narcissa, or The Cost of Empire,* an epic based on the life of eastern Washington missionaries Narcissa and Marcus Whitman, who were killed by Cayuse Indians in 1847.

Carr hoped to take *Narcissa* to New York, but "New York managers looked upon a westerner and a woman . . . in the light of a joke." Impresario John Cort did not; with his intercession Moore got an audition with National Music Society president Arthur Farwell, a fervent apostle of American art music since the 1890s. After hearing a run-through with Moore at the piano and two singers, Farwell exulted that "America now has a grand opera of national spirit." Still, no New York production resulted, but the work did get four performances at the Moore Theater in April 1912, with Moore herself conducting. Critics were ecstatic: "Cries of 'Bravo!' so seldom heard in an American theater, broke the silence of the Moore, for it was recognized that . . . the musical spirit of the great Northwest had been caught by Miss Moore." The score's abundant "Indian" themes were particularly well received; Moore aimed to evoke Native American song rather than adapt it literally, although she did visit a Nez Perce reservation near the site of the Whitman mission and quoted judiciously from the chants she heard (her mother, Sara Pratt Carr, wrote the libretto). The bravos died, Moore resumed teaching, and in the twenties she returned to California, where she composed eight more operas and attained prominence as a music educator and journalist. The most important work by one of a handful of American women to compose art music in the early twentieth century, *Narcissa* received only two subsequent stagings, both under her direction. The opera awaits revival in the city of its creation.[24]

Narcissa faded but the opera bug did not, and in 1914 Mr. and Mrs. Berthold Sprotte and Montgomery Lynch founded the Standard Grand Opera Company. Mrs. Sprotte was an eminent concert vocalist (and had sung a leading role in *Narcissa*), and she and her husband were old hands at producing opera in Europe. The couple hung out their shingle on Music Row and announced an ambitious coming season: *Faust, Carmen, Rigoletto, Martha,* and *The Merry Wives of Windsor.* Claude Madden, a distinguished composer/violinist/chorister, was engaged as choral director, and John Spargur as conductor. Dozens of singers and musicians, few of whom had ever performed an opera in its entirety, plunged into a summer of intensive rehearsal. Rumors of feuds between Spargurites and Maddenites flew, and *Faust's* Moore Theater opening night approached amid predictions of disaster. But Gounod's warhorse was a smash, and critics were agog over the fact that Seattle artists actually pulled off "an extraordinary achievement—a personal triumph for each and every one of them . . . scoffers and the supercilious have been routed . . . the indifferent have been roused to lively interest." Those familiar with Seattle's choral groups might not have been so amazed (the Amphion Society, of which Madden was director, was one of the West Coast's top male choirs), and in October 1915 he and the Sprottes outdid even this with a Seattle debut of Wagner's *The Flying Dutchman* that was hailed as a landmark in the city's musical development. The sternest critics judged the orchestra and staging superb, and praised H. H. Tuttle (the Dutchman) and Mrs. George F. Russell (Senta) as equal to the best professionals. So, however, was the mounting deficit; as the prospect of world war loomed, subscribers grew cautious, and the Sprottes paid off what they could and slipped quietly away to San Francisco.[25]

Riding the classical music boom was the *Town Crier,* the first periodical to offer in-depth Seattle arts coverage. Debuting in 1910, its existence seemed to prove that Seattle had reached her cultural coming of age. Not so much, sighed publisher Miller Freeman: "The 'Seattle Spirit,' whatever that means, has never found place in the music life of the city. The city is noted for its lack of support of local artists and musical ventures." A mite harsh for a city that mobbed the musical events of the Alaska-Yukon-Pacific Exposition, sustained a symphony orchestra (Los Angeles, a substantially larger city at the time of Freeman's writing, would not see its own philharmonic for another nine years), and provided economic incentive sufficient to boost the resident musician population from 293 in the 1900s to 923 in 1910. Perhaps he only meant to shame the you-know-who-you-are's into pulling their share of the load. In any case, two years later he was calling upon Seattle to "create an artistic atmosphere of its own . . . to foster musical appreciation among the masses and so create a new concert-going public."[26]

The city was actually doing just that in a public school system that, under Superintendent Frank B. Cooper, treated the arts as an integral part of the curriculum. Between 1903 and 1922, Cooper's school orchestras, bands, and choral groups did more than editorial harangues to create new generations of music lovers. This yielded buyers aplenty for symphony and opera tickets—"the masses" were indeed doing their part in the genteel movement. But ticket sales alone do not keep symphony orchestras afloat; real money was, and is, required. Seattle's early twentieth-century gentry, small compared to the great eastern aristocracy, was also less rich, less class-conscious, and closer in its interests and self-identity to the business-and-professional middle class. As the city grew and exclusive new neighborhoods developed, something like high society began to appear, and the Skinners, the Stimsons, and the Blethens could generally be counted on to cover the symphony deficit, a fact of life even with full houses. But not always, and over succeeding decades that indispensable but inconsistent elite support would give the Seattle Symphony a fiscal roller coaster ride that made its survival an annual cliffhanger. There were many on all rungs of the socioeconomic ladder who agreed with populist former mayor W. D. Wood when he grumbled, "Let us have payrolls and wealth now, luxury and art when we can afford them."[27]

David Scheetz Craig chose to look on the bright side. Proclaiming "the morning of musical opportunity" in the Pacific Northwest, he launched *Music and Musicians* in 1915. "We believe," said Craig, "that Seattle, Portland, Spokane, and Tacoma are bound to become centers of intensive and progressive musical activity." Craig and Miller Freeman turned up the heat on lagging donors, called for broader community support, and kept Seattle connected with the music world beyond the Cascades. They also defended the genteel bastion against barbarian invasion. "The menace of the popular song looms big," warned the *Town Crier*, "and . . . the need for its suppression is woefully apparent." Bernard Brin, who opened his Seattle School of Popular Music at the Pantages Building in 1911, disagreed: "Musicians may deride ragtime all they please, but it remains the national expression of a love for music . . . and it has brought music to the masses more rapidly than any of a hundred schemes devised by musical societies and great artists."[28]

Genteel Seattle had a fling in July 1916, presenting what it hoped would be the first annual Northwestern Musical Festival. The three-day event in the Arena at Fifth and University was intended to supplant the raucous parades and lodge-brother high jinks of the previous all-city bash, the notorious Potlatches. The sponsors targeted the middle class with Brahms, auto tours, Scandinavian folk dance demonstrations, and band concerts at Volunteer Park. Amateur and church choirs were in abundance, and child fiddlers mingled with housewives in Swedish peasant costume and frock-coated symphony veterans. Nine-year-old Jean Kantner sang "Le Saran Rose," Mrs. K. O. Miracle crooned "Minstrel Boy," and violist E. Hellier-Collens (a forty-crossing veteran of White Star Line steamship orchestras) roused vigorous ovations. Claude Madden's orchestral ode to Native Americans, *The Dying Race*, got such tumultuous applause that the piece had to be repeated. John Spargur and the festival orchestra and chorus brought things to a spirited finale with Handel's *Messiah*. The press trumpeted the festival as a triumph of Seattle talent, even as it reluctantly acknowledged that it had not quite replaced the Potlatch in the popular affection. Of greater concern was the short shrift given contemporary American composers. The *Dying Race* ovation certainly proved that there were ears aplenty for local composers, and critics agreed that any such future event should make room for them, and "give us some of the fine modern music . . . that belongs to our own day and meets our present needs."[29]

But the first festival was the last. In 1917 the United States entered the First World War, rousing an ugly nationalism that condemned anything German. Violinist Fritz Kreisler was denounced by the Daughters of the American Revolution, and scores of "enemy alien" German and Austrian musicians, most notably Boston Symphony conductor Karl Muck and Cincinnati Orchestra leader Ernest Kunwald, were interned for the duration. Theater owners who did not play the "Star Spangled Banner" before every performance risked boycott (even though it was doubtful most Americans could sing the anthem through), and a leaden atmosphere of suspicion settled over the land. Seattle was not immune to hysteria, and John Spargur quietly dropped German composers from his philharmonic programs. The *Town Crier* deplored the "danger zone of hate," noting that not every place had gone to such extremes: "Down in San Francisco they are hearing Wagner. Can it be that those cities and many others . . . are less patriotic than we?" Nevertheless, the paper tartly approved Muck's jailing, and writer Welford Beaton echoed popular sentiment when he grumbled, "I want no German music or German anything else, and it will be a long time after the war before I will."[30]

The war siphoned musicians into military and defense work, but as manufacturing boomed, so did entertainment, and wages for remaining musicians rose. The influenza epidemic of October 1918 forced a month-long closure of dance halls, restaurants, theaters, and even churches, but things rebounded swiftly, and as the decade dwindled, the music was livelier than ever. Said critic Alfred Dyer,

> Music in Seattle is permeating the whole of the city till it promises to become indeed a city in which music shall be not merely an amusement, but in which it is an integral part of city life. There are more pupils and more teachers than at any period of Seattle's existence. The programs show a wider range and merge into each other, being no longer esoterically classical or cheaply popular.

In the coming decade, the melding of art and popular genres would produce some of the twentieth century's greatest music. And, while the genteel tradition would meet competition and setbacks, it would continue to gain ground.[31]

■ ■ ■

Bill Douglas peeled the shiny black Model T into the roadhouse parking lot. Wafting through the thin walls of the dingy frame building came a braying cornet, a clanking banjo. A giggling couple lurched out of the lighted doorway. The union secretary slammed the door on his new flivver and marched toward the entrance. This joint, out twenty miles of brick and dirt road from Seattle, in the little town of Bellevue, had a pretty good record of hiring union music. But that record was maintained only through constant vigilance and persuasion. These methods suited Douglas fine—they didn't call him Bulldog Bill for nothing. The doorman grinned: "Well, well, here's Bulldog, right on schedule!" "You bet, Sam! Who we got tonight?" Douglas peered toward the bandstand and scowled: Fengler's Famous Five, a nonunion band out of Kirkland. Allen Fengler and his daughters were crackerjack musicians, all right, and for months Douglas had been after them to join the union. But old man Fengler wouldn't budge: "Aw, go jump in the lake," he'd growled. And now, sitting there next to young Gretchen (admittedly, a whiz on the saxophone) was Forrie Hart, a banjo player and a union man. A union man sitting in with a nonunion band! Douglas grunted and pulled out his little black notebook. Come Monday, Hart would have some singing to do before the union board. Up on the tinsel-draped bandstand, Hart's eyes drifted to the door. "Rats," he muttered to Gretchen Fengler, "it's Douglas."

■　■　■

Chapter 4

Musician's Dream

THE 1920S WERE A MUSICIAN'S DREAM. Furred and tuxedoed audiences crowded the theaters and nightclubs, cafés jumped to hot jazz, and every neighborhood had its movie house, complete with organist. Radio and phonograph records, both initially derided as job-stealing "canned music" by musicians' unions, stimulated popular demand for live entertainment. But it didn't happen overnight, and the decade immortalized as the Roaring Twenties began with a moan. The first years were bleak with recession, and many a hard-luck musician headed for greener pastures. To pep up its members, the Musicians' Association started a newsletter, *Musicland*, in September 1921. "Let us make HARMONY our keynote," exhorted editor Clyde Dunn, "and keep it in tune." Harmony would not come easy. Acknowledging the "misery and depression in recent years," *Musicland* assured the membership that their union would vigorously resist threats to wages and conditions. Those threats were immediate; confronting their own stringencies, theater owners banded together in 1921 as the Allied Amusement Interests of Washington, demanding that the musicians' union accept a 10 percent wage cut, from fifty dollars for a six-day week to forty-five for sidemen, as well as extend the work week from six to seven days. Local 76 said no and held out for scale, even as it lamented the lengthening lists of those suspended for not paying their dues.[1]

Slack times or no, there was no slack for members who transgressed union rules. Working with nonmembers or in nonunion venues was strictly forbidden, and there was to be no unpaid sitting in or auditioning. When

United front: Members of the Musicians' Association of Seattle pose at the union headquarters at 2025 Fourth Avenue during the 1920s. White-mustached Dad Wagner stands front and center, at his left is Charles "Tiny" Burnett, and William J. Douglas stands at the far right in the second row. On the porch beneath "Musicians" are Ida Dillon (*left*) and Hattie "Mother" Titus. The old house continued as union headquarters until Local 76 erected its own building at Third and Cedar in 1955. Courtesy of Paul Dorpat

Chinatown restaurateur King Choy refused to hire union music, Dunn wrote, "King Choy better come around and come around in a hurry, or somebody is going to take the 'choy' out of his life." That somebody was indefatigable union secretary/sergeant at arms/business agent/managing editor William J. Douglas. The hard-charging Bulldog talked smooth to the police, the city council, and the mayor, and tough to recalcitrant club owners. In 1920 the union bought him his own Model T, and he glee-fully hustled the Tin Lizzy from café to theater to roadhouse ferreting out unfair owners and union rules violators. After being nailed by Douglas for sitting in with the Fenglers at the Bellevue roadhouse (well within Local

76's ten-mile jurisdiction), bassist/banjoist Forrie Hart told the union board that he had only wanted to "jazz a little." No matter; his escapade cost him a stiff reprimand and an even stiffer twenty-dollar fine. Douglas was often successful (only much later would *Musicland* hint darkly at his less-than-genteel methods of persuasion), but invariably, as soon as one King Choy had been dealt with, another would pop up. Nevertheless, credit for an average union membership of 75 percent of all Seattle musicians, and among the best wages of any local union workers, must in large part go to William J. Douglas.[2]

By the end of 1922 the twenties began to roar. Construction, manufacturing, and consumer sales turned skyward, and war and recession were forgotten as Seattleites had children, built houses, and bought automobiles. And now, even more than previously, they went out at night. Once again, Seattle musicians faced rising demand. Under this happy circumstance, Local 76 could enforce its wage scales, minimums, and the long-sought six-day work week—possibly the first in the land to do so. The six-day week spread quickly to Tacoma, Portland, San Francisco, and the East, and was a hallmark of union music for decades thereafter.

It was a paradoxical age. Seattle's economy had long thrived under the old wide-open policy, and people were readier than ever to enjoy good times and good music. At the same time, however, the forces of reform grew stronger, and in the twenties they came down hard on gambling, public drunkenness, racial mixing, and dancing. The Seattle Council of Churches and the Seattle Federation of Women's Clubs kept a close watch on nightlife, and when they felt things were getting out of hand they succeeded in obtaining anti-taxi-dance ordinances and periodic dance hall closures. The embodiment of reform was Bertha Knight Landes, who served on the city council and was elected mayor for one term in 1926. One of her first acts as a new council member was to pass the "Landes ordinance" of 1923, requiring dance halls to obtain licenses, hire police matron chaperones, and discontinue taxi dancing and "suggestive" lighting effects. This was followed by a blue law prohibiting public dances on Sunday. Butler Hotel owner John Savage challenged the law, held an open dance, and was fined $100, with jail promised if he did it again. In 1929, at the very apogee of the Jazz Age, Landes's successor, Mayor Frank Edwards, summarily closed Seattle's dance halls. Bill Douglas reasoned with Edwards that hundreds would be thrown out of work by his action, but the mayor stood firm, calling dancing a public menace. The city council proved more tractable, and let the dance halls reopen if they promised to behave. They did, and the Landes ordinance, with its licenses and chaperones and no-moonlight clauses, remained on the books into the 1960s. The Musicians' Association fought long and hard to convince legislators that public dancing and live music were not forces of evil, and for decades lobbied against blue laws—statutes that proved extraordinarily resistant to repeal.

Hypocrisy was guaranteed by Prohibition, the total ban on the sale and consumption of alcoholic beverages within the United States as decreed by the Volstead Act, which Congress adopted in October 1919 as the Eighteenth Amendment to the U.S. Constitution. Prohibition became law on January 16, 1920, and was promptly flouted by supporters and opponents alike. Police, local officials, and "dry" members of Congress kept bootleggers' order books full (a moonshine still was found on the property of one of the senators sponsoring the act). Booze was banned but could be easily purchased from your neighborhood bootlegger or the corner druggist (and in a back room of the Washington State Capitol), and it ran in rivers in illicit barrooms—speakeasies. In Seattle, successive administrations flatly refused to enforce Prohibition, and so the "speaks" of Chinatown and the northern outskirts flourished, the cacophony of cocktail shakers and jazz bands only occasionally interrupted by pro forma police raids. The thirteen-year reign of the "noble experiment" perfectly symbolizes the tortured ambivalence of American attitudes toward public morality and recreation in the 1920s.

JAZZ AGE

Flappers and bathtub gin notwithstanding, the twenties clung to many earlier notions of propriety. Among these was the equation of "legitimate" music with European classics. The elephant in the conservatory was that strange and raucous new phenomenon, jazz. Brought to the popular ear late in the teens by the Creole Orchestra and the Original Dixieland Jazz Band, hot music was all the rage by 1920. Getting Seattle in sync with syncopation downtown were Jack O'Dale's Purple and White Jazz Band, F. W. Baitinger's Novelty Jazz Trio, and the Fox Syncopated Five, while up on Yesler Hill Noodles Smith and Jimmy Woodland opened their Entertainers Club with the West Coast's hottest jazz unit, Benjamin "Reb" Spikes's So Different Orchestra, and a return swing by Jelly Roll Morton.

The twenties did not become the Jazz Age without a fight. The press ignored jazz almost completely, while the guardians of the genteel tradition pulled their long hair and condemned "ragtime and racket." In July 1921 *Music and Musicians* publisher David Scheetz Craig announced that he was banning jazz as "a menace to the community, detrimental to the advancement of music in the home and in school . . . it is proved that the effect of jazz is to tear down the moral fiber and to destroy the highest ideals of youth." Pianist Cecilia Augspurger, composer Claude Madden, and prominent educators signed a resolution calling for the ouster of jazz from all state schools. The musicians' union didn't like jazz either. As black syncopated bands enjoyed rising demand, Local 76 howled "unfair" at their playing under scale and working for tips (even as it continued to keep black musicians from wage jobs in downtown theaters and restaurants). The new fad of jamming and sitting-in rankled old-liners: "It is not much of a trick," said *Musicland*, "for a man to sit in for another man who has been grinding away for four or five hours, and put up a flash that attracts the attention of the boss, with the result that the relieved man suffers by comparison." But the trend would not be stopped, and even as Craig imposed his ban, the *Post-Intelligencer* ran a column from the *Musical Courier* praising jazz as the new American folk music: "From the slums of New Orleans come ballads as imaginative and alive as any seventeenth century ballad. The famous jazz, duly slandered, is a vigorous subconscious reaction against . . . sentimentality. . . . A world of beautiful melody is hidden in the heroic moans of the saxophone."[3]

Seattle's African American community grew slowly after its early 1900s spurt and in 1920 numbered 2,894, 1 percent of a general population of over 313,000 and living mostly in the Central District east of downtown. An equal accommodation law passed in 1890 made Washington one of the few non-segregated states in the Union—in theory. In practice, segregation in Seattle was all too real. African Americans were barred from residence in most neighborhoods and unwelcome in many downtown hotels, restaurants, and dance halls. Employment opportunities were limited, and, as in most trade unions, black musicians (Powell S. Barnett excepted) were shut out of Local 76. Symphony, theater, radio, and virtually all downtown restaurant work was off-limits. Beyond the pale of legitimacy, black musicians turned their talents elsewhere.

Twin poles of good times were Chinatown's Golden West and Coast hotels, owned and operated by Russell "Noodles" Smith, the self-anointed ward boss of the Jackson Street strip that ran from Chinatown up into the largely African American neighborhood to the east. The Golden West and Coast fit the classic Prohibition pattern of respectable hotel up front, speakeasy in back, catering to mixed crowds with hot black jazz bands. Two years after launching the Entertainers Club at 12th and Main, Smith opened his Alhambra at the southeast corner of 12th and Jackson in 1922, and for the next four decades the Alhambra (in 1932 renamed the Black and Tan) would be the epicenter of the Jackson Street scene.

Noodles Smith's chief rival was John Henry "Doc" Hamilton, who arrived from Mississippi around 1915 and started a string of restaurants that culminated in the Barbeque Pit, which opened in 1926 at 908 12th Avenue. By virtue of Doc Hamilton's courtly manner and secret sauce, the Pit (later named the 908 Club) jumped for six lively years. Politicians, policemen, and gangsters mingled in sweaty ribaldry, momentarily united by lively music.

Star of Doc Hamilton's and all of Jackson Street was Oscar Holden. Born in 1886, Holden moved from Nashville to Chicago with his family early in the twentieth century, and as a young man played both piano and clarinet aboard Mississippi riverboats. In 1919 Holden organized a dance band for a Canadian tour, hiring Jelly Roll Morton to play piano while he led the band on clarinet. The group played their way to Vancouver, then turned south to Seattle. Morton played the Entertainers Club and moved on, but Holden stayed behind and took his place as a founding member of the city's pantheon of piano legends. A facile sight reader, Holden loved playing both Chopin and jazz, but on the job he favored the crunchy, two-handed New York piano style known as "stride." With his huge hands and sophisticated harmonic sense, Holden sparked bands and as a solo player delighted speakeasy crowds with a skill equal to any of Harlem's piano lions.

Oscar Holden's son Dave affirmed that

Dad was one of the greatest piano players to have ever lived in Seattle. For one thing, he could read any type of music *right now*. Many a time he'd hear something on the radio, like "Flight of the Bumblebee," and say, "I'm gonna learn that." He'd go get the sheet music and spread it out all the way across the piano, and run it down—*bbbbrrrrrrr!!!* No hesitation at all. Dad played what I call stride, but he also modernized his playing in the sense that he would play the modern arrangements that were

Oscar Holden at home in 1952. Photo by Al Smith, 002–015–0147, courtesy of the Al Smith family

on the music sheet, whatever it was. So he would play like the modern guys would play, and whatever the job demanded.[4]

Asked if his father had ever expressed frustration over being excluded from "legitimate" music work due to his race, Dave said, "No. I don't think he was frustrated, for the reason that there were times when people actually would call on him to play that kind of music, because he could *read* it. Dad was so prolific in what he did that he would get called out of the area to work at the Seattle Tennis Club or the Orpheum Theater, whereas a lot of other musicians weren't able to work anywhere else." Oscar Holden anchored the black music scene for decades, his warm smile and tireless good humor at the piano giving little indication that by day he worked at Todd Shipyard, tuned pianos, and liked to unwind with a brisk swim across Lake Washington. In 1929 Holden married Leala Coleman, herself an accomplished pianist, and the pair raised a large family that included several notable musicians. Oscar Holden remained the elder statesman of Seattle jazz until his death in 1969.[5]

Worthy rival to Holden was Archie Jackson. Hailing from St. Louis, Jackson absorbed the influences of ragtime and stride and in the twenties led the Odean Jazz Orchestra. The group found steady favor at the Lodge and Nanking cafés, and the fact that they were allowed to work these downtown restaurants is testimony to the talents of Jackson and the band's star saxophone player, Frank Waldron. The high-living Waldron played both trumpet and saxophone as a youth but put away the trumpet after losing his lip. For Waldron, it was no loss, for the twenties were the decade of the saxophone, that curious hybrid which up till then had been largely a vaudeville novelty and supporting player in military bands. Inspired by the famed Six Brown Brothers, C. F. Rush organized his saxophone quartet, the Washingtonians, in 1915; the group made a brief stir, but it was Waldron who inspired a generation to embrace Adolph Sax's wonderful invention, and for decades aspiring jazzers—Ronnie Pierce, Jabo Ward, Buddy Catlett, Dick Wilson, Quincy Jones—flocked to his home studio.

Third of the great twenties piano trio was Palmer Johnson, who stepped off a steamer from Los Angeles in November 1928 and into a gig at the Maryland Tavern on the Bothell Highway. He was soon befriended by Oscar Holden and under his tutelage developed into a formidable keyboard talent. Johnson made the north-end hot music scene happen, accompanied by a group of LA players that included guitarist Freddy Vaughn and Sally Harper, a male vocalist who, not long after the gang's arrival, popularized the Klondike gambling song "Ace in the Hole." Women were not absent from early jazz, and Topeka-born Edyth Turnham made big waves in Seattle and down the coast with her Knights of Syncopation and Black Hawks. Turnham was a no-nonsense businesswoman as well as an entertainer, and knew how to work both black and white audiences. When she snagged downtown gigs at the Strand Dance Hall and fashion shows at the prestigious Frederick and Nelson store, Local 76 grumbled, but even Bulldog Douglas couldn't check the redoubtable Turnham. Coming up alongside her was Evelyn Bundy, a student of Frank Waldron who led her own band while singing and playing banjo, piano, and saxophone.

In creating and popularizing a radically new way of making music, these artists continued the transformation of American music and American society begun by minstrel shows, spirituals, and ragtime. In its improvisations, jazz breached the old wall implied by arrays of music stands

The artistry of the Odean Jazz Orchestra made it one of few African American bands able to work downtown in the twenties. At the Nanking Café, the group includes saxophonist Frank Waldron, pianist Archie Jackson, and either Ralph Stevens or Ralph Gibbs on drums. Black Heritage Society of Washington State, Inc., 2001.14.2.15E

holding the written scores of traditional music, and made music less formal and more accessible. It also breached the wall between races, and gave a northern European city new connection with America's largest minority group. Lured by the exotic word "jazz," whites discovered and heard with growing appreciation Oscar Holden and Edyth Turnham, proud of their remote city's connection with the latest New York musical trends, and perhaps just a little proud, too, of their hometown jazz musicians. And if that pride did not lead to immediate social revolution, those musicians found strength in jazz music as one of the few professions that could bring them both a good living and acknowledgment, and used their talent to build lives that were, in places such as Seattle, relatively secure.

The speakeasies where most African American musicians worked paid them at best a token wage. Their real source of income was the kitty: in pretentious establishments a plaster of Paris cat with eyes that lit up when a coin was pitched in, but more commonly an upturned hat. Either way, tips often paid far more than union scale. Beyond kitty's power to provide, though, was the security that came with a steady job paid by a set wage, backed by a strong union. Seattle's black musicians had had their own union since 1918, but it had not flourished. Local 458 founder Powell Samuel Barnett had tried, but in 1922 he was called before the mother local to answer a slug of complaints: his local had failed to uphold scale wages; it had failed to hold regular meetings; and its books were a shambles. Threatened with revocation of his charter, Barnett appealed for one last chance: Lack of legitimate work for black musicians, he told the stern-faced white board, had left the 458 treasury empty, and the incompetence and backbiting of a handful of officers had caused a lot of the trouble. Bill Douglas and his colleagues nodded, and in October 1924 Local 458 was reconstituted as Local 493, with Powell Barnett as its first president. The reborn black musicians' union was no more independent than its predecessor, but for the following three decades it danced deftly around its parent's stern supervision as its members continued jamming and playing for tips. The mother local could only wring her hands and moan, as strict enforcement of union rules across the color line would have deprived the white establishment of the music and allied recreational activities it deemed desirable. Kitty kept purring, and the jazz blared loud and late on Jackson Street.[6]

As jazz insinuated itself into American culture, theater orchestras held firmly to their pretensions of legitimacy and remained dominated by the violins and repertoire of the classics. But wishful predictions of the imminent demise of the "jazz craze" were belied by field reports from theater operators around the country saying that vaudeville audiences were going wild over hot licks. By 1924 the success of the Paul Whiteman Orchestra and the dramatic premiere of George Gershwin's *Rhapsody in Blue* opened the mainstream to jazz, and musicians' unions acknowledged that it was here to stay. In March 1925 the Coliseum Theater timidly announced that a select unit from its thirty-piece orchestra would present brief jazz concerts, while stoutly denying that the new policy would "interfere in any way with the present policy of maintaining a . . . 'legitimate' concert orchestra." Bandleaders who failed to get in step found themselves outside looking in; the Fox Theater had not been long open in 1929 when its symphonic orchestra was supplanted by a jazz band. Still, the very nature of jazz, as both improvised music and the expression of a repressed minority group, ensured that it would remain a largely fringe phenomenon. Army bandmaster Randall Wells could have been speaking for the majority of Seattleites when he observed, "Mister Average American citizen likes a smooth, flowing melody with just a suspicion of syncopation in the ensemble." In the coming years, many a musician would find success following Wells's dictum.[7]

SOUNDS OF THE SILVER SCREEN

As speakeasies jumped, so did theaters at the height of the Silent Era. Vaudeville continued to hold its own, and no fewer than four Seattle theaters—the Orpheum, Palace Hip, Pantages, and State—presented variety shows and a solid diet of musical comedy and light drama. But movies were the big draw, and for millions the mighty Wurlitzer was *the* sound of the twenties. Now a bloated, Baroque monster bristling with ranks of special effects, the great "groan box" was a far cry from the traditional church organ. It ran on higher air pressure, its stops were arranged differently, and, with the aid of couplers and "second touch" mechanisms, was more expressive of human emotion than its pious relation. Purists hated it, especially the tremulant feature that gave the theater organ its characteristic throb. "This leaky, wind-driven instrument . . . from the standpoint of the traditional and established organ is really not an organ at all," sniffed Seattle church organist Harry Colwell. "Where the regular organ is dignified, sonorous, reverent, and pastoral, the theater organ shouts, wails, screams, sobs, moans, cries, barks like a dog, and shoots itself with a bass drum."[8]

Oblivious to such distinctions, the public flocked to the great unit orchestras. Arms and legs flailing away at ranks of keyboards and foot pedals, Wurlitzer practitioners worked with one eye on the screen, the other on the bewildering array of effect stops—a fumble could land an automobile klaxon in the middle of a torrid love scene. Contrary to the carping of traditionalists, musicianship of the highest order was required of theater organists. Some major productions, such as *Intolerance* and *Seventh Heaven*, came with full scores, but most had little more than skeletal cue sheets, and organists were on their mettle to provide suitable accompaniment, drawing from commercially produced "musician's Bibles" of stock musical phrases and improvising liberally as the action and mood changed. "We wouldn't see the picture first before we'd put music to it," recalled Gaylord Carter, who worked six days a week from noon till midnight as head organist at Los Angeles' Million Dollar Theater.

> The cue sheet would give a few bars of suggested music. . . . It would say, probably, "Screening," when the picture hit the screen. Then it would call for a fanfare. Then "Opening titles," and during this maybe one of the themes was used. Then it would say, "Boy and girl in boat," and it would indicate a barcarolle type of music. Then, "Boat tips over." . . . I'd go over these things and make some little marks, and then about the second time I'd play the picture, I'd know pretty well where I was going.

Organists had their own strategies for fighting tedium. According to organist John Muri,

> Small audiences on off-days had a way of drying up one's musical faculties, and you would then have to rely on pieces drawn out of the filing case of memory. It got boring at the console hour after hour . . . especially if the organ was out of tune or had dead notes. Many organists brought food, candy, and drinks, and stored them in the ample handy side storage coves. . . . Most organists I knew played with the console lights on, but some played in the dark, and it was they who probably had easiest and most frequent access to the *nosherei* while working.[9]

More than a decade after his arrival in Seattle, Oliver Wallace remained King of the Keyboard, packing the Liberty Theater for his Sunday prologue concerts. Albert Hay Malotte offered stiff competition, and, like Ollie, was a tunesmith, producing songs that appealed to the twenties' taste for the moony and exotic: "In Spain," "Melancholy Moon" (with Harold Weeks), and "What Would Be the Use of Living if You Never Had a Little Girl to Love?" Perhaps most significant of his works was a musical setting of the Lord's Prayer that was widely circulated at the time. Malotte moved to Los Angeles in 1927, opened a theater organ school, and wrote film scores. Women were also prominent on organ benches: Betty Hilton accompanied spectaculars at the Fifth Avenue and led singalongs out at Ballard's Bagdad, while Martha Foosness earned twenty-five dollars a week riding her bicycle across town to cover shows at the Liberty, the Egyptian, and the Neptune.

The Castor and Pollux of the Seattle theater galaxy were Renaldo Baggott and Donovan Moore, who as "Ron and Don" melted thousands of

"Talented, progressive, and full of pep," organists Ron and Don—
Renaldo Baggott and Donovan Moore—enjoyed great popularity with
picture palace audiences. Author's collection

hearts in their brief but glorious career at the new Seattle Theater (later
the Paramount), which opened in 1928. As the lights went out in the cavernous French Baroque auditorium, the gilt-and-white Wurlitzer 4/20
Publix 1 rose majestically from the basement on its hydraulic lift, aglow
with colored lights and blasting furiously. The crowd gasped—there was
no one at the keyboard! Hidden in an alcove, Ron pealed out a fanfare on a
small "slave" console, while Don stepped out from the wings, mocked surprise at the unmanned organ, then introduced his partner to laughter and
applause. The two worked the $46,000 instrument in tandem, dazzling
patrons with a blizzard of musical and sound effects. (In the seventies a
tearful Baggott would return to the Paramount and play a nostalgic revival
concert on his old instrument.)

Supplementing the organists in all of downtown Seattle's major theaters were full symphonic orchestras. Whether scored for organ or for
orchestra (and in many scores both were intermingled), the music accompanying silent films was invariably a pastiche. William Axt's score for *Ben
Hur* mixed original themes with quotations from Borodin's *In the Steppes*

of Central Asia and Dvořák's *New World* Symphony. To the theater-going public of the day, it was all of a piece; pep was as pertinent as perspicacity, and a snappy rendition of "Get Out and Get Under (the Moon)" carried every bit as much weight as *The Merry Widow*. Smiling out from the orchestra pits were conductors such as George Milton Lipschultz, who worked as a soloist and guest conductor with orchestras in Cologne, Paris, and Los Angeles before settling into his Seattle career. Taking the baton at the new Orpheum Theater in 1929 was Charles "Tiny" Burnett. Eighteen years with the Orpheum Circuit and one of the city's most popular musicians, the dapper and diminutive Burnett came from St. Joe, Missouri, by way of Tacoma and was hired as musical director at the old Orpheum Theater at Third and Madison, conducting with one hand and playing a harmonium with the other, while singing and hamming it up in false noses, mustaches, wigs, and crazy hats.

The Coliseum Theater outdid everybody with its thirty-piece orchestra led by crusty Arthur Kay. A widely respected old-school maestro from the Royal Opera Orchestra of Berlin, Kay had been a favorite conductor of Victor Herbert, assistant conductor of the Boston Symphony, and director of the Grauman's Chinese Theater orchestra in Los Angeles. His starchy Teutonic discipline sometimes rankled (he habitually bawled out sidemen in front of audiences), but it got results; the orchestra was hailed as being of symphonic quality and kept the Coliseum packed. As jazz took hold, Kay permitted his boys to cut loose a little, and on hot numbers smiling Ernie Gibson delighted audiences with his cheerful fiddling and toe-tapping arrangements. One who did not suffer Kay's discipline was clarinetist Nicholas Oeconomacos; when the conductor dared criticize a clarinet passage, the haughty Greek simply packed his instrument and walked out of the pit. Brought before the union, Oeconomacos declared, "I like and respect Mr. Kay, but I will not be corrected by him or anybody else." The union admonished Oeconomacos to obey his conductors, and ordered Kay to stop bawling out his musicians.[10]

In quick succession, picture palaces sprouted like tropical flowers, and with them an army of musicians beloved by generations of Seattle audiences. (Realtor Henry Broderick and his wife occupied the same Orpheum Theater seats every Saturday night for decades.) Trombonist-vocalist Gale "Gobby" Claggett was a pit band regular from the twenties to the fifties, and adored by his peers. "Gobby was a wonderful old-time vaudeville musician," remembered reed player Dick Rose. "He wore a sailor cap and brought his little dog with him to the job and sat him under his chair. He was a fine trombonist of the old school and could make all kinds of funny sounds and animal noises." After the Palomar Theater ended its live shows in 1951, Claggett moved to Yakima and became an instrument repairman. He died in 1952 just after marching in the Independence Day parade.[11]

Abe Brashen and Leonard Hagen were just two of a distinguished coterie of theater fiddlers who kept the legitimate sound alive and well amid the bray of saxophones. Hagen, a Boston Conservatory graduate, came west in 1919 and became John Spargur's concertmaster in the symphony. He led the orchestra at John Hamrick's Blue Mouse Theater from 1922 until 1928, then walked across Fifth Avenue to direct the action at the new Music Box. Hagen's consummate musicianship had much to do with the sound and success of the Seattle Symphony in the late twenties, and he remained in its ranks until 1936. Section mate Abe Brashen was a theater and café orchestra favorite who landed a ten-year gig directing the studio orchestra at KJR Radio, then led dance bands through the forties. Hermie King, "Seattle's King of Melody," presided at the Palace Hip and Moore theaters, where his glossy piano stylings, smooth vocals, and debonair persona spelled "Broadway" to New York–obsessed Seattle. And soaring out into the Chinese Baroque cavern of The Fifth Avenue, Earl Gray's lilting alto and C-melody saxophone solos inspired a generation to become dance-band reed players.

In the thick of it all was dashing young clarinetist Ronald Phillips, a star of theater pit, symphonic stage, and bandstand for nearly seventy years. When interviewed in 1992, the youthful, eighty-six-year-old Phillips smiled as he considered the benefits of longtime school superintendent Frank B. Cooper's emphasis on the arts:

I started school at University Heights Elementary. They had a forty-piece orchestra there! I picked up my first clarinet when I was five years old and took to it right off. My cousin played cornet at the Cowen Park Theater for a dollar a night. I was ten years old, and I thought, "Heck, I can play better than he can," so I went in there on amateur night and played a solo. Then I sat down to watch the movie, and an usherette came up and asked me, "Are you the young man who played the solo?" I said yes, and she put five dimes in my hand: my first music wages.[12]

Phillips's natural talent quickly landed him offers of dance and theater work. "In the fall of 1924 I auditioned for first clarinet in the Coliseum Theater. They were going to send down to California for somebody, but I got the job and held it for two years. At the same time I played in the six-piece orchestra at the Frederick and Nelson tearoom, where all high society ate. Oh, I was making big money, about the equivalent of $1500 a week now!" It was at the Coliseum that Seattle first heard George Gershwin's anthem of the twenties, *Rhapsody in Blue*, and Ronald Phillips was in the band. "I must have played *Rhapsody in Blue* fifty times. My first was at the Coliseum Theater in 1926, just two years after it came out. I didn't play the famous opening—jeez, I didn't know how to make a glissando on a *clarinet*! I don't think *anybody* did."

The man who got the glissando was Trygve "Tommy" Solberg, who picked up the clarinet at age nine and never put it down. By fourteen Solberg was a fixture in World War One–era dance bands in Seattle and Everett, then in 1920 settled into the Seattle Symphony. Like Phillips, he filled out his time in theater pits, radio studios, ocean liners, and the Frederick and Nelson tearoom. Tommy Solberg kept playing until he was a hundred, proudly carrying his union card: number 1 in the American Federation of Musicians.

HOTEL STYLE

While less glamorous than theaters, hotels were high-prestige proving grounds that launched many a musician's career. In the teens, hotels followed the trend set by restaurants in featuring live music as a prerequisite of "tone." Shaking off the soot of a week's train journey, eastern visitors with visions of Seattle as a log cabin village were soon disabused of their preconceptions when they entered elegant, fireproof, and otherwise fully up-to-date hotels and found orchestras playing Tchaikovsky. Locals, too, could take pride in the cosmopolitanism that hotel musicians so vividly embodied.

For years after its 1893 opening, the Butler Hotel at Second and James was Seattle's pre-eminent hostelry. By 1920, though, the city's epicenter had gravitated away from the Pioneer Square district, and the Butler was losing ground. Nonetheless, its proximity to railroad and steamship terminals continued to weigh in its favor, and, best of all, the Butler had the Rose Room. Opening at the start of the decade, the Rose Room soon developed a reputation for illicit high jinks among the college set and slumming businessmen. Tiny Burnett kicked things off with a jazzy dance band of hometown stars: violinist Leonard Hagen, cornetist Frank Bradley, saxophonist Jim Eames, trombonist Andy Ward, banjoists J. Bruce Macdougall and Ernie Anderson, and drummer Marvin "Slats" Risley. Following Tiny was Tex Howard, who came from Spokane in 1924 and spent much of the decade in the Rose Room. Howard's band ostensibly numbered five pieces, but the novelty song was at its peak, and plenty of musical firepower was considered requisite for entertaining a public spoiled by the theater organ's vast array of sound effects. Most popular bands of the twenties included sidemen who could "double" on two, three, or more instruments, and Tex Howard's boys took the art to its apex: trumpeter Billy Stewart had seven instruments at his disposal, and trombonist Gobby Claggett claimed no fewer than nine doubles. The band could field a marimba quartet or a male vocal quartet, and most of Howard's boys doubled on strings.

The soul of the Rose Room was Victor Aloysius "Vic" Meyers. A smooth, pencil-mustached operator, the Montana-born Meyers (1897–1991) started out on drums and saxophone, led bands in Portland during the teens, and in 1921 headed for Seattle as the Rose Room was taking off. Meyers was a perfect fit for the naughty nightspot, and his nine-piece band rapped out peppy foxtrots guaranteed to keep the flappers flying. "Mean, Mean Mama," "Burmalone," and the timely hit "Rose Room" offered a winning formula of syrupy saxes, "wah-wah" cornet, and raunchy trombone breaks. Adding to the fun were frequent raids by local police and federal liquor agents, a well-known fact that did nothing to diminish the Rose Room's raffish image or its popularity. When the inevitable G-men appeared, Meyers gleefully swung into "How Dry I Am," and if a contingent of out-of-town collegiates happened by, his boys belted out the University of Washington fight song "Bow Down to Washington," guaranteeing a full-bore melee. It was all in good fun, but neither the best lawyers nor Meyers's glib tongue could prevail against federal agents determined to make an example of the Butler, and the Rose Room was enjoined from operating after nine in the evening for much of 1928–29. It enjoyed a brief comeback before the Butler closed for good in 1933.

In 1924 doors were opened on the establishment that would become the seat of Seattle high society, and more than any other institution would symbolize the city's rise to cosmopolitan maturity—the Olympic Hotel. The Olympic's sumptuous Marine Room and Venetian Gardens were

Late in the twenties, young Jackie Souders and his boys play a radio broadcast from the Olympic Hotel's Venetian Room. Walt Haines plays bass and Forrie Hart finally gets to "jazz a little" on banjo. Courtesy of Taylor Bowie Jr.

the place to be in Jazz Age Seattle, and filling them was a new musical fashion. Born in the orchestras of Paul Whiteman, Isham Jones, and Art Hickman, the emerging hotel or "sweet" band sound featured crooning saxophones and a gloss of strings hinting at classical respectability, spiced with just enough syncopation to sound "up to date." The hot crowd would shortly dub such bands "Mickey Mouse" and "schmaltzy," but the majority of the bill-paying public was not so judgmental, and the formula was wildly successful and widely emulated.

Unlike a later age that would see rock and roll divide the generations, dancers of all ages flocked to the Olympic and forked over a stiff cover charge—fifty cents on weeknights, one dollar on Saturdays and holidays—to hear Eddie Harkness, Cecil "Cec" Smith, Johnny Robinson, and, most notably, John R. "Jackie" Souders. The jovial trombonist with the ready quip came from St. Louis in 1920, by way of Minneapolis and Spokane. He attended Queen Anne High School and at age sixteen took his first music job in a trans-Pacific steamship orchestra. Back in Seattle, Souders jobbed with Cliff Campeau, Hilda Anderson, Hermie King's Palace Hip Orchestra, and Vic Meyers, and in 1924 launched the first of almost a half-century's worth of bands, the Collegians. In short order he was working Charles Blanc's toney Chanticler Café six nights a week and making stage appearances as a "peppy jazz band" at the Pantages Theater. Short, bubbly, and full of beans, Souders hit it big with the public and landed a contract with Columbia Records; the band's takes on "Gonna Get a Girl" and "Maybe Sometime" further enhanced his growing cachet as a bright new light in the West Coast scene. In December 1926 Souders inaugurated the Olympic's swank Venetian Gardens, beginning four decades of steady appearances at Seattle's premier hostelry. The trombone-playing bandleader boasted that he was leading a trend away from novelty, toward a "lowdown" sound emphasizing melody and danceability. The formula, which in later years he branded Music with a Heartbeat, was embraced by generations of Seattleites.

THE NEW WOMAN

The twenties were the decade of the "new woman": short of hair, flat of chest, striding briskly forward in her chosen profession. If it was a stereotypical image, it was also real. Washington State women got the vote in 1910, leading a national trend that culminated in passage of the Nineteenth Amendment to the U.S. Constitution nine years later, making women's suffrage universal. Two years later, Bertha Knight Landes was elected to the Seattle City Council, and in 1926 she became the first woman mayor of a major American city. And in cafés and theaters, more women would make music professionally during the twenties than in any preceding or succeeding decade.

"Girl bands" were at their peak. Early in the twenties Polly Butler's jazz band kept things hopping at the Plantation, while entertaining at Scandinavian dance halls was vivacious pianist Katherine Jacobsen, just then embarking upon a three-decade career. Pianist Hilda Anderson took charge of the all-male Hippodrome orchestra in 1921, while Viva Ford was appointed director of the Winter Garden Theater orchestra—an unusual combination of Ford on violin, Martha Foosness on piano, Marie de Laney on cello, and D. D. Rexford on timpani. Ford directed the orchestra for several years, then led groups at restaurants, society functions, and aboard Alaska steamers.

Monique Thomas's violin was heard often at society functions, restaurants, and on the airwaves. Her 1927 KJR Radio band, the Collegians, included, from left, Gretchen Cade (née Fengler), pianist Helene Hill, and Thomas. Author's collection

The infant medium of radio offered women a new forum, and in 1922 the Harding Sisters—singer Betty and pianist Louretta—were among the first to broadcast locally, making their debut in Radio KFOA's Bothell garage-studio. Violinist Monique Thomas was another early radio stalwart; starting at the busy Puss 'n Boots Café with cellist Iris Canfield and pianist Mabel Mohrman, by 1925 she was leading her Collegians (not to be confused with Jackie Souders's Collegians) on Radio KJR. Busier than anybody were Gretchen and Julie Fengler, from the Kirkland family that would make music around the Sound for three decades. As the region's top female saxophonist, and possibly as influential as Frank Waldron (it's a shame no recordings were made of either), Gretchen Fengler (later Cade) was in constant demand and appeared occasionally with the Seattle Symphony. She and her pianist sister, Julie, led their own combos for years, and, like Viva Ford, enjoyed great popularity at society functions.

Their increased legal standing and strong presence in the city's musical life notwithstanding, women remained a minority in a male-dominated profession. (In 1926 the *New York Times* described Seattle as "a hustling, bustling, materialistic city . . . essentially masculine in spirit and activity.") Women were accepted as musicians in restaurants because they were still considered a novelty and were attractive to prospective customers of both sexes, and also because restaurants were seen as appropriate venues for female musicians. Unlike their counterparts in other professions, female union musicians received the same pay as men. If the Musicians' Association ever had any objections to women members, they were unrecorded, and the substantial female contribution to the Local 76 treasury was certainly welcome. But women being educated and trained in music, though growing in numbers, continued to find themselves barred from theater and symphonic jobs; they were frustrated by the long-standing perception that they were less technically proficient than men, by the assumption that domestic duties would interfere with practice and rehearsal, and by society's continuing prejudice against women doing "men's work." Despite their prominent role in creating and sustaining the Seattle Symphony Orchestra, very few women made it onstage—in 1929's orchestra of fifty-five, there were four women: cellist Iris Canfield, violist Wilma Wills, pianist Cecile Barron, and harpist Eleanor Beck. It would take another world war to alter this equation. Meanwhile, British conductor Thomas Beecham spoke for many men when he declared, "I do not like, and never will, the association of men and women in orchestras and other instrumental combinations."[13]

The leadership of the Musicians' Association during the twenties upheld the male prerogative, with two significant exceptions. Embracing both the piano and progressive politics at an early age, Hattie White "Mother" Titus moved from Boston to Seattle in 1914. With her husband, Rev. H. F. Titus (who founded the *Seattle Socialist*), she eagerly joined the fight for labor rights, playing piano and organizing charity work at his Baptist ministry. For years Titus served as Local 76's representative on the King County Central Labor Council, organized fund-raising events, smoothed the always ticklish relations between unions, and gently but insistently pressed lawmakers to consider the interests of professional musicians. No less influential was Ida B. Dillon, a musicians' union stalwart for four decades. In the twenties Dillon played piano on steamers to Alaska, then became musical contractor for the Alaska Steamship Company (hiring trios of female musicians almost exclusively). In 1926 she was elected Local 76 business manager, then joined Hattie Titus on the executive board. Dillon held this post, and edited *Musicland*, until 1959.

Women's associations continued to exercise a powerful influence, but most potent of all was a one-woman band. During the teens Cecilia Augspurger was one of dozens of aspiring young pianists giving occasional society recitals. She won a spot in the Northwestern Music Festival of 1916, then plinked indifferently away toward anonymity. In the twenties, however, and now married, Cecilia Augspurger Schultz (1878–1971) decided that her real interest lay in the music business and began a long and colorful career as a concert promoter. She learned fast; paying a slippery agent five hundred dollars for a soprano, she was chagrined to discover that she could have gotten her for fifty, swore she'd never be burned again, and became her own booking agent. The opening of the Olympic Hotel presented the perfect opportunity, and in 1926 Schultz launched her celebrated Olympic Matinee Musicales, where Seattleites met on intimate terms pianist Ossip Gavrilowitsch, violinist Efrem Zimbalist, and composers Maurice Ravel, Sergei Rachmaninoff, and Ottorino Respighi. In four decades as the Northwest's premier impresario, the sharp-tongued Schultz ruffled many a feather (*Time* magazine said her voice was "sometimes compared to the sound of tearing canvas"), but she was a tireless fighter for great music and at times almost singlehandedly kept the genteel tradition alive. Editor Louis Guzzo opined that Cecilia Schultz gave Seattle "a 50-year jump culturally on most American cities."[14]

FALL AND RISE OF THE SYMPHONY

After a happy honeymoon in the teens, the Seattle Symphony came to grief in the early twenties. Buoyed by solid ticket sales after the war, the orchestra moved into the University of Washington's Meany Hall just in time for the 1920 recession. Patrons found Meany remote and acoustically challenged, and as attendance slumped, the board of trustees squabbled. Owed several thousand in back wages, John Spargur laid down his baton. This story was being played out even in Boston and Chicago and Philadelphia, as hard times and the federal income tax instilled in the wealthy a new parsimony toward arts funding. In 1922 Cecilia Schultz and friends organized the Seattle Musical Art Society in a bid to resuscitate the orchestra, but society and business support failed to materialize. The Seattle Symphony was dead.

Lack of money was compounded by the fact that much of the symphony's audience was already enjoying symphonic music at the movies. For those who demanded something more substantive than background music to *The Vamp*, there was Madame Mary Davenport Engberg. The "only lady director in the world," Engberg (1880–1951) made her Seattle concert debut in 1908 as a violinist, getting warm reviews (the *Town Crier* called her "one of the most interesting figures in the musical world of our country today"). In the teens she led the Bellingham and Spokane symphonies, then moved to Seattle in 1920 and with her husband, Henry, established the Engberg School of Music on Capitol Hill. On April 24, 1921, Engberg led the debut performance of the Seattle Civic Symphony, a mixed group of ninety amateur and professional players. Though unpaid, the orchestra had the quiet sanction of Local 76, which saw a greater good in promoting the long-term viability of a professional symphony. Musicians found Engberg a hard taskmaster, and a woman waving a baton at a virtually all-male orchestra was a dicey proposition. Nevertheless, they bore with her until the last concert in May 1924, when the oboist missed a cue in *Scheherezade*. Engberg had words with him backstage, he accused her of slapping his face, and no more was heard of the Civic Symphony. Thereafter, Seattle went to the movies, and "factionalism, financial losses . . . and sundry wheels within wheels . . . resulted in a period when to talk 'orchestra' in Seattle was to risk being forcibly ejected from a prospective guarantor's office."[15]

During the symphony's wilderness years, classical music was kept alive by Cecilia Schultz, the Ladies' Musical Club, and the Cornish School of Allied Arts. Twenty-four-year-old Nellie Centennial Cornish arrived in Seattle in 1900, a hopeful music teacher who found the city teeming with "artists, musicians, businessmen, and dreamers alike . . . carried along by [a] stream of pulsating energy." Cornish (1876–1956) set up shop in the Holyoke Building, determined to change the old, dry ways of teaching music. She adopted the Montessori Method of piano instruction, and by 1914 she had all the students she and two assistants could handle and a school of her own on Capitol Hill. "It's a wonderful school," sniffed a New York critic, "but what in hell is it doing in Seattle?" By 1920 Cornish's student body numbered eight hundred. Seeking a unifying force, Nellie Cornish found it in Calvin Brainerd Cady, who preached a holistic philosophy that viewed music as essential to human happiness and fully the equal of other disciplines. The result was a democratic and individualistic educational culture that became a Cornish hallmark. But there was no time for frivolity; the mandatory six hours of daily classroom study included solfège, eurythmics, voice, harmony, and regular performance. Cornish cautioned her students that they were there to learn—and work.[16]

Seeing that they did were some of the West's most illustrious musicians: pianist/composer Dent Mowrey, baritone Brabazon Lowther, cellist George Kirchner, violinist Francis Armstrong, flutist Glauco Meriggioli, and pioneering eurythmics instructor Julia Mary Canfield. Lending Old World color was a contingent of refugees from the Bolshevik Revolution: violinist Peter Meremblum and cellist Kolia Levienne (both veterans of the Imperial Conservatory) and opera coach Myron Jacobson, lately of the Moscow Art Theater. With pianist Berthe Poncy Jacobson, Levienne and Meremblum formed the Cornish Trio, which at times provided the only classical music heard in Seattle and brought the school considerable prestige. None of this brought in much money, however, and it was only through emergency transfusions from a wealthy few (notably banker Axel Soelberg and Seattle arts pillar Harriett Overton Stimson) that the school survived. In her office, Nellie stared down Harvard Avenue dreaming of an endowment fund and fuming at the stinginess of the Seattle elite. Famed Russian dancer Anna Pavlova and New York financier Otto Kahn both visited the school and came away marveling at the treasure Seattle had in her midst (and Kahn chiding the establishment for its paltry support of it). "There was little recognition from them of what Miss Cornish had achieved," said historian Roger Sale, "and of what she needed from those who would have to sustain that achievement." The achievement was sustained, however, and Cornish endured, fitfully but proudly, as a beacon of the fine arts in the Pacific Northwest.[17]

Admirable as the Cornish Trio was, it was no symphony orchestra. At the beginning of May 1926, Cecilia Schultz and Harriett Stimson rallied their forces, met William Douglas and Local 76 vice-president Harry Pelletier at the Olympic Hotel, and informed them that they were prepared to throw their combined financial and social clout behind the union if it would support a reconstituted symphony orchestra. Pelletier and Douglas agreed and with the ladies organized the Seattle Philharmonic Society. A trial concert was scheduled for May 14 at the Metropolitan Theater, and

The Spargur String Quartet (from left, Albany Ritchie, John Spargur, E. Hellier-Collens, and George Kirchner) was Seattle's most distinguished classical ensemble of the early twentieth century. The quartet was founded in 1912 and rehearsed for two years in the Lincoln Hotel before making its first public appearance. After disbanding in 1937, Spargur continued teaching and performing until his death in 1955. Author's collection

at the suggestion of Stimson the group hired conductor Karl Krueger, who had recently guest-conducted in Portland to good reviews. With a reassuringly Teutonic name but born in Atchison, Kansas, Krueger (1894–1979) was a cellist and organist of international stature who had studied in Paris and Vienna conservatories, served as assistant conductor of the Vienna Opera Orchestra, and by 1924 was in Los Angeles directing his own chamber orchestra. The trial concert came off well, but, uncertain of its next step, the society lapsed into bickering.

The Musicians' Association refused to accept this. "We have an orchestra of sixty-five artists ready for rehearsal," announced Bill Douglas (who stepped up as symphony business manager), "and we will give Seattle a permanent symphony if we have to hire a hall." Douglas's statement drew notice in the national press and led an impressed Karl Krueger to speak out: "The situation is unique. Where else in the United States . . . would the musicians' association feel the lack of a symphony orchestra so keenly that they would take the initiative into their own hands?" With a little prodding from Douglas, the ladies settled their differences, and Cecilia Schultz began selling tickets for the upcoming fall season (and few were the socialites who could resist; an invitation was even wired to Queen Marie of Rumania, who, in the midst of her U.S. tour, regretfully declined). The gala opening concert on November 8, 1926—a daunting feast that included Tchaikovsky's Sixth Symphony, Borodin's *On the Steppes of Central Asia*, and an old Seattle favorite, Sibelius's *Finlandia*—was a triumph.[18]

Krueger at the helm, the Seattle Symphony Orchestra entered its first golden age. The maestro's international stature and podium manner drew full houses and maximum results from the musicians. Krueger established a new precedent in community outreach, speaking at Rotary Club luncheons and high school assemblies as well as from the concert stage, an unusual gesture that brought the orchestra and its music closer to a public which discovered that classical music need not be cold and aloof. The pop concert tradition continued, and Krueger added children's performances (no adult admitted without at least two kids in tow) and junior evenings that allowed student soloists and choirs to sit in with the orchestra. His regular programs mixed the familiar (he was one of America's foremost interpreters of Tchaikovsky) and the lesser known, such as Manuel de Falla's *El Amor Brujo* and Charles Roussel's *Le festin de l'arraignee*. "Krueger was a very good conductor," said Ronald Phillips, who played second clarinet, "and we did a lot of the new things soon after they came out: Ravel's *Bolero*, Respighi's *Pines of Rome*, Richard Strauss, Igor Stravinksy." Ten years after the Great War, though, what the symphony-going public wanted most was its old friends Beethoven, Brahms, and Wagner. Krueger gave them plenty, and his successors would do the same. [19]

An audience favorite was first clarinetist Nicholas Oeconomacos. Born in Sparta, Oeconomacos studied at the Paris Conservatory and played in the French Grand Opera Company, crossing the Atlantic with them in 1903. Remaining in America, he spent two seasons with Sousa, who praised him as one of the best in the world on his instrument. In 1906 he came west and joined Franz Adelmann's Rathskeller orchestra, then took his own string orchestra into the Butler Hotel. In 1909 he joined the Seattle Symphony, a position he would hold for more than twenty years.

Tall and imperious, the great Greek drew smiles as he strode Fifth Avenue in his flowing cape and slouch hat, then gasps of amazement at transcendent readings of the Mozart Clarinet Concerto. Krueger called him the finest solo clarinetist in the country, and an Oeconomacos performance invariably concluded with multiple curtain calls. Other orchestra luminaries were violinists Mischa Levienne, Abe Brashen, and Albany Ritchie, cellists Kolia Levienne and George Rogovoy, first flutist Glauco Meriggioli, and Harry Nelson, who when not playing principal bassoon worked as a firefighter. Along with their conductor, these leading players raised the standard of Seattle musicianship and made many new friends for the symphony. "What decided strides forward the orchestra has taken," said the *Town Crier*, "and how greatly it has improved in quality and finish, especially in the violin section." Morale also improved, not least due to the fact that the orchestra was put on salary for the first time.[20]

Krueger's finest hour came in August 1927, when the Musicians' Association (again spearheaded by the indomitable Bill Douglas) and the University of Washington's Wayfarers' Pageant Society collaborated on a breathtaking production of Verdi's *Aida* at the university stadium. For four nights squawking flivvers converged on the open bowl, where five principal singers from the Metropolitan Opera, a five-hundred-member chorus, an augmented symphony of one hundred musicians, and a fifty-piece band laid on the grandest musical spectacular Seattle had yet seen. It was an enormous gamble, but Krueger and chorus master Jacques Jou-Jerville overcame the lurking pratfalls of any outdoor performance, melding instruments and voices—spread out over nearly half an acre—into a gratifyingly soul-stirring whole. Audiences of twelve to fifteen thousand gasped at technical director Burton James's towering sets and tingled at the waves of soaring music. All agreed that *Aida* was a triumph; unfazed by the vast space, lead soprano Frances Peralta declared, "I have never seen anything superior to Seattle's production," and one of dozens of Boy Scout ushers pronounced it "splendid." Never mind that two of the four evenings were rained out and had to be rescheduled; it was some of the most fun Seattle would have between two world's fairs.[21]

CANNED MUSIC

John Philip Sousa called it "canned music" and predicted that it would kill live performance. Musicians' unions cursed it. But the phonograph that Thomas Edison developed in the late nineteenth century brought recorded music into the homes of millions. Iowa farmers discovered opera, New York housewives the Virginia Reel, and music commenced its mutation from live performance to portable property. After 1910 the 78 rpm record disc began supplanting wax cylinders, a technological advance that joined with improved phonograph players in stimulating demand for all kinds of recordings. Then came jazz bands and hotel orchestras, and consumers couldn't purchase Victrolas fast enough. In the short term, the new technology and live music stimulated one another.

By the 1920s the big New York–based recording companies had made the happy discovery that Americans were desperate to own every kind of music imaginable, and the companies began committing anything and everything to disc. Scrambling for product, they assembled the latest equipment and dispatched field crews across the country. From the West Coast, slick new dance orchestras beckoned: Abe Lyman in Los Angeles, Herb Wiedoeft in San Francisco, and Vic Meyers in Seattle. The Brunswick Record Company was first off the mark, and in August 1923 their engineers arrived in Seattle, set up "a complete reproducing room," and immortalized Vic Meyers's Hotel Butler Orchestra, capturing on their first disc "Mean, Mean Mama" and "Shake It and Break It" (BR 2501). These original songs by band pianist/accordionist Earl Gibson and saxophonist Robert Gordon were by no means lowdown blues (many twenties "blues" songs were blues in name only, even if they did end on a dominant seventh), rather bouncy foxtrots laden with simpering saxes and peppered with trombonist Jim Taft's respectably hot solo breaks and Bill Zimmerman's impish "talking" cornet. The first commercial recording made of a Seattle band, Brunswick 2501 sold well and led to more sides for Brunswick and Columbia, including "Isle of Dreams" (with Oliver G. Wallace and Harold Weeks), "Ada" (with Weeks and Danny Cann), and "I'm Happy Now That You're Gone" (with Al Thompson and Harry von Tilzer). Joining Meyers on shellac were Johnny Robinson's Varsity Vagabonds, whose "Night" and "Under a Blanket of Stars" (BR 4989) found many buyers in Seattle and Portland, and Jackie Souders, who in 1926 and 1927 recorded ten sides for Columbia, including "Gonna Get a Girl" and "Maybe Sometime." Brunswick's experiment with mobile recording was not repeated (though a Columbia mobile unit recorded Meyers again in 1928), and virtually all subsequent big-label recording sessions were held at permanent studios in Los Angeles or New York. Not until after World War II would Adolph Linden's Linden Records market a commercial recording in Seattle.[22]

Taking music of all kinds to places it had never before reached was another modern marvel that E. B. White called "the godlike presence" of the twenties: radio. The first public broadcasts in 1921 ignited a wireless mania that in two years put sets in 400,000 homes. Like the phonograph but on an immensely vaster scale, radio made music more accessible, and in greater variety, than ever. Millions, among them single women and senior citizens who may not have otherwise been inclined to drop in on their neighborhood speakeasy or don formal dress for a night at the symphony, eagerly forked over $23.50 for Montgomery-Ward receivers. In Seattle, Vincent Kraft began experimenting with vacuum tube transmission late in the teens, and in March 1922 inaugurated Puget Sound's wireless age from his Ravenna garage studio, which carried the call letters KJR. Over his five-watt transmitter, Kraft broadcast his favorite phonograph records and invited musically talented neighbors in for turns at the microphone. By 1925 KJR had professionalized its programming with the Mendelssohn Trio, Wagner's Band, and the S.S. *President Madison* dance orchestra. Other stations—KTLC, KXA, and KTW—sprouted from department store roofs and office building cellars, and Seattleites purchased receivers as fast as the manufacturers could churn them out.

Local 76 reacted to the wireless "menace" with predictable apoplexy, moaning that radios were even replacing orchestras at dances. The union would soon discover that radio was in fact a gold mine for musicians, as studios began hiring soloists and orchestras by the dozens and publicizing their air times in the daily papers. Seattle broadcasting hit the big time in 1926, when the Fisher family launched KOMO Radio. At three o'clock in the afternoon of December 31 the station bowed in with Sousa's "Stars and Stripes Forever," played by Seattle's first in-house studio orchestra. Listeners were promised music "of the highest class," in keeping with the dignity of the numerous sponsoring companies. Eager to dominate the regional field, studio chief Orin Fisher built the Northwest's most modern broadcast facilities around large, well-insulated music rooms and combed the state for instrumentalists and singers, making KOMO the largest single musical employer in Washington. Radio brought to people in the far crannies of Puget Sound and the Cascades a kaleidoscope of local music and made scores of Seattle musicians—Warren Anderson, Viva Ford, Ivan Ditmars, Henri Damski, Monique Thomas—household friends.

Classical music got a huge boost from radio. Commercial sponsors embraced the medium as a means of advertising, and naturally turned to the classics to stress their corporate dignity and the wholesomeness of their products. Happy to oblige were scores of Seattle string and woodwind players, who enjoyed welcome new job opportunities bringing Brahms and Mozart to thousands who otherwise would not have heard them. A landmark in the history of broadcasting and American classical music was the Standard Oil Company of California's "Standard Symphony Hour," which debuted in 1928 and presented in turn every West Coast symphony orchestra, including Seattle's. Many doubted that a classical program would go over, but after several years the verdict was clear: "Contrary to all pessimistic predictions," said the *Town Crier*, "it has been an outstanding success from the start. . . . Today it stands, with other programs of similar nature, at the top of the list of popular radio musical entertainment." The Standard Oil program won the orchestras thousands of new listeners, both on the air and in the concert hall, along with increased appreciation of their social value. Those who wanted something peppier could tune in the live "remote" broadcasts of dance orchestras from the Olympic and Butler hotels. Remotes brought local bands to an audience far bigger than what could fill the largest dance halls, and lured eager recording companies to Jackie Souders and Vic Meyers. The nation tuned in, discovered new sounds, and then turned out to hear those sounds live and purchase phonograph records of them.[23]

Radio revived music long overshadowed by Tin Pan Alley pop, and in another paradox of the age, Northwest listeners discovered "old-time" music on radio waves: dulcimer player Elmer Hardy, reprising the tunes he had played for Seattle dancers in the 1880s; Hugh "Cowboy Joe" Poore, introducing Puget Sound to country-western; accordionists Bert Lindgren and Zac Kalbach, playing Scandinavian and Continental melodies; and Pietro Carrabba, purveying traditional Italian song with his mandolin-violin duo. The new medium made the world sounds tasted briefly at the Alaska-Yukon-Pacific Exposition an everyday reality, and for several years Hawaiian music was among the most popular of local air offerings. Radio had made America more music-conscious than ever, and *Post-Intelligencer* arts writer Everhardt Armstrong observed, "My friends among the music teachers report that . . . never in the past have there been so many young Americans seriously intent upon unlacing the polyphonic complexities of Johann Sebastian Bach, or mastering the profound utterances of Beethoven, as we find in the schools and studios today." Radio was to a great extent responsible.[24]

CLOUDS

In 1929 few musicians anywhere had it better than Seattle's. "The Seattle musician holds an enviable position in the American Federation of Musicians today," boasted Bill Douglas. "He has not only been able to hold the conditions that he has so long strived for, but has progressed with the times and gained more and more of his just share of American prosperity. Many of our sister locals have not been so fortunate. Lacking that militant spirit which pervades our organization, many of them have lost ground until their condition has become almost deplorable." Still, the profession was as vulnerable as any to social and technological change, and the Musicians' Association labored ceaselessly to defend its hard-won gains. When the Seattle Police Band was hired for a civic function instead of a union group, Douglas lamented, "We do not feel that the police who are paid for protecting the public should compete with the musician who is endeavoring to earn his livelihood from the same public for which the police band plays gratis. Certainly they would not be allowed to go out as carpenters or stone masons, so why allow them to go out as musicians?" Douglas and Hattie Titus lobbied stage federal representatives to prevent encroachments, but despite occasional concessions it remained an ongoing battle that would never be fully resolved to the union's satisfaction.[25]

Just as troublesome was the fundamentally fragile nature of the American economy, even in the apparent good times of the twenties, particularly in those industries dependent on discretionary income and sensitive to seasonal fluctuations. The theater business was one of these, and throughout the decade it was characterized by an undercurrent of instability and anxiety. The profits of a good month could be easily wiped out by a bad one, and managers were constantly on the lookout for ways to cut overhead. A running and often bitter battle with the musicians' union over house minimums and wage scales was one part of this reality. In 1921, and again seven years later, the owners of the Liberty, Winter Garden, and Palace Hip all complained that their theaters were losing money and asked Local 76 for permission to reduce their orchestras or use organs only. No dice, said the union, so the owners locked out the bands and hired nonunion musicians, including students eager for professional experience. "With such competition," the union lamented, "we have no means to cope." That this declaration would later prove prophetic is a gross understatement. The nightclub business was just as fickle, more dominated by shyster operators, and even in flush times bands were not infrequently paid with bad checks or asked to be "good fellows" and rebate wages or accept promissory notes in return for keeping a job—only to find themselves called on the union carpet to explain why they did not observe the price list.[26]

There were darker clouds on the horizon. In the autumn of 1926, the Vitaphone Corporation began showing sound motion pictures at Grauman's Egyptian Theater in Hollywood. Seattle theater owner John Hamrick (who was scrupulous in maintaining good relations with his musicians) wired the Blue Mouse and on March 18, 1927, ushered in the sound era with *Don Juan*. The Fifth Avenue and the Pantages soon followed suit, sending shivers of horror through the professional music establishment. Local 76 sounded frantic alarms, while persuading itself that field reports of Vitaphone breakdowns would lead to public revolt against mechanized movie music, even as newly wired theaters began laying off their musicians.

Not so fast, said Bill Douglas: Existing contracts had to be honored, and premature firings would be met with legal action and boycott. Douglas had done his work well. "In many of our eastern and Pacific Coast cities, the musicians have lost out completely because of the Vitaphone," he declared. "Sensing months ago what was in store, your officers immediately took steps to protect the membership of this local from the inroads of mechanical devices, with the result that we secured signed agreements that our members would not be replaced by them." This, along with the high cost of installing sound equipment and the imperfections in the new technology, kept live music in Seattle theaters for several more years. Not desiring to completely alienate the operators, the union demonstrated some flexibility. Summer was customarily a slack time for movie theaters, and when in June 1928 the Coliseum asked to temporarily cut its orchestra from fifteen to eight pieces, the local agreed. The full orchestra returned in September, but in November the dread Vitaphone was in place and management was pressing hard to fire most of the orchestra and the second organist. Angling for any possible mitigation, Local 76 passed a resolution that sound movie projectionists be members of the musicians' union, but was overruled by American Federation of Musicians president Joseph Weber. As more theaters wired up, the tumble went into free fall. Desperate to rally public opinion against canned music, the American Federation of Musicians formed the Musical Protection League and circulated petitions opposing the elimination of theater music. But the

Vitaphone would not be denied, and Local 76 president Harry Pelletier sounded a sad coda to the era of theater orchestra and Wurlitzer: "Sound has been our nightmare this last year. Hope is held out that synchronized sound is a fad and that the revolving cycle will again demand musicians in the flesh." It was a vain hope, and though it lingered in a long twilight, the Silent Era was over.[27]

■ ■ ■

It was a city within a city, a shantytown of cardboard, tarpaper, and tin. On Seattle's weedy southern waterfront, the Katzenjammer jumble was derisively named "Hooverville" for the president many held responsible for America's collapse. In the jumble lived hundreds of jobless men, men who had sold insurance, run locomotives, and built houses. A handful of women lived there, too: secretaries, waitresses, and musicians. At least, they used to be. Each morning, the residents of Hooverville emerged from their makeshift homes and walked uptown in search of food and work. Each evening they returned, some successful, more not. As darkness descended, smoke rose from hundreds of cooking fires, and deep within the little improvised city a cornet sounded taps. A stocky, ruddy-faced man put his beloved Antoine Courtois back in its case, settled wearily onto his cushion, and lit his pipe. Who knew how things would pan out? Not the cornet king on those steamer excursions when he made that horn sing! Not when the young blades sidled in close and the smiles of the gals all but blinded you! What had it all led to—the smiles and the music? The ruddy-faced man grunted; he hadn't played a real job in over a year, and now he didn't care if he never played another. Still, his Hooverville neighbors did seem to get a kick out of hearing old Tom Brown play "Taps" and, when the mood struck him, rip off a slightly sardonic fragment of "A Hot Time in the Old Town."

■　■　■

Chapter 5

Easing Depression

I N OCTOBER 1929 THE TWENTIES BOOM went bust in an implosion of overextended credit and falling market confidence. The aftermath, twelve years of misery wrapped in the singularly apt description "the Great Depression," was the worst social and economic disaster America has ever seen. Three million Americans lost their jobs in 1930, and within three years they were joined by twelve million more. Mortgage and rent money evaporated, construction and manufacturing stopped, and Hoovervilles sprouted in cities across the country. Though diverse, Seattle's economy was dominated by interdependent industries—fishing, logging, shipbuilding, light manufacturing, and retailing—that were acutely sensitive to seasonal and market fluctuations. They languished, and as the Dirty Thirties shuffled on, unemployment hit 26 percent, breadlines lengthened, and labor organizers clashed with police. There were heartening distractions: The soaring new Exchange Building was Art Deco proof that Seattle was becoming a "world city"; the papers were proclaiming that local banks were "liquid"; and even at a stiff $222 ($3.75 per month on the installment plan), Victor's Radio-Electrola Phonograph was finding buyers. But on the rain-sloshed sidewalks of Pioneer Square, lines of men stood waiting at soup kitchens and relief shelters, their gray suits matching skies that had never looked grayer.

For musicians, the Depression was a time of feast and famine, and every good gig was too often followed by weeks of scuffling. Saxophonist Andy Piatt got lucky:

I was a pretty average musician, but good enough that I could always find a job playing music when I couldn't do anything else. When I was in my last year in high school, I started playing the saxophone, and after graduation a bunch of us went over to Yakima to pick apples. One night I went into a tavern; they had a three-piece combo, so I asked if I could sit in and play a tune—"Sure, kid, come on." When I finished, the owner came over and asked if I wanted a job. You bet I did—playing music beat picking fruit! I worked in that little tavern band for a while, then went over to Coulee Dam and played two and a half years at Whitey Channin's and Jack Lewis's Silver Dollar—six nights a week for a dollar an hour. Those Coulee Dam joints ran twenty-four hours a day and would hire anybody carrying a musical instrument. The dam workers would come in and throw silver dollars in my horn. Then I came over to Seattle, and there was plenty of dance band work here.[1]

HARD TIMES

Work there was, but a musician had to be versatile. Those accustomed to the security and sheet music of legitimate music found the going tough, and former theater musicians had the worst time of anyone. The beginning of the Depression coincided cruelly with the end of the Silent Era, and by 1929 only 5,000 of the nation's 22,000 theater musicians employed in 1926 still had their jobs. As if that weren't enough, more technological innovations intruded: Jukeboxes and prerecorded "piped-in" music bumped bands from restaurants, and electrically recorded transcription discs allowed radio stations to dispense with staff orchestras. The American Federation of Musicians signed collective bargaining agreements with film studios, radio networks, and record companies, but this covered only a tiny fraction of professional musicians. For millions more, the new decade dawned bleak.[2]

Seattle's theater musicians fared better than others, because the transition to sound movies was slow. Virtually all downtown theaters were in the midst of five-year contracts with Local 76, and operators themselves were hedging their bets; early sound technology was by no means perfected (*Variety* magazine was full of tales of embarrassing synchronization failures), and as late as 1932 studios were issuing films in both sound and silent prints. Under these circumstances, retaining live music and letting the sound transition take a deliberate course was seen as good business. Organists, too, had long been a popular draw, and theaters were loath to move too far ahead of public taste. Moreover, pipe organs had been very expensive investments, and many operators preferred to see them earn their keep as long as the public kept coming.

Come, they did. Well into the thirties, Albert Hay Malotte drew good crowds to the Paramount, Herb Kern roused flagging spirits with singalongs at the Fox, and other theaters that had laid off musicians in 1929 subsequently reinstated them. In 1932 most downtown houses were still employing orchestras and organists at least part-time to provide intermission and "prologue" music. Despite its parent company's bankruptcy, the Fox retained old symphony hand John Spargur and a thirty-five-member orchestra, and the Egyptian hired cellist George Kirchner and a small band for the afternoon "curtain-raiser," an attraction that evidently drew well enough to warrant a switch to the prime evening spot. Vaudeville continued at the Fifth Avenue and Orpheum, backed by the orchestras of Jules Buffano and Owen Sweeten, and in 1933 the revived Pantages (later renamed Palomar) brought back vaudeville along with five-piece house bands and organist Harry Reed. Reed, who was also a pioneer DJ at KJR Radio, presided at the Palomar console for the rest of the decade and beyond, becoming one of Seattle's longest-serving and most popular organists.

It was a last gasp. By the autumn of 1935 the clock had run out; the orchestras vanished, and the great organ consoles were left to gather dust in theater basements or were sold (the Liberty Theater's landmark Unit Orchestra went to Pacific Lutheran University, then to Spokane's First Church of the Nazarene). Only the Palomar vaudeville carried on the grand theater music tradition. A few of the theater veterans who had enthralled Seattle audiences got lucky, most notably Albert Hay Malotte and Oliver Wallace, who found work scoring films in Hollywood. Keyboardists always had an edge; pianist Jules Buffano slipped easily from conducting theater orchestras to leading small dance bands, enjoying a long run at the Washington Athletic Club and serving as Seattle's leading musical contractor before moving to California.

Others weren't so fortunate. Once the star of theater pits and praised by Sousa, in 1931 Nicholas Oeconomacos was just one more underemployed theater musician. Unable to pay his rent or light bill, he was reduced to teaching a handful of students by candlelight. Never one to accept fate passively, Oeconomacos packed his clarinet and went busking downtown. Perched on a suitcase at Fourth and Pike, he piped his old favorite, "The Sweetest

A Seattle legend, Nicholas Oeconomacos was considered one of the
nation's finest clarinetists by Karl Krueger and John Philip Sousa. To
protest the firing of theater orchestras in the early thirties, Oeconomacos
busked on downtown sidewalks, but preferred to entertain the children of
his Cascade neighborhood. Museum of History and Industry 86.5G2241

Story Ever Told," to the passing throngs, opera cape around his shoulders
and wide-brimmed hat turned over on his knee. "It is hard to do this," he
told a reporter, "it makes me feel like a beggar." Oeconomacos wasn't busking for himself alone, however, but to publicize the plight of all musicians:
"Thousands are walking the streets. The public will forget what living music
is. Our children may never hear it." He stirred consciences by saying,

> During my twenty-five years in Seattle I have played for hundreds of
> organizations. They never thought of sending me a check. . . . Our
> wealthiest families often invited me to dinner and receptions with the
> invariable postscript: "Don't forget to bring your clarinet." With the lone
> exception of our late, beloved Mrs. C. D. Stimson, none ever sent me a
> check. They pay dance musicians but we artists must live on air![3]

The spectacle of the beloved celebrity playing for change was a shock.
Children mailed him coins, a laborer placed a hundred dollar bill in his

hand, and embarrassed society matrons sent long-overdue checks. But many just shrugged—what could one do, when *everyone* was out of work? Oeconomacos had an answer to that: form a Federal Bureau of Fine Arts to ensure that no artist went hungry and that great music always had a place in America. Increasingly cantankerous and unwilling to take direction, Nicholas Oeconomacos was fired from the symphony in 1933 and evicted from his small house. Somehow (there were rumors of a fortune hidden in a mattress), he managed to purchase an even larger dwelling in Cascade, and with coins earned from coaching school bands ("Be alive! When you play, let people look into your face and see the sparkle!"), he transformed it into a fanciful House of the Terrestrial Globe, complete with a Greek theater where he entertained his neighbors. Still a musical force to be reckoned with, he joined flutist Glauco Meriggioli, violinist John Spargur, and cellist E. Hellier-Collens in presenting Musique d'Ensemble recitals that dazzled listeners until a few years before his death in 1945. Oeconomacos's symphony successor, Ronald Phillips, told me,

> Oeconomacos had great phrasing and tone, but he played his way. The leader could just follow along and hope it came out all right. Finally, [conductor] Basil Cameron wouldn't have him, and made me first chair. It was only years later that he grudgingly accepted that. Oeconomacos was a powerful man—the most colorful character of all. I put flowers on his grave every Decoration Day.[4]

As it had in the Panic of 1893, the musicians' union circled the wagons. Bill Douglas chased down scabs and unfairs, while ballroom and nightclub operators complained that hard times made paying union scale impossible. Hat-passing returned, and Local 76 granted dues exemptions to unemployed members and marshaled food and shelter for hardship cases. Even so, by one estimate, the Seattle union lost as much as one-third of its members. Still, depression or not, society craved music, and for every out-of-work musician there was another who managed to ferret out a gig. The end of Prohibition in 1933 and President Franklin Roosevelt's New Deal coincided to bring better times to barrooms and ballrooms.[5]

SEATTLE SWINGS (AND POLKAS)

As theaters went talkie, live music retreated to ballrooms and nightclubs, where people flocked to forget their troubles. Opening on May 20, 1927, the Trianon boasted the largest dance floor in the West, a capacity of 5,000, and brought big-name bands—Ted Fiorito, Fletcher Henderson, Jimmie Lunceford—while local groups kept dancers happy during the week. Elward "El" Arseneau hit it right with his unpretentious but consistently crowd-pleasing orchestra, and worked steadily through the decade. "El's was a good, solid dance band," Arseneau trumpeter Hugh Bruen told me. "It wasn't what you'd call distinctive. We played stock arrangements like most of the bands at the time, but we were tight, we swung pretty good, and El had a personality that the club bosses and the dancers liked. It was enough to keep us busy when a lot of bands were scuffling." On the other end of town, in suburban Burien, the Spanish Castle (initially called the Highline Spanish Ballroom) opened in 1931 with Vic Meyers's orchestra, but would shortly become synonymous with the sweet band of trumpeter Frankie Roth. The short, dapper Roth idolized Henry Busse, the Paul Whiteman Orchestra cornetist who had a big hit with "Hot Lips," and delighted in whinnying away Busse-style as his sidemen rolled their eyes. People loved him, though, and for twenty years Roth *was* the Spanish Castle, and his name in neon over the marquee proved it.[6]

Epitomizing Jazz Age Seattle (though it opened on December 18, 1929, after Wall Street laid its famous egg) was Vic Meyers's Club Victor, at 2221 4th Avenue. The pomaded, wisecracking Meyers provided a dash of Gotham glamour in hard times, enhancing it with a regular radio remote on Walter Winchell's "Lucky Strike Hour." (According to newspaper radio schedules, Meyers got the most airtime of all Seattle bandleaders during the period.) What he didn't bring was money. From the day Club Victor opened, its wily owner played a running game of cat-and-mouse with Local 76 over back wages, and with creditors and prohibition agents pounding at the doors, the nightspot closed in the spring of 1931. Meyers continued to front (and stiff) bands, then in November 1932 entered a colorful twenty-year career in politics, convincing the public to elect him lieutenant governor ("I won't tell any lies about my opponent if he won't tell the truth about me"). As the erstwhile bandleader took up his duties in Olympia, Club Victor reopened but was no more profitable than before, and Meyers ran up a hefty tab of back band wages before folding for good

The Vic Meyers Orchestra strikes it up for the photographer early in the thirties. Museum of History and Industry 86.5.35776.2

in 1936. Politics, rubber checks, and the loss of his nightclub did not spell the end of Vic Meyers's musical antics, and he would continue to work as a part-time bandleader into the 1960s, leaving a generation of musicians ruefully shaking their heads.[7]

Increasingly popular, especially after Prohibition was lifted in early 1933, were nightspots catering to a population that was expanding beyond the city limits. On Saturday nights dusty Fords and glossy Duesenbergs converged on a cluster of suburban highlife at 85th and Bothell Way: the Old Plantation, Chinese Castle (later the Jolly Roger), and Jungle Temple Inn. Fred Owens's Jungle Temple led the pack with the Jungle Temple Syncopators, featuring female pianist Babe Hackett, vocalist Eddie Rucker, and clarinetist Joe Darensbourg. A light-skinned Creole from Baton Rouge, Louisiana, Darensbourg enjoyed a peripatetic career that brought him to Seattle in 1929. The wry and dapper musician was among Seattle's first notable purveyors of the New Orleans–style jazz that later came to be known as Dixieland. At the Jungle Temple, though, Darensbourg and band were strictly up-to-date, and that meant not the raggy jazz of the twenties but the streamlined, four-to-the-bar sound that would shortly be dubbed swing. Referring to the "chamber jazz" then popular in New York, Darensbourg recalled, "We were playing stuff something in the John Kirby style. Not quite as technical as Kirby . . . but definitely swing. It wasn't Dixieland." But vocalist Rucker was the big draw: "People came from all over the Pacific Northwest to hear Eddie," said Darensbourg. "He used to do a lot of . . . off-color tunes. . . . We would average seventy-five or a hundred dollars a night in that kitty!" Twice-weekly live radio broadcasts beamed the Jungle Temple band across the state. Darensbourg went on to work the boats to Alaska and Asia and scuffled around the decaying saloons of the western outback (in Prescott, Arizona, he played clarinet while pumping a player piano with his feet). But he preferred Seattle, and spent most of the decade whirling from job to job: banging out blues with pianist Vic Sewell at the Spinning Wheel, dispensing dance music with Oscar Holden at the Blue Rose, and cutting loose with singer/saxophonist Tootie Boyd at the 908 Club. To Darensbourg, the city on Puget Sound was a special place: "There's never been a town like Seattle . . . Seattle and New Orleans is the two distinct towns in the U.S.A., so different from any others."[8]

Working alongside Darensbourg were old pros such as William Rayne "Bus" McClelland, a genial ex-theater organist who led combos at Cap's Old-Time Dance, the Silver Slipper, and countless restaurants before moving to Portland late in the decade to man the organ at Oaks Park. From the twenties through the forties, pianist Gordon Kilbourne fronted radio orchestras and played solo at the Garden of Allah and the Spinning Wheel, backing Seattle's early female impersonators. Danny Cann's Melody Boys worked the same circuit, and so did stride pianist Delle Alexander and her Alexander's Ragtime Band. Able to segue easily from "The Liechtensteiner Polka" to "A Good Man Is Hard to Find" (in all its variations), these hardscrabble, six-night-a-week bands exemplified not only the sound of Depression-era Seattle but the music found in taverns and dance halls into the 1960s. Down-to-earth yet versatile and musicianly, they offered consistent, accessible conviviality and the emotional connection of a musical language shared by people of all ages and backgrounds.

The foxtrot may have dominated the dance floor, but Seattle's large northern European population had one foot in the past. As early as 1910, the Musicians' Association noted the enduring popularity of the "old songs" being played by string bands. In following decades, Seattle's old-time music was distinguished by Scandinavian-accented dance orchestras that mixed contemporary songs with schottisches and hambos. The time was ripe; by the mid-twenties Columbia and Victor were producing at least as many ethnic as domestic records, Scandihoovian artists Hjalmar Peterson and the Olson Sisters were playing to packed houses, and the culture of recreational dance eagerly embraced the polka. "Old-time ethnic music," says musicologist Victor Greene, "had . . . substantially broadened its appeal and in fact was on the verge of becoming an integral part of our national culture."[9]

In Seattle, accordionist Al Sjodin's ten-piece Scandinavian-American Dance Band packed Norway and Vasa halls and hosted regular old-time nights at the Trianon Ballroom. Bert Lindgren started out as a theater organist, then in the thirties became a bandleader and opened a dance hall in suburban Bothell that became a bastion of old-time and Scandinavian dancing. One of the stars of Lindgren's Pavilion was young Norwegian-born accordionist Harry Lindbeck, who began his bandleading career in the Mount Vernon area then worked a steady circuit of lodge, granges, and ballrooms throughout the Northwest with what was probably the most popular Scandinavian American dance band between 1930 and 1960. These bands featured not the traditional Hardanger fiddle but saxophones and in particular the piano accordion, an instrument that rose to popularity in the twenties and became a generic voice of European dance music. Seattle's Scandinavian dance bands were not literal ethnic ensembles bent on preserving old traditions but a new type of "international crossover" orchestra formed to make money by satisfying diverse audiences. The Scandinavian sound never found the broad and enduring popularity that Polish and German bands did in the Midwest, but it did give a distinctive flavor to Seattle's dance music scene.[10]

PACIFIC RIM

Northern Europe did not completely dominate Seattle's international community. In the summer of 1896 railroad magnate James J. Hill began regular steamship service to and from Japan, establishing a connection with Asia that would create a new Pacific Rim community of trading partners and promote cultural exchange between hemispheres. Despite prejudice, the need for cheap labor and the relaxation of immigration laws after

1900 invited new waves of Asian settlers to head for western Washington.

Seattle's first major immigrant group, the Chinese, enjoyed a big come-back in the twenties and thirties, and so did their music. Even though the 1882 Chinese Exclusion Act would not be repealed until 1943, a new gen-eration began settling in Seattle. Among them was Portland-born restaura-teur Charlie Louie, and in 1923 he opened a theater at Seventh and King, hired native musicians, and revived traditional opera. Louie's Chinese theater lasted longer than its predecessor, but by the end of the decade the plaintive wail of the *erhu* gave way to the shouts of boxing matches. Unlike the commercial music of neighboring speakeasies, Chinese music was strictly art music and not an adjunct to the sale of liquor and other "products," and so had little economic foundation. A businessman first and traditionalist second, Charlie Louie traded the theater for the Chinese Garden Restaurant—with jazz bands.

Chinese music found a lasting Seattle home in 1938 with the found-ing of the Luck Ngi (Musical Arts) Musical Society. The Luck Ngi Musi-cal Society became the successor of the backroom groups of the 1880s, its membership mostly single waiters, laundrymen, and merchants who met to discuss business, play games, and perform Cantonese opera and songs into the wee hours. Among them was Henry Lip Louie, a Toishanese who studied Cantonese opera in China and became a master of the erhu. Giving public performances in Chong Wa Hall, Luck Ngi thrived in the late thirties, surviving attrition and war to become the oldest and largest Chinese organization in Seattle. "Seattle's Cantonese opera company was considered the best anywhere," Chong Wa regular Pete Leinonen told me. "Families brought picnic lunches, children ran around, and the musicians played nonstop, smoking and slumping like jaded pros. Woman sang along with the arias, men smoked, and everything was seasoned with generous splashes of Chinese cymbals. It was a rich sensory feast that I wish every music lover could experience." As the founding generation began passing away in the 1980s, the association's days appeared numbered. New genera-tions have discovered the beauty of Chinese music, however, and both the Luck Ngi Musical Society and the Chinese Arts and Music Association keep cymbals and erhus resonating.[11]

In the 1890s, Japanese immigrants began to fill the void left by their Chinese predecessors, leasing farmland in the Green River valley and set-ting up shop in Seattle. Though it was illegal for Japanese to become natu-ralized citizens or own property, their numbers grew steadily, and by the

A traditional Japanese orchestra accompanies a kabuki performance at
the Nippon Kan Theater late in the thirties. University of Washington
Libraries, Special Collections UW 21330

1930s the Japanese American population topped 8,000 residents—by far the
city's largest minority group. Many Japanese immigrants desired both new
opportunities and the preservation of old customs. The Meiji Restoration
of the late nineteenth century imposed radical change upon feudal Japan.
One upset came in 1880, when the emperor ordered the Japanese school
system to adopt Western music. Traditional music—high art/court music
(*Gagaku*), and folk/entertainment music (*Zokugaku*)—was summarily
banished to the countryside, geisha parlors, and private schools. To preserve their native culture in the new world, the first Japanese immigrants
established a strong network of schools and community associations. In
1901 the school at the Seattle Japanese Buddhist Temple was established,
becoming a haven for traditional music. It was soon joined by the Society
of the Lotus in presenting stage plays and musical ensembles for the Set-
subun festivals of Buddha's Birthday and the New Year.

In 1909 the Nippon Kan Theater opened on the hill overlooking
Nihonmachi (Japantown), and for the next three decades Japantown was

a major American center of Japanese music, dance, and Kabuki and No drama. Local and visiting musicians brought Seattle the sound of the three-stringed *koto*, zither (*shamisen*), and flute (*shakuhachi*). Japanese music flourished during the Depression, mesmerizing audiences of all nationalities at the Nippon Kan and at Japan Days at the Playland Amusement Park. In August 1932 the first annual Bon Odori festival was held in Nihonmachi, where 2,000 people enjoyed the music of kotos, shakuhachis, and drums. Sadly, the eviction and imprisonment of virtually all people of Japanese ancestry during World War II ended this renaissance of traditional culture, and the Nippon Kan went dark. Seattle's Japanese community struggled to revive itself in the fifties, embracing Western customs and reserving traditional music for study and rare special occasions.

COLLEGE RHYTHM

Insulated from the worst ravages of the Depression, the University of Washington (UW) was a musical world in itself during the thirties. The big noise on campus was Cecil "Cec" Smith, whose sweet band dominated Husky functions throughout the decade. Drummer/xylophonist/trumpeter Smith hailed from Bellingham, worked his way through law school as a bandleader, and wrote one song—"Let's Write a Song"—that received airplay by the Tommy Thomas Orchestra. Smith's orchestra was one of the most in demand among off-campus society as well, and joined the Olympic Hotel's "collegiate circuit" alongside Jackie Souders's Collegians, Johnny Robinson's Olympic Varsity Vagabonds, and the orchestra of pianist Center Case. "Center Case was a real nice guy who played decent piano," said bassist and Case alum Ed Gross, "and we played a lot of college functions at the Olympic Hotel. Center had an excellent book of arrangements, most of which he transcribed off records. A lot of guys did that during the Depression, when there was no money to buy music." Sororities favored the Jimmy Crane Orchestra, whose Guy Lombardo sound made the coeds swoon, and the frats cavorted to Robert Tomlinson's Madhatters. "The Madhatters came out of Ballard High," said Mitchell Taylor Bowie, who matriculated in the Tomlinson band as a top alto sax player. "It was a Sammy Kaye–style hotel band and very big with the college crowd. Robert had a thing for instrument-swapping; the book was full of quick changes, and, jeez, you were constantly switching instruments. If you weren't careful you'd knock your teeth out."[12]

"Kid bands" were a hallmark of swing-era Seattle, and among them was Edmonds High's Cavaliers. In this 1939 photo, trombonist Ken Cloud sits on the far left, Doris Hellwig stands at the microphone, and playing sax are Dick Giger and a grinning Johnnie Jessen. Johnny Wittwer is at the piano. Courtesy of Ken Cloud

Obverse of the sweet bands was the exuberant aggregation of pianist Gaylord "Gay" Jones. A UW graduate struggling to break into the music business with something new, Jones wrote some arrangements, formed a band, and burst onto the scene as the headliner at Seattle's first jazz festival on March 2, 1939. Organized by UW junior Norm Bobrow's Husky Hot Club, the show was a sensation. A buoyant, gregarious New Yorker, Bobrow (1917–2008) brought to Seattle an enthusiast's love for jazz and swing that evolved into an evangelical desire to take it to a wider audience. "I would like to see swing music attain in Seattle the same respect with which it is regarded throughout most of the country," Bobrow declared. "Swing is an American music and Seattle an American city. Why shouldn't we accept the music of our own country—or at least try to understand it?"[13]

The Hot Club show launched Bobrow's long career as Seattle's leading jazz impresario, and it made Gay Jones's the hottest band in Washington. It also netted him a three-year run as house band at the Trianon. On Saturday nights the lines would stretch a block long, while inside, the famous dance floor would pound to the feet of hundreds of stomping jitterbugs. Small combo jam numbers gave the dancers a respite, then the heat was steadily turned up by the high notes of trumpeters Carle Rising and Pete Barrington and the propulsive drumming of Gordon Challstedt, who took inspiration from Jimmie Lunceford drummer Jimmy Crawford's distinctive two-beat "lope." Jones got people on the floor with stock Artie Shaw, Count Basie, and Benny Goodman numbers, then hit them with his original charts: bright, propulsive scores with the extended harmonies just then creeping into use in big-name bands. Cooling things down with romantic ballads was Jones's wife, Marilyn, who sang under the stage name Mars Mercer (and for a time performed locally with a Boswell Sisters–inspired vocal trio). The success of the Gay Jones Orchestra both as a jazz band and as a commercial dance orchestra was an effective demonstration that the two need not be mutually exclusive.

Excitement notwithstanding, jazz remained a pariah to old-schoolers. University of Washington president Lee Paul Seig asked Bobrow if he couldn't give the Hot Club a less suggestive name, and saxophonist Milt Kleeb found the atmosphere similarly stuffy:

> Tiny Martin and I had attended summer music school at the UW in 1939. The program at the time was strictly classical. We put together a jam band, and one day all the guys who were supposed to be in music class were jamming with us instead. Tiny and I were branded "disruptive," and the dean of music threatened to expel us. Of course, Tiny later became first chair bass in the Boston Symphony. But back then jazz was still not accepted as "legitimate" music.[14]

JACKSON STREET JUMPS

For most African Americans the thirties were hard times and then some. Seattle's black community was small, concentrated, and largely invisible to a white society that kept blacks from virtually all opportunities for advancement. Nonetheless, against a background of pervasive prejudice, black music had been embraced by America, and for some African American musicians the decade presented a wider field of opportunity than ever.

This still did not extend to mainstream pop and classical realms. Powell Barnett, the resolute founder of African American musicians' union Local 493, remained determined to change that. In 1931 he led another assault on the ramparts of Local 76, petitioning for integration. Again he was rebuffed, although the local did name him delegate to the annual American Federation of Musicians convention in 1933. There he made his case to federation president Joseph Weber, who was receptive to the idea. But it wasn't enough to budge the Seattle union establishment, and Local 493, which averaged some forty members during the thirties, remained firmly under the thumb of its thousand-member mother local. A musicians' union amalgamation was opposed as well by some blacks who felt that they were better off away from the close supervision and restrictive rules of the white parent. Integration would take another quarter century.

The way barred in one direction, African American musicians found fulfillment in another. Marching eastward up Jackson Street from Chinatown, then north on Twelfth Avenue, the Ubangi Club, the Black and Tan, the Blue Rose, the Hi-Hatters' Club, and Club Royale blared from dusk to dawn. This now-legendary Jackson Street scene offered black Seattleites fine entertainment and reassurance that their culture could stand fast in an overwhelmingly white city. It also offered work aplenty for black musicians such as saxophonist Earl Whaley. A Bay Area transplant and Seattle swing pioneer, Whaley and his Red Hot Syncopators ignited the Black and Tan and the short-lived Cotton Club on East Marginal Way, then sailed to Shanghai and wowed the Far East with the Jackson Street beat. Some reverse pollination also took place. "A lively jazz scene on Jackson Street," wrote Michael Segell, "was largely responsible for producing a generation of fantastic Filipino saxophonists: the owners of Japanese ocean liners hired Filipino workers . . . and the laborers discovered a special affinity for the instrument, which they studied at Jackson Street speakeasies and practiced on board. The popularity of the instrument in the Philippines hasn't waned since."[15]

Turning up the heat was Gerald Wells, who led what some considered Seattle's best jazz band. The reed-and-flute player hailed from the West Indies and had come to Seattle via Los Angeles and Benjamin "Reb" Spikes's So-Different Orchestra. In Noodles Smith's Ubangi Club, said to be the largest black-owned business north of Los Angeles, Wells and his ten-piece band backed Cotton Club–style floor shows and dispensed vivacious Harlem jump that had mixed audiences on their feet till sunrise. Another new face was enigmatic pianist Julian Henson, who by age eighteen had absorbed the stride technique of his mentor, Archie Jackson, and had added to it the intricate ornamentations and advanced harmonic ideas of the new king of pianists, Art Tatum. Henson played the Seattle clubs for twenty years, garnered a high reputation among insiders, and then moved to Portland, where he remained active.

The Benny Goodman Orchestra is often credited with igniting the swing craze, but many Seattle musicians took inspiration from Gene Coy. The Texas bandleader was an apostle of the bluesy Kansas City style hitting its stride with Jimmie Lunceford and Count Basie, and in a series of shows at Washington Hall, Coy's Eleven Black Aces left black and white musicians shaking. One of Coy's stars was Dick Wilson, a light-skinned reed player who went to Broadway High School, played with Joe Darensbourg, and in a too-short life became a widely heralded tenor saxophonist. Paul de Barros labeled Wilson (along with fellow tenor man Corky Corcoran) the Northwest's most significant swing-era figures. Only thirty years old, Dick Wilson died in 1941.

Palmer Johnson opened his own Jackson Street joint, the 44 Club, in 1937 and invited a young stripling fresh off the train to spell him on the piano bench. Jimmy Rowles took his cue from Julian Henson and built up his chops at Sunday jam sessions that occasionally welcomed a visiting Louis Armstrong or Duke Ellington. Norm Bobrow befriended Rowles, who also worked briefly with the Jimmy Crane and Kenny and Charles Reisdorf bands at the UW. "Jimmy was a marvelous jazz player," Norm said, "but he listened to everything, and he didn't limit himself to just being a 'jazz musician.' He used to brag that he owned every record Guy Lombardo made!" Rowles was not long on the Seattle scene, and by 1940 was off to Los Angeles. For a short time, too, Johnson featured trumpeter Herman Grimes, who many believed out-blew Louis Armstrong himself. Grimes took his place in the ranks of Seattle near-legends who burst bright for an instant then faded.[16]

Up on Twelfth Avenue, Doc Hamilton's 908 Club was hopping, a magnet for political and business leaders and their not-always-well-behaved offspring. (Hamilton would occasionally have his limousine haul inebriated college kids back to the dorms after a wild Saturday night.) The genial Doc was a diplomatic businessman who knew how to walk the precarious tightrope of the successful African American in white society. Musicians, too, had to know how to look happy, and one of the most knowledgeable was pianist-bandleader Winfield King. Son of LeEtta Sanders King, herself a dance-band pianist and an influential music teacher in the black community, King and his bands enjoyed strong favor in African American social circles, and he later became active in Local 493. "Winfield was a real, entertainer-type piano player," said trumpeter Floyd Standifer, who worked with King in the fifties and sixties, "somewhat in the nature of a Bobby Short, only more blues-oriented. He would play Cole Porter side by side with the get-down blues, and do them both beautifully. Winfield was in possession of a fabulous singing voice—he had an ebullience about him that just reached out and *grabbed* you. Winfield King taught me a lot about how to get along."[17]

Getting along was crucial. Not seen by the happy hordes at the 908 Club were the stone-faced beat cops in the back room, pocketing their payoffs while Doc Hamilton did his best to maintain his dignity. As long as they kept smiling at their patrons' often crass behavior, Hamilton and his musicians remained on the good side with the downtown whites who claimed the best tables and (illegal) liquor. Eventually, however, reality caught up with him, and in 1932 Hamilton was arrested by federal authorities who were shocked to discover that gambling was taking place on his premises. He appealed, charging the presiding judge and the system with racism, and lost. Doc Hamilton bowed out of the Seattle nightlife in his inimitable style, driving his big limousine to Walla Walla, where he spent ten months in the state prison. He emerged in 1941, bitter and broken, and died in poverty the following year.

With the percolation of black dance music deeper into the cultural soil, and blacks and whites mixing (in black-run establishments outside downtown), it is tempting to see in the thirties the beginnings of a coming together of society. Seattle's racial climate was indeed more moderate than Atlanta's: "Black Seattleites had long prided themselves on being in the most racially tolerant city on the Pacific Coast," observed Quintard Taylor. Nonetheless, integration and true tolerance lay far in the future, and in the thirties Seattle's black newspaper saw things getting worse, not better: "One time the city of Seattle afforded employment to many of its [African American] musicians and entertainers. During this period of employment every strata of community life was far better off than it is today. Pressure has closed this line of endeavor." This pressure sent Doc Hamilton to prison and, in March 1939, allowed the capricious and antiblack Liquor Control Board to temporarily close the Black and Tan. These actions threw many African Americans out of work, aggravating already bitter feelings. Only the outbreak of a new world war, and its social consequences, would begin to change things for the better.[18]

THE CLASSICS DIG IN

Maybe it took profound social tension—strikes, breadlines, street brawls—and the equally profound new voices of Steinbeck and Dos Passos. Or a new eye for the contrast between affluence and poverty, old and new, natural beauty and human squalor. Whatever the impetus, the arts bloomed in Depression-era Seattle. A Northwest school of painters coalesced around Dr. Richard Fuller's new Seattle Art Museum, modern dance took its first steps at the Cornish School, an opera company was born, and the symphony found lasting stability. Not that it came easy; Seattle Symphony subscriptions hit an all-time peak in 1930–31, only to plummet a year later. A disillusioned Karl Krueger announced his resignation in December 1931, taking his final bow at the Metropolitan Theater as a capacity crowd sang "Auld Lang Syne." Krueger's departure was a heavy blow, and critic Richard Hays praised the maestro as "a musician whose individual achievement in the cause of music in this city has been the most brilliant that has come into my observation." Karl Krueger went on to midwife the symphony orchestras of Kansas City and Detroit, then settled in New York and founded the American Arts Orchestra and the Society for the Preservation of the American Musical Heritage.[19]

The Krueger era was over, but good luck waited in the wings. Through the first of many public "Save the Symphony" fund drives, the orchestra was able to meet its $28,000 target and hire English conductor Basil Cameron, co-director of the San Francisco Symphony, to take Krueger's place. Arriving in November 1932 to begin rehearsals, the new maestro got a frosty reception from an orchestra full of Krueger loyalists, but won them over with his unaffected demeanor, efficient rehearsal technique, and impressive knowledge of the repertoire. The public also took to Cameron, and box-office phones starting ringing.

Cameron mostly avoided modernists such as Stravinsky, Schoenberg, and even Mahler, and stuck to the path well-worn by Krueger: plenty of Mendelssohn, Schubert, Beethoven, Tchaikovsky, and especially Wagner, who seemed to exercise a Svengali-like hold over successive Seattle conductors. A smattering of exotics—Rimsky-Korsakov, Debussy, Berlioz—spiced things up, and Cameron now and then ventured to the far fringes with Percy Grainger's "Green Bushes," Uuno Kiami's "3 Beaufort," Arcady Dubensky's Fugue for Eighteen Violins, and Francesco Malpiero's *Elegiaca* Symphony. Bach was touch and go, Grieg surprisingly rare in a city with a large Scandinavian population, and little was heard of Elgar, Vaughan Williams, Saint Saens, Bruckner, or—surprisingly—Verdi.

American and local composers got even fewer innings. Across the country, critics, conductors, and organizations such as Seattle's own American Music Society, formed in 1909 with Mary Carr Moore as president, would labor for decades to get domestic composers equal opportunity in the symphonic repertoire. Mostly, they would fail, and when it came to challenging the hegemony of the Three B's, Seattle was no more progressive than the rest of the country. After a symphony program of works by George McKay was ignored by the mainstream press, critic Paul Ashford sighed, "Had a similar occasion been thrust upon either Portland or San Francisco the . . . news services would have carried the news all over the country. . . . With the best of faith in the ability . . . of Mr. McKay and his associates in their work of educating Seattle into an understanding . . . of modern music, I must confess to a sad lack of faith in the musical potentialities of Seattle."[20]

Nonetheless, the thirties were good to classical music. Kreisler, Toscanini, and Stokowski became cultural icons, inspiring millions to tune in, head for the concert hall, or take up an instrument. Patent nostrum of the genteel tradition, "good music" was now accepted as a social and civic necessity. Radio was an elixir for classical music's popularity, and Basil Cameron got the Seattle Symphony regular broadcasts on the "Standard Oil Symphony Hour" and on NBC's Pacific Coast Network. "At the beginning of radio popularity," an observer noted, "it was feared that it would lessen the attendance at theaters and concert halls. Just the opposite has been the effect: not only have the radio audiences increased . . . but concert hall audiences have grown enormously. . . . The public wants to *see* the artists that they have heard over the air." Cameron encouraged that public with children's and pops concerts, and ticket prices of a depression-friendly twenty-five or fifty cents. Visiting artists—Sergei Rachmaninoff, Lauritz Melchior, Percy Grainger—filled the Civic Auditorium, and by 1936 critics were nodding: "Basil Cameron has literally made the Seattle Symphony Orchestra . . . the sections play with better balance than ever before, with superior precision and flexibility, altogether more musically. . . . Today judgment does not climb wearily upward from the bad to the fair, but dips from the very good to the not quite so good."[21]

The Cameron orchestra was in its glory in December 1936, when George Gershwin came to town. The man many considered America's greatest composer arrived from Los Angeles with a bad cold. He warmed up in a KOMO Radio interview with Vic Meyers, took in a symphony performance, then on the night of the 15th played his *Rhapsody in Blue* and Piano Concerto in F Major, and conducted excerpts from *Porgy and Bess*. The city that began life named New York eagerly embraced the urbane sound of its namesake's favorite son, and more than seven thousand excited listeners filled the Civic Auditorium. "Gershwin's music may be either praised or condemned," mused J. Willis Sayre, "but no one can be indifferent to it, and no one can call it dull." Now, too, it was Ronald Phillips's turn to play the *Rhapsody*'s famed clarinet introduction. "I practiced it constantly," he told me in 1992, "and when Gershwin came here in 1936, I nailed it. We had one rehearsal, and after the glissando he said, 'That's great, Ron! Go ahead and boot it right out there. It's a big place.' I think I'm the only clarinetist still living who actually played *Rhapsody in Blue* with George Gershwin." Starchy socialites tapped their toes, the composer did three encores, and the giddy crowd clapped to the brink of exhaustion. A musical comet had blazed through Seattle, and those lucky enough to have been present would never be the same. Within a year, thirty-eight-year-old George Gershwin was dead of a brain tumor. The *Seattle Times*'s James Wood mourned the composer's "suppressed genius," echoing the thoughts of others who felt that Gershwin had been "caught in the whirl and pressures of commercialism, and in the truly fine spirit that moved him has yielded . . . more froth than substance."[22]

Between bright moments, the symphony struggled. Seattleites turned out handsomely for their orchestra, but ticket revenues alone were not enough to sustain it, and broad-based financial support remained elusive. "A very small minority has paid the piper the rest of us hope to dance to," lamented the *Town Crier*. "Subscriptions in the recent campaign for a guarantee fund were almost entirely divided into two classes—the very large and generous donations, and the very small but equally generous kind. The great middle class of Seattle sat back and shirked as usual." Former conductor John Spargur grumbled that the city was still in the thrall of "too much fish and timber" to be a truly cultured metropolis. The *Town Crier*'s Paul Ashford had a radical suggestion: Why not open a bar in the lobby? "A five-cent glass of beer included in the price of each admission would win our symphony a new audience." Unfortunately, this admirable proposal was not adopted, and Save the Symphony campaigns became an annual ritual. Raising the $30,000 to $40,000 needed each year to keep the music playing was an enormous task in a time of short money and plenty of movies and dance bands competing for that money. It is to the credit of its dedicated volunteer drumbeaters and the ones who repeatedly stanched the deficit that the orchestra never missed a season.[23]

Equally challenging was survival for orchestra musicians, especially those whose instruments did not cross over to dance bands, and the short symphony season compelled players to find other income even in good times. Some taught, while others were forced to cadge whatever part-time work they could. "It is . . . no secret that it has been pretty tough going for musicians for the last two or three years," said a critic in 1934. "Artists of the highest type have been barely able to eke out a living. Some of them have not even done that well." Even the conductor was not immune; the winter 1938 fund-raiser fell flat, and the crestfallen trustees informed Cameron that his contract would not be renewed. For an abbreviated 1938–39 season, they turned to Russian conductor Nikolai Sokoloff, who had founded the Cleveland Orchestra and led it for fifteen years (he had also headed the Federal Music Project). Sokoloff retained most of his predecessor's policies, and the public responded enthusiastically. Some critics praised his work, but James Wood, a Cameron admirer, panned the Sokoloff regime as "the dullest stretch in the history of the Seattle Symphony."[24]

Beginning a forty-year career as a symphony trombonist in 1939, Ken Cloud found Sokoloff anything but dull. "Getting in the symphony was a lot easier in those days than it is now," the wry and diffident Cloud told me.

Ed Krenz and I were in the union hall one day in 1939, and there was a card stuck up on the bulletin board: "First chair trumpet and trombone wanted for Seattle Symphony." We went in and played some parts like we'd done in the school orchestra—no screens or juries—and they hired us both. Being that we were green kids, we were accepted on the condition we study our parts with Louis Rotter, the symphony librarian and viola player. He was an old-school Viennese, and we really woodshedded that first program. Pay was $42.50 a week for an eight-week season from November to February. I saw it as a few extra bucks, not as a career. We called Sokoloff the Russian Bear, because he was big and overbearing.

A meticulous musician, Ken Cloud was not above chuckling when things went wrong: "During the war we played a popular radio show. They used two fanfares to open the show, both the same but in different keys. The program started and Sokoloff whispered, 'Fanfare! Fanfare!' But he didn't say which one, so naturally half the orchestra played one key, and half played the other. Sokoloff practically tore his hair out."

Also tearing their hair out were those who, since the departure of the Sprottes in 1915, craved opera. Roused by 1927's *Aida,* opera fans were galvanized by the March 1931 visit of the Chicago Civic Opera Company, which filled the Civic Auditorium with no fewer than four big productions, including *Die Walkure* and *La Traviata* (ironically, the company would itself fall victim to hard times and fold within a year). Cecilia Schultz swung into action, and the Seattle Civic Opera Association was born. The mostly amateur group rehearsed for six months, and in the spring of 1932 took the Civic Auditorium stage with Wagner's *Tannhauser.* Principal singers included sopranos Mildred Eyman and Vera McBain, tenor Ernest Goddard, and baritone Edward Scriven. Mary Davenport Engberg directed the orchestra in its first season, assisted by her son, Paul, who sang a leading role and took over as conductor for subsequent terms. Grandson Ralph joined the fun, and, as they had in *Aida,* the Svea and Nordica choruses filled out the chorus. Amazingly, the company survived the Depression and a second world war (giving its final performance in December 1946), and critic Richard Hays declared the 1938 presentation of Karl Goldmark's seldom-seen *The Queen of Sheba* "a new high for local grand opera performances. . . . Time and again a verdict of 'cold, unresponsive' has been returned against Seattle audiences, but no one sat on their hands or seemed afraid to ruin their white gloves at *The Queen of Sheba.*"[25]

Late in 1938, the Metropolitan Theater hosted a different kind of opera. Hated by wealthy Americans who called him a traitor to his class, President Franklin D. Roosevelt was adored by many more whose lives were saved by his New Deal social programs. Foremost of these was the Works Progress Administration, which put millions of people to work building roads, painting murals, and making music. Seattle was not a major beneficiary of the WPA's Federal Music Project (whereas Los Angeles enjoyed a WPA symphony orchestra, a dance band, a light opera company, and a black chorus), but federal money did pay for a twenty-eight-member Seattle WPA Band, directed by John Spargur, and allow the Seattle Symphony to expand to seventy members.

Most importantly, WPA money bought *An Evening with Dunbar.* A musical celebration of the life of poet/philosopher Paul Lawrence Dunbar, the "folk opera" was developed by the Negro Repertory Company of the WPA's Federal Theatre Project. University of Washington student Howard

Biggs composed the incidental music, wrote original songs ("Angelino" and "Good Night") based on Dunbar poems, and directed the twenty-two-voice chorus, while the WPA Band provided accompaniment. The show, wrote J. Willis Sayre, was "good enough to be copied all over the country. . . . If any Hollywood talent scout fares this way and sees that male quartet, it will certainly be nabbed for pictures." The *Northwest Enterprise,* Seattle's sole African American newspaper, also praised Biggs's harmonic mastery along with the work of soprano Doris Booker and baritone Joe Staton. *An Evening with Dunbar* ran only one week, then faded into history and, like other classically inclined black musicians, Biggs found little opportunity in Seattle's restricted legitimate sphere. Migrating to New York, he produced for doo-wop and R&B bands and composed a string of minor hits including "Write Me a Letter" and "Get a Job." Howard Biggs died in 1999, having made his own distinctive mark on American music.[26]

Filling in between symphony and opera was the indefatigable Cecilia Schultz. Her illustrious Olympic Hotel soirees continued, and in 1935 she leased the Moore Theater and established herself as one of the nation's top impresarios. In her fourteen-year term, "Cissy" regaled Seattle with the likes of Jascha Heifetz, Fyodor Chaliapin, and the Don Cossack Chorus. Tall and imposing in her trademark furs, ornate hats, and pince-nez, Schultz was born to the job, and her annual talent searches became legendary among New York and London agents. "These big business tycoons are just little boys when it comes to music," she scoffed, and legend has it that when a drunk fell through a window into her office, she laughed, "You're the only person to get into my theater free in twenty years!" The Schultz empire got a boost with the formation of the Seattle chapter of Pro Musica, a national organization dedicated to presenting less familiar art music. Pro Musica delivered Bela Bartok, Martha Graham, and Ottorino Respighi, and in February 1936 gave Seattle's first early music concert with lutenist Suzanne Bloch and recorder player Carl Dolmetsch. (Dolmetsch's father, Arnold, led the early music revival in England during the 1920s.) All this activity belies the reality that Seattle's classical music season lasted only from October through March. The balance of the year, violists and bassoonists taught, worked day jobs, presented recitals at Cornish, or moved east. As arts observer Maxine Cushing Gray said, "By April nothing was happening. One went out in the sun. In the summer, one stayed in the sun."[27]

■ ■ ■

Again, the police. Billy Tolles was on his way home that night when the patrol car pulled up. "Where ya goin', boy?" the officer barked. Tolles bristled, but he knew his lines. Putting his saxophone case down, he removed his hat. "I'm goin' right on home, sir. Yes, sir, I'm goin' home right now." The hard face relaxed. "That's right, boy. You go right on home." The squad car eased off, and Tolles, his heart pounding, walked home. Sitting at the kitchen table as the sun came up, the young musician shook his head: At least he'd missed the draft, but the cops and all the new crackers up from the South made life way too hard. The next night, on the stand at the Savoy, he poured his anger into his saxophone. "Man, you sure goin' at it tonight," laughed pianist Buddy Brashear. "Yeah, man," muttered Tolles, "I'm goin,' all right. I'm goin' home."

■ ■ ■

Chapter 6

Wartime Whoopie

THE BEGINNING OF THE 1940S offered little promise that the Depression would soon end. Only the all-out mobilization after the bombing of Pearl Harbor brought America out of her slump and a new boom time to Seattle. Even before the first shots were fired in World War II, workers and their families from across the country descended upon the town to take defense jobs at Todd Shipyards and "Boeing's." Hotels and restaurants were jammed, and First Avenue gin mills swarmed with green (and green-gilled) recruits. Once more evoking the city's ancient namesake, newspapers boasted of traffic jams "rivaling those you read about on Broadway in New York" and bragged that restaurants and nightspots were busier than ever. In the century's most turbulent decade, music was transformed by war, social upheaval, and politics. Even the staid symphony could not escape the excitement.

DANCING THE WAR AWAY

The military draft made staffing bands a constant challenge, but the music business flourished, and musicians immune to conscription found work for the picking. Even so, many 4-F players did their part in defense jobs (symphony clarinetist Ronald Phillips and oboist Whitney Tustin worked side by side as pipefitters at Todd Shipyards) and bandleaders scuffled to fill empty chairs. Clever strategies were needed to contend with the gasoline and rubber rationing that made traveling to jobs difficult. "Elward

Arseneau had swing shift gigs out at Juanita Beach," recounted his pianist, Bob Hill, "and he came up with a very creative way of keeping them: He got a day job in the Todd shipyard, and because it was defense-related, it enabled him to get a C ration for unlimited gasoline. So he bought a couple of big sedans and ran car pools to the shipyard, then used them to haul the band to his gigs."

Even lowly draftees found that being a musician opened doors. Before the war, Queen Anne High graduate Hill had led a popular kid band, Bob Hill's Noteworthys, but in 1943 he was just another musician with a 1-A notice. "I took my valve trombone with me down to Fresno for basic training," the tall, soft-spoken Hill told me,

and the horn was my pass into the Signal Corps, which was where they stuck lots of musicians. They figured using Morse code would be easy for someone with a sense of rhythm. From there I went to officers' candidate school in Tomah, Wisconsin, where a bunch of us musicians were designated an "authorized" band. Our duties were to inhabit a barracks, which was about a half-mile from anything else on the base, keep the place clean, get up at a decent hour in the morning, and then rehearse for eight hours and play for whatever event needed playing. From Wisconsin I was ordered to DeRitter, Louisiana, where I played piano in the officer's mess for dinner. A first lieutenant said, "I like the way you play. How'd you like to join my outfit and form a band?" Swell! I assembled a twelve-piece band, and because there were only stock arrangements in the book, I spent every cotton-pickin' night writing an original arrangement and copying it out for twelve pieces. It was a great opportunity for a twenty-one-year-old kid. We had only three reeds, so I filled out the reed section with, say, a muted trombone. I loved the Les Brown band, so I copied that, and also Glenn Miller. The Miller sound was always salable—it's salable today! With that band we played squadron parties at Beaumont and Port Arthur, Texas; they'd rent the floor of a hotel and invite USO gals. It was a perfect setup, and I couldn't figure out where this first lieutenant got all his pull. Then we found out he had a certain "Uncle Omar"—General Omar Bradley! When the Battle of the Bulge broke, they disbanded us and sent me to the regular GI orchestra. I wrote a pretty good Glenn Miller–type book for that outfit, too, and at the end of the war we went to Andrews Field in Washington, D.C., and played the separation ceremony for the actual Glenn Miller Orchestra.

In some places, war seemed very far away. An oasis of serenity, the Olympic Hotel gave the Northwest a new musical institution when it hired two musicians who for nearly thirty years would epitomize Seattle sophistication. Pianist Freeman "Tubby" Clark was born on Whidbey Island in 1914 and by 1929 was playing piano in Vic Meyers's Butler Hotel band and working in staff orchestras at KOMO and KJR radio. Erstwhile silent movie organist Eddie Clifford spent the thirties leading small bands and in 1941 teamed up with Tubby in the Olympic's Marine Room. Clifford and Clark soothed the nerves of officers, businessmen, and diplomats, and sent jaded travelers on their way with perhaps a greater appreciation for Seattle than they had arrived with.

While the brass sipped martinis at the Olympic, GIs headed for the Trianon. The Gay Jones Orchestra kicked off the decade at the second of Norm Bobrow's big festivals on February 4, 1940. The band enjoyed a brief twilight in the Northwest's premier ballroom, then the draft intervened and Jones yielded the scalloped Trianon bandshell to (but kept his sound alive in) the Curt Sykes Orchestra, which occupied the stand for much of the duration. Dick Giger played reeds with Sykes: "Curt's checks weren't always good, but his band was. Sykes was not much of a musician; he played piano and celesta, but we were too loud for him most of the time, anyway. He did have some hot Gay Jones arrangements, and it was a fun, enthusiastic band." Bert Lindgren's Old Timers kept traditional dancers happy every Tuesday, and big name bands—Ozzie Nelson, Kay Kyser, and Jan Garber—routinely drew crowds of four and five thousand that had the vast dance floor groaning. Long lines snaked down the sidewalk, outdoor canteens served coffee, and the endless nights resounded with taxi horns, wolf whistles, and laughter. Swing-shift dances were instituted, and the music never stopped. Standing guard over all was tall, music-loving policeman Elmo Hudgins, whose after-hours parties for visiting bands became legendary.[1]

Up on Pike Street a lively strip of greasy spoons—the Caballero, Golden Egg, Golden Pheasant—served up hamburgers and swinging combos. Frenetic saxophonist Bud Storm featured (and risked a union fine for doing so) black trumpeter Leon Vaughn on the Bunny Berigan classic "I Can't Get Started" and played up a storm himself. Storm gave young reedman Ronnie Pierce one of his first jobs. "Anson 'Bud' Storm was a sweet guy with curly red hair," Pierce told me, "but on tenor and clarinet he was an absolute wild man. He would take off, man, and be *gone*—outer space time! We all know the road, right? So why not fly? Bud was that kind of cat." Pierce laughed over another fact of Seattle nightlife, which club owner "Russian John" Lasso transgressed:

> I did six nights a week with Bud at the Havana Club, one of Russian John's joints. Russian John was a skinflint. He hated paying off the cops, but he had all these illegal bottle clubs, so every Saturday night, in comes Sheriff Callahan to get his money. One day, Russian John said, "I'm not gonna pay off them blankety-blank cops no more." Okay, next night, in comes the wrecking crew—they tore that place to *pieces!* Ten thousand dollars worth of booze down the drain. After that, Russian John paid.

The Japanese attack on Pearl Harbor on December 7, 1941, created a new America. Overnight, blackouts were thrown over coastal cities, Japanese American citizens were imprisoned, and heavy industry frantically retooled to produce tanks and bombers. Seattle's strategic location, its Boeing plant, and its shipyards made it a vital West Coast outpost of President Roosevelt's arsenal of democracy, and a flood of southern black and white laborers inundated the sleepy metropolis. Friction was inevitable, and as "No Colored" signs began appearing in hotel and restaurant windows, the city's relatively soft racial divide hardened. The region's largest single employer, the Boeing Airplane Company, began accepting black applicants in 1942, and in two years the African American population soared from 3,879 in 1939 to over 10,000. At last the black community found real money and numerical strength.

But few black faces were to be seen in the ballroom hordes. Like all downtown dance halls, the Trianon enforced a rigid whites-only policy. In November 1940, however, an impending visit by Lionel Hampton's orchestra spurred black local 493 president Gerald Wells to pressure management to admit blacks. No deal, barked owner John Savage, who considered African American patronage "bad for business" and took refuge in the fiction that mixed dances were illegal. Savage did, however, grudgingly permit "colored only" dances on Monday nights (and who heard him complain at the bank come Tuesday morning?). The black community's Trianon was Lemuel Honeysuckle's Savoy Ballroom, which opened in the old Gala Theater at 22nd and East Madison in December 1941. As it often did with black concerns, the liquor board dithered on granting Honeysuckle a cabaret license, so he began with Saturday afternoon dances. Seventeen-year-old tenor sax player Billy Tolles kicked things off with his Savoy Boys, a "kid band" featuring pianist Buddy Brashear and his reed-playing brother, Gerald, who would mature into one of the most formidable jazz musicians to come out of Seattle. In 1946 the city council finally granted the Savoy a license, and thereafter the ballroom resounded to swing and the brash new explosions of bop and rhythm and blues. On Jackson Street, in Chinatown, and in Russian John's First Avenue joints, jazz and swing music echoed till dawn in what some called a permanent Mardi Gras.

King of the night was Al Pierre. A suave stride pianist, Pierre jobbed around LA, Portland, and Tacoma before settling in Seattle in the thirties and opening his own club, Al's Lucky Hour, at 12th and Yesler. The Al Pierre Orchestra was a jazzy swing unit of seven to ten players that included reed players Jabo Ward and Terry Cruise, trumpeters Bob Russell and Leon Vaughn, trombonist Major Pigford (one of the few notable black trombonists of any era in Seattle), and drummer Vernon Brown. Table singers—Harry Fox, Dee Dee Hackett, and Russell Jones—gave the spots torchy ballads, blues, and rounder tunes such as "Ballin' the Jack" and "Ace in the Hole." Several were seasoned southwestern territory musicians, giving the Pierre band a bluesy, Kansas City beat. "Al had that old, slick style, like Jimmie Lunceford and Duke Ellington," trumpeter Floyd Standifer told me. "Oh, man, he'd swing you into bad health! He was a very large and energetic factor in the after-hours scene." The end of the war ended the high times, and as peace settled in, bookings dwindled, and Al Pierre scuffled up and down the coast before passing away in 1951.[2]

DUSTBIN

Under Basil Cameron and Nikolai Sokoloff, the Seattle Symphony reached a mature adolescence. If some felt that the orchestra had lapsed into dullness under the Russian Bear, this was one ingredient conspicuously absent from the term of his successor, Sir Thomas Beecham. During his season-and-a-half tenure, the bombastic Brit was a society editor's dream, bringing to town not just stellar musical talent but flamboyance and an unbridled tongue.

Beecham (1879–1961) was one of the world's most celebrated conductors. Heir to the Beecham's Liver Pills fortune, he fell in love with classical music as a youth and learned to conduct by the simple expedient of hiring orchestras to practice with. At sixteen he made his public debut with the first of several Beecham Symphony Orchestras, and in the years to come he guest-conducted virtually all the world's great orchestras and directed both the London Symphony and the BBC Symphony. In 1941 the Seattle Symphony offered him a year's engagement; he accepted (taking only the autumn half of each season, allowing him to conduct the Metropolitan Opera and other orchestras during the winter), and on October 20 a capacity crowd settled into their seats at the Music Hall Theater in eager anticipation. That such a celebrity would actually deign to lead their provincial symphony was both flattering and a little unsettling. Would the orchestra rise to the challenge? Would Seattle?[3]

Beecham bolted from the gate with a mesmerizing "Midsummer Night's Dream" Overture by Mendelssohn. On the podium, the liver pill heir hissed, grunted, flailed, danced, and seemed at times to levitate off the stage altogether. In the second half, he was not a minute into Delius's "Walk to the Paradise Garden" when *Seattle Post-Intelligencer* photographer Arthur French snapped a picture with an all-too-audible click. Beecham stopped the orchestra and glowered at the lensman. "You can go home now! You are an insult to the audience." The audience gasped but at the conclusion leaped to its feat with a mighty roar and brought Beecham back for a dozen curtain calls. In subsequent rehearsals, the maestro's barbed wit ("Will someone kindly introduce the gentleman back there to the intricacies of that horn?") took the musicians some getting used to, but they warmed to him. "Thomas Beecham was a delight!" said principal clarinetist Ronald Phillips, smiling.[4]

> I did my very first solo piece, the Mozart concerto, with him. He used my pocket score for three rehearsals, then handed it back—"Thank you very much, Mister Phillips, I won't be needing this anymore"—and conducted from memory. It dawned on me later that I was playing from memory, too, and I got a little chill thinking about what would have happened if one of us had lost our place. But under Beecham we put on some truly memorable concerts, and the orchestra played way over its head. We knew no fear!

Coming and going in a nimbus of exploding flash bulbs, Sir Thomas embodied the cosmopolitanism Seattle had always craved. His goateed visage dominated newspapers, and for the first time the Seattle Symphony sold out its season subscriptions. As the nation went to war, Beecham did

Ron and Tom: Sir Thomas
Beecham and Ronald Phil-
lips confer over a matter of
interpretation during a Seattle
Symphony rehearsal in 1942.
Philips was preparing for his
first solo performance of the
Mozart Clarinet Concerto in
A Major (K-622), with which
he would end his fifty-six-year
symphony career on March 7,
1983. Courtesy of Paul Dorpat

his part, making V discs for Armed Forces Master Records, which sent
them to servicemen around the world. A Symphony Studio was opened in
the Fisher Studio Building, with records, phonographs, magazines, and
even musical instruments for musicians in uniform to play. Servicemen
were welcome at rehearsals, and Beecham delighted military audiences
with droll tales of life in the musical trenches. He cheered everyone with
his favorite composers: Delius, Sibelius, Wagner, and Mozart (Beecham
staged Seattle's first Mozart Festival in 1942).

Ironically, in view of his disdain for women symphonists, Beecham's
arrival coincided with a mass influx of women musicians, necessitated by
the draft. In 1943 almost half the orchestra was female, including a number of first-timers in the string bass and woodwind sections. By this time
women had all but vanished from pop orchestras. During the Depression
most of the female bands of the twenties dissolved as restaurant work dried
up, musicians married, and male-dominated swing bands became the
vogue. War took women into defense plants, not onto bandstands, and

by 1944 Helen Hart claimed that her Melo-Dears was the only women's orchestra in town. The novelty had worn off.[5]

Beecham had scarcely settled into his rooms at the Marlborough House before he was enveloped in controversy. Sued by the British government for back taxes, he was nabbed by delighted press photographers accepting the subpoena in his bathrobe. Two weeks later, on November 14, 1941, he addressed a meeting of civic and culture nabobs at the Washington Athletic Club. Seattle, he told the assembled luminaries, had great potential. Why should she take her cue from New York or San Francisco? Her people must get serious about the arts, get out their wallets, and give their all to symphony, opera, and theater. "Set your shoulder to the task," he declared, and he would make its "embryonic" orchestra as good as any. After all, he smiled, "If I were a member of this community, really, I should get weary of being looked on as a sort of esthetic dustbin." People left the meeting not quite sure of what they'd heard, within days the press was twisting admonition into pejorative, and urban legend has taken it as an insult ever since. Rubbish, said Ronald Phillips. "Beecham was most notorious for allegedly calling Seattle an 'esthetic dustbin,'" he told me. "I was at the luncheon where he made that speech, and he didn't say that at all. What he said was, Seattle should take care not to *become* a cultural dustbin. Beecham never disparaged Seattle that I'm aware of, but even now some people still twist it around to make it sound like a put-down."[6]

There were other issues in play. Phillips continued,

> Beecham attracted a lot of attention to the symphony, but he also attracted the attention of William Randolph Hearst. Hearst had been kicked out of England as an undesirable. The upshot of that was, the critic from the Hearst-owned *Post-Intelligencer*, Suzanne Martin, started needling Beecham: the orchestra didn't rehearse enough; he was unreliable; he was erratic. I don't know if all this was on Hearst's orders or not, but Beecham didn't renew his contract. He wouldn't have stayed anyway; I know he was planning to go back to England.

To be fair, Martin had been as ecstatic as anyone over Beecham, saying that he had given Seattle the best symphonic music the city had ever heard. In November 1942, though, Martin lobbed a backhanded compliment at "the pompous little Britisher's conductorial magic" and went on to decry the orchestra's skimpy rehearsal time, low pay, and its director's habitual flitting off to New York rather than standing with Seattle as he had all but promised in the "dustbin" speech. Another reviewer had the temerity to criticize thin strings and blobby brass, and Beecham went on the warpath: Seattle critics were nothing but incompetent gossipmongers, he raged—"If this action . . . continues, I shall close up shop and leave."[7]

Then there was the Other Woman. Arriving shortly after the conductor in 1941 was a young British pianist, Betty Humby, who performed several times under Beecham's baton. By February rumor had the maestro in love. Nonsense, Beecham snorted—but in August he sued his wife, Utica Celestia, for divorce. All of this delightful business yielded record ticket sales until, on November 3, 1943, the great man pleaded illness and handed in his resignation. Two weeks later, sixty-four-year-old Sir Thomas Beecham and twenty-nine-year-old Miss Betty Humby boarded a train for New York, where they were married in February. Seattle Symphony boosters sighed and wondered what was next. The *Post-Intelligencer* pleaded once more for broad community support and ran a letter from Donald MacArdle, a visiting army officer and conductor of the Westchester, New York, opera, who predicted that the orchestra would languish until it found the

> missing component . . . a conductor who succeeds or fails in his life's ambition as the Seattle Symphony Orchestra succeeds or fails. . . . A few thousand dollars a year—far less than the price of a famous name—and the opportunity to turn a second or third-rate orchestra into a first-rate one would be the great break of his career. Finding that young man . . . and supporting him as the permanent conductor . . . would be the great break of the Seattle Symphony Orchestra.[8]

A break was sorely needed. Newly assigned to Seattle in 1942, young GI Louis Guzzo caught the symphony at the Moore Theater. Used to the "far kinder sound" of his hometown Cleveland Orchestra, he found that, even with Beecham doing his best, the Seattle Symphony was "an offense to the ear." This was due in part to the draft, which had reduced the orchestra from eighty-three members to as few as fifty-five, many with little experience. The symphony limped through the 1943 season with Albert Coates, then for the next season turned to Carl Bricken, a pianist, composer, and educator who had developed music programs at the universities of Chicago and Wisconsin. Bricken arrived in the summer of 1944, put the orchestra through a stiff rehearsal regimen, and was rewarded by respectable attendance and good notices. An October 1945 opening night performance of Dvořák's *New World* Symphony got a standing ovation, followed by gratifying ticket sales and some of the best reviews in the orchestra's history. The conductor stepped up radio broadcasts and brought the orchestra back to nearly full strength. And, the treasury was full.[9]

Late 1946 gave a hint of things to come when the Seattle Civic Arts Commission recommended that the city purchase land near the Civic Auditorium complex north of downtown for a new concert hall and opera house. The Auditorium itself was the product of a bond issue, and its 1928 opening was greeted with great fanfare and its acoustics pronounced "perfect." But it was a Spartan, steel-girt facility (folding chairs had to be set up on the main floor), and pride turned to frustration as concertgoers craned their necks and strained to hear violins in the echoing concrete barn. As the symphony became more popular, however, it was the only space in town big enough to accommodate everybody. To use the Moore, Orpheum, or Metropolitan theaters meant holding concerts (and expensive guest artists) over a second night, a prospect that had bookkeepers seeing red. Patrons fumed and symphony management experimented with auditorium fixes: a temporary sloping floor, an acoustical band shell, swaddling the entire room in curtains. Nothing satisfied, and Mayor William Devin accepted the arts commission resolution. The concept of a grand new civic cultural center began to take shape in the public consciousness.

Such a positive development had to be offset by trouble, and, at the end of the 1946 season, a quorum of symphony musicians informed the trustees that Bricken would have to go. He was inexperienced, they said, and not up to the standards set by his august predecessor. Never mind his two successful seasons and public acclaim. At the instigation of orchestra manager Philip Hart, the Seattle and Tacoma symphonies were merged under the joint direction of Bricken and Tacoma conductor Eugene Linden (who also played second flute in Seattle) and christened the Pacific Northwest Symphony Orchestra. Protests flew ("Oh, it just makes me sick!" yelped Cecilia Schultz), but the unified orchestra bowed in on November 17, 1947, and Bricken's performance was cheered. The following January, however, he announced that the end of the season would be the end of his stay in Seattle. His supporters begged him to reconsider, but he was adamant. Eugene Linden continued as associate conductor, but in February the Seattle contingent pulled out of the combine.[10]

After more months of trustee bickering, the fed-up musicians told the Symphony Association in August 1948 that they would run the orchestra themselves. Ron Phillips confided to me,

> Carl Bricken was not a good conductor and I'm afraid the orchestra gave him a rough time. We called him "the shoemaker." After two seasons we staged a revolt against him and reorganized the symphony as a co-op. We insisted on seventy-five players, chose our own music and who played what, and had a committee to audition new players. That's how they run the Berlin Philharmonic.

The musicians named their new co-op the Seattle Orchestra and retained Eugene Linden as conductor, and Cecilia Schultz stepped in as manager. Linden was backed by *Seattle Times* critic Richard Hays, Dr. Hans Lehmann and Thelma Lehmann, and their friend Alexander Schneider. "Sasha" Schneider was a violinist with the Budapest String Quartet, a Walker Ames professor at the University of Washington School of Music, and a wily musical politician. "[Schneider] acted as a catalyst in Seattle," remarked Hans Lehmann. "Not only did his teaching have a great impact on . . . the string players . . . but his deft hand masterminded what is often called the '1948 revolution' in the symphony." Schneider held up the Israel Philharmonic as an example of what could be accomplished under the co-op system.[11]

Horrified at creeping socialism, conservative trustees condemned the rebellious musicians as "musical mobsters," cursed Cecilia Schultz ("She has always wanted to get her clutches on the orchestra!"), and announced that the symphony would proceed with its regular season using guest conductors. For the second time in forty years, Seattle found itself with two competing symphony orchestras. Musicians agonized over which one to cast their lots with, while each side vowed to boycott the other and an amused *Time* magazine wondered that any music could be made at all, "when there was so much caterwauling backstage, in the boxes, and in the business office." The Seattle Orchestra gave six concerts before making the astonishing discovery that a city hard pressed to support one symphony orchestra could certainly not sustain two. Chamber of Commerce executive Joseph Gandy brokered a truce between the factions, and in January 1949 the two were reunited as the Seattle Symphony Orchestra Society, under Eugene Linden's direction. At his side was Cissy Schultz, whom many disliked but all agreed was indispensable. "All those board members have been pretty good about this," she barked. "I guess a lot of them aren't crazy about me, but they want to give the musicians a good break, and that's what's important."[12]

Still, the drama wasn't over. At Linden's invitation, French conductor Manuel Rosenthal, then composer-in-residence at Puget Sound University, was engaged to guest conduct. Predictably, a new fight broke out over the relative merits of the two conductors, and Rosenthal emerged victorious. It was a hollow victory; public confidence was exhausted, and ticket sales headed for the cellar. As they had in the twenties, the musicians took up damage control, offering to fill the 1949–50 budget gap by waiving salaries and playing for the door. Pickings were slim—some got by on as little as nine dollars a week. A December 1949 Beethoven Festival had to be canceled after it became evident that the orchestra and chorus would outnumber the audience. Seattle was "a beautiful body without a brain," lamented Rosenthal. "Civic leaders and groups appear enthusiastic about music, but when it comes to buying a ticket or contributing, they run." The public was given a chance to redeem itself; the festival was rescheduled at a dollar a head, and the Civic Auditorium sold out to standing-room only.[13]

By this time, Seattle actually had two permanent symphony orchestras. In 1943 Hungarian violinist Francis Aranyi and a small group of students founded the Seattle Youth Symphony, one of the first such organizations in the country. Now, young musicians had an outlet of their own, one that would take an increasingly important part in the Northwest's musical life. And Cecilia Schultz continued her one-woman cultural movement, sweeping into New York booking agencies every summer and returning with a purseful of talent. Thanks to Cissy, Seattle heard numerous African American artists—Marian Anderson, Roland Hayes, Paul Robeson—and 1943's touring Broadway production of *Porgy and Bess* set a Moore Theater attendance record. In October 1945, Seattle's first lady of classical music offered Helen Traubel, the Don Cossack Chorus, *and* the von Trapp Family Singers, all in the space of a week. Seattle seemed in little danger of becoming an esthetic dustbin.

POSTWAR DANCE BANDS

The year 1946 was one for the books. The war was over, and the seething crowds that had mobbed ballrooms had gone home. New musical trends challenged the supremacy of big band pop. Drastic actions by the American Federation of Musicians portended a future of unintended consequences. And, possessed by something like mass hypnosis, a flood of young men packed up their instruments and headed for Seattle.

Popular taste does not change overnight. Dance bands continued to draw and new ballrooms opened, among them Byron Scobey's and Howard Crow's Palladium in north Seattle. Scobey had been a sporadic bandleader since the late twenties, when he played Cole McElroy's short-lived Spanish Ballroom one block south of the Trianon. Ronnie Pierce was in the Scobey reed section on the Palladium's opening night:

> Byron was drunk. He was drunk a *lot*. He'd count things off by waving his baton, but not in any kind of tempo you'd recognize, and Norm Hoagy would bang his foot so we could start together. Byron's family owned the land, and I guess he just thought being a bandleader would be a kick or something. He had the money to hire the best guys, so the band was actually pretty decent.

Ronnie Pierce was a whirlwind in the postwar scene, and in 1946 he made his big splash with an orchestra that whipped youthful audiences into a frenzy. "I was sixteen and totally into Stan Kenton and Claude Thornhill," he recalled.

> This *sound* came together in my head. I mowed lawns and delivered papers seven days a week, and when I'd get $150 together, I'd drive my 1933 Chevy over to the corner of 45th and University. Bob Hill would be standing on the corner, and I'd pull over and hand him the $150, and he'd give me an arrangement with an official red union stamp on it, and *bam*! there it was: my dream band. Ten brass, six reeds, wandering French horn obbligato—"I'll Remember April," "My Old Flame." Nobody, I mean *nobody*, here had anything like it, and for one year we were the biggest thing around. We played every high school prom in town—the kids just went *nuts!*

Pierce honed his chops in Roosevelt High "kid bands" that rode the swing wave of the thirties and forties: trumpet prodigy Pete Barrington's Men About Town, and the Noteworthys (not to be confused with Bob Hill's Noteworthys). A child of absentee parents, young Ronnie got no encouragement at home. Instead, he was taken in hand by saxophone master Johnnie Jessen, who as a teen played steamships and Seattle nightclubs before entering the rarified world of Hollywood radio and recording orchestras. Pierce shook his head in wonder telling me about Jessen.

Johnnie Jessen saved me. I was in grade school at Lake Forest Park and got the bug to play the trumpet. Then I got hit in the face by a baseball. *Blam!* So here I am with this gaping hole in my teeth. Kronenberg, the music teacher, told me to forget the trumpet and handed me this seven-dollar-and-fifty-cent clarinet. The thing fell apart. But I noticed my buddy Owen Nelson was playing great. I asked him, "How did you get so good?" "I take lessons from Johnnie Jessen." So I went downtown to Sherman Clay on Fourth Avenue and found Johnnie's studio, and here's this big, tall guy in high-up pants and suspenders. He'd just come up from Los Angeles after working on Phil Harris's band for the Jack Benny Show. Big-time cat! I must have weighed all of seventy pounds, there's nothing but beer in the ice box. Johnnie took one look at me, this little tiny kid with a gap in his teeth and eyes rolling back in his head, and right then and there he took charge of my life. "Sit down," he says, and when I went home, I could play "America" on my seven-dollar clarinet. Johnnie took me into his home at Christmas and fed me. We would go to the A-1 Soup Company and for twenty-five cents get a bowl of hot water with a carrot in it. I had no money, and he charged $2.50 a lesson, which was a *lot* of dough for a kid in those days. I was living way up past Lake City, and sometimes I wouldn't show up for my lesson. Johnnie would be right on the phone: "Why aren't you here?" I'd say, "Well, Johnnie, I don't have bus fare." He says, "I don't care! You get down here for your lesson!" So I take my clarinet and hitchhike down to Sherman Clay and have my lesson. Johnnie Jessen was a saver.

Jessen taught his new pupil (and many others, including Kenny G) a technique that yielded a supremely lush sound: glottal, or "open-throat," tone control. Jessen himself learned it from Seattle's top instrument repairman, Joe Lusier, who spent fifty years on Music Row working miracles with battered brass. Open-throat is difficult to master, but the results are worth it, and to listen to Pierce in 2009 is to hear the saxophone of Adolph Sax's fondest dreams: a blast of enveloping resonance that can rattle martini glasses. As Pierce told me,

Most horn players never learn to breathe, and their sound goes *plop* ten feet in front of them. With open-throat, you create a ball of sound—a *projectile*. Throw it five hundred feet out, BLAM! Hit 'em in the second balcony. I worked on open-throat for six years, and at the end of six years, I was *gone*, brother! There were only three guys in Seattle that ever learned open-throat: Fred Menzie, Taylor Bowie, and me.

Limited to a few practitioners, the technique that might have significantly enhanced the sound of Seattle dance bands never took hold. "With all the closed-up cats," Pierce chuckled, "I had to hold back in bands so I didn't blow 'em all away."

With sidemen scarce during the war, bandleaders were desperate for musicians, and Pierce was hired almost as soon as he could string two notes together.

I got into the Noteworthys, and this guy from out of nowhere asked if I could play saxophone. I told him I didn't own one, so he says, "If I get you one, can you make the Greenlake Fieldhouse Saturday night for a PTA dance?" " Well, gee, I don't know. . . . " I was fourteen and never played a gig in my life! He found me a beat-up alto and I took it down to Johnnie, and he worked on the keys and showed me the fingerings. I went to the job, they gave me a jacket and tie, and we started working every Sunday at the USO on Second Avenue for ten bucks a week. At fifteen I joined the union and got in Stanton Patty's UW band, the Chevaliers. Stan was a decent trumpet player, and the whole band got thirty-two bucks a night for playing sorority dances. Being one of Johnnie's students, I started getting calls; I played the Palladium with Scobey, then Bud Storm called me to work in Russian John's Havana Club. Six nights a week, sailors, girls, bottles. I was still in high school! Jeez, I'd wrap up at five in the morning, park in front of Roosevelt High in my 1933 Chevrolet, and sleep until 7:20. Then go to class until three, drive home, go to bed, wake up at eleven, go back downtown, and go to work again. My grades went in the toilet.

After his big band broke up, Pierce went back in time to the pit of the Palomar Theater. A magnificent holdout, the stately former Pantages was one of the last surviving vaudeville houses in the country.

In 1947 I got called for the Palomar to sub for each of the reed players on their days off, and worked for three different leaders—Guy Parks, Chuck Gould, and Leon Plath. I was there for a year and learned all the reed parts. Angelo Recchia played lead alto there for thirty years, and I almost got fired for fluffing his part. It was harmony with the other saxes, but I was twenty years old and thinking Charlie Parker, and Guy Parks points his finger at me: "Listen, you! If you don't have that right in the next show, you can pack up and get the hell out of here!" I went into one of the dressing rooms and woodshedded the thing, and an hour later, three-part harmony, clear as a bell. Parks didn't even look at me. I guess that's what being a pro is—when nobody notices you. The Palomar worked a twelve-piece band onstage, seven days a week. Start at ten in the morning with a movie, then a variety show, six acts, four times a day, five on weekends. The union minimum there was twelve pieces, and often the act didn't have a book for that size band, so we'd do little fillers and intermission music, then sit there while these visiting acts did their thing. Sammy Davis didn't have a book; he'd come running out—"Vamp till ready!"—and do a Jimmy Cagney imitation and dance and tell jokes. I backed up Sarah Vaughn, Billy Eckstein, Hank Williams, the Mills Brothers nineteen times. Each act had a different book, and at nine a.m. opening morning they'd have a quick rundown: "Tacit this, cut that," *I'm gonna buy a paper doll that I can call my own.* . . . I'm living in that tuxedo, but I'm making more money than I'd ever made before, and thinking—how'd I get *here?* I mean, this saxophone's really paying off!

Ronnie Pierce had fast company in the reed section. Tacoma-born tenor sax prodigy Gene Patrick "Corky" Corcoran hitchhiked to Seattle in 1940 to jam at after-hours joints. He was picked up by Jimmie Lunceford before going on extended tours with Sonny Dunham and Harry James, all the while keeping his hand in the local scene. Corcoran's career, like so many, would run "on the rocks" of alcohol dependence, but by his death in 1979 he had become recognized as one of the Northwest's top jazz talents. Jimmy Shevenko ventured north from the LA studios in 1946 (rumor had it he was fired for being uncontrollable), fell into the Seattle jobbing scene, then formed his own combo, which enjoyed a long run at the New Chinatown at 6th and Main. A hard-drinking, big-toned tenor and clarinet shouter who also loved to sing ballads in a sweet tenor voice, the "Mad Russian" was one of the hardest-working sax players in postwar Seattle, playing (often with his friend Ronnie Pierce) in everything from country western to Scandinavian bands. Another "class of '46" reed standout was Bob Winn. Trombonist Mike Hobi told me,

> When he came here just after the war, Bob Winn was playing bop when not a lot of people were playing it yet. He had a glass eye; I was sitting right behind him on a job, and every now and then, when he'd be playin' hard, that eye would pop out. Land on the stage with a *clack* and roll around at our feet. Bob picked it up, popped it back in, kept right on playing like nothing happened. I thought I was gonna fall out of my chair. But Winn was fabulous on alto, and also one of the best flute players around.

In that confluential year 1946, two more tenor players showed up: Freddie Greenwell and Rollie Morehouse. Both had played with legendary pianist Claude Thornhill's navy band in the Pacific. Delaware-born Greenwell worked in Curt Sykes's band, while Morehouse joined Wyatt Howard at the Town Ranch and would become known as a first-rate jazz clarinetist as well. Both were acclaimed top reedmen by their peers, but Ronnie Pierce was emphatic:

> Of all sax players out of Seattle, Freddie Greenwell was *it*. Great sense of humor and high intelligence in his playing. He was the master. Every year, he got called to go to New York and play this big coming-out party with Lester Lanin. Here's this fabulous jazz cat who can play anything he wants, taking this crummy society gig. I asked him, "How do you do it?" "Ronnie," he says, "you put on your suit of armor every night, and make sure there's not a single crack in it."

It was a philosophy that served Pierce well in fifty years of dance and show bands. A case in point was the Frankie Roth Orchestra, house band at the Spanish Castle until 1950. Roth's corny trumpet playing was an object of derision among his sidemen, but he taught Pierce a valuable lesson in showmanship. "Taylor Bowie got me on Roth's band after I left the Palomar," he recalled.

> Frankie was a good guy to work for once he decided he liked you. He'd play his trumpet and sing, both badly, and people loved it. He put on

A trumpet solo by bandleader Frankie Roth evokes mixed responses on New Year's Eve 1947. From left are Gale Snyder, Lee Naylor, Roth, unknown, Gene Harmon, Alex Gomavitz, Taylor Bowie, unknown, Andy Piatt, unknown. Courtesy of Taylor Bowie Jr.

this man-of-the-world act, standing up in front of the band smoking his pipe, and I'm thinking, "*This* is the music business?" Then one night we opened for a big-name act at the Civic Auditorium in front of five thousand people. Roth picked up his trumpet, cold, and played "You Made Me Love You," and he brought that house *down!* Biggest hand of the whole evening. It was because he *communicated* with those five thousand people. That set me back—"Oh! Okay!" I'll never forget that.

Like many a jobbing musician, Ronnie Pierce often met himself coming and going, resulting in episodes that some co-workers tolerated better than others. Ronnie proudly keeps a running tally of how many times he's been fired by every bandleader he's worked for, but Roth is not on the list. "I was amazed at my own longevity on that band," he laughed.

One night I left my clarinet in the street—right in the white center line. I get on the job, and we're playing down a chart, and here comes a section for four clarinets. Only mine is sitting out in the damn *street!* So I duck out and get the clarinet, which is still sitting out there in the road, and come back and jump in like nothing ever happened. Frankie looked at me like I had to go to the john or something. But he never fired me.

In 1950 a group of Roth sidemen decided that they couldn't take it any longer and defected to the camp of trombonist Gordon Greene. Soon after, Greene took Roth's Saturday night slot at the Spanish Castle. Holding down the foundation on bass was Ed Gross:

Frankie hired me to play bass for Gordon Greene, his substitute bandleader. His book was mostly commercial hotel-style stuff, but very good. Gordon married the daughter of one of the owners of the Spanish Castle. Not long after that Roth got into a spat with the Castle management and Gordon got the gig, which lasted fourteen years. The Spanish Castle drew huge crowds every Saturday night, and lots of people met there and ended up as husband and wife. The Castle was a wooden structure, and when a mob of dancers started doing the Bunny Hop they would get the whole building shaking. At Christmas time the management would throw a big party for all of us. That was a dream job for a musician.

The tall and dignified Gross played string bass and tuba in dozens of bands beginning in the late twenties, and was an innovator in more ways than one. In 2003 the ninety-year-old bassist told me,

I started amplifying my bass in the early fifties. I had to; Shorty Clough was playing drums with Gordon, and he was so loud I couldn't keep up with him otherwise. I bought an early Ampeg box amp, and the only problem with it was that the pickup was actually a microphone, and it would feed back and squeal like crazy. I used two Ampeg B-15 bass enclosures with my amp for stereophonic bass, so both sides of the band could hear me. One bandleader didn't want to pay me extra to haul the things around, so I went to the union and made the case that bass players, drummers, guitarists, and keyboard players should be getting cartage money for hauling all their gear. My suggestion was adopted, and cartage became part of the union price list.

A distinctive postwar musical trend, one that retained the essence of the big band sound, minus the overhead, was the tenor band: four reeds, a lone trumpet or trombone, and rhythm. Tenor bands dominated Seattle dance music between 1945 and 1965, and prime exponents of the formula were Norm Hoagy and Vern Mallory. Lanky Norm Hoagy landed in 1945, fresh from the bands of Herbie Kay and Shep Fields. Hoagy (his name was spelled "Houge," but he pronounced it "Hoagy" and subsequently adopted that spelling) jobbed around, then settled into a long engagement at Harry Lew's China Pheasant. With Hoagy doubling on sax and vibraphone, the group featured a cool, "semi-bop" sound and innovative Latin numbers that won them kudos in *Down Beat* magazine. From the China Pheasant, Hoagy took a twenty-year stand at the Magic Inn. With distinctive arrangements and a wry stage presence, Hoagy built a loyal following among musicians (young Quincy Jones was a Hoagy student) and the public. The Hoagy sound became a hallmark of Seattle dance bands. Sax player Dick Rose told me, "Just about every tenor band in town—Jackie Souders, Vern Mallory, Archie Kyle—wound up with some of Norm's arrangements. They were wonderful to play."

Before jumping on the tenor bandwagon, Vern Mallory headed one of Seattle's hottest postwar white bands. "We had some excellent jazz players on that band, and it really swung," said trombonist Don Glenn. "Except for a couple of 'older' guys in their twenties, we were all just teenagers." Like Bud Storm, Mallory hired black sidemen when he could. "Jabo Ward played tenor and baritone and sang," Glenn told me. Moreover, Mallory's was the only white band to regularly play the Savoy Ballroom. "We played Ellington, Lunceford, Dorsey, Kenton, and had a rocking sound that the dancers loved, and they packed the place. Vern was a very solid piano player and was a handsome matinee-idol kind of guy and a shrewd, aggressive businessman who worked hard to get bookings. He was a father figure for us kids." Quick to see where things were heading after the war, Mallory dissolved his orchestra, started a tenor band, and went after high-paying society work. He succeeded handsomely, becoming a fixture at the Olympic Hotel and at military bases.[14]

Nineteen-forty-six was a momentous musical year in the black community. New players who would become Seattle legends moved in, and colored Local 493 moved its headquarters out of the home of longtime president Gerald Wells and into its new clubhouse/nightclub, the Blue Note, at 14th and Jefferson. Now members had an all-hours meeting place

Billy Tolles and his Men of Jive rock a dance in the mid-forties. Left to right: Buddy Brashear, Delbert Brown, Don Alexander, Tolles, George Francis, Major Pigford, and Gerald Brashear. Photo by Al Smith, 002–035–0157; courtesy of Al Smith family

close to the Jackson Street strip, and the Blue Note became a music Mecca where African American musicians could network and jam.

Taking the mantle of top black bandleader from Al Pierre was Robert A. "Bumps" Blackwell. "Bumps couldn't play anything," chuckled trumpeter Floyd Standifer, "but his talent lay in the fact that he could sell snow to an Eskimo. He was an absolute *marketer*. He knew how to open doors. He'd take that band places no other black band could go, man, and play for white audiences." The Bumps Blackwell "senior" orchestra featured veterans of the Al Pierre band and singer Tommy Adams, to whom Standifer ascribed "a beautiful voice, like a cross between Prysock and Eckstein." Standifer, a neophyte trumpet player and himself a 1946 arrival, learned much of his stagecraft from Blackwell: "That band was successful because Bumps was a total professional and knew what to do and, more importantly, what *not* to do. He always had his bands dressed up well and taking care of business. Consequently, Bumps was able to open certain doors to us and get us before white audiences. Out at Cottage Lake, on old Highway 99—they *loved* him out there!"[15]

But it was the Bumps Blackwell "junior" band that raised a ruckus, and one of the reasons sat beside Standifer in the trumpet section: a sixteen-year-old from Chicago named Quincy Jones. Blackwell's band had actually been launched by Jones and tenor saxophonist Charlie Taylor, and it was no casual affair: "We elected a president," wrote Jones, "a vice-president, a secretary/treasurer (me!) who took minutes, we had fines for drinking, fines for being late to rehearsal, fines for not looking cool. Everything was aimed at being cool." But looking cool was one thing, getting gigs another, and when the smooth-talking Blackwell told the youngsters he'd find them work, they turned the band over to him. Blackwell was a tireless promoter ("He had . . . a taxicab business, a jewelry business, he worked off-nights at the Boeing aircraft plant, plus he ran a butcher shop") who knew how to walk the fine line, and he soon had his young charges playing places—the Seattle Tennis Club, the Broadmoor Golf Club, college fraternities, and county fairs—that had never before seen an African American musician. Liquor and drugs were strictly off-limits on the Blackwell band, and the leader demanded absolute dedication to the business of entertaining the public on all sides of town. Bumps drilled his pupils in ensemble playing, singing, reading a crowd, and how to get girls. Then he laid it down with infectious music and a floor show that included shake dancer August Mae, dancers "Chicken 'n Giblets," and a comedy duo starring Jones and trombonist Major Pigford as "Dexedrine and Benzedrine."[16]

Encouraged by his school music teachers, among them Garfield High's influential Parker Cook, Quincy Jones plunged into the art of musical arranging early in his teens and became a star pupil of the great Frank Waldron, delighting his mentor by rattling off exotic scales on demand. Standifer told me,

As just a young stripling Quincy was already writing good music, stuff that had a little bit of that Louis Jordan jump sound and a little bit of

Count Basie. Blues-based, yeah, except that Quincy was a very intellectual cat and he understood that sound was everything. He didn't just stick with the blues, for the simple reason that Bumps, with all his talent, encouraged him to realize that the public responded to variety and pop songs, not just blues.

Like Standifer, Jones took from Bumps Blackwell life lessons that would see him through a minefield of racism and venality and into a stellar career. "Music made me full," he wrote, "strong, popular, self-reliant, and cool. . . . Jazz gave black men and women dignity." As much as he loved Seattle, Quincy Jones was ready to swim in deeper waters, and in 1951 he headed for the East Coast and growing recognition. Bumps Blackwell went south to Los Angeles, where he assisted young Sam Cooke and "Little" Richard Penniman in their rise to fame.[17]

BEBOP AND BEYOND

In the 1940s two men named Norm took jazz into the concert hall and made it "respectable." In Seattle, Norm Bobrow presented Fats Waller and orchestra at the Moore Theater in 1941. Three years later, Norman Granz launched Jazz at the Philharmonic in Los Angeles. In April 1946 Granz brought Jazz at the Philharmonic to Seattle with a solid swing lineup of Coleman Hawkins, Lester Young, Meade Lux Lewis, Buck Clayton, and Helen Humes. By then, however, swing was being edged aside by a brash and angular music incubated in New York by Dizzy Gillespie and Charlie Parker. Technically dazzling and aimed at the head and not the feet, bebop quickly found an ear among young musicians and listeners. Though never widely popular, bop had a strong influence on popular music, making the big band sound in particular less dense, more contrapuntal, and, to the dismay of many, more cerebral.

What Oscar Holden made of bop can only be imagined, but by 1947 records by Parker and Gillespie were circulating among excited Seattle musicians. And when Norman Granz (now represented locally by Norm Bobrow) introduced Charlie Parker to Seattle the next year, the Metropolitan Theater was packed. Floyd Standifer was in the audience:

When I came up to Seattle just around '46, at the age of seventeen, I started runnin' into people that were actually starting to play a little bop.

Yeah, we'd take our horns and jam there at the Y at 21st and Madison. The big bands like Reggie Crabtree and Don Cherry rehearsed at Birdland, and all us young kids would lay back and soak it in. I went into the UW, and pretty soon I was exposed to a group of white musicians who were doing their own take on jazz. I was probably one of the few African American beboppers around here in '46. Most of the guys I was playing with were white; the blacks were all swing musicians, and it wouldn't be another four years before all that bop would begin to get here.

Also in the Metropolitan audience was alto saxophonist Roscoe Weathers. After hearing Parker, he woodshedded, took a trio into Basin Street, and made his reputation as the Charlie Parker of Seattle. He and Kenny Boas shared an apartment near the Washington Social Club that became bebop central for aspiring players. A moody and introspective artist, Weathers lost faith in the music business and faded from the scene, to be whispered about in awed tones decades later. Others stuck with it: Pony Poindexter, whose tenor sax mixed bop and blues, and Vernon "Pops" Buford's more laid-back tenor keeping things sultry in the Yesler Hill–Jackson Street "chitlin clubs." Standifer remembered another who enjoyed a brief fling before fading:

Rolo Strand played tenor in the mold of Stan Getz and was truly one of the greats. Unfortunately he was also one of those guys that lost it early on to mind-altering substances. This is in that period of time where, in order to play like Charlie Parker, a lot of people thought they had to *act* like him. But here in Seattle we all knew each other and respected each other. If you played bebop, fine. If you played swing, fine! Just appreciating each other and working with each other, you learned how to adapt. That's how you survive as a musician.

Alongside bebop came a warm wind from Latin America. With a baton in one hand and his pet Chihuahua in the other, Xavier Cugat drove America mambo-mad in the early forties, and after the war jazz lovers went wild over the bop-tinged Afro-Cuban sound of Dizzy Gillespie and Chano Pozo. Seattle caught the fever in 1949 when the pair raised the roof at the Senator Ballroom. By then, ex-Los Angeleno Daryl Harpa was in residence at the El Rancho with his popular Latin-flavored band. Musicians soon discovered that Harpa was neither Latino nor much of a musician, but they also discovered that he was good at finding work, and that he had a smouldering rhythm section in conga drummer David "Dacito" Niego and pianist Eddie Diamond. Pianist Jack Hungerford later started his own band with Niego and told me,

> Dacito was the greatest performer in town. He was a Cuban who had played in Xavier Cugat's band, and he stirred up a lot of excitement around here. He could put a glass of water on his head, play his congas, dance, jump up on the tables, and never spill a drop. Dacito nicknamed me "Pancho" and told me I was the only pianist in Seattle who could play Latin. Somehow he got a gig at the Georgian Room, so we rounded up a bunch of guys and used my tenor band book, and wore ruffled shirts to look "Latin."

Bop and Latin were joined by a third trend set by pianist Nat "King" Cole, guitarist Oscar Moore, and bassist Wesley Prince, who with skilled arrangements and subtle chord voicings took the combo beyond the realm of loosely structured jam band into a sophisticated new realm. The King Cole–style piano trio was epitomized in Seattle by Elmer Gill, who took his early inspiration from gospel pianists in his native Indianapolis and rode the wave of '46 to Puget Sound. At the new Rocking Chair at 14th and Yesler, he settled in with tenor saxophonist Jonas Weir, bassist Johnny Warren, and vocalist Juanita Cruse. The group was an archetype of both the piano lounge combo and early R&B bands, and with it Gill established himself as a top man on the scene. The sound was jazzy and bluesy; as he told Paul de Barros, "Sometimes we'd start in playing the blues at twelve o'clock, and at four o'clock in the morning we were still playing the same blues." For the patrons of the black clubs, many of whom came from the South and Midwest, Gill's formula was a winning one, and he enjoyed long runs as a regular at the Black and Tan, Spinning Wheel, and Mardi Gras. Elmer Gill added vibraphone and vocals to his palette and reigned for years as a king of sophisticated Seattle nightlife.[18]

TURNING POINTS

His middle name was not Caesar for nothing. In his younger days, James C. Petrillo played the trumpet in Chicago kid bands. Then he found his calling in the smoky backrooms of union politics, and by 1940 he was head of the American Federation of Musicians. He had his work cut out for him, for just as John Philip Sousa had warned, canned music had proven to be a wolf in sheep's clothing. In the thirties, radio stations discovered the economy of using "transcription" discs rather than live orchestras, and an alarmed AFM joined a long fight for royalties from prerecorded programs. Relieving the long-serving Joseph Weber, Petrillo declared that, unless musicians were paid for transcribed broadcasts, live music was doomed. He promptly demanded that records for radio use be produced under strictly prescribed procedures that gave musicians suitable compensation. All other records must be labeled "for home use only."

The record companies refused, and the United States Supreme Court backed them, saying that artists had no inherent right to control their product once it entered the marketplace. All right, Petrillo shot back; if musicians could not get their share of the recording pie, there would *be* no recordings. On August 1, 1942, the first AFM recording ban went into effect. Benny Goodman and Tommy Dorsey vanished from the airwaves, and were allowed to record only "V discs" for the military. It did not take long for industry resolve to crack; lacking inventory backlogs, small record labels began making concessions, and in 1943 the Recording and Transcription Fund was established, funneling 2 percent of record sales into an AFM fund that would essentially subsidize live music. Watching sales plummet, the major labels capitulated.

The ban was lifted, but not for long. Smarting from Petrillo's lash, Congress (many of whose members owned interest in radio stations) swore vengeance and in 1946 passed the Lea Act banning restrictions on the sale and use of records, and outlawing "exactions" for rebroadcasts of recorded programs. The following year the legislators passed an even tougher measure, the landmark Taft-Hartley Act, which banned sympathetic boycotts and payments to unions for "work not done." The Recording and Transcription Fund was effectively nullified. Petrillo erupted furiously at the "fascistic" death blow directed not just at the AFM but at all of organized labor, and in August 1947 he called a second recording ban. Caught in the middle were thousands of musicians, such as Ronnie Pierce, whose 1946 "dream band" foundered under the ban. "We recorded fourteen sides," Ronnie told me, "and in August of '47 I had an agent take it all to Chicago. He was in the office at Sonora Records signing the contracts when Petrillo called the ban. The same day! It wiped us out."[19]

After a year of negotiations, and under mounting pressure from the rank and file, Petrillo proposed a compromise: Live performances would be funded out of a combination of recording industry profits and AFM dues, to be deposited in a recording industry Music Performance Trust Fund (MPTF). The MPTF was set up to be run by a trustee appointed by the recording companies. Federation locals would designate which venues and events would get MPTF funds. Some dismissed the Music Performance Trust Fund as a slush fund, but for union musicians it would prove to be a godsend—a cushion against the many forces encroaching on their livelihood. As an antidote to canned music, the MPTF brought live music to thousands of events every year that would have otherwise used recorded music or none at all. To this day, musicians argue heatedly over whether Petrillo's actions helped or harmed their livelihood (many blamed the demise of big bands on his bans), but in Seattle, the MPTF meant concert music in the parks, pep bands at sporting events, and singalongs at nursing homes. As it did in all segments of labor, though, Taft-Hartley wrought profound changes in the music profession.

Local politics also took a hand. In 1946 the state supreme court declared bottle clubs illegal, opening the door two years later for the sale of mixed drinks in public places, something musicians and club owners had long hoped and lobbied for. There were catches: Establishments selling liquor had to sell food, too, and unaccompanied women were not allowed to sit on barstools. Then, in the spring of 1949, the Washington State Liquor Control Board defied the high court and summarily denied Class H, liquor-by-the-drink licenses to roadhouses, cabarets, dance halls, and nightclubs. The musicians' union lodged a strong protest, but to little avail, and under growing pressure from downtown cocktail lounge owners and the Jackson Street Council, the age of the bottle club slowly passed to the age of the cocktail lounge. And in those lounges, strange metal boxes aglow with flickering black-and-white images began to appear. Music would have to adjust.

■ ■ ■

It was a slow night at the Trianon. The modest audience had been all but lost in the vast ballroom, but then, the band business had been slumping for a long time. Now the famed dance hall was on its last legs. Management had summoned Vic Meyers for one last dance before closing the joint. And Meyers was well known for stiffing his bands. Ronnie Pierce eyed his friend Jimmy Shevenko: Would Vic stiff them, too? A figure emerged from the office at the far end of the hall: Vic Meyers, sleek in a white dinner jacket, strolled slowly toward the stage, holding something in outstretched palms. Reaching the bandstand, he gingerly placed the small object on the edge of the stage. It was a stack of bills. Without a word, he spun on his heel and walked out of the room. The musicians of the Vic Meyers Orchestra eyed each other warily, then one of them stood and began to distribute the wages, one bill, one man at a time. Quickly— too quickly—the little pile vanished. This time, the band was not exactly stiffed, but shorted all the same. Pierce turned to Shevenko and laughed, "Ya gotta love it!"

■   ■   ■

Chapter 7

Dizzy Decade

IT BEGAN WITH "MONA LISA" and ended with "A Big Hunk of Love."
It looked ahead, it looked back; it revered yesterday and worshipped
tomorrow. The fast and frantic fifties were a schizoid decade, a dynamic
decade, and mostly a decade dizzy with change. Freeways, suburbs, pres-
surized airliners, and television transformed landscape and culture. The
generation that danced in downtown ballrooms moved to Levittown to
raise families and watch "I Love Lucy." Cold War paranoia and twenty
years of privation spawned blacklists and materialism.

Music reflected our nervous energy, looking wistfully backward and
anxiously forward. Strains that had long been simmering—folk, country-
western—bubbled over into mass popularity, while classical music and
jazz enjoyed wider acceptance than ever. Backed by the Taft-Hartley Act,
the recording industry stepped up its campaign to transform music from
a live to a prepackaged medium, marketing "product" to an increasingly
fragmented consumer population. The educational system and a strange
new sound would begin the transformation of music from profession to
hobby. In the middle of the decade Jacques Barzun proclaimed an American cultural revolution: "Music has become for many people a passionate avocation. . . . The amateur now mingles with the professional and
tends, while usurping his place, to surpass him in devotion." Thanks to the
phonograph, movies, the radio, the jukebox, and then television, music
became all-pervasive and virtually inescapable.[1]

INDIAN SUMMER

Nationally, the demise of the ballrooms hastened the decline of the big bands, but Seattle lost relatively few. Byron Scobey's Palladium was converted to a bowling alley in mid-decade, and May 1956 saw the last dance at the Trianon. John Savage invited the ballroom's "old friends" to a gala final fling with the Vic Meyers Orchestra. Fifty years later, Ronnie Pierce still laughed at the memory of that night:

> You had to *love* the guy! Vic Meyers was a "man of the world." That's the image he built up of himself, and that's how everybody saw him. He was an absolute con artist. You couldn't help but like him, even though he stiffed everybody and you knew he was going to stiff *you*. So we played the job, the crowd left, and the band sat there knowing Vic would try to cheat us. He always did. I mean, to be this big shot bandleader and lieutenant governor for thirty-three years and not have a buck! So here he comes with that little stack of bills, like it's some kind of holy offering. And of course, it's short. But *everybody* loved him!

The clamshell bandstand was dismantled and the Trianon became a discount store, while Parker's and the Spanish Castle remained far outposts of ballroom culture. Hotels, school dances, trade shows, and the Music Performance Trust Fund took up the slack, keeping the big band sound bright in a long Indian summer.

The fifties were good to Ronnie Pierce, who happily revived his bandleading career to accommodate the continuing demand for dance music:

> I was in fat city! From 1957 to 1960 mine was the most popular band in Seattle. I had gigs coming out of my ears, three dozen white Palm Beach jackets, and signed contracts. One Valentine's night I had forty bands out— forty *big bands!*—all of 'em in white jackets. I was a *machine!* I took the Olympic Hotel from Jackie Souders. This got to be too much for the old guys at the union, and they gave me a lot of grief. I gave 'em the finger.

Pierce and pianist Jack Hungerford were regulars in each other's bands. A lifelong jazz lover, Hungerford smiled ruefully as he recalled the low esteem in which non-classical musicians were held:

Dad wouldn't allow any popular music in the house. I came up from Stadium High, Tacoma, class of '37, and after school I'd go down to the basement and practice jazz until my mother yelled, "Your father's coming!" I'd stop and put everything away. Years later I was leading my own band at the Pier 91 officers' club, and my folks came out. Dad was completely flabbergasted—"Where did you learn to play the piano like that?" In 1952 I got my first band into Parker's Ballroom, but I billed myself as "Johnny Sherwood." I didn't use my real name because I was working for a machinery company and my boss was a real square guy. I was afraid if he heard I was playing music at night he'd fire me. He never found out, and we worked there almost a year. There was a general feeling then that musicians were just no good.

But people liked Hungerford, and he pleased them with a well-proven formula:

I wanted a distinctive sound, and I noticed that there weren't any bands around Seattle playing the Glenn Miller sound, which was about the most popular style going. I took a bunch of current pop tunes and arranged them Miller-style, and of course we played schmaltz for dancing, but we also played as much jazz as we could get away with—"Four Brothers," "Disc Jockey Jump." I wouldn't play any two tempos alike, and we kept everybody happy.

For forty years trombonist Ken Cloud played first chair in the Seattle Symphony and led one of the busiest of white-coated dance orchestras. "I really got rolling after the war," the tall, soft-spoken Cloud told me in 1991. "I found an agent willing to take me on, and in 1949 we went into the Trianon subbing for Curt Sykes. Society jobs came to me pretty steady after that, mostly by word of mouth. I usually worked with eight or ten men, and most of my book was stocks." Cloud added a distinctive sound with his own writing, and rather than resist new trends, he made them work for him: "I wrote arrangements when I felt like it: specialty things, a Hawaiian medley, a little of this, a little of that. When rock came in I thought, 'This will never last.' Swing lasted ten years, but rock keeps on going. Even Lawrence Welk plays rock arrangements, and we do, too. People like it! You have to be versatile." Ken Cloud was Seattle's leading apostle of one of the twentieth century's most popular musicians: "My model was Tommy Dorsey, the greatest trombone player ever. I've been playing his theme song, 'I'm Getting Sentimental Over You,' since it first came out. Glenn Miller only had to play 'In the Mood' for four years—we've been playing it for fifty." With fellow symphonists Ronald Phillips and Vaughn Abbey at his side, Ken Cloud was the personification of musical excellence to the many who enjoyed his artistry in both classical and pop contexts.

It was another trombonist, however, who was widely acknowledged as the fifties' Mister Music, and no big society or civic function was considered complete without smiling Jackie Souders. The Souders band hit its height during the decade, pleasing young and old with happy sounds, from swing to Dixie. Souders's Violettes—Seattle Symphony violinists Evelyn Hunter, Corinne Johnson Odegard, Jean Olson, and Evelyn Roderique—added a genteel polish to the horns, and the leader's trombone chimed in with winsome Russ Morgan glissandos. Lush and light-footed, the Souders band was a dancer's dream, keeping the momentum flowing with that hallmark of hotel bands, the medley: several songs of consistent tempo strung together by composer, title, or theme. An airborne medley of "Beyond the Blue Horizon," "Skyliner," and "Flying Down to Rio" constituted just one of dozens in the Souders book, while charts such as percussionist Bruce Ford's "Drums along the Duwamish" added a modern note. Mickey Mouse his band may have been, but an evening with Jackie Souders was never dull.

NIGHTCLUBBING

Seattle in the fifties was not exactly Times Square. The wartime crowds were long gone, leaving behind blue laws and a largely staid and stay-at-home population. Few new buildings went up downtown, anticommunist paranoia encouraged people to keep their heads down, and the city seemed to withdraw into its sleepy, prewar self. Still, there were bright spots. Vic Naon opened his Magicians' Club in the basement at 602½ Union in 1946, just in time for piano-and-trombone-playing ex-GI Bob Hill to join Joe Parente's combo in the cool, dimly lit cavern. "The Magicians' Club was the typical gambling joint run under the fiction of a 'private club,'" said the tall, avuncular Hill. "You paid your 'membership' at the door and bought scrip, which was redeemable for a bottle of your preferred liquor. Many places used this ploy." In 1951 the Magicians' Club was reborn as the Magic Inn, and with Norm Hoagy presiding, it remained a downtown hot-

Twenty-nine years after opening the Olympic Hotel in 1926, Jackie
Souders is in his element at the hotel's Spanish Ballroom in 1955. Front
row (left to right): Dean Curtis, Max Pillar, Dick Rose, reeds; Souders;
Jean Olson, Evelyn Hunter, and Evelyn Roderique, violin. Back row:
Jim Weaver, Don Anderson, trumpet; Chris Schafer, trombone; Murray
Sennett, drums; Mickey Ingalls, piano. Playing bass is old Souders hand
Forrie Hart. "Jackie Souders treated you like family," said longtime saxo-
phonist Dick Rose. "He paid better than anybody, his music was first-rate,
and he worked a *lot*." Courtesy of Dick Rose

spot for twenty years, serving up T-bones, dancing, and floor shows. Musicians used the Inn as a networking base, and snide comments aimed at the
bandstand were guaranteed to evoke a witty Hoagy rejoinder. "Norm was
a seasoned musician and slightly cynical," smiled bassist Tamara Burdette.
"My dad was playing with Norm one night and a lady came up and said,
'Can't you play something we can dance to?' Norm says, 'Lady, how 'bout
you dance something we can *play* to!'"[2]

The Magic Inn got hefty competition in 1954 when Norm Bobrow
opened the swankiest nightspot since Club Victor, the Colony. An eter-

Vocalist Sally King and the Norm Hoagy Orchestra anticipate another evening of musical merriment at the Magic Inn in 1950. Left to right: Lee Howe, trumpet, trombone, violin; Dave Stettler, drums; Al Wied, bass and baritone sax; Hoagy; and Cass Arpke, piano/trombone. Courtesy of Sally King

nally restless jazz promoter and publicist, Bobrow was at loose ends when opportunity knocked. "This was a job that came looking for me," Norm recalled in his downtown apartment.

I was living in cords and sneakers—I didn't know what the hell I was doing! A friend called and said, "Norm, there's a man who has a club that's just made for you. You've got to come down and see it." I met Ted Tickton in his place at Fourth and Virginia, which had been Mori Simon's Clef Club, and I figured, okay, what have I got to lose? I said yes and got a band together: Walt Tianen, a very good modern trumpet player; pianist Johnny Wittwer, and drummer Max Nosich. I borrowed three thousand dollars from my father to put up as a good-faith gesture, we opened dead broke on a Monday, and by Saturday both the club and the till were full.

Bobrow's timing was right, and so was his location:

What really put us over was the fact that the Moore Theater was only two
blocks away. All the traveling stage shows played the Moore, so I got the
idea to comp the cast members to drinks and food. I figured if we could
get show people to come in, everybody else would follow. Boy, was I
right! We were busy every night, and I never bought one cent of advertising. We did theme nights around the current Broadway hits and whatever
show was in town. When *The Pajama Game* was big I had the band dress
up in nightshirts with poker figures on them. All the big money in town,
all the people who wanted to be thought of as high rollers—they just beat
down our door!

The Colony will forever be known as the launching pad for the first
Seattle musician to achieve stardom, Pat Suzuki. Child of Japanese American parents in Cressy, California, Chiyoko Suzuki was in her twenties
when she landed a small role in the road show of *Teahouse of the August
Moon. Teahouse* and Suzuki arrived in Seattle in 1954, just after the Colony's opening night. "Everyone called her 'Ponytail,'" smiled Bobrow.

One Saturday afternoon I was tidying up around the club and I saw this
ponytail sliding along over the booths. I called out, "Can I help you?"
She said, "I'm casing the joint. I've got a walk-on part in *Teahouse*, but
what I really want to do is sing." She explained that she had never sung
professionally but the piano player on the show, Jules Stein, had seen
something in her and encouraged her to start. I told her, "Why don't you
come in after your show tonight and do a couple of numbers?" So that
night she got up on the stand and sang "Fine and Dandy" as a ballad,
half the normal tempo, and just knocked everybody out. Pat left the show
and settled in with us and made herself a singer. We billed her not as a
singer but as a singing *star*, and from her first night the crowds went nuts.
She did her solo numbers, and she and I and Dallas Dixon, our maître
d', sang Broadway numbers. Pat worked 2,000 consecutive shows with us
and was completely responsible for the success of our club.

Word of the Seattle phenomenon spread, and show business heavies
began stopping in to see what the excitement was about. "Bing Crosby
came in," Bobrow told me,

and was so impressed he endorsed the liner notes to her debut album, *The Many Sides of Pat Suzuki*, which came out on RCA in '57. Lawrence Welk had her on his TV show, and then she was on George Gobel, Patti Page, Pat Boone, and Frank Sinatra. Frank asked Pat, "Will you marry me?" I'm glad she said no! Jack Paar had her on ten times—he *never* had anyone on *ten times*!

Kings of Broadway in the fifties, Richard Rogers and Oscar Hammerstein were as impressed as everybody else, and in 1959 they signed Suzuki for their new show, *Flower Drum Song*. "She had never sung anywhere else," exclaimed Bobrow, "and she went directly from singing in a Seattle night-club to Broadway. It was unprecedented! I went along as her personal manager, and Pat was the hit of Broadway—the toast of the town." Pat Suzuki was a phenomenon not only in talent but in making it big in Seattle *before* moving to New York. After *Flower Drum Song*, Pat Suzuki married, settled in New York, and used her magnificent voice sparingly, mostly in the service of Japanese American causes. The young woman people called "Ponytail" will remain a legend on Broadway and in the city that first nurtured her talent.

Between the showy Colony and the subterranean Magic Inn was *the* place for big-name talent and lush dance music, the Seattle Town and Country Club. Presiding over the "T&C" was gruff, hard-driving Wyatt Howard, son of bandleader Tex Howard. "During the war George Cook and I were partners in the Town Ranch," the ebullient Howard reminisced,

but George saw how things were going go after the war, and he sold his share to three businessmen. They thought they were getting something because during the war the place was packed every night. Sure, it looked like a goldmine. But after the war, it died. These guys didn't get it. They came cryin'—"Where did we go wrong? How can we turn the joint around?" They'd been using small bands, so I told 'em, "You need a full orchestra." Then I said, "Gentlemen, you gotta do something the other places aren't doing. People are tired of goin' out to buy their booze and payin' a buck for water. Get a private club license." That cinched it; in 1946 the Town Ranch became the Seattle Town and Country Club. And it was one hell of a place.

The fifties saw the final flowering of the floor show, and the T&C didn't disappoint. Sammy Davis Jr., Bing Crosby, Bob Hope, and the Ink

Norm Bobrow presents a new way
of nighte life for Seattle

Dining, dancing and cocktailing for Seattle's
smartest set...with the Latin and
American rhythms of the Colony Musicians
...and Johnny Wittwer at the lounge
piano...every night

The Colony

"The place to go after the show!"

NOW TWICE NIGHTLY
her name is
Suzuki

...direct from the Teahouse of the August
Moon in her American Singing Premiere

FOURTH AND VIRGINIA IN THE CLAREMONT HOTEL

Pat Suzuki made Norm
Bobrow's Colony a West Coast
hotspot during the late fifties.
Courtesy of Norm Bobrow

Spots were just a few who headlined in the more than twenty years of the club's existence. For the professional musician, the T&C was one of the best jobs in town. "We were the only club in town that worked a ten-piece band six nights a week for twenty-five years," Howard proudly recalled. "We rehearsed, which was very unusual for a Seattle band, and the musicians got a week's paid vacation every year. That was unheard of."

Cherry gig the T&C may have been, but sidemen earned every penny. "In Wyatt Howard's band, you lived in a state of constant fear," sighed Don Smith, who played trumpet at the club for six years.

Wyatt was an alcoholic who'd completely lose control—you never knew when he'd start screaming. He'd single out one guy and stick the needle in him all night long: criticize his playing, his clothes, his attitude. Then he and his wife would start in screaming at each other right there on the

bandstand. The audience stared in disbelief, and onstage we'd be cring-
ing with embarrassment. One night people were talking during the act,
so Wyatt yelled at 'em, "Why don't you bastards go down to the Magic
Inn? That's where you belong!" He actually threw them out and locked
the door! But for a musician, it was one of the only full-time jobs in town,
paying an honest-to-goodness living wage. I bought a house, a car, and
paid for the delivery of our first child all on that one paycheck. One-
thirty-five a week. Try doing that today.

Disdaining the corn and commercialism of the uptown clubs, jazz
lovers gathered in a coterie of intimate joints that offered a taste of the
smoky shoeboxes on New York's fabled 52nd Street. First among these
appeared in 1952, when Dave Levy opened Dave's Fifth Avenue near the
weedy backwater that a decade later would be the site of Seattle's second
world's fair. With a Bohemian ambience that attracted young listeners,
Dave's presented local artists—Billy Tolles, Ernestine Anderson, Elmer
Gill—and occasional touring names. One afternoon early in 1957, a young
bassist named Monk Montgomery wandered in, discovered a packed
house enthralled by Cal Tjader, and was inspired to launch a band of his
own. Soon after, Montgomery debuted a brash, electrifying new group,
the Mastersounds, with himself on the still-novel electric bass, his brother
Buddy on vibes, pianist Reggie Crabtree, and drummer Benny Barth.
Contrasting with the loose jam format most jazz groups favored, the Mastersounds presented show and pop tunes and jazz obscurities alike in a
meticulously arranged and rehearsed ensemble sound that nonetheless
swung hard and packed Dave's for months on end. Between 1957 and their
breakup in 1960, the Mastersounds were the young lions of Seattle jazz;
their standing didn't suffer, either, when the third Montgomery brother,
Wes, joined in on guitar. Some found the Mastersounds overly structured,
but they are still considered among the best-selling of all recorded Seattle
jazz ensembles.[3]

Brass bands and barrelhouse pianos were long gone from Pioneer Square
by 1957, and the grimy brick buildings of the old tenderloin glared down
wistfully on the quiet streets. That year, however, twenty-one-year-old Pete
Barbas opened Pete's Poop Deck on the waterfront at the foot of Main
Street. The appropriately funky atmosphere was heavy on apple crates and
peanut shells, beatniks read poetry, artists drew in shady corners, and Barney Kessel and Cal Tjader alternated with locals such as Bob Winn. The

saxophonist and his stellar combo—pianist Jerome Gray, tenor sax/vocalist Gerry Brashear, bassist Milt Garred, drummer Bill Richardson, and singer Jewel King—were in the vanguard of musicians who helped revive the dusty heart of old Seattle, attracting young listeners amazed to discover that such a neighborhood existed. Freight trains clanked by, gulls shrieked, and the salt air gave jazz a unique Puget Sound flavor.

MODS AND TRADS

The fifties were the true Jazz Age. Duke Elllington made the cover of *Time* magazine, Dave Brubeck and Miles Davis packed clubs and sold albums by the millions, and in 1957 future Seattle radio announcer Jim Wilke was a student at the University of Iowa: "Jazz was the popular music on campus in those days. My jazz group played fraternity parties, our homecoming dances were played by Woody Herman and Count Basie, and when you walked down a dormitory hall, jazz was the music you heard coming out from under peoples' doors." In Seattle, jazz clubs were *the* place to be for anyone with aspirations to hipness, and the place to hear the abundant and abundantly talented local artists.[4]

A regular at Pete's Poop Deck and every Seattle club since was Floyd Standifer, who in his half-century career became the city's most revered jazz musician. Arriving in that fateful year 1946, the young trumpeter built his lip with the boppers on East Madison and by 1950 was solidly established as a first-call man in Local 493. In 1955 Standifer started a Monday night gig at the Flame Tavern at Northgate with Milt Price (guitar, piano, sax, and flute), pianist Ernie Hatfield, and drummer Dave Stettler. If he didn't think it would amount to much, Standifer was pleasantly surprised when a handful of hard-core jazz buffs swelled to standing-room-only crowds. Local and nationally known musicians began sitting in, and the ecstatic club owner extended the gig by weeks, then months. In 1959 Standifer joined his friend Quincy Jones on a European tour and departed the Flame, leaving legions of ears ringing with a new jazz sensitivity.

Standifer's heroes were Dizzy Gillespie, Fats Navarro, and Clifford Brown, and he distilled these voices into his own vibrant sound on trumpet and tenor sax. In 2004 I met Floyd at a Yesler Hill coffeehouse; surrounded by Al Smith's classic musician portraits, he relived his early years in the business.

I was born in Wilmington, North Carolina, and in 1936, by which time I'm seven and a half years old, I had started to play the trumpet. My father, Floyd Standifer Senior, was a minister in the African Methodist Episcopal Zion Church. He was a good preacher—in fact, a little too good. See, the church is big business, and when you get to be a *liiittle* too much of a threat, boy, they'll ship you to the hinterlands in a minute! So they sent Dad out to Portland to "civilize" the West Coast. The church became unable to support a minister, especially one who had five children, so we picked strawberries and ended up saving all that money and buying a farm. That was my first knowing exposure to the work ethic. Dad said to me, "Son, if you can eat, they can't control you. You cannot be controlled if you're not *hungry*." I learned that. I also learned that, if you want to eat regularly, you got to put it back in the ground. All that checks out later in your real life, as you will find.

Like so many upwardly striving African American parents, the senior Standifers held certain aspirations to gentility, along with a not-uncommon ambivalence toward earthy music.

We did not have jazz at home. Nope! Dad secretly loved the blues, though. He *loved* it. He loved Leadbelly, he loved Josh White, and he secretly loved Duke Ellington. And what made it possible for him to like Ellington was that Ellington was well-spoken, well-dressed, and intelligent. See, this was an era when most African Americans were trying to get away from the blues, 'cause amongst the black elite blues was considered to be trashy music. They had spent their entire life trying to get away from that element and *"be"* somebody. *Except*, they secretly *knew* that this was *really* where they came from. All that made it kind of tough for me, because it took Dad several decades to accept me as a *jazz* musician. He wanted me to be a teacher. About the only time he became happy with me was when I became *both*. Finally, some years before he passed away, he told me, "I keep hearing about you all the time—I guess you've done some pretty good things." When your dad is from the Edwardian Age, that's about as good as it's gonna get!

The Standifer home was nonetheless full of music. "Mom'd tune into this 'Lippman and Wolf Hour' on our little Atwater-Kent radio, and there would be Wagner and Mendelssohn. The fact that I didn't hear jazz or blues at the house didn't make any difference to me—it was still beautiful music." Standifer's father may have preferred that his son choose another career, but he opened wide the door to music:

Dad, he happened to have a *trumpet* just sittin' there in the hall doin' nothing. He said he was gonna learn it "sometime." Uh-huh. I kept lookin' at it, sittin' there on the floor, and after three months I ask, "Are you gonna play that?" He said, "I wish I could, but I can't find the time." "Can I try?" "Sure, go ahead." So I did. Now, you have to be more or less fearless to play the trumpet, and in those days I was—well, not arrogant, but just totally *confident*. It got to be I was just pushing music through that horn! We were out on the farm, and we had a big ol' hill out there, and it's nice and quiet. You could aim at that hill, play a scale, and thirty seconds later, back it would come, clear as a bell. Yeah! That was my "recording machine."

Despite his parents' preferences, jazz and pop seeped out of the radio and into their son's ears.

Well, okay, along came Frank Sinatra and those guys on the "Lucky Strike Hit Parade," and then I'm getting wise to Louis Armstrong, Coleman Hawkins, Roy Eldridge, and *then*, this guy named Charles "Yardbird" Parker. And John Birks Gillespie. Uh-*ohhh!* From then on, I was all bebop. Hoo boy, I'd be playin' with the school band and just take off onto something I heard in my head. Everybody'd stop and turn around and stare at me. It just occurred to me that this would fit— never mind about what the *composer* wanted! Later on I learned that's a no-no. But the thing was, I could *do* it. It's kind of like, why do they climb mountains? 'Cause they're *there*, right? "Why you playin' that?" "Cause I *can!*"

Arriving in Seattle, Standifer found a music scene in transition, with partisans of two styles bidding for his talent.

As soon as we got here, I was jamming with the boppers and gigging in the black swing bands of Terry Cruise and Bumps Blackwell and Joe Gauff. Terry Cruise had an eight-piece orchestra and was a very accomplished saxophonist with the sound of Johnny Hodges, but almost like a violin. Plus, he sang like Louis Jordan, so he had a lot of that kind of stuff in his book: hot jump music, what you might call early R&B. No bebop at all.

The young musician did not let his eagerness to play bop get in the way of his education. He enjoyed working with older swing players, incorporating their drive and warmth into his playing, and their musical experience into his own ability to cross musical boundaries. "I'm digging on learning from these old musicians about all the stuff you do and *don't* do," he emphasized.

> Like dissing each other: If you don't like the way a guy plays, you don't call him on it. Take for example, "Muskat Ramble": It's got three or four parts, and if you can't negotiate all of those parts at the right time, and with the right spirit and the right phrasing, you're stepping all over yourself. And if you got any pride at all, you say to yourself, "Nah, man, if you're gonna do this, you better practice up and do it right." Playing with these guys, I was easing myself into the pro scene. Coming straight off a farm like I did, you don't acquire sophistication right away. You got to pay some dues. And so it took me about a year and a half of rubbing some of the corners off. But once you got into it, and they discovered that you could play, you were in. The name of the game always has been and always will be, *Can you play?* Look at Louis Armstrong, when he went with Fletcher Henderson: He walked into rehearsal the first day, and all these dudes looked at this cat with this big round head and these big ol' thick-sole shoes and black suit with white socks on, and they said, "Who is *this*?" About the third note he played, they said, "Ohhh—*that's* who this is!"

Standifer enrolled at the University of Washington. Into the thirties the UW had been no more receptive to African Americans than the rest of society, and some departments simply refused to admit black students. After the war, though, the climate was thawing, and Floyd found his white peers less interested in skin color than in performance.

> For black and white people to interact was not all that common in Seattle, but you *could* do that at the U. Amongst us there was no such thing as inferiorities. You get into a jam session and somebody says, "Hey,

man, you sound good. We got a dance comin' up—can you make it?" My first gig was a bar mitzvah, and the guys paid for me to get my union card in Local 493.

For moving gracefully through a segregated society, Standifer applied the wisdom of his elders and devised strategies of his own.

What with the union being segregated, it wasn't *illegal* for white guys to hire me, but it was not the *policy.* Norm Hoagy said to me, "I'd love to hire you, but man, the union would really nail me." Okay, I understood that! I worked around it. Powell S. Barnett fought the system for years, trying to get African American musicians accepted. He was a very powerful man, and I admired him greatly—in private. In those days, I did not feel able to speak out publicly. We knew what we were up against, see, and we went about our business in more of a subtle way. Wherever I was, I had always been the only African American kid in school. Consequently, I developed the education that allowed me to go back and forth without feeling ill at ease. So what that did for me was get me into the big band scene around Seattle, where a lot of other black musicians couldn't do it. Either they couldn't read music, or they weren't comfortable, or they didn't have the technical skill on the instrument.

The seamier side of nightlife offered its own instruction, and to get along at Basin Street and the Black and Tan, one went along. "By about 1960 the after-hours scene was just about dead," Standifer mused, "but it took a long time dyin'."

Those were the days when they had a little saying: "Stay with your party so your head don't get knotty" [a spin on Basin Street's bromide, "Stay with your party and our service is yours"]. Meaning you had best tread lightly! That black Elks Club came about as close to being a bucket of blood as I've ever seen. You had a big flight of stairs, and one night I was just openin' the door when down comes a body—*bump-bump-bump!* Working in them kind of joints was kind of iffy; you *might* get your money, and you might *not* get your money.

Standifer found in Seattle a congeniality that kept him from bigger ponds.

Among musicians, there was kind of a respect around here that you didn't run into in New York. In New York you *never* tell anybody where you're playing, man, because, instead of *having* a gig, you just *had* a gig. You meet some guy on the street: "Hey, man, how ya doin'?" "Well, I'm working at so-and-so." "Yeah, who got the band down there? Oh, man, haven't seen him in years!" Well, 'soon as he leaves you, he's right on the phone: "Look here, man, I understand you got so-and-so playin'. I don't care what he's playin' for, I'll do it for *half*!" That was not the case out here. That's because everybody knew each other. There was no such thing as anonymity, because Seattle was too small a community for you to alienate anybody. It wouldn't be all that many years before that would begin to change. But Seattle always had, underneath the segregation thing, a tendency to be civil. We all knew we were here in the Northwest because everybody's fiercely independent, and so, if you didn't cooperate, you weren't gonna get anywhere. How do you maintain your independence? You don't maintain it by separating—you maintain it by cooperating to an extent with those who have *like* causes to yours.

Floyd Standifer reached his twentieth year of playing every Wednesday night at the New Orleans Creole Restaurant in Pioneer Square, when he passed away in January 2007. A modest yet brilliant musician who might have attained wider recognition, Standifer chose to stay in Seattle. And Seattle was more than happy to have him.

Since his Husky Hot Club days in the late thirties, Norm Bobrow was synonymous with jazz. Bobrow's warm yet scholarly manner opened doors across society and attracted talent to a city previously considered too far off the beaten path by many booking agents. Handsome, witty, and possessed of a pleasantly hip tenor voice, Bobrow sandwiched turns as a bandleader/ vocalist/bassist/conga player among careers as a disc jockey, journalist, and publicity agent, and "Norm Bobrow Presents" attained a local cachet rivaling that of international impresario Sol Hurok. In the late forties and early fifties Bobrow promoted jazz on two radio shows, presented rising stars—Dave Brubeck, Charlie Parker, Stan Getz—and hosted weekly jazz jams at the Repertory and Cirque playhouses. "I never had bands at the Cirque," Norm told me. "I only hired individuals, and I always preferred to have people play with others that they didn't usually play with, or had never played with before."

In his eighteenth year of Wednesday nights at the New Orleans Creole Restaurant, Floyd Standifer takes a solo during a Hurricane Katrina benefit in September 2005, backed by pianist Bob Hammer, bassist Phil Sparks, and drummer Clarence Acox. Photo by Kurt E. Armbruster

In October 1951 Bobrow presented one of the most sensational jazz performances ever heard in Seattle, featuring a young man he had just plucked from obscurity. Bobrow recalled,

> I was working at the Palomar hosting vaudeville acts for Zollie Volchok, and accompanying a tap-dancer—*accompanying!*—was this *killer* piano player named Cecil Young. He was a cat of about thirty-five from New Haven, and he struck me right off as a major talent going to waste. I talked to him backstage, after which he and the tap dancer parted company, and I started lining up dates around town for him, not as an "agent" but as his friend. For a year and a half, Cecil Young was the king of jazz in Seattle.

He was crowned that October evening when he ignited a crowd in the genteel surroundings of the Ladies Musical Club. With him was an all-star band: tenor sax phenomenon Gerald Brashear, an alumnus of Billy Tolles's Savoy Boys, who matched Young with blazing bop solos and jaw-dropping scat vocals (critic Leonard Feather thought Brashear's scat singing the best anywhere). Young in age but an old-school believer in *entertaining* his audiences, Young worked both sides of the aisle, mugging and tap dancing to the Madison Park squares, and wowing the cats with his lightning speed and advanced keyboard harmonies. Bobrow's King label recording of the evening roused the interest of the prestigious William Morris Agency, and the group headed east. In Chicago and New York Young and company enjoyed a short, heady fling then flamed out, a classic example of the heartbreak and arbitrary nature of this cruelest of professions. Only a few copies of Bobrow's recording remain as evidence of an incandescent moment in Seattle music history. Normally reluctant to make comparisons, Bobrow told me flatly that "the Cecil Young Quartet was the greatest jazz ensemble ever to work in Seattle."

Even as the young bop lions roared, an echo of the past was reaching new ears. New Orleans–style jazz—a three-horn "front line" taking turns improvising extended variations over popular and traditional tunes—peaked in the twenties, then was swept aside by swing. Late in the thirties, however, a group of young Chicago musicians—Eddie Condon, Bud Freeman, Muggsy Spanier—discovered that freewheeling "trad" jazz provided a happy alternative to heavily orchestrated big band fare. By 1938 the Dixieland revival had bloomed in New York and Chicago, and six years later it took root on the banks of the Duwamish River when jazz-loving Harry Lew, owner of the China Pheasant, hired pianist Johnny Wittwer and his band.

As a UW music student, Wittwer formed what may have been Seattle's first Dixieland band with trumpeter Lee Howe and drummer Murray Sennett. Wittwer took off for Hollywood, where he accompanied Shirley Temple's voice lessons, then toured briefly with Jack Teagarden. Returning to Seattle, he hooked up with New Orleans veteran Joe Darensbourg, and the duo soon attracted the attention of "jazz doctor" and amateur recording engineer Dr. Frederick Exner. "Doc Exner loved New Orleans–type jazz," Wittwer told Pete Leinonen in 1989, "and he brought Joe together with me and Keith Purvis as the Johnny Wittwer Trio. He did his recording in a little radio station in the basement of the Northern Life Tower." Subsequent sessions saw Wittwer and Darensbourg teamed with New Orleans trombonist Kid Ory to wax classics such as "Tiger Rag," a move that revived Ory's long-dormant career. "Joe put Exner in touch with Kid

In 1951 the Cecil Young Quartet gave one of the most exciting jazz performances ever heard in Seattle. Backing pianist Young were drummer Jimmie Rogers, bassist Traff Hubert, and saxophonist/vocalist Gerald Brashear. Courtesy of Norm Bobrow

Ory," said Wittwer, "and he went to LA and recorded Ory, Joe, and me with some of his old friends he'd played with years before. Those Exner records really had a lot to do with the New Orleans revival."[5]

On the heels of the recording sessions came the seminal China Pheasant gig. Darensbourg's exuberant personality and woody clarinet spurred Wittwer and the rest of the band to play up the Dixie sound, and the band attracted a large following. "We were at the China Pheasant for about a year," Wittwer added. "We didn't just do Dixieland, but dance music, too. That was expected in those days. I switched back and forth between piano and trombone." In 1946 Wittwer moved to San Francisco and joined Lu Watters's seminal Yerba Buena Jazz Band, most famous of West Coast Dixie groups, but was back in Seattle for most of the fifties. In February 1959 he veered into another realm altogether when he brought poet Kenneth Patchen to Seattle for one of his fabled Poetry and Jazz sessions, teaming him in two performances at the Musicians' Association headquarters with "the New Bed of Roses"—Floyd Standifer, Lowell Richards, Bob Gilkeson, and George Mullaly.

Seattle Dixie made its big splash with the Rainy City Jazz Band. Gordon Greimes was a UW freshman with no musical background when he wandered into the university music building one day in 1941 and found a recording of "I Wish I Could Shimmy Like My Sister Kate." Intrigued, he put on the old '78 and was hooked. With trumpeter Dick "Boots" Houlihan, trombonist Jack Sheedy, pianist Barry Vye, drummer Dolph Bleiler, and tuba player Lowell Richards, he scavenged second-hand instruments and old records and set about mastering the New Orleans idiom. After war's temporary interruption, they reunited and caught the ear of Doc Exner, who recorded them in 1948. *Down Beat* highlighted the "patriotic project in musical archaeology," quoting a fan who proclaimed Rainy City "the only band north of the Golden Gate and west of the Mississippi now playing hot jazz in the pure New Orleans idiom."[6]

Rainy City dug in at the Lake City Tavern and created a lively musical oasis in Seattle's otherwise sedate north end. On the heels of Rainy City came Don Anderson's Seattle Rhythm Kings, otherwise known as the Shakey City Seven. A first-call trumpeter in Los Angeles studios during the thirties and forties, Anderson played on dozens of movie soundtracks and radio shows before "retiring" north. Johnny Wittwer was in the band and so was trombonist Mike Hobi. Hobi told me,

> A fraternity brother of mine bought the Lake City Tavern around 1955 and turned it into a Shakey's Pizza franchise. We played some Dixie, but just as many standards. We didn't read music—we all knew the tunes. In fact, Don Anderson had been a studio player so long that we had to have rehearsals to teach him the songs. When we were on the radio, I'd tell jokes like, "Here's a tune Teddy Roosevelt *dug*." Then we'd play "Panama."

Puckish, Aberdeen-born Hobi got hooked on music as a teen when he won a Horace Heidt talent contest playing "Twelfth Street Rag" with his foot. He put his natural talent to work gigging around Los Angeles, played in the first Disneyland band of 1955, then got bored and returned to Seattle, where he landed in Don Anderson's band. Clarinetist Rollie Morehouse won Hobi's special affection:

> If Rollie Morehouse wasn't the best clarinet player in Seattle, I don't know who was. We'd do "Tiger Rag" as a flagwaver, so fast you could hardly make out the melody, and Rollie would not only do these intricate figures you thought were impossible, he'd embellish the embellishments! Everybody that ever heard him came away shaking their head.

A full house digs Don Anderson and his Dixieland band at the Lake City
Tavern in 1956. Left to right: Dave Coleman, Chuck Metcalf, Anderson,
and Mike Hobi. Courtesy of Mike Hobi

All scenes eventually burn out, and Lake City was no different. According
to Hobi,

> Shakey's was a good gig, but we decided to hang it up. The blue laws
> were being more strictly enforced, ASCAP started hounding the owner for
> royalties, and there was plenty of other work, anyway. I liked variety and
> hated being typecast as a "Dixie" player. Sure, I enjoy trad jazz, but actu-
> ally I'd rather play more modern stuff. Jeez, you get stuck with a bunch
> of Dixie guys who only know a bunch of ancient tunes, and a crowd that
> wants dance music, and that makes for a long night!

Dixieland ("traditional jazz" became the preferred term in the seventies) remained popular among a small but persistent group of fans, and in
1960 it found new headquarters in Pioneer Square's Blue Banjo. To this
day, Trads have never been fully accepted by the jazz mainstream (boppers

dismissed them as "moldy figs"), and when the Blue Banjo closed in 1965, traditional jazz became an endangered species. Ten years later, though, the Puget Sound Traditional Jazz Society was formed to perpetuate the New Orleans sound, and the group's regular concerts continue to present superb hot music.

PIANO JAZZ

By the middle of the twentieth century, Earl Hines, Art Tatum, and Oscar Peterson had taken the piano places unimagined by Charles Constantine. Though the light and nimble style of Nat King Cole was ascendant, still very much in play was the swinging descendant of classic, bass-heavy Harlem piano known as "stride." From Oscar Holden to Palmer Johnson, the line reached Ernie Hatfield, a genial Pennsylvanian who had worked with Ella Fitzgerald and played New York's fabled 52nd Street before hitting Seattle on tour with the Jimmy White Trio. "Ernie was more of a swing player than bebop," said friend Floyd Standifer. "He had a marvelous sense of harmony and was a beautiful singer, too." Hatfield delighted generations, who heard him everywhere from the Washington Social Club to the Seattle Tennis Club, and was playing at the Roosevelt Hotel when he died in the late 1990s.[7]

Though Art Tatum had roots in stride, he transcended it with florid and impossible-sounding treble excursions. Jazz players—and many classicists—idolized him. Benny Witte was, in Norm Bobrow's words, "the nearest thing to an Art Tatum we had in Seattle. Some say he was the greatest, and he certainly was as good as they come. But Benny was very, very shy. He never played with anyone else, and when he was still a young man he gave up performing and just hid away." Another Tatum emulator was Bob Dyke, who floored everyone with his technique and his penchant for spicing solos with chicken cackling or Wagner arias.

By 1950 Bud Powell had joined Nat Cole in advancing a new and bop-flavored piano, and among its early apostles was Gerald Wiggins. "Gerry was a wizard and still is," remembered Bobrow, who often hired Wiggins for his Cirque concerts. "He'd put a book up on his piano music rack and read while he was playing. He bragged he could read a novel a week that way!" Another of the "class of '46," Wiggins arrived as an impatient young firebrand, only to be properly humbled by the legendary Julian Henson, who helped him develop his own virtuosic style. Wiggins worked with Al

Hickey's postwar jump band, the Jive Bombers, and moved to Los Angeles in the middle of the decade.[8]

Taking Wiggins's place in the Jive Bombers was Johnny Moton. At seventeen, Moton had just arrived with his mother from Texas when he was inducted into the pro music scene by the great Oscar Holden. Soon after, he joined the Jive Bombers. The popular dance and show band originated in a Sand Point Naval Air Station group led by New York–born tenor saxophonist Al Hickey. Moton said of his bandmates,

> Those guys came here from Chicago, and they were in the navy together during the war. Al Hickey was desperate for a piano player, and somebody led him to my mom's house. I was still living at home and not even considered grown up yet! What we played was straight-ahead jazz, pop tunes, a little blues—one of our big numbers was "Flying Home." On bass we had Al Larkins, who came from Baltimore and was just about the best bassist anywhere. Up there at the Rocking Chair, he'd pick up his bow and throw in a solo from *Claire de Lune*! We were flashy, but still mostly a dance band, so we were big in all the black clubs.

Johnny Moton made himself a first-call jazz player and a distinguished gospel pianist. He had deep roots:

> Benny Moten, the famous Kansas City drummer, was my great uncle. Mom got me into playing music for church at around age six, and I started right out reading music. Mom didn't expect me to go as far as I did; in fact, she tried to discourage me from going professional—she held the opinion that all professional musicians were pimps, and I had to work hard to convince her that I would not go in that direction. By age sixteen, when we moved up here, I was listening to everything on the radio and copping what the jazz players were doing. That's how Oscar Holden found out about me; he came by to visit and heard me tinkin' around on the piano and he says to Mom, "We need a piano player. Can he come play with us?" First thing she asks: "How much you gonna *pay*?" She wanted me to get right out and make some money! He says, "I'll pay scale." Ten dollars for a three-hour sideman job, which was not bad at all, then. Still, she had to think hard on it, and I did a lot of fast promising that I would not be straying into bad habits.

Pianist Johnny Moton had recently joined the Jive Bombers when
this 1952 portrait was snapped. From left to right: bassist Al Larkins,
trumpeter Dave Bachman, drummer Ralph Davis, Moton, tenor sax Al
Hickey, and alto sax/vocalist Bobby Braxton. Courtesy of Johnny Moton

Anxious to better himself, Moton dabbled in classical music but found
that avenue closed to him, not to mention unprofitable.

Back in the South, people would tell me how good I was. But I knew I
wasn't, so I went out to Cornish School to get some training on Bach and
Beethoven. Quincy Jones and I were out there at the same time, which
helped to make me a little more seasoned. The headman at Cornish
didn't like jazz—the only one he halfway admired was Duke Ellington—and I almost got a flunking grade 'cause I played jazz. You had to
give concerts there, and afterwards you got a letter telling you how good
you did. I played a Bach piece, and the verdict came in: Rotten! The
principal said, "I couldn't tell if it was Bach or Moton." I didn't like that
at the time, but then I began to analyze myself, and to think maybe he
was right. Sure, I played the notes, but it wasn't anything like what Bach
had in mind. Ultimately, I came to the conclusion that jazz was where I
needed to be. Classical guys weren't makin' the money that we made in

jazz. Not only that—I was black. Mom wanted me to stay with classical, but I said, "I got to go where the money is." I knew one black person who maybe had the chance to become a classical player, Edith Bowen. She was at Cornish with me, then she went back east to Juilliard.

Johnny Moton found friendship and inspiration in another southern transplant. Georgia-born pianist/singer Ray Charles Robinson and duo partner Garcia McKee decided they'd had enough of working the South and in 1948 left Florida and drove as far as they could. The road ended in Seattle, and the pair went to work at the black Elks Club, where their slick Nat King Cole sound made them the new lions of Jackson Street. Adding bassist Milt Garred, they took the name "McSon Trio" (for McKee and Robinson) and moved up to the Rocking Chair. Robinson had the kitty overflowing with his prodigious talents not only on the piano but also on the drums, bass, and saxophone—feats all the more phenomenal considering he was blind. Once in a while, he set aside the King Cole cool and broke into a blues, rocking it with a shuffling, gospel accompaniment. He did this warily; the wartime migration of southern African Americans to Seattle had enlarged the audience for blues, but many northern blacks continued to disdain blues as a reminder of bad times. So the shrewd Robinson kept the blues mostly to himself, and when pressed to get funky, as Johnny Moton related, he shrugged, "Oh man, you can't make a nickel singing like that." In 1950, he decided to take his chances in Los Angeles, and four years later, as Ray Charles, he broke into the big-time with "I Got a Woman."

In Seattle, though, R. C. Robinson was still finding himself. "RC— that's what we called him—and me, we used to steal off each other," Moton chuckled.

Like the song "Georgia on My Mind": I started that! He used to come to my house and set down on one side of the piano, and me on the other, and we'd both try to outplay each other. He'd show me different little things. That's how I got my blues touch, was through Ray Charles. He played these modes, which I didn't hear at the time. Me, I taught him a lot about execution, because I had better hands than he did. No doubt he had to feel his way, 'cause he couldn't see the keys, but I started him to feeling them a little bit more.

It was thanks to Ray Charles that Moton learned a valuable lesson in nightclub economics. Moton said,

I was one of these guys who, if the scale was ten dollars, I played for ten dollars. Not seven, not five. Now RC, he'd call me up on gigs when he'd get a better one, and ask me to take the one that he's turning away. That's how he called me to play for him down at the Tuxedo Club. But then he said, "Okay, now I'm gonna warn you: this guy B_____, the owner, he don't wanna pay. You gotta get your money up front." I go down there to the Tuxedo Club, and he's got a house full of people, and Milt Warren and his cats were all there on the bandstand waitin'. B_____ comes up and says, " Oh, you the guy RC sent?" "Yep." "Well, I'm gonna tell you, I'm only gonna pay seven cents." That's what we called it in those days— "cents," not dollars. I said to him, "If I'm playin' at all, you're payin' ten." We took it in the back office for quite a while, and if he had had the time to look for somebody else, he would have got 'im. But he was stuck! So he says, "Okay, I'll give you ten, but under one condition: Don't tell those guys out there that's what I'm payin' you." I agreed, but when I got back on the stand, I told 'em, "Guys, he's payin' me ten." They all walked right back into the office to have a little conference with B_____, the upshot of which being the entire band got scale. Oh, B_____ was furious! When we was done, he told me, "Don't bother comin' back!" That was fine with me. I found out later that the rest of the guys went back to playin' for seven.

The fiscal realities of the music business remain a sore point with Moton, who, not unrealistically, insists that a musician should be compensated as any other professional.

Nowadays the guys play for practically nothing and the clubs all sweet talk 'em: "Come on and give us a freebie, and you'll get a crack at the gig." Only, you never do, 'cause the owner just keeps rotatin' 'em in and out and gets nothin' but free music all the time. That's what prompted me to go into the finance business. I've always been finance-minded anyway, and musicians here, they just want to play. Don't care about earning anything for it. If you don't believe me, just open up a place, and see all the musicians land on your step! A woman friend opened a place down in Renton and she let all these musicians come in, and they just line up waitin' to play. You talk about "pay," you're liable to get yourself put out of there.

Pay was serious business for Elmer Gill, who made himself one of the West's outstanding jazz artists in the fifties. At the start of the decade the ebullient pianist took a week's stand at the Spinning Wheel, one of the few downtown nightspots that booked black bands, with singer/alto saxophonist Bob Braxton and guitarist Milt Green. The crowds grew, and the week stretched into two years. Gill aimed for a distinctive ensemble style and got it, adding marimba and vibraphone and creating an airy, boppish sound that delighted jazz fans while keeping dancers happy. Gill never forgot his roots, singing earthy blues and harmonizing with Braxton ("Seattle's Billie Eckstein") on popular standards.

Gill called his band the Question Marks, but he was in no doubt over one issue. Discovering that the Spinning Wheel discouraged black patronage, he insisted that mixed audiences be required in all his contracts. "You'd be surprised at the number of people that wouldn't sign that contract," he later told Paul de Barros. He would continue to press for integrated venues and was a major force behind the forthcoming amalgamation of black and white musicians' unions. In 1952 Gill tested the LA waters, played in Lionel Hampton's band, then returned north to open what he hoped would be a new kind of nightspot at Fifth and Jackson. The Ebony Club had mixed audiences, good food and drink, a refined atmosphere, no gambling, no knives—and no kitty. Black musicians, Gill insisted, were entitled to regular wages, the same as white musicians. The Ebony house band lived up to its promise with a mixed trio of Gill, white guitarist Al Turay, and bassist Al Larkins. End-running the after-hours tradition he disdained, Gill instituted "Jam for Breakfast" sessions on Saturday mornings, another innovation that drew surprisingly well until the club closed in 1957 after its financial backers failed to pay their taxes. The club reopened several months later and survived into the early sixties, while Elmer Gill swung on into the eighties as one of the greats of Northwest jazz.[9]

THOSE OTHER KEYBOARDS

The majestic roar of the theater organ was stilled by sound movies, but the 1930s saw the birth of a cousin (some called it a poor relation), the Hammond electric organ. Slow to take hold, the Hammond became a nightlife staple in the fifties. Seattle was full of cheery islands—Bon's Congo Room, Garski's Scarlet Tree, the Firelite Lounge—that invited weary souls to come in out of the rain and let the warm tones of the Hammond wash away their troubles. Earline Hunt, Derneice "Melody" Jones, Dick Dickerson, and Esther Farrar were just a few of the descendants of the Lava Beds saloon pianists who restored spirits at the end of the day. Most of these cocktails 'n' keys artists spent their nights fielding requests, and many encouraged singalongs. Dick Schrum was one of a long line of regulars who dispensed cheer in the organ lounge of one of Seattle's favorite watering holes, the Dog House. After Schrum played several years at the "canine club," Harriet McGlothern took his place and he opened his own Capitol Hill restaurant, the Plaid Piper, where he provided the kind of intimate live entertainment that has since become virtually extinct.

Almost as popular as the Hammond was the accordion. Invented in Central Europe in the mid-nineteenth century, the modern piano accordion was embraced by dance bands in the 1920s, and in the forties Joe Mooney and Art Van Damme made it a serious jazz voice. Rich overtones and harmonic warmth (and perhaps Old Country connotations) made jazz played on the accordion more accessible to many listeners, and its mobility and dynamic range encouraged its use in combos.

Possibly the first to play the accordion in Seattle was Guido Deiro. Deiro came from Italy shortly before the Alaska-Yukon-Pacific Exposition, worked Pioneer Square saloons (one wonders how his operatic excerpts went down with the loggers), then hit the vaudeville circuit, where he took the instrument to national prominence. Following Deiro, Taylor P. "Zac" Kalbach started out in the early twenties playing clarinet in the symphony and working as relief organist at the Strand Theater, then sang and played accordion at Blanc's Café, Seattle's oasis of Continental cuisine, where he remained a beloved fixture until the early fifties. In the twenties, Seattle's Frank Iacolucci toured the country as an accordion soloist before settling down at home, where his fleet-fingered virtuosity with jazz and classics made him a restaurant and party favorite until his early death.

Inspired by Iacolucci was Frank Sugia, who at age sixteen got his union card, worked with Betty Taylor and her Beaus and Jackie Souders, and after the war hit his stride at the Trianon and the 40 and 8 Club. In 1950 Sugia hosted a weekly Channel 5 television show and began thirty years of leading the Christmas minstrels at the Frederick and Nelson department store, a local tradition that would introduce countless children to music. "Frank Sugia was the classic bandleader," said longtime colleague and fellow minstrel Floyd Standifer. "He brought with him a certain amount of the old-school baggage, particularly where women were concerned. Frank could be the face of evil and the face of piety, and when he got to drinking that red wine with his buddies, you learned to make yourself scarce! But Frank was a superb musician: a great devotee of Ravel, and he turned me on to Delius." Frank Sugia's virtuosity, and a vast repertoire spanning bebop to opera, allowed his accordion to transcend categories and produce a hallmark Seattle sound as sophisticated as any.[10]

Queen of the accordion was Lucia "Lucy" Carrabba, who found her opportunity thanks to World War II. The ebullient entertainer told me at her Hood Canal home,

> I was just out of Franklin High School in 1941, and Seve Hagstead called. He was working swingshift dances every Saturday for shipyard workers at the Kingston Grange, and he needed me because his regular guy got drafted. Seve had been a Columbia recording artist doing Scandinavian stuff, and we played standards along with polkas, hambos, and Swedish waltzes. I met Curly Johnson, a tenor player, on that band; we got married, started a band, and landed a thirteen-year contract with the Arthur Murray Dance Studios.

Lucy came up in a musical family. Seventeen-year-old Pietro Carrabba left Sicily for the United States shortly after the turn of the century and landed a place in Liberati's band. In 1909 he headed west and was hired as first clarinet in Wagner's A-Y-P band, then led orchestras of his own during the next three decades. "Dad landed in New York with two dollars in his pocket," said Lucy.

> He worked up a vaudeville act where he'd come onstage in a street cleaner's costume, pushing his trash can with a broom sticking out of it. The "broom" was actually made up of a clarinet, a mandolin, a flute, and an ocarina; he'd take the thing apart and play each instrument. In the twenties he had an eight-piece dance band that was featured on KOMO radio, and he took the Everett Elks band to a national contest in San Diego and won first prize.

Peter Carrabba remained a Seattle musical mainstay until the late forties, dying in 1951.

Lucy Carrabba (now Mitchell) proudly walked in the footsteps of an illustrious legion of women keyboardists, and did not find her gender a handicap. "Being a woman was never an issue for me. I feel I have always been treated with the same respect that a man would be. I was never discriminated against in that way—if I was, I was too stupid to know it." Lucy did find that with her lineage came high expectations: "Guys'd say, 'Oh, if you're Pete Carrabba's daughter, you must be good.' When I was a green kid that kind of thing would tie me in knots. You have nights when you flub something, and stewing over it keeps you awake all night. Well, forget it; nobody's ever going to hold that stuff against you, if they even notice in the first place. You have your good days and bad."

The music business dealt Mitchell some good hands and a few hard knocks. "For ten years I was at King Oscar's on Aurora," Lucy recounted.

> I started at two nights a week, but I brought in so many people that they upped it to three then four nights. That joint was jumping, and people would say, "Wow, you must have an interest in this place." That's a laugh! I was just the working musician that brought the money in, and got screwed for it. The bookkeeper never withheld my pension payments like he was supposed to. I guess he figured he was helping the management, but he sure didn't help *me*! I didn't know until eventually someone got on them about it. I managed to salvage some little thing, but I should have had a lot more. That's my livelihood, messed up by some stupid little bookkeeping mistake! Still, the music keeps me young. Most recently I've been working at the North Shore Inn in Belfair on Sundays, and doing casuals. These days I just like to relax and play standards, medleys, and funny stuff—*I'm so happy I'm so gay, and I'm that way every day, I'm on Prozac.* I like to entertain people.

Scandinavians dominated Seattle's demographic in the first half of the twentieth century, and the international dance bands of Al Sjodin, Bert Lindgren, and Harry Lindbeck made Old Country echoes a Puget Sound trademark. Nordic heritage found its ultimate voice in Stan Boreson, for two decades Puget Sound's most beloved television personality. Still going strong in 2005, the puckish entertainer took a well-earned break to visit with me:

In 1925, when I was twelve, Mom took me into Buehl Music in Everett to take guitar lessons from Mel Odegaard. He put this guitar in my hands and said, "Okay, we'll start with fingering, then learn some songs." I told him, "I'm *not* singing!" "Well," he said—"how 'bout an accordion?" Okay! My cousin, Harry Lindbeck, had been playing the accordion a long time, and I always loved to hear him play polkas and schottisches. By the time I was in high school I was pretty decent, and I'd gotten over my inhibitions and was singing, too. My other cousin dared me to do "Oh, Johnny" in Norwegian at a school assembly, and that was the start of my Scandinavian comedy. It was natural—all my relatives talked that way.

Boreson got his lesson in music economics early:

At age sixteen I joined the union and started playing dances. My first job was with Les Elsbury at the Snohomish Grange. We got $2.50 a night, and they told us if we filled more than twenty-five tables they'd pay us an extra fifty cents. It took me a while to figure out that they couldn't get more than twenty-five tables in the place! After that, I started playing with Harry; he had a ten-piece orchestra that played without reading a note of music, and owned the Seven Cedars Ballroom on Highway 99, north of Mt. Vernon. It was an old barn, and he installed a dance floor and made it a bottle club. Seven or eight hundred people would show up on a Saturday night and dance to the old Norwegian and Dixieland tunes. They *loved* Dixie—"Clarinet Marmalade," "South Rampart Street Parade"—and I'd throw in my Scandinavian novelty songs like "It Vas Yust One of Dose Tings."

Television entered American life in the late forties and began costing musicians work, edging bands from taverns and keeping onetime jitterbugs glued to the sofa. For a select few such as Boreson, though, the new medium offered a golden opportunity to present their own kind of music.

After the war I went to the UW and joined Club Encore, the student performers' association. I met Art Barduhn, himself a superb accordion player, there, and we formed a duo. Television was just getting hot, and Dorothy Bullitt started KING TV. She grabbed the NBC franchise away from the Fisher family's KOMO by sneaking back to New York and riding William Paley's commuter train with him every morning—boy, were they furious! Then she hired Lee Schulman to come up from LA and develop some local shows, and he auditioned some of the Club Encore talent. Art and I were hired, and we presented a fifteen-minute show, "Two B's at the Keys," which was expanded into "Clipper Capers." I had to memorize five songs a week, many of which I wrote or customized with humorous lyrics. I had an old blackboard with a hole in it, which I called my "Norwegian Teleprompter," but I'd sometimes forget the words, anyway. When that happened all you could do was smile, or bust out laughing. That ran six years, then Art moved south and "Clipper Capers" became "The Stan Boreson Show," which ran eighteen years. At first, Doug Setterberg and I were *it*: we wrote the script, planned the skits, and acted the parts. Doug was Uncle Torvald, I was Grandma. Mike Rhodes was the Old-Timer—the old man in the closet. We never let him out, 'cause if we did, we would have had to pay him. Out of eighteen years of work, the studio saved only two hours of videotape. The rest went in the trash.

To Boreson's dismay, the accordion's heyday came to an abrupt end. "In the fifties I opened a music store in Ballard," he ruefully recounted, "and started my accordion schools. We had five teachers and fifty students a week, and one year I hosted a concert of one thousand accordions at the Civic Auditorium. Then Elvis hit, and closets all around town started filling up with accordions." On his TV show and with his popular dance band, Boreson kept the Scandinavian sound alive. "I had a dance band into the eighties, and we were big with all the fraternal groups. Now the Elks and the Moose have just about died off. The younger crowd doesn't care about all the initiations and mumbo-jumbo; they'd rather just go to a tavern and shoot pool. A young person going into music today would find it very, very tough. I was lucky to make my break when television was just getting started."

THE GUITAR CATCHES UP

It's hard to believe that the most popular instrument of the late twentieth century was ever obscure, but the guitar took a long time to attract a following. Essentially unchanged since developed in eighteenth-century Spain, the guitar of Victorian America had gut strings, a soft, intimate voice, and was played most often in parlors by young, middle-class women with pretensions of gentility. Late in the century, however, the instrument began to be adopted by southern blacks, who found it an ideal accompaniment for the songs that would come to be called the blues. With metal strings and sturdier construction, the classic American flat-top was born and, with the mandolin, took its place in small string bands exemplified in the early 1900s by the Zoe Peabody and Wang Doodle orchestras. Long in decline, the banjo regained ground in the dance bands of the twenties (it recorded better on acoustic equipment, and it was *loud*), but by 1930 electrical recording had been perfected, Eddie Lang and Jimmie Rodgers were showing what the guitar could do, and the erstwhile parlor instrument was reasserting itself. The rhythm sections of the Count Basie and Benny Goodman orchestras owed much of their infectious energy to the quiet but crunchy strum of the guitar.

Still, to be a guitarist in the big band era was to court anonymity, and mechanically chunking away amid blaring horns was a far cry from the six-string heroics of the rock age. For four decades among the busiest of Seattle guitarists, Carl Challstedt enjoyed the freedom of being a quiet loner in a sea of section players. "I did a lot of winging," he told me in 1991.

I got my first gig at the old Civic Auditorium in '41 with El Arseneau. Elward didn't have a guitar book, so I had to wing it. I played an Epiphone Emperor, a wonderful guitar, and used a thirty-five-watt amp. Nowadays the kids would laugh at such a thing, but it let me hold my own even in the Civic Auditorium with a fifteen-piece band. Then I went with Bob Harvey at the Trianon; he had 552 tunes in his book and wrote most of the arrangements himself. A great band, but again, no guitar parts. I preferred combos, where I could play a bit and be noticed. In the mid-fifties I loved playing with Lois Apple, a wonderful pianist with a style very similar to Bob Harvey's, and I was with Bob Bachman's combo a long time at the Queen City Yacht Club. In the fifties I was averaging $1,200 a month just on casuals at private clubs and hotels.

For all-around best, Challstedt deferred to another: "Of all Seattle guitar players, none could touch Al Turay. He was a master who used wonderful and distinctive chord voicings, always smooth and interesting." Turay played his first jobs on Alaska steamers during the Depression, then worked downtown in clubs. In 1953 he took a four-year gig in the house band at Elmer Gill's innovative new Ebony Club and opened a Wallingford studio that would spawn innumerable Northwest rock guitarists.

A guitar original was Paul Tutmarc, a tall, dashing man who started as a saxophonist/vocalist in the late twenties and was featured as the "Silver-Toned Tenor" in Fox and Fifth Avenue theater orchestras. Tutmarc accompanied George Stoll's Syncopators to Los Angeles in 1929, where his voice and good looks snagged him singing roles in two motion pictures. By 1931 he was back in Seattle teaching guitar, when, at the suggestion of Art Stimpson, he put a telephone transmitter on a steel guitar, built a crude amplifier, and became a musical revolutionary. It did not make him rich: "I blew about $300 in patent offices before attorneys convinced me I'd have to go all the way back to Alexander Graham Bell to find something patentable." Tutmarc had plenty of company in developing the steel guitar, but he created a sound he could with some justification call his own, and he ranks as one of the region's significant musical inventors.[11]

After the war Tutmarc married another six-string innovator, Bonnie Buckingham. A woman playing the guitar professionally has always been a rarity, but Buckingham had dreamed of doing it since childhood. "At about age twelve I knew that playing the guitar was what I wanted to do in life," Bonnie reminisced in her Soap Lake home.

In my family we had four boys, me, and one Gibson guitar, which was passed down from the oldest to the youngest. That meant I didn't get my hands on it until I was fourteen. Then I bought an instruction book and taught myself. My father liked Jimmie Rodgers and Irish tenors, but we happened to have a record by a guitar player named Nick Lucas, and that really got me going. I learned his solos off the record, then I discovered Charlie Christian, the fabulous guitar player with Benny Goodman. There was a big dance hall near our home in Federal Way, and I would sneak out at night and listen to Bumps Blackwell and Duke Ellington under the window. I loved those Ellington musicians! Ben Webster's saxophone had the most velvet, all-consuming sound you would want to hear.

By the late forties Bonnie had taken her playing public.

I like to think I have a unique style. It had to be, I guess, because I never really did learn the "proper" techniques. I just listened to a record and took a song phrase by phrase and learned my own ways to finger it. When I turned twenty-one I began playing in private clubs like the Elks with three and four-piece bands. Paul Tutmarc was playing the same circuit, so we got married and I adopted the name Bonnie Guitar.

The pair toured the Northwest with their band, the Islanders, and Paul's keening pedal steel and Bonnie's twanging electric hollow body did much to popularize Hawaiian and country music in the postwar years.

In 1957 a wistful ballad written by Ned Miller gave Bonnie Guitar her first and biggest hit. "Dark Moon" shimmers with Bonnie's crystalline vocals and her trademark echoing guitar bass line, a device that she helped make a hallmark of late fifties western and rockabilly. "On 'Dark Moon' and my other early recordings," Bonnie recalled, "I played a white Gretsch Falcon, which I think was one of the first ever made, and a Gretsch Cadillac Countryclub. They were both solid body electrics, but they had a big, resonant tone and could sound like a regular hollow-body or flat-top. I mostly used a Fender amp with a built-in vibrato, but 'Dark Moon' was just straight." Not content with just playing, Bonnie eagerly involved herself in all aspects of music, especially recording:

Very early on I became fascinated by the recording process and began producing my own and other peoples' records. Fabor Robison recorded me on "Dark Moon" with as many as twelve musicians; we must have done it a hundred times, with different combinations, and still he wasn't satisfied. Then one night Fabor and Ned Miller and I went into the studio and did it as a quartet. I asked Ned to play just a straight rhythm on acoustic guitar, I played lead guitar, and we had a bass. That simple version was the one we ended up using.

Bonnie Guitar's "Dark Moon" saga is a cautionary tale of all too common music business pitfalls, but one she cast in a positive light:

I had been working in Seattle, and a woman asked me to demo seven or eight songs she'd written. I recorded them, and she sent the disc to Fabor Robison, a producer in LA. Fabor called: "How soon can you get down here?" I flew down, and he hired me as a staff musician in his studio in Malibu Canyon. I played on, and helped produce, every hit record he had. One day Fabor said, "I have a new song that I'm recording with Dorsey Burnette. I want you to hear it." Dorsey had had a big hit and was on his way up the charts. Well, Fabor played me this song, "Dark Moon," and I was knocked out. I had to have it! I told him, "I'll forgo all my royalties to record this song. It's going to be a smash!" So I recorded it, and sure enough, it hit big. And I didn't get one cent in royalties. Well, that was my own doing. But what I didn't know was that Fabor had already recorded the song with Dorsey and didn't like the result. He didn't bother telling me that.

Nor did Robison tell Bonnie that his shopping trip with "Dark Moon" wasn't ending with her, either. Even as Bonnie's version, on Robison's own Fabor Records label, worked its way up the charts, he peddled the song to Dot Records, which had television star Gale Storm under contract. Storm knew a hit when she heard one and appropriated "Dark Moon" for herself. Thanks to an agreement giving her right of first refusal over all material *and* preferential promotion, it was her version that went to number four, leaving Bonnie at number six on the charts. Bonnie was philosophical about this and other setbacks:

> Gale Storm's husband was her manager, and he was looking around for a hit. He found "Dark Moon" just as my version was coming up, so she had the big hit with it. Some people would call that a bad break, but it gave me a wonderful break. Fabor was being a little sly, you might say, but I made up my mind to turn it to my advantage, and after "Dark Moon" I had a pretty good string of hits.

Like many other Seattle artists who might have found wider recognition, Bonnie made the decision to stay home rather than embark on the lonesome road to stardom.

> I sacrificed many opportunities to be a star, but my preference was always to be in the studio, not out on the road. I was in LA with Paul, playing clubs and recording, and Fabor Robison wanted me to go on the road and build my name. General Artists wanted to sign me, but required me to go on the road at least fifty weeks out of the year. Bob Hope asked me to tour with him, Gene Autry wanted me to do the "Annie Oakley" TV series. I turned them down. By then I was married and my husband put his foot down: "We're going home." We had a young daughter, so we went home.

A young family woman in a ruthless and male-dominated business, Bonnie Guitar was determined not to let adversity spoil her fun.

Some musicians complain that music is an unfair business. I say it's a wonderful business! But there is so much emotion involved; for example, after "Dark Moon" came out, Bill Gavin wrote that I was the top A&R person of 1957. Well, I was partners in Dolton Records with Bob Reisdorf, and Bob got absolutely irate! He didn't want me to get any of the credit for producing "Dark Moon"—*he* wanted it. But he had nothing to do with the production. He *couldn't* have—he was a refrigerator salesman, not a record producer! So he started a deal with his other partners to sell off Dolton Records behind my back. I had no idea what they were up to, and I never thought they'd do that to me. You can say, "That's a dirty deal." But that's *part* of the deal! In music, you just have to swallow the disappointments, don't you understand? That doesn't mean you let yourself get walked over. So many things can go wrong—if one person drops the ball in the chain of producing and distributing a record, that record can be *over*. Period! That's why I have always preferred to believe that one opportunity lost is another waiting. I would never waste my energy being negative, and I don't have anything to be negative about. Every little thing that happened to me that was unpleasant built me to a pleasanter plane.

SINGERS TAKE THE SPOTLIGHT

Big band vocalists got no respect. "Girl singers" suffered the pinches and passes of male sidemen, and both sexes endured endless evenings for a few minutes of attention. "You're just an appendage," said vocal veteran Sally King: "Run onstage, smile, sing one slow song, one fast song, then hang around for the next show. Gets kind of old after a while." The AFM recording bans of the forties changed things. Not considered "musicians" by the union, singers were free to make records. While big bands cooled their heels, vocalists assumed new importance, and by the end of the decade singer-dominated combos were in the ascendance.

In Seattle, women singers dominated pop and jazz. Naomi Weat Foote launched her career at age six, singing in Walt Haines's orchestra under the vigilant eye of her mother before graduating to Bob Harvey's orchestra in the 1940s, billed as "Carol King." Lola Sugia (later Lola Tebelman) sang with virtually every Seattle dance band and combo including her brother Frank's, at times under the name Lola Ray, and Polly Freeman was a familiar voice with Jackie Souders, Archie Kyle, and Norm Hoagy. Of the new generation of combo singers was University of Washington voice student Joni Swartz, who both sang and played piano. In 1953 she caught the ear of Norm Bobrow and became a regular at his Jazz at the Cirque concerts. Swartz recalled,

> Norm wanted me to perform, but I was about eight months pregnant with my first child, and it was too hard to sit on a piano bench for very long. Norm talked me into it: "We'll turn out the lights and have a candle on the piano. Somebody will help you up on stage, and you'll sit right next to the candle. Nobody will see you." So I got up there, obviously pregnant but with all the lights out, and sang "Love for Sale." I finished— and Norm turned up the lights. Everybody howled with laughter.

Swartz married bassist Chuck Metcalf, and as Joni Metcalf was a popular solo and combo performer into the 1980s.

The woman Quincy Jones and many others proclaim Seattle's greatest singer arrived in 1944. Twelve-year old Ernestine Anderson was the daughter of a blues-loving Texas transplant, and was wild about the blues herself. At jam sessions she impressed saxophonist Gerald Brashear and trumpeter Sonny Booker, who got her father's guarded okay to hire her as long as she kept her grades up. At the Washington Social Club and Basin Street, Ernestine learned how to work a crowd, and Bumps Blackwell bumped her up to headliner. By 1950 she was singing with Lionel Hampton, and Norm Bobrow was presenting her as the next Ella Fitzgerald. "I took some heat for calling Ernestine 'the next Ella,'" Bobrow told me. "This 'Seattle girl'—how dare I! I proved them wrong; she was every bit as good as Ella, but with her own style." In 1952 Anderson left for New York's fabled 52nd Street clubs, recorded the first of twenty solo albums, and became a world artist. Ernestine Anderson's home always remained Seattle, however, and her radiant voice has continued to spread joy from one century into another.[12]

Jazzy vocal groups—the Modernaires, the Hi-Lo's, the Four Freshmen—were big in the fifties, and Seattle jumped in with the Signatures. Inspired by Stan Kenton's Pastels, Bob and Ruth Alcivar started their own group at the end of the forties; the Signatures—the Alcivars, Cathi Hayes,

Lee Humes, and later Gus Mancuso—created hip scenes at chic down-town restaurants and lent contrast to the Dixie bands at the Lake City Tav-ern. The end of the fifties spelled the end of the Signatures; Hayes found modest success as a solo artist in San Francisco, and the rest of the group went to Los Angeles and recorded two albums for Warner Brothers. Bob Alcivar took his talents to New York and LA, writing for The Association and the Fifth Dimension.

In a class all her own was Sally King. Born Sally Lang in gritty McKeesport, Pennsylvania, the elegant, honey-toned vocalist took the stage at an early age. "Radio was my inspiration," Sally told me. "Right from practically infancy I'd sit glued to the radio. Ella Fitzgerald was my idol, and Frank Sinatra and Sarah Vaughn. I learned all their songs as they came out of the box—my mother even named me after her favorite song, 'I Wonder What's Become of Sally.'" Graduating high school in 1944, Sally joined the road band of Jack Teagarden, whose trombone playing was as legendary as his drinking. "Jack didn't like the band business," Sally said, "and he never should have tried. He'd get in his cups and I'd have to nursemaid him—'Come on Jack, it's time to catch the train'—and his wife would get mad at him and split, and take the money with her. We were stuck in New York one night, couldn't even check out of the hotel. His wife had run out with the money."

Fed up with babying Big T, Sally worked as singer-for-hire for the Music Corporation of America, touring with Johnny "Scat" Davis and Bernie Cummins. She was singing in a Chicago gin mill one night when a sax player named Terry King walked in, introduced himself, and before long convinced Sally that Seattle should be her next stop. A year later, she headed west and found a congenial welcome in the little city by the bay. Breaking in with Jackie Souders, she graduated to long runs with Norm Hoagy and Wyatt Howard. King was in her element at the Magicians' Club (later the Magic Inn):

Norm Hoagy was a fabulous musician and his band had a very hip sound. He also had a very dry sense of humor, and some nights we'd giggle our way through an entire evening over something somebody was wearing, or some obnoxious drunk. We did dance sets and floor shows six nights a week, and most of our tunes were "head arrangements"—made up in our heads as we went along. You could get away with that then because Seattle was full of good musicians. Wyatt treated me all right, and the

Town and Country Club had a great band. I had a chart up at home showing what gown I wore each night so I wouldn't repeat an outfit in less than a week.

King preferred roots to the road, and her voice helped her stay in one place.

I didn't like to job around too much—I liked to build a clientele in a nice place where folks would come in all the time. I had a seven-year thing going: seven years with Bob Mayfield's Topnotchers at the Lake City Elks, seven years with Frank Sugia at his club, the After Five, and seven years with the Jazzabouts. Bob Mayfield was a *nut!* He did the Earl Bostic thing on "Honky Tonk" and jumped over chairs and clowned around. The Elks crowd loved it. Sugia was a superb musician, and he made you feel like you were just as important as any sideman—that you were an artist. We all sang on his band; Gene Sargent, Sugia's bass player, wrote wonderful vocal arrangements that were inspired by the Modernaires, and they made us sound like a full band. Besides singing, I played cocktail drums. That's sort of a lost art: just a light snare with brushes, maracas every now and then. It beat just standing there doing nothing when I wasn't singing. Those were the perfect jobs, because I still could be a mother. I guess I might have been "big," if I'd wanted to, but to do that means you have to give up everything else. I wanted more of a "normal" life.

Inevitably, Sally had to endure the jibes of less-than-enlightened male co-workers.

Aside from getting hit on once in a while, my being a woman was not usually an issue. But there were exceptions. Sugia was a real chauvinist; he'd try to tell me who I could and could not sit with during breaks, and make very obvious snide remarks about me in Italian with his buddies, as if I couldn't guess what he was saying. I could tolerate that because he was such a great musician and we had so much fun in his bands. But there was a certain other bandleader—whose initials were B. S.—who would make me sit way in the back, or wherever he thought I wouldn't get any attention. He'd try to tell me how to sing into the microphone, and when I was singing he'd do things like hold up a rubber chicken behind me. Real class act. He tried to tell me, "You don't work for any-body else—you're *my* singer." I told him, "Do you think I just fell off the turnip truck?"

Sally King wrote no songs. She made virtually no records (unfortu-nately), and she did not become famous. Rather, she spent six nights of every week spinning that great golden thread of twentieth-century Amer-ica—the standard song—into webs of connection with her listeners. "I must know a thousand songs," she smiled, years after her last gig, "and they still pop right back. I'm an entertainer first—I don't sing for *me*. I still get people who call and ask me, 'Where are you singing now? We miss you so much!' I loved connecting with the audience. I loved the joy of it."

FOLK REVIVAL

Seattle has long had an ear for old-time music. In 1910 Zoe Peabody's string orchestra played Stephen Foster at the Cherry Grotto, hundreds hamboed in the Trianon Ballroom at the peak of the Jazz Age, and by 1930 "folk music" was being programmed by local radio stations. It was in the tail-finned fifties, though, that roots music came of age in the American consciousness, and Seattle was an early and avid center of the folk revival.

The working men who drove the economy and furnished the audience for music in old Seattle also provided a key component of the folk reper-toire, one growing out of the Northwest's dependence on extractive labor. Miners, loggers, and longshoremen suffered appalling working conditions and management abuse, and in the early 1900s Seattle was a center of labor agitation. Formed in Chicago in 1905, the Industrial Workers of the World (IWW), otherwise known as the Wobblies, embarked on an aggres-sive organizing campaign. Song was an essential weapon in the Wobbly strategy of stirring the emotions, and its *Songs of the Workers*—the famed Little Red Songbook—was first published in Spokane in 1909. Familiar hymns and ballads were rewritten with sardonic, class-struggle lyrics and deployed in street harangues and motivational meetings dubbed "hoote-nannies." From the teens into the Depression, the intersections of Sixth and Main and Washington and Occidental were "Free Speech corners," where militant oratory and song rose defiantly into the gray air.

Wobbly activist Joe Hill visited Seattle on his West Coast agitating tours and wrote two songbook classics, "The Preacher and the Slave" (a parody of the hymn "In the Sweet Bye and Bye") and "Workers of the World, Awake!" It was a West Seattle native who popularized Hill's songs and became one of the most influential of American folk musicians. In the early thirties, Earl Robinson (1910–1991) was a student of composer George Frederick McKay at the University of Washington, then left for New York, where he studied with Aaron Copland. He wrote scores of songs, most notably the iconic "Joe Hill" of 1936, "The House I Live In," and "Hurry Sundown," tunes that inspired Woody Guthrie and Pete Seeger and buoyed progressive and civil rights movements in repressive times. Robinson was the archetypal folksinger, strumming his guitar in his trademark overalls and offering visions of peace and justice. He was also a prolific art music composer who wrote concertos for banjo and piano, dozens of cantatas— "The Lonesome Train," "Ballad for Americans"—and tone poems such as "A Country They Call Puget Sound," which was performed in 1963 by the Seattle Symphony. In 1989 Earl Robinson returned to live in West Seattle, where he was killed in an automobile accident.

It was songs of the sea and forest that inspired the enigmatic man who became Seattle's first folk celebrity. Born in 1905, Ivar Haglund was the scion of a musical family. Staking a claim on Alki Point in 1867, grandfather Hans Martin Hanson fiddled at Saturday night dances on a violin reputedly once owned by legendary Norwegian violinist Ole Bull.

Ivar's uncle Edmund inspired him with humorous ditties and tall tales of the Old Country, and his cousin, Hans Martin, played piano and led his own dance band. Ivar followed their lead, teaching himself to play guitar and tap dance, and setting old songs to funny original lyrics. Haglund spent young adulthood as a landlord, beachcomber, and amateur musician, and in 1938 opened an aquarium on the Seattle waterfront. Two years later Haglund got a call to pinch-hit on a KJR Radio program; he grabbed his guitar, warbled a few sea chanteys in a winsome tenor voice, and was a hit. Landing his own Sunday morning show, Haglund offered a refreshing respite from big band pop while rousing new feelings of regional identity.

Stories differ on how Haglund discovered the hoary Puget Sound anthem that he would make his own. One says that Francis Henry's "The Old Settler's Song" was mailed to him in 1930 after he ran a newspaper ad requesting folk material; another comes from Pete Seeger, who claimed in his autobiography that he taught Ivar the song when he and Woody Guthrie came to Seattle in 1941. However he picked it up, Haglund staked his claim; when he opened his famed waterfront restaurant in 1946, he

Northwest icons: Ivar Haglund gave many Puget Sounders their first taste of Northwest folk song. Courtesy of Ivar's Restaurants, Inc.

Stan Boreson (*right*) and Doug Setterberg (*left*) ham it up Scandihoovian-style on KING TV early in the fifties. Courtesy of Stan Boreson

named it Acres of Clams and put the last verse of "Settler" to work promoting the place. With the advent of television, Haglund continued his singing career on Don McCune's popular "Captain Puget" show, drumming his adoptive theme song into the regional consciousness.

Among the Ivar-inspired was Don Firth, a singer-guitarist and himself a folk revival leader:

> Dad and I used to listen to Ivar Haglund's Sunday morning radio show.
> He'd sing "The Old Settler"—the "acres of clams" song—and tell tales
> about seafarers and stump ranchers. He brought in guest singers like
> James Stevens, who collected a lot of the Paul Bunyan stories and who
> also wrote songs like "The Frozen Logger." Ivar collected these old songs,
> and whenever we folkies would have a hootenanny, we'd invite him. But

Ivar was very standoffish and didn't want to be associated with the folk crowd at all, even though he insisted on being considered Seattle's "folk singer emeritus." Pete Seeger claimed that he taught Ivar "The Old Settler's Song," and Ivar claimed *he* taught the song to Pete. I tend to believe Pete. Ivar *may* have picked it up someplace around here, but Pete said that *he* learned it from one of the Lomaxes in the late thirties, and not from Ivar. Either way, Ivar made a *lot* of dough off that song!

In the early fifties folk music swept campuses across the country. And again, it was a man with western Washington roots who lit the fire. Portland-born Harry Smith moved with his family to Bellingham in the early thirties and by the end of the decade was recording the songs and legends of the local Lummi and Samish tribes. He briefly attended the University of Washington before heading to San Francisco, all the while haunting second-hand shops and voraciously collecting old records of American rural music. By 1950 Smith was a struggling painter/filmmaker/professional eccentric in New York. Short on money, he asked Folkways Records president Moses Asch to buy some of his huge collection of rare records. These included sides recorded in the twenties and early thirties by long-forgotten artists such as Blind Lemon Jefferson and Mississippi John Hurt. Asch had a better idea: Why not reissue them in a compilation album? In 1952 Harry Smith's epic eighty-four-song *Anthology of American Folk Music* was released, fostering a new appreciation of America's music heritage.

As Smith's anthology hit the stores, folk music was hitting it big in Seattle's University District. Lead singer was Walt Robertson, a Bainbridge Island–born guitarist with a light, old-fashioned voice (complete with rolled r's) and a mammoth repertoire ranging from Elizabethan ballads to Wobbly agitprop. Robertson (1928–1994) was the main attraction at Seattle's new folk music central, the Chalet, and his radio show, "Wandering with Walt," beamed ballads and work songs across Puget Sound. Robertson's inspirations were eclectic: "Walt attended Haverford College in the late forties," said Don Firth, "and just down the road at Swarthmore they had folk festivals with John and Alan Lomax, Seeger, Richard Dyer Bennett, Leadbelly, and Josh White. Walt hung out with them, then came back to Seattle and passed their songs on to the rest of us." Like many, Firth first heard the diminutive and charismatic Robertson at the Chalet, and was spellbound.

Walt Robertson. Courtesy of Bob Nelson

Our folkie headquarters was the Chalet, a little coffee house in the basement of Eagleson Hall. On Friday and Saturday nights there'd be a "Closed" sign in the window, when there was obviously activity inside. They didn't have an entertainment license, so they would officially "close" the place while jazz groups played. It was dark and candle-lit, and out came Walt, a skinny, hawk-faced guy with the biggest guitar I'd ever seen. He perched on the table, planted his feet on a chair, and sang for three hours. Ballads, labor songs, blues. I was spellbound, and I decided, "*I* want to do that!"

Firth was also present at the re-creation of an American institution. "About 1952 one of the guys at the Chalet said, 'Let's have an old-fashioned hootenanny.' We all looked at him: 'What the heck's a hootenanny'? 'Well, they used to have union meetings in Seattle where they'd sing solidarity songs. They called 'em hootenannies.' The original hootenannies around here had no separation between audience and performer, and anybody could haul off and sing if they were so moved."[13]

Also taking inspiration from Walt Robertson were fraternity brothers Bob Flick, Dick Foley, Mike Kirkland, and John Paine. After catching him at the Chalet, they hauled out guitars and began working on vocal harmony. One day in 1958 a friend told them that someone at Norm Bobrow's Colony had heard them singing and wanted them to appear. The foursome dashed downtown, only to be met with blank stares. But as long as they were there, they might as well come in that night and do a few numbers. They did, were hired, and quickly impressed the Colony crowd with their fresh, youthful sound. Within a year the boys were on their way to San Francisco, where they hoped to turn heads at the West Coast's reigning folk venue, the Hungry i. They got the attention of producer Mort Lewis, and the resultant record, "Greenfields," propelled the Brothers Four to national fame.

The folk revival got a big boost from two university community members, UW English professor David Fowler and store owner Gordon Tracie. "Professor Fowler was quite influential in propagating the ballad tradition," affirmed Firth.

> In his English ballads class he introduced us to the Child collection, which dates from the seventeenth century. Our term paper assignment consisted of researching a ballad, which we would pick from Child, and then go digging for all the background information we could find. I did Child number 20, "The Cruel Mother," and came up with about twenty different versions. Bob Sessler, otherwise known as Moose, picked "Lord Randal" and found something like 1,013 different versions, extending from Scandinavia, Continental Europe, through the British Isles and down to North Africa—even in modern parodies and radio commercials. Joan Clark, an Irish harper-singer, was in Fowler's class; she hosted "hoots" at her place, and Dr. Fowler and students would gather there and swap songs.

Born on Bainbridge Island in 1920 of Swedish parents, Gordon Ekvall Tracie fell in love with his ancestor's songs during a wartime visit. As a UW student after the war, he started an informal Scandinavian dance group, which in 1948 was formalized as the Scandia Folkdance Club. The group took off, becoming a major repository of traditional Nordic music, and in 1950 Tracie opened the Seattle Folklore Center in the Pike Place Market (it later moved to 41st and University Way). His store was a Mecca for singers and musicians, offering obscure folk recordings unavailable anywhere else and hosting evening hootenannies.

In 1950 Senator Joseph McCarthy began his anti-Communist witch-hunt in the U.S. government, and for the next five years a cloud of fear and suspicion darkened America. The events elicited little protest from Seattle's budding folk music community. "Most of us had an apolitical interest in folk music," Firth told me. "The old labor songs in the IWW 'Little Red Songbook' still had some currency, and most of us were sympathetic in spirit to what the IWW was all about. But generally, we just wanted to enjoy a variety of songs and appreciate them as music. There were a couple of folks who tried to dominate hoots with lefty songs, but someone would always grumble, 'Okay, let's move on.'"

In a time when not even "Lincoln Portrait" composer Aaron Copland was safe from the hysteria, however, folk artists were not immune from suspicion. Pete Seeger was cited for contempt of Congress for refusing to answer questions, and his band, the Weavers, was suspected of "Communistic" associations. Don Firth related,

In 1953 a bunch of us formed two groups, the Pacific Northwest Folklore Society and the East 42nd Street Arts Association, and we put on concerts in the Wesley House. Walt Robertson heard that Seeger had not been getting many performances since he had been "under suspicion," and so in '54 he asked him if he'd come out here and do a concert in Seattle. We were not interested in Pete's politics—we wanted to hear him sing. On October 4 he did his show at the Moore Theater, and then performed for another three hours in the Wesley House auditorium for a crowd of about ninety people. Pete wanted to hear some of the local singers, so after the Wesley House show about a dozen of us congregated in someone's living room and passed the guitar around—"How does Leadbelly do that?" "Hand me the guitar, I'll show you." Well, the following day the Chalet, which was the unofficial office of the Pacific Northwest Folklore Society, started getting phone calls: "Take me off your mailing list!" They had a list of 200 people and in three days it was down to a dozen. Those people were *that* afraid of being linked to the "suspect" Pete Seeger.

But the folk movement could not be stifled, and songs of protest rang into the next decade, helping millions keep their faith in better times coming.

THE CITY GOES COUNTRY

The summer of 1927 was hot and dry in Tennessee. For years, RCA Victor engineer Ralph Peer had been tramping the South, capturing the sound of backwoods musicians on his primitive recording gear. Neither the heat nor the slowness of the music industry to respond to his efforts discouraged Peer—he knew he was onto something. And in Bristol he found it: Answering his latest call for rural talent was a young man named Jimmie Rodgers, and Alvin, Maybelle, and Sara Carter. By the beginning of August, Peer had recorded six sides by the Carters and two by Rodgers. Modern country music was born.

Spread by records and radio, country ("hillbilly," it was called at first) appealed to a peculiar American emotion not tapped by slick, New York pop: nostalgia for pioneer roots and a persistent desire to remain connected with the earth in an industrial age. "Urban migrants often grew nostalgic for the country," said music historian Ronald Davis, "and found comfort in songs that reminded them of home and a vanishing past. Other urban dwellers who had never cared for hillbilly music before found that with repeated exposure the country songs offered a warmth and simplicity that were appealing, particularly in rapidly changing times." Country-western music reached maturity in the fifties, aided by TV westerns and a craving for an antidote to the gray flannel straitjacket of modern life.[14]

Hillbilly came to Seattle as it did elsewhere, by radio. As early as 1925 KJR aired singer/guitarist Hugh Poore, alias Cowboy Joe, in a half-hour slot that was popular enough to continue into the forties, and in 1939 NBC beamed the Grand Ole Opry to Puget Sound. Six years later Bob Wills and his Texas Playboys packed the Civic Auditorium on two consecutive nights, and by the end of World War II western bands were playing a widening circuit of granges and dance halls throughout the state. Southerners who came to Seattle to work in defense plants furnished a new audience for country music, as did Northwest natives who had never heard it before. With "Sagebrush Serenade" and other programs, KVI Radio led the country trend after World War II.

The irrepressible pioneer of Northwest country was Marion "Buck" Ritchey, an ex-Missouri carny hired in 1942 as a singer and disc jockey. Ritchey formed a band, the K-6 Wranglers, to tour the state and promote KVI at dances. The Wranglers were joined late in the forties by steel guitar inventor Paul Tutmarc and his wife, Bonnie Guitar, who had been leading

Buck Ritchey's K-6 Wranglers enjoyed a year's run on Seattle's first live television broadcasts. In this 1950 view at the KING TV studios are (left to right) Dave Stubbs, Gil Ross, Marty Dahlgren, Floyd Thomas, Vic Martin, Bonnie Guitar, and Ritchey. *Courtesy of Marty Dahlgren*

their own country-western movement with distinctive interpretations of cowboy songs. Arriving on the scene in 1950 were country music veterans "Texas" Jim and "Jack" Rivers Lewis. The rambunctious brothers made a big splash in the thirties with their touring band, the Lone Star Cowboys, produced several early western hits ("Seven Beers with the Wrong Woman," "Too Late to Worry, Too Blue to Cry"), and starred in a string of B-movie westerns. Landing in Seattle, they waged a two-man country revolution, hosting the popular "Sheriff Tex" TV show (nervous cameramen kept wary eyes on Texas Jim's waving .44) and building a huge following on the bar circuit.

By the mid-fifties Seattle was dotted with taverns—the Silver Dollar, the Brown Derby, the Owl, the Tik Tok—hosting country bands. And for many a two-stepper, *the* place to be on a Saturday night was at the Circle Tavern, dancing to Lafe "Curly" Booth and his Swingtime Cowboys. A hearty, silver-haired bull fiddler, Booth arrived in the flood of defense workers in 1942, working at Boeing by day and by night in a combo at the Rodeo Tavern. With him were Booth's longtime sidekicks, accordionist Phil "Skeeter" Schwendt and lead guitar/vocalist Dale Starcher. Junior member of the band was Richard "Sandy" Sanderson, who joined the Cowboys at the Circle in 1953.

Sanderson's roots all but guaranteed a future in music. His father, Alvin S. Sanderson, was a Montana railroad man and one of the nation's top old-time fiddlers. "By the time he was 70," Sandy told me, "Dad had won first prize for the senior division in the national fiddle championship four years in a row. Finally the judges said, 'Alvin, you're takin' it every year, so we're just gonna have to retire you undefeated.'" Sandy's uncle, Engwald S. Sanderson, was a Yakima Valley rancher who loved to play Hank Williams and Bob Wills songs at family gatherings. He was a regular at regional talent shows, prompting his nephew to join in. "I was very shy around people and didn't have a lot of friends," Sanderson said, "but I gradually got brave enough to do some shows."

> I'd put on my cowboy outfit, sing a song or two, and darned if I didn't come away with some wins. Earl See, a piano player, hired me for his variety band, the Stylettes, and we played military bases, and I really scored big with NBC Radio's "Talent Search, Country-Style," which had a larger radio audience than the Grand Ole Opry. In 1951 they offered me a week at the Village Barn in New York, but by then I was stuck in the army.

The tall, sandy-haired young musician was not to be sidetracked:

> I got out of the service in '53 and went back to my job at Western Union. Curly Booth's wife happened to be a Western Union delivery person, so the next thing I knew I was playing in his band. Curly assigned me the newer stuff, including some Elvis Presley, 'cause it was on the jukebox. Curly and Dale Starcher sang the older tunes. We never rehearsed; I'd just put a new piece of sheet music on the stand and tell 'em I was gonna do it in the key of something or other. The guys'd say, "Okay, just stomp 'er off and we'll take it from there." And they sure did! Skeet Schwendt was a marvelous musician who had been playing accordion since he was a kid, in Hollywood and around the country before moving to Seattle. Curly was out of Spokane, and had worked on Coulee Dam and played in the bars over there. He had a fine baritone voice and was a good

Lafe "Curly" Booth and his Swingtime Cowboys are all smiles at the Circle Tavern in 1955. The drumless Cowboys feature Booth's slap bass and harmonica and Phil "Skeeter" Schwendt's accordion—instruments long since banished from mainstream country. From left are Schwendt, Dale Starcher, Booth, and Richard "Sandy" Sanderson. Author's collection

harmonica player, but he couldn't really play the bass at all. Couldn't even tune it—Skeet had to tune it for him! But Curly played slap-bass, so it didn't really didn't matter what notes he was playing; he had a good strong beat, and it sounded fine. Curly was a terrific front man who could put over a song very well and keep the energy up in a place. He'd do novelty songs and get folks laughing, and then the more traditional Eddie Arnold–type songs. We played the Circle Tavern six years straight; the place held over 200 people, and many's the night folks'd be lined up clear around the building. We had people from Canada, Oregon, all over, and they just loved dancing to that beat and that kind of music. There were other country joints going then, but the Circle was *the* place.

Taking the reins from the country pioneers was Jack Roberts, who with the region's most popular country band and his "Evergreen Jubilee" TV show made country-western a mainstream phenomenon in Washington. "At home my brothers all used to sit around in the evenings playing guitars and singing country songs," the guitarist/singer/bandleader/promoter told me over coffee near his Kenmore home.

> I listened to the Grand Ole Opry and took to Eddy Arnold and Elton Brett. Elton had the big hit "Chime Bells" and his yodeling style was widely imitated by many country artists, me included. In 1949 I was still in high school when I started my first band with a guitar player buddy of mine; a couple other guys joined in, and pretty soon we had ourselves a real western swing band. That was something very new in the Pacific Northwest. Western swing was just barely starting to be recognized here in 1950; Hank Thompson and his Brazos Valley Boys were the big thing, a slicker version of what Bob Wills had been doing, and our kid band took directly after him. In 1954 we were hired to play Saturday nights at Heiser's Shadow Lake Resort. By then western swing was taking hold, and we packed Heiser's every Saturday night. We called ourselves the Evergreen Drifters, a name I held on to the rest of my music career.

Roberts took a risk when he decided to add drums to the band.

> After about a year I got Mac McFarland to play drums, and boy did that cause an uproar! Drums were not accepted in western swing at all—they were not allowed on the stage of the Grand Ole Opry. Only in Texas and Oklahoma were drums considered acceptable in country-western music. When I hired Mac, my rhythm guitar player, Bud Jennings, read me the riot act: "We don't need any drums in our band!" I tried to convince him that it would work out, but he quit. Well, Mac's drumming made us *the* top western swing band in the Northwest. There's a big difference between drumming for western swing and for other styles, and Mac had it down. He knew when to lay back and when to really sock it, when to play in two and when to play four-four—when to swing, and when not to. And he had such a good, clean *whack!* Then along came a fiddler who *really* put us over, Marty Dahlgren. After Marty joined us, people said we were the best western swing band anywhere. We were certainly as good as the best. We played Shadow Lake till 1964, then went up to the Spanish Castle and packed that place, too.

Strangely, Roberts got the cold shoulder from the medium that had done so much to create modern country music. "Getting into radio was tough," Roberts nodded.

Buck Ritchey had a regular radio show on KVI for a while, but it went off the air. Buck was a very smart, savvy old-time radio DJ, and he was into *radio*, not just country music. When Gene Autry announced he was going to buy KVI, some folks got all excited: "Oh boy, now we're gonna get a real country station!" But they didn't know what I did: that Gene owned about a dozen radio stations around the country, and *none* of 'em was western! He may have been a country artist, but he was also a businessman, and they just didn't think there was a market for country back then. About 1955 I went to KAYO Radio to pitch a three-hour country show. After all, here we were packing them in at the Shadow Lake Resort every Saturday, and I tried to show the studio heads that this was a major trend. No dice. It wasn't till about three years later that KAYO hired Buck Ritchey, and that show made country music a big thing here. In 1958 I started my own "Evergreen Jubilee" show on KOMO TV, and it lasted for years. We started in black and white, but because we had a lot of colorful sets and costumes, we became one of the first color shows broadcast in the Seattle area.

Roberts preferred straight-ahead western swing to the later "Nashville sound":

The early artists—Roy Acuff, Ernest Tubb, Lefty Frizzell—were, I think, much more individual than the folks that started coming up later. And women were very, very scarce in country music in those early days. They just didn't have an audience. You'd think maybe Patsy Cline would have been a big deal, but she wasn't. On concert dates, even someone like Patsy would have to be carried as an "extra attraction" to the male stars. It wasn't until much later that she got to be considered a big star on her own, in fact not till after she was gone, unfortunately. Overall, I would say that country might not have a really *big* audience, but it is a *consistent* one. Consistent and loyal.

The fiddler who sparked the Evergreen Drifters, Marty Dahlgren, carried on the Seattle tradition founded in the 1860s by Mart Lewis and

Charles Testman. His artistry has had generations of bandleaders knocking on his door, and he has kept his finesse well-honed into his majestic eighties. A performance at the Centrum Fiddle Tunes Festival at Port Townsend in the summer of 2006 left a packed hall gaping in wonder at Dahlgren's tour de force treatment of "Listen to the Mockingbird": swooping, soaring, and double-stopping in the best hoedown style, then sliding into rococo excursions reminiscent of the great Joe Venuti. "In the thirties we lived in Arlington," Dahlgren told me,

> and on weekends folks'd gather at each others' homes and the fiddlers would start sawin' away. Later we moved to Edmonds, and I started violin lessons. By then I was listening to the radio and picking up on the country artists just starting to be played by some of the local deejays. Bob Wills was my hero, and I memorized most of the solos by his fiddle player, Joe Holly. I about wore out a 78 rpm recording of Fiddlin' Red Herron playing "Listen to the Mockingbird." Pretty soon I began playing for fun with some of the bluegrass guys in Edmonds, and was strongly influenced by Buss Boyd, a wonderful Everett fiddler. When I was about twenty, I got a call from a man who had heard about me, who asked if I could play for the Wednesday night square dance lessons at the Everett Elks. That was my entrance into professional music. The piano player there was a great jazz guy, and he started teaching me songs and how to improvise and take jazz solos, which really was no different from what Bob Wills was doing.[15]

After World War II, Dahlgren joined the Washington country-western movement.

> About 1948 I began to play taverns with some of the bands around Seattle. One of the first was Ray Johnson's Western Melody Boys, with Pete Thorsen, a very fine lead guitarist. Ray was an excellent singer and rhythm guitar man—most of the country singers then also played rhythm guitar. Vic Martin's Western Merrymakers was another top early band; Buck Ritchey played with him, along with Bonnie Guitar, Dave Stubbs, and Floyd Thomas. Dave Stubbs was an excellent bass player and singer, Floyd wrote some very good songs, and we worked quite a while at the Brown Derby Tavern on Empire Way. In 1950 I started playing with Jack Roberts and his Evergreen Drifters at taverns, granges, and Kinney's

Barn outside of Snohomish. The owner's daughter led the house band, Kinney's All-Star Western Swing Band, and they also sponsored a touring group, the Cascade Hillbillies, which I played and recorded a couple of sides with.

Marty chuckled as he pondered the vagaries of musical style and public taste.

A couple hundred people was a small crowd for Kinney's on a Friday or Saturday night. But some people, no matter what you give them, are not going to be satisfied. You'll be playing a standard country tune, nothing fancy, and somebody will come up: "We're leaving because we can't dance to your music." Well, okay. There's a hundred others out there on the floor dancing and not complaining, so what do you do? Most of our country bands here were pretty similar in style, although they did develop some individual styles according to the talents in the band. Jack Roberts would hang a sign behind the stage, "Requests Welcome," and it had the effect of making folks feel like they were part of the music, not just spectators.

Asked if there is any fundamental difference between improvising country and jazz, Marty was emphatic: "No. A lot of country players are really playing full-out jazz, just with a country beat behind them." And he had no beef with rock and roll: "One reason might be that rock had more in common with western swing than other pop music. A lot of Bob Wills's songs had the same rock feel that Elvis songs did, so we didn't consider it anything unusual. The country bands I was in started doing rock numbers fairly early; in fact, people started requesting them."

A GREAT BREAK

Manuel Rosenthal sighed. Seattle was a long way from Paris! Why was money for a symphony orchestra so hard to come by—here, in this richest of all nations, with its luxurious automobiles, its supermarkets full of food? Certainly, the public could not be faulted for its attendance, especially if ticket prices were kept low. Rescheduled after dismal ticket sales, the big Beethoven festival in January 1950 had filled the Civic Auditorium (execrable barn that it was) at a dollar a head. Even so, musicians were still playing for the door! "It is so ghastly," Rosenthal moaned, "always going over the same tracks begging people for money." As for the government (which in France generously subsidized the arts), here it could be depended on for one thing only: to tax an orchestra into bankruptcy. A May 1950 guest appearance by Arturo Toscanini and the NBC Symphony had cost its Seattle sponsors more than $5,000 in city, state, and federal taxes. Oh, well; there was one thing Seattle and Paris had in common: The backstabbing and bickering were as bad as anything he'd seen at the Conservatoire![16]

Rosenthal, at least, brought a touch of the old Beecham glamour. A hero of the French Resistance during World War II, he had studied with Maurice Ravel and directed the French National Radio Orchestra. Even the notoriously prickly Virgil Thomson praised his orchestral suites, *Magic Manhattan* and *Musique de Table*. Rosenthal "humanized" the Civic Auditorium with in-the-round seating, and his exuberant Seattle premieres of Modest Mussorgsky's *Pictures at an Exhibition* and Hector Berlioz's *Symphonie Fantastique* were cheered. Still, despite extensive fund-raising efforts, including the first annual "Symphoneve Ball," orchestra executive vice president John Hauberg Jr. reported in December 1950 that the sustaining fund was $30,000 short. Unless more could be raised, and soon, the season would end with the year. After that, who could say?

Desperate, the board of trustees frantically wired other orchestras for advice. Dallas offered the helpful reply that maintenance money was raised "almost in one luncheon . . . from banks, utilities, newspapers, department stores . . . and others who think the orchestra is necessary to complete the picture of metropolitan Dallas." The rest came, as in Seattle, from a small group of wealthy music lovers. Indianapolis wired that their city government guaranteed a yearly $25,000 in return for their orchestra performing at city high schools. Thus fortified, the Seattle Symphony trustees asked the city council for $20,000 to stave off disaster. "There is nothing new or unusual about a municipal subsidy of this character," editorialized the *Seattle Post-Intelligencer*. "Music is more important in Seattle than it is in any other city of its size . . . as attested by the vast number of choral and instrumental groups." No, said the council; the city charter expressly forbade it.[17]

To the rescue came Norm Bobrow. On December 29, he and deejay Hal Davis set up a microphone, two chairs, and a cot in a show window at the big Frederick and Nelson store, and invited Seattleites to phone in pledges. Taking turns napping in full view of the passing throngs, Bobrow and Davis begged and browbeat their neighbors into buying the symphony another season. As midnight neared, they clanged cowbells and shrieked, "We're in!" Two weeks later, Bobrow and Davis hosted "Jazz vs. Symphony—A Musical Bout in Two Rounds" at the Civic Auditorium. Mozart's *Jupiter* Symphony squared off against Bobrow crooning "The St. Louis Blues," while popcorn vendors patrolled the aisles. The year was further brightened by guest artists Marian Anderson, the Vienna Boys Choir, Isaac Stern, and Oscar Levant (delivering Beethoven's "Moonlight" Sonata with his "customary arthritic abandon"). Then, on October 16, 1951, Seattle opened its morning papers to find out that Maestro Rosenthal had two wives.

Jaws agape, society gasped at the lurid accounts of how Rosenthal and the woman he had been representing as his wife, Miss Claudine Verneuil, had been detained at Ellis Island after "some people who didn't like me in Seattle" had reported to the State Department that he was in fact married to a woman other than Miss Verneuil. Rosenthal was denied entry on grounds of perjury and moral turpitude, and it was revealed that he was indeed still married to one Lucie Traoussier. From Paris, Madame Traoussier explained that she and Manuel had been separated since the war, and that, after all, "he is a great artist, and artists face many temptations." The two were later divorced, and Rosenthal and Verneuil lived happily ever afterward. In the meantime, the Seattle Symphony was once again leaderless. Into the breach stepped University of Washington music director Dr. Stanley Chapple, who, with only four hours' rehearsal and several new first chair players, led the orchestra in a triumphant "Standard Oil Hour" broadcast. Guest conductors—Yehudi Menuhin, Maurice Abravanel, Leopold Stokowski, Arthur Fiedler—took up the slack, and while audiences enjoyed some of the world's greatest conductors (and bookkeepers appreciated the black ink resulting from not having to pay a permanent director), symphony boosters looked wistfully back on the days of Karl Krueger and Basil Cameron—days when the symphony advanced under the vision and consistent discipline of a resident maestro. Where was that young man, looking for a big break?[18]

In January 1953 another conductor passed through the revolving door. Born in 1909, Milton Katims grew up in a musical Brooklyn family, began playing the piano at age six, and completed Columbia University as a grad student in viola and conducting. Moving to Woodstock, New York, he began dating cellist Virginia Peterson. Peterson was a student of Alfred Wallenstein, musical director of Mutual Broadcasting System's Radio WOR. (Wallenstein would also take a turn guest-conducting the Seattle

Symphony in the fifties.) When Wallenstein mentioned that he was look-ing for an assistant conductor and solo violist, Virginia told her swain, who threw down the phone, rushed 100 miles to the station's Manhattan stu-dio, and landed the job. During his eight years with Wallenstein, Katims immersed himself in the classical repertoire and was rewarded with solo and guest conductor spots. The warm, intimate tones of the Katims viola were enjoyed across the nation in homes and in hundreds of churches, which piped in the station's Sunday Bach program. Milton Katims was clearly a young comer in American classical music.

In Katims's radio audience was a music legend. By the 1930s, NBC Sym-phony leader Arturo Toscanini had become the most famous orchestra con-ductor in the world. His face of a thousand moods, his passionate podium balletics, and above all his soaring interpretations of the masters had done as much as radio itself to popularize classical music. Among the millions who worshipped the fiery maestro was Katims, who as a teen had eavesdropped on Toscanini rehearsals by sneaking into Carnegie Hall and lying quietly on the floor of a box. Naturally, when the NBC Symphony announced a vacancy in the viola section in 1941, Katims immediately asked for an audi-tion. He was stunned when the personnel director informed him that no audition would be necessary; Toscanini was a regular listener to Katims's broadcasts—the job was his. So began Milton Katims's lifelong friendship with Toscanini, who embraced his adoring fan and groomed him as his assistant. By 1950 Katims was guest-conducting the NBC and other orches-tras around the country. The maestro was feeling his age, and when he hinted to his young associate that retirement was not far off, Katims knew that the NBC Symphony would probably not long survive its director. Qui-etly, he made it known that he was at liberty as a conductor. Offers began trickling in: Dallas, Indianapolis, Rochester, Detroit, Seattle.

Fed up with guest conductors, the symphony trustees had put Dr. Hans Lehmann in charge of finding a new Karl Krueger. Impressed by a Katims performance with the NBC Symphony, Lehmann asked a mutual friend—none other than Sasha Schneider, mastermind of the symphony's 1948 "revolution"—to arrange a dinner meeting. By the end of the eve-ning, Lehmann was smitten: "Milton, you must come out and conduct in Seattle." Katims frowned: "Maybe. But where exactly *is* Seattle." He was kidding, of course; Katims was eager for his own orchestra, and a date was set. In January 1953 and again in November, Katims scored impressive per-formances with the symphony, and he and his new wife, Virginia, sailed through a battery of Meet the Maestro luncheons, dazzling the cultural elite. Among the most impressed was new *Seattle Times* arts writer Lou Guzzo, who urged the symphony board to start a short list of prospective conductors at the letter K. "He's like a Greek God!" gushed Hans Lehmann. They were resistant; all but Lehmann—the one European on the board—wanted a European conductor. Katims himself wasn't sure. Direct an obscure, provincial orchestra three thousand miles away from the New York music world he loved? Yes; Seattle "held the most potential for growth. A few guest-conducting visits confirmed my conviction that it would be an ideal city in which to live and . . . bring up our children." Milton Katims signed for the full 1954–55 season. The Seattle Symphony had finally gotten its great break.[19]

Where Arturo Toscanini was the archetype of the Old World maestro, Katims was young, approachable, and spoke in terms that both musicians and chamber of commerce types could appreciate. "These days," he told a reporter, "an orchestra conductor must be all things to all people." Still, the youthful face masked an iron will, a prickly temper, and a conducting style taken whole cloth from his old school mentor. Before signing his contract, Katims made clear that he would strive for a new standard of music making: "I would make no concessions to the fact that the orchestra was comprised of a mixture of experienced professionals, schoolteachers, and housewives." The musicians listened somberly as he charted their future: He would enlarge the group (at eighty members, no larger than the Kegrize orchestra of 1910), extend the season, increase the geographic reach, lobby hard for a concert hall that would accommodate not only concerts but opera and ballet (encouraging those art forms would give the musicians vastly more work), and, most of all, elevate the quality of the orchestra itself. "Just sitting around holding each others' hands is not real security," he declared—"I want to make us such a fine orchestra that people will *want* to come and hear us." Then came the clincher: He would not work his revolution by committee. The conductor must be able to hire and fire musicians as he saw fit. The cooperative must go; if not, Katims would. Other cities, he reminded his patrons, would pay handsomely for his services.[20]

The musicians debated hotly whether to accept the new dispensation; tears were shed, friendships severed, and the majority voted to go along. Sweetening the deal was a 15 percent pay increase and the guarantee of a longer season, with one hundred rehearsal and concert "services" a year, thirty more than previous. (The wage scale—$1,250 to $2,000 in 1957—

still lagged behind other major American orchestras, prompting bassist Leslie "Tiny" Martin and a handful of others to take more lucrative offers elsewhere.) Milton and Virginia settled into a Laurelhurst home with a fine view of Mount Rainier and pitched into a ceaseless round of Coffee-with-Katims socials, dinners, corporate luncheons, and school lectures. They were essential. "The financial problems of the Seattle Symphony Orchestra constituted a paradox that was uncommon in communities possessing such musical organizations," noted orchestra historian Esther Campbell. "Ticket sales were among the largest . . . in the United States, but large business and industrial firms of the type that contributed liberally elsewhere gave comparatively meager support to Seattle's orchestra."[21]

Nonetheless, the fifties were ripe for promoting classical music. The rise of the middle class banished old assumptions that "the arts" were an elite province, and as radio had been the great equalizer of the thirties, the long-playing record of the fifties made extended symphonic works marketable and popular on vinyl. "We owe our contemporary knowledge of Bartok and Berlioz to the long-playing disc and frequency modulation—nothing else," mused cultural historian Jacques Barzun. "In 1934 the Beethoven Ninth Symphony was bought by about 500 people a year; in 1954 over 130,000 bought Toscanini's recording of the work." In Seattle, an informal group of musicians, artists, and architects calling themselves the Beer and Culture Society began considering ways to pep up Seattle's languishing cultural environment. All agreed on one thing: If big business would not support the arts, then government should. Adopting a more suitably sober name, Allied Arts of Seattle, they convinced the city council to establish the Seattle Municipal Arts Commission in 1955. The commission considered a broad plank of Allied Arts recommendations, which included reducing the city admissions tax for the symphony and other "organizations performing a public service," and grants for symphony and parks concerts. These measures were adopted, and public moneys began to fix more than potholes.[22]

One cause Katims took up with a vengeance was his adoptive city's lack of a suitable concert venue. After playing the Civic Auditorium in 1953, violin legend Jascha Heifetz told Katims that he should not bother inviting him back until Seattle had a decent hall. Seventy-six-year-old Anna Falkoff stepped up, offering the gift of one of her three apartment buildings, worth $150,000, to a concert hall kitty. Heavier artillery was brought to bear in November 1956 when a $7.5-million Civic Auditorium conversion bond issue was placed before the voters. The campaign also proposed that the civic center grounds be enlarged, and that Seattle host a world's fair within the next decade. "I would like to talk about Toronto, Montreal, and Detroit," Katims admonished at a businessmen's luncheon. "What do they have the Seattle has not? They now have concrete plans for concrete halls ["I like that word 'concrete'!" enthused a cement plant executive]. Where in Seattle are all the people who share the vision . . . held by one lone woman who offered her apartment house? If we don't build NOW, when will we have a more propitious time?" The maestro marshaled friends and family into honking motorcades, their cars festooned with "Vote YES!" banners. Seattle said yes. The Katims charisma, and the now general feeling that classical music was no longer a luxury but a civic necessity, won the voters, and a seventy-two-acre site was designated around the Civic Auditorium and National Guard Armory.[23]

A happy future beckoned, but it was not to be reached overnight. The 1957 symphony fund drive fell $30,000 short of its $120,000 break-even goal, scotching Katims's ambitious plans for an extended season, a Northwest tour, the commissioning of new works, and recording sessions. Privately, Katims cursed the businessmen he had been wining and dining. Why couldn't Weyerhaeuser and Paccar see that they stood as much as anyone to gain by a having a first-rate symphony? In December came the rumor—from where, no one knew—that Katims was again considering offers from other cities. Shock and recrimination exploded among symphony backers who had struggled to extract nickels and dimes from the "fish-and-timber" barons. Smiling grimly at the challenge of cracking every nut in town to build his orchestra, Katims enlisted friends from NBC days—Heifetz, Isaac Stern, Arthur Rubenstein—in the cause, dangling them as guest stars as if to say, "Do you really want to give this up?"

Katims took the orchestra into the neighborhoods and schools, and Virginia fed the city's need for connectivity by telling amusing stories of teaching European friends how to pronounce "Seattle." Impressing many was the fact that this stellar musician did not run when faced with crisis (and offers of more money), but instead stood with Seattle. Had the rumors of Katims's leaving been a ruse? Perhaps Sasha Schneider had again worked his canny wiles. If so, it worked. Ever so slightly, corporate coffers began loosening, average folks switched off their TV sets and went to the concert hall (and because Seattle didn't actually *have* a concert hall, they began to want one), and their children came home from school raving that the symphony had actually come to play for *them*. Slowly but surely, Milton Katims bent Seattle to his will, making her the city she had always wanted to be.

SLIPPERY SLOPE

In 1955 Tiny Martin was scared. Seattle had been good to the portly bass player, a familiar figure in the symphony and dance bands. And Seattle had always been a good union town; the previous year Local 76 opened its new headquarters at Third and Cedar, complete with café and show-room—for the first time in its history, the musicians' union owned its own building. But now, even as *Musicland* ballyhooed the excitement, work was drying up. The Spanish Castle and Trianon had cut their bands to weekends only, and taverns were replacing bands with TV sets and juke-boxes. The blackboard in the new union office was thick with "at liberty" notices, and members, some of whom had been playing since Dad Wag-ner's day, were grumbling.

Just elected Local 76 president, Martin's smiling portrait went up beside Wagner's in the new boardroom. But the beaming bassist could offer only a grim prognosis: "The music profession is in a state of tran-sition," he wrote in the union paper. "Unemployment is more stringent than ever before due principally to the influx of television and the pres-sures of the 20% amusement tax. . . . Taft-Hartley and Lea Act legislation and the newer 'Right to Work laws' . . . have set trade unionism back on its heels." The encroachments of amateur, military, and especially school bands had become a flood, along with a growing number of recreation alternatives, many of them publicly funded. When the Woodland Park Zoo was expanded two years earlier, the union grumbled, "We seem to have taxpayers' money for bear grottos . . . and for those who would like to master the art of horseback riding, but . . . money is always scarce when FREE music for the public is suggested." By 1960 it was only thanks to the Music Performance Trust Fund (MPTF) that union musicians were able to continue appearing in Seafair parades and other events being overrun by school bands. Professional music was now compelled to take money from one pocket and put it in the other, to keep its members working. What had gone wrong?[24]

Enemy number one was the hated admissions tax, which discouraged the hiring of live music. Seattle city ordinance 88748 was passed in 1943 to enforce a federal 20 percent tax on cover charges at all places of amusement, including dance halls and nightclubs. During the booming forties, the implications of the levy were apparent to only a few, such as AFM president James C. Petrillo, who lobbied hard against it. Ten years later, though, the consequences had become clear, and musicians' unions across the country were clamoring for repeal. They got nowhere. Sticking the needle in further was the pesky 1920s Landes ordinance, still on the books, which required teenagers attending public dances to be accompanied by a parent. There went the teen market. And maddeningly obtuse were the three bureaucrats who constituted the state liquor control board. When the agency nixed a trio at Bon's Congo Room in 1955, it freely admitted that its decision was based on "no fixed policy." The union protested what it termed a de facto "music control board," but to no avail, and decades later the liquor control board continues to exercise arbitrary and anti-music authority.[25]

Another culprit was the union itself. Even as Martin editorialized, the AFM began diverting payments to recording musicians into the MPTF, evoking furious protests and a mass resignation by Los Angeles studio players, who then formed an alternative union, the Musical Guild Association. The fracas sent shock waves through the union, followed by lawsuits and expulsions that worsened the AFM's already negative public image. Three years later Petrillo resigned amid widespread grumbling that the day of the union was passing along with him. In Seattle, complaints of cronyism and favoritism mounted.

A somber AFM took stock. Pollsters for Dr. A. W. Zelomek's Research Company of America fanned out over the country and discovered that the position of the professional musician in American life was precarious. "American musicians have suffered from the worst possible public relations," said Zelomek, who had been an economic adviser to President Roosevelt,

> largely caused by the failure to effectively answer the many unwarranted attacks that have been leveled the past several years at James C. Petrillo. . . . Nothing positive has been done to counteract the preposterous picture of the musician as either an eccentric longhair or degenerate jazzbo. . . . A good musician is an artisan, employed at essential work, and deserves to be so rewarded.

Instead, taxation, automation, legislation, television, and changing tastes had caused the loss of some 50,000 professional music jobs across the country. Zelomek presented his findings to a congressional Ways and Means committee. Would they listen?[26]

On September 9, 1956, a young singer banged out a guitar chord on the "Ed Sullivan Show," and music was forever changed. Lip acurl, Elvis Presley led the charge in the great teen takeover, and by 1958 the first wave of Seattle rock bands—the Frantics, the Adventurers, the Continentals—began shouldering white-coated orchestras out of the ballrooms. Local 76 had little official comment, but members were not so reticent: "Hated it," frowned Stan Boreson; "simplistic," shrugged Floyd Standifer; "corruptive noise," scowled Ed Gross; "yecchh!" grimaced Nick Potebnya. Struck dumb by the big beat, the music establishment at Third and Cedar could only encourage the rank and file to redouble their efforts to keep gigs coming. "Musicians in general have become lazy," lectured new president Chet Ramage. "Musicians don't want to rehearse anymore. . . . More musical aggregations should be organized, rehearsed, and professional. . . . Every musician should ask himself: 'What am I doing to improve the live music situation?'"[27]

One change had been a long time coming. By 1950 AFM president Petrillo had made integration a national policy, and the locals slowly began to fall into line. Long resistant to mixing, Local 76 continued to fine members for playing with black musicians, prompting several white members to join black local 493 in protest. Three successive joint committees developed recommendations for a merger; the third group, with Tiny Martin, Harry Reed, and Alvin Schardt representing Local 76, and Local 493 officials Powell Barnett (whom Petrillo personally named), Bob Marshall, Gerald Wells, and Emmett Lewis, succeeded. Fines for mixed bands were abolished, and in December 1956 the memberships of locals 76 and 493 voted in favor of union. Bandleader/club owner Elmer Gill gave the movement a shove that year when he staged his own integration of the Brigadier Room in the New Washington Hotel. The fact that Gill regularly packed the place influenced the hotel's management to acquiesce, and one more brick toppled from the wall. In January 1958, Local 493 was absorbed into Local 76 by unanimous vote of the memberships, and Local 76 became Local 76–493. Pianist Johnny Wittwer celebrated: "The musicians of Seattle are greatly relieved that this stupid situation is over. . . . There are plenty of non-musicians who are pretty happy about it, too."[28]

Not all African American musicians were happy. Under the terms of the merger, Local 493 was obliged to hand its assets over to the combined union. These were not large, but they did include the Blue Note, the nightclub that since 1946 had been Local 493's unofficial union hall. Within weeks of the merger the Blue Note closed, depriving the black musical community of a vital support venue. Nor did integration equate to increased opportunity in the white music world. "When we went into Local 76," grumbled saxophonist Jabo Ward, "we got crumbs." Floyd Standifer offered a different perspective: "Seattle was one of the last to amalgamate unions," he told me.

They foot-dragged up a storm—there were some guys who were just out-and-out rednecks! But James C. Petrillo said, "If Truman can integrate the armed forces, we're gonna integrate the musicians," and that was that. It took a long time to work out the definition of "full membership." In other words, if you came in from 493 and you had, say, ten years of longevity, are you eligible for retirement or lifetime membership? At the same rate as anybody else? For those of us who knew how to read music, how to carry ourselves in certain situations—among white people, let us say—the amalgamation worked out all right. Many of the other black musicians, however, never were able to cross over from music as they had known it in the after-hours clubs. At that time, the after-hours scene was coming to an end, and by around '61 it was gone. A lot of those cats were used to jamming and blowing the blues all night, and had no experience reading music and cutting "legitimate" gigs. So they found themselves hung out to dry. You saw it happening in sports, too. Yes, it did represent a loss of the old way. But I was for it. This was America! Everybody should have the opportunity.[29]

Johnny Moton agreed.

Most of us black and white musicians was already brothers, anyway. This just made it official. It was happening all over, and I was glad. Amalgamation did not make things any worse for the black musician, and it did not make things any better. After the combination, some complained that the work wasn't coming. But it wasn't coming anyway—it was drying up! Amalgamation didn't cause that. The after-hours clubs were closing. Rock was becoming popular. It all comes to economics in the end, and I don't care if you're a black musician or white: In the economics of the music business, you're gonna be livin' on the short end most of the time.

■   ■   ■

A cold rain pummeled First Avenue. A man in a sodden trench coat ducked furtively into the Green Parrot Theater. In a passing patrol car, a heavy-lidded policeman yawned. This leaden winter of 1969, downtown Seattle was quiet, even bleak. The bustling evening crowds and glowing theater marquees of another era were long gone, and the ghost of Charles Constantine walked unmolested through a deserted Pioneer Square. But from a bright oasis on First Avenue, a saxophone wailed bravely into the night: the Soul Cellar was rocking! Sailors and pimps lined the bar, young women in beehive hairdos sat like sparrows along the wall, and on the dance floor, two couples lurched in boozy embrace. On the little bandstand, Boss George Hurst pumped out wry insinuations on his big, hollowbody guitar: Listen here! I'm talkin' to you! Booker Williams shouted back on his fur-lined tenor saxophone: Well—talk all you want, mister man. I got what you need! On the rain-slick sidewalk, a skinny seventeen-year-old kid stopped, slouched into an alcove, and listened.

■ ■ ■

Chapter 8

Groovin' High

SEATTLE SAILED INTO THE SIXTIES in a roar of jet engines and bulldozers. The Boeing Company's prototype 707 jet airliner took to the air in 1955 and by 1960 was radically accelerating the pace of travel. Up and down the hourglass-shaped city, bulldozers gouged out the artery that would soon tie it to the Interstate Highway System. Gleaming glass boxes intruded into long-unmolested brick blocks, and in a weedy backwater, three great steel prongs inched skyward. When that huge stem blossomed into the Space Needle, *Life* magazine hit the newsstands with the new Seattle icon on the cover. Inside was an eye-popping preview of the city's second world's fair in less than a hundred years, the Seattle World's Fair–Century 21 Exposition. Seattle was reborn.

Conceived in 1955, Century 21 began as a businessmen's scheme to pep up the sleepy city with a fiftieth-anniversary celebration of the Alaska-Yukon-Pacific Exposition. Two years later, though, the Soviet satellite *Sputnik* threw America into a panic that it was falling behind its Cold War adversary, and fair boosters pitched a new concept to Congress: a "Space Age World's Fair" that would employ visions of a bright technological future and inspire the nation to retake the high ground. Opening on April 21, 1962, the fair attracted three times as many visitors—9,609,989—as the Alaska-Yukon-Pacific Exposition, and at its October 21 conclusion Seattle heaved a sigh of satisfaction that the show had delivered the city to the front rank of modern American metropoli.

Music for the twenty-first century. If there were few surprises left by the time the second Seattle World's Fair opened in 1962, this was one of them. French composer Jacques Lasry, sculptor Francois Baschet, and associates perform on electronic instruments at the United States Science Pavilion. Baschet and Lasry's "Structures Sonores" made a splash in France, a center of electronic music, but few ripples in the United States. University of Washington Libraries, Special Collections U W 27672

Century 21 looked ahead technologically, less so musically. As opening day crowds poured in, Broadway baritone John Raitt crooned "Meet Me at the 'Needle, Nellie!" to the tune of Kerry Mills's "Meet Me in St. Louis, Louis" (twelve-year-old daughter Bonnie held his sheet music), and Ronnie Pierce's combo (alias Skinny Malone and his Hot Bananas) blared Dixieland. Jackie Souders's thirty-seven-member World's Fair Marching Band was Wagner's Band reincarnated as it strutted the grounds in cream and gold uniforms, serenaded international days, and backed Elvis Presley in *It Happened at the World's Fair*. To a public that had pretty much heard it all by 1962, there were fewer surprises this time around. Still, the new Opera House laid out a musical cornucopia: Van Cliburn, Ballet Folklorico de Mexico, Theodore Bikel, the Foo Hsing Theater, and Josh White. Counterpart to the Alaska-Yukon-Pacific Exposition's Natural Amphitheater, the World's Fair Stadium reverberated to the pipes and drums of the Royal Canadian Tattoo, while in the Food Circus fairgoers munched Danish frankfurters as a red-wigged clown belted out the 1912 hit "Row, Row, Row." A big band blared for strippers at Gracie Hansen's Paradise International, and on Sundays folk guitars strummed in the United Nations Courtyard. Adding a welcome note of carny hokum was Alden Bice's circus calliope.

For musicians, the early sixties soared as high as the Space Needle. "The world's fair was a dream come true," exclaimed drummer Howard Gilbert. "I think we all bought houses that summer!" Gilbert played in the Souders marching band and then some. "I worked three jobs a day," he remembered,

> and often more: parade through the fair in the morning, do an afternoon concert, then another parade. After that, go home, practice an hour, have a beer, then hit the road again and play maybe Dick Parker's Ballroom with Jackie Souders, in the German band at the Hofbrau, or Vern Mallory's combo at the Drift Inn. And after *that*, pack up and run down to the New Chinatown Café, go up the stairs, and play until sunrise.

Practice, I asked Howard—after all that? "Absolutely! I'd do an hour of warm-ups and hand movement every day. Otherwise, with that intense activity, your hands and wrists fail. Just lock up. I knew a lot of guys who got in big trouble from overplaying and not practicing. If you're fighting your own muscles, it destroys you."

Playing the fair was a grind rewarded by steady money and a few laughs. "Jackie Souders could be irascible," Gilbert affirmed, "but he was an honest man."

> You started on time, finished on time, and got your check on time. But being leader of the fair band, there was a lot of pressure on him. We were playing fanfares and national anthems at the Flag Plaza one day for the governor and a group of international dignitaries. Microphones broadcast

us across the fairgrounds. A priest started giving the invocation. We were sitting there behind all these dignitaries, and somebody down in the woodwinds got bored and starting talking and messing around with his music. Souders very loudly barked, "STOP F***ING AROUND DURING THE G**D**N PRAYER!" The mikes carried it all over the fairgrounds.

There was no gig Howard Gilbert would not take—except a nonmusical one. "I never thought about another profession," he told me proudly, "and I never had a day job."

> My folks accepted it. Even before I had a driver's license, my dad would pick me up at two o'clock in the morning and bring me home from a job. If you can lower yourself and be versatile, you work. The New York jazz cats didn't just play 52nd Street; they'd report to the union hall and go out and *work*. Miles Davis used to play Polish weddings! My closet was full of lederhosen, a cowboy outfit, Hawaiian shirts, world's fair band uniform, musicians' union uniform, and two or three tuxedos. There were a lot of players in Seattle who didn't work because they wouldn't take every gig. But to survive and not have a day job, you had to play everything. And that was *fun*, because you had to master all the different styles. There is always something to be learned on every job, no matter how mundane you might think it is. You can correct your own playing and you can learn to make a bad band sound good—and making lousy musicians sound good can darn well keep you working! But if you stick your nose in the air—"I'm a *jazz* musician"—you might as well get a day job.

The art of trap drumming evolved briskly during the twentieth century, from the temple blocks and rat-a-tat of the teens to the intricate subdivisions of bebop. Seattle had her share of percussion greats: Ralph Gibbs and Marvin "Slats" Risley pepped up Jazz Age escapades; Jackie Wolcott and Ray Watkins punched vaudeville shows and circuses; Bruce Ford and Dave Stettler propelled dance bands from Vic Meyers to Jackie Souders; Dave Coleman and Bill Kotick pleased the most discerning jazz fans. Howard Gilbert learned his craft from an old school master:

> In high school at Portland I studied with one of the great drum technicians, Joe Amato. People came from all over to study with him. He was a Sicilian, and he didn't care if you learned or not. But if you didn't prac-

tice, you'd better not show up. He would teach in an undershirt with tux pants and suspenders and a cigar between his jaws, and if you made too many mistakes, he would knock the sticks out of your hands. You'd bust out crying, and he'd call downstairs: "Mama! Bring up a cookie!" Then, "Okay, kid, start over again." We learned through *fear*. And if you're really dedicated, fear works! That kind of training gave me the endurance and ability to play *anything*. I was still in high school when I played my first professional gig, then I started working with German bands, which were very big here in the late fifties and sixties. Herb Marks and Hans Reinert had one of the top German bands; they were both accordion players, and we worked during the world's fair six nights a week at the Hofbrau on Fifth Avenue. These bands were mostly Rhinelanders and Austrians: button accordion, key accordion, tuba, drums. We cooked!

Like all pro musicians, Howard Gilbert was not always paid what he was promised. Unlike many, he refused to take being stiffed philosophically. "One night before we went on at the Hofbrau, the chef told me, 'My paycheck bounced.'"

I went into the office and demanded to be paid immediately. The place was full, and they needed a drummer, right? So the boss starts writing out a check. I say, "Cash." He paid cash. A group tried to stiff my wife, Pamela Roberts, who was a concert cellist; she picketed the office with our little daughter in her stroller, and I went in and walked out with a typewriter. She got her money.

Century 21 was a bright beginning to a new decade. But even as the fair closed in October 1962, the national mood was darkening. President Kennedy faced down Soviet premier Khrushchev over missiles in Cuba, and television cameras brought the beatings of civil rights marchers into American living rooms. The musicians' union bemoaned the disappearance of jobs, the proliferation of canned music, and the encroachments of amateur bands, while fighting the eternal fight against the admissions tax and blue laws. More ominously for traditionalists, the music many said would never last was proving disturbingly tenacious. The Wailers and Ventures bumped Gordon Greene from the Spanish Castle, and fellow bandleader Bob Harvey lamented, "I've got a whole trunkful of tunes written, good dance music just waiting to be played, once this rock and roll craze ends—I hope." It was a vain hope, and the man who had once led a popular ten-piece dance band was reduced to part-time gigs—when he could get them—with an "orchestra" consisting of himself and longtime bandmate Carle Rising tripling on trumpet, guitar, and drums.[1]

The music establishment may not have liked rock, but business was business. At the tail end of the fifties rock musicians began joining the union, and in 1960 the annual Musicians' Association picnic hosted its first rock band, Tom Larson and the Dynamics. From playing hard bop at the Flame, Floyd Standifer found himself blowing raunchy tenor sax for the go-go girls at the Pink Pussycat. Eagerly or not, others jumped on the rock wagon. Pete Leinonen played in early rock bands and told me,

> What many people forget is that there was a strong continuity between the older generation of pro musicians and the first generation of rockers here. Many of the early rock drummers studied with Shorty Clough, Howard Gilbert, and Dave Coleman, while Al Turay had a huge influence on guitar players. The first Northwest rock bands brought this to their music, and most of those bands were highly sophisticated in both their material and their presentation. A lot of us jazz players caught the wave, too—Dave Press had a little ceremony where he burned his tux in his front yard.

WHITE COATS IN THE GO-GO DECADE

The rock revolution did not change the old order overnight, and most musicians kept their dress suits pressed. "I used to say 'Rock is a crock,'" recalled Burke Garrett, who unabashedly proclaimed his Burke Garrett Orchestra "the workingest band in town" during the sixties.

> We never played rock on my band. I thought Elvis was totally raw and uncool. Not till much later did I gain an appreciation for his talent. My band's interpretation of rock was more of an R&B treatment of things like "Watermelon Man" and "Summertime." We'd throw on a heavy backbeat, and the dancers'd do the Boogaloo. We kept 'em happy, but remained musical. Lots of dance bands dealt with rock the same way.

As a young man in 1960, Garrett was unfazed by the dwindling opportunities for dance bands. Instead, he attacked the music business like a military campaign, studying what the established groups were playing, watching their moves, noting audience response, then launching a frontal assault that took many of the old-timers' gigs.

I was twelve years old when I saw *The Glenn Miller Story* and I thought, "I'm gonna be a bandleader!" I bought a sax at a hockshop and began studying with Johnnie Jessen and Ron Phillips. At fifteen I started a band, and within a couple of years I had more work than I could handle. I also discovered that there were lots of bands around, but no organization *selling* them. I *liked* selling, and I was way into being a bandleader as opposed to being some kind of jazz cat.

Barely out of his teens, Garrett took his cues from the old guard:

My strategy was, one lick at a time. I'd ask myself, "What do I need to get to where Wyatt Howard and Jackie Souders are?" I was young, we hadn't been in the business twenty years, so everything was scripted. I even wrote out all my announcements. How else do you learn? The old guys said, "Oh, he's just a flash in the pan," but after a while I was *hiring* those guys. Jackie Souders had the most successful band in town, so I hired his arranger, Bernie Press, to write similar things for us. Schmaltz. Bernie was a good arranger, but we'd camp the hell out of his charts and exaggerate the Guy Lombardo vibratos. Most of the time we were playing for audiences twenty years older than we were; they caught on to our vibe but saw that we were having fun, and so *they* had fun. I was proud as could be to be playing for the "moneyed elite"—me, a kid from Federal Way High!

Unlike many musicians, Burke Garrett had no problem being an entertainer as opposed to an artist, and so was able to enjoy being both: "I was a stickler for playing what the people who hired us liked. But we'd push the envelope a little and get into some jazzy things, and when people wanted to rock, we'd play head arrangements of 'Jose Outside' and 'Day Tripper.'" Garrett prided himself on hiring some of the best players in the Northwest:

Sarge West, on trumpet, was fantastic. He worshipped Miles Davis and could do a respectable mimic of him, and play bass, vibes, and organ, too. Corky Corcoran played tenor in the Zoot Sims or Ben Webster caliber—an absolutely *huge* sound. Keith Mirick, who was practically unknown because he only played with me, was a superb lead trumpet player and singer, and a great front man. Drummer Bill Kotick was a very demanding, meticulous musician. He had little patience for incompetence in others—he'd yell at you right on the stand if you were doing something wrong. Then again, sometimes he'd just sort of go nuts; one night he stood up and sang "Hello, Dolly!" at the top of his lungs, hitting the snare drum at the same time. We had a custom sound and lighting system, which few bands had in those days, and we'd do a black light show with ultraviolet lamps, with the band in fluorescent costumes that glowed in the lights. We were *stunning*! In the late sixties I got into booking and bought Northwest Releasing; that was a lot of fun, but nothing beats rolling into a student union with all our gear, setting up, then hitting the downbeat and seeing all the dancers come out onto the floor. I *loved* being a bandleader!

So did Garrett's chief rival, Jackie Souders. For many, Jackie Souders was still Mister Music, and in the early sixties his orchestra held its seemingly permanent place at Parker's Ballroom, the Olympic Hotel, and the Washington Athletic Club. Souders and his fellow bandleaders were thrown a bone in 1963, when the Century 21 fairgrounds reopened as the Seattle Center and the recording industry Music Performance Trust Fund began thirty years of Saturday night big-band dances at the Food Circus. Fittingly, Souders kicked things off, and new generations discovered the big band sound. By mid-decade, though, rock's grip was tightening; the fiddling Violettes were let go, and Mister Music was getting desperate. "I got $52 a week in 1923 with Vic Meyers's band," Souders moaned to his old friend, Tiny Burnett—"now I feel lucky if I can make that in a month."[2]

Taking a job as a court bailiff (where he delighted in crying "Hear ye! Hear ye!"), Souders kept his hand in with small combos. "Jackie could play decent trombone," trumpeter Harley Brumbaugh told me, "but he was no ad-libber. He made up for that by being unpredictable. One night he just started playing—didn't tell us what tune it was, just sailed off into it, then turned around and whispered, 'Hey, guys, make me look good'! We stood there going 'Whaaat?' until he segued back to the book like nothing had happened." Unlike some bandleaders, Souders never accepted the new musical dispensation. "Jackie *hated* rock!" Harley continued.

We had a combo date out in Renton, and a fellow started pestering him: "Hey, do you know any rock and roll?" Jackie ignored him, but the guy kept after him: "Come on, play some rock!" Finally, Jackie threw his trombone on the floor—*BANG!* "G**d**n it, I've been playing this horn since before you were born, and I damn well know what my band can and can't play!" Then he picked up his bent trombone and asked, "Anyone know a good repairman?"

Jackie Souders was clearing brush from his land in Issaquah on February 14, 1968, when a heart attack overtook him at age sixty-four. With his passing, Seattle lost a little bit of its identity. "Jackie was eternal youth," said old friend Don Duncan. "He could make you tap your feet and thaw your frozen face. Music and people having fun sustained him."[3]

In one sense, there was nothing special about the Jackie Souders Orchestra. It was a generic dance band cut to a common cloth and duplicated by thousands. It broke no musical or sociological ground. It did, however, excite emotions: not the screaming passion evoked by Benny Goodman or Elvis Presley, but innumerable quiet, private passions that produced marriages (Souders called Hoagy Carmichael's "Stardust" "Cupid's favorite weapon"), families, and that sense of solid, middle-class success that was so dear to twentieth-century Seattle. Like other big-bands, the Souders orchestra played music of inclusion and shared experience—of connection. "The big bands did so much for musicians and for society," said Stan Keen, who played piano with Souders and led his own show and theater bands. "They served as a very important bridge between people in those days, and between jazz and dance music. Big bands were the music of adults *and* young people, not like today. Kids and their parents listened to the same music." This alone did not make Souders and his band distinctive. What did was longevity. In a time when endurance was seen as a virtue, decades as Seattle's top bandleader made Jackie Souders a face of music and continuity that businessmen, policemen, politicians, and housewives could all relate to, never mind that, by 1960, that face was no longer young. Souders gave the would-be Gotham on Puget Sound music as opulent as that heard on the Hudson River, and, like Dad Wagner's, Souders's longevity made his ostensibly ordinary orchestra something Seattle could call her own: as uniquely local as the Smith Tower and Ivar's Acres of Clams.[4]

Carrying the Souders torch was his old sideman, Max Pillar. A gregarious reed player, Pillar formed his own orchestra in 1957 and started giving his erstwhile boss a run for his money. In the 1960s the Max Pillar Orchestra became a Saturday night institution at Parker's Ballroom, easing in as Souders eased out. Souders's trombonist/arranger, Bernie Press, came over, too, and wrote much of the Pillar library. The bands actually differed sharply. Souders liked variety, dabbling in Dixieland and even a little cool jazz. None of that for Pillar: "Max worshipped Guy Lombardo," said longtime sideman Dick Rose, "and he stuck very closely to that style. Souders was more in the Russ Morgan style, and more diverse in his presentation." In the rocking sixties the Max Pillar Orchestra became a bastion of tradition for the still-considerable audience of adults who liked to dance to the music of *their* youth. "Max had the smoothest band of any," declared Harley Brumbaugh. "He loved to ham it up and strut around the stage waving his baton, and go into his Ted Lewis bit with the top hat and wobbly clarinet, shouting 'Is everybody happy?' His saxophones had to play that wide Guy Lombardo vibrato—the wider the better. He called it the 'womb-tremblor': 'Lemme me hear those *womb tremblors!'"[5]

Plodding along in the shadow of Garrett, Souders, and Pillar was Archie Kyle. A student at Queen Anne High, Kyle started his first band in 1926 and played continuously for over sixty years (in 1986 the American Federation of Musicians saluted him with a plaque of honor). The drumming bandleader was no showman but played current hits and standards in simple arrangements made even simpler with lead-foot percussion. Some called him stodgy. "I was with Archie for a long time," Brumbaugh reminisced.

> He was a sweet guy to work for and he loved music, but his drumming was strictly old hat. We tried the Tijuana Brass's "Music to Watch Girls Go By," but Archie could not play that rock beat to save his life. He sounded like a broken-down locomotive! Finally I said, "Okay, Archie, we're gonna have a little music lesson," and I wrote out the beats right on his snare drum head. He finally got it. But everybody liked Archie; he was big with the police and fraternal associations, played the prestigious Fireman's Ball every year at the Olympic, and he became a fixture at the Seattle Center. If Jackie Souders was Seattle's white-collar bandleader, Archie Kyle was the blue. Souders was more musical and his band was slicker and more danceable. Archie was all "boom-chuck," no matter if it was a ballad or a rock tune. But Archie had the common touch, and a lot of folks liked that. A lot of folks *like* "boom-chuck."

THE HOUSE THAT KATIMS BUILT

The Century 21 Exposition left Seattle many legacies: a world-famous civic icon, new restaurants, international recognition, Heinz pickle pins, and the feeling we'd had a heck of a good time. Seattle Spirit lived! But arguably the greatest legacy of Century 21 was the building Seattle had dreamed of for decades. Those who had once craned their necks and strained their ears in the old Civic Auditorium gasped in disbelief at its transformation into a glittering showplace of luxurious box seats, mahogany paneling, and golden chandeliers. (At Cecilia Schultz's insistence the makeover was named Opera House, and not architect Benjamin Marcus Priteca's proposed Multipurpose Hall.) The April 21 opening night concert was suitably spectacular: Van Cliburn performing Rachmaninoff's Third Piano Concerto and Igor Stravinsky conducting his *Firebird* Suite.

The fair and its Opera House set off an arts explosion that continues to reverberate a half century later. The fuse had a long delay. Arts writer Maxine Cushing Gray noted pointedly that Century 21 had been stingy with local arts groups: "If Washington State carpenters and plumbers and even architects had been bypassed as prodigally as were our people in the performing arts, there would have been protests. . . . The Seattle Symphony . . . was hired by the fair exactly once, for the April 21 opener." Nonetheless, the Musicians' Association of Seattle reported that the fair had netted its members more than half a million dollars.[6]

But the fuse *was* lit, and it was lit by Milton Katims. Under his direction the Seattle Symphony entered a new golden age, and brought with it opera, ballet, and theater. Big, bold, and brash was the Katims style, and he was the perfect fit for a born-again city. Arriving at the Opera House in his yellow Corvette, the maestro liked to stride briskly out from the wings, leap onto the podium, and without so much as a pause for breath, sweep the orchestra into action with his baton. As promised, Katims enlarged the orchestra to eighty-five musicians, twenty-eight of whom were women (three in the string bass section); he lengthened the season (in 1954 a mere eight concerts, in 1967, twenty-four, not including family, school, and special performances), added pops and young people's programs, wooed business leaders, harangued chamber of commerce dinners, and backed movements to attract major league sports. And with a grant of $50,000 from the Weyerhaeuser Foundation, he also began recording. For Milton

Milton Katims leads the Seattle Symphony on opening night 1965. At left is concertmaster Henry Siegl. Old friends from the NBC Symphony, Katims hired Siegl in 1956 and the first fiddler anchored the orchestra for over two decades. Museum of History and Industry 1986.5.309171

Katims, the sky was the limit if it expanded his audience and made Seattle more livable for his musicians.

Women loomed large in the Katims orchestra's success. Virginia Katims, whose vivacious facade masked shrewd diplomatic wiles, proudly declared, "I live every phase of the symphony with my husband. We spend twelve months a year planning, thinking, and almost eating music." She played her exquisite cello for women's clubs, wined executives at Candlelight with Katims dinners, and matched her husband in rallying community support for the symphony. In the 1930s the symphony presciently hired one of its staunchest and most effective advocates, manager Ruth Allen McCreery. Ravishing in the latest Paris fashions, McCreery continually pressed the orchestra and its directors to do things in high style, giving the symphony an aura of chic that served it well in glamour-hungry Seattle. Both women made legions of friends, soothed musicians' egos, loosened pocketbooks, and encouraged the conductor to lead his audience into new musical territory.[7]

Reflecting his Russo-Hungarian heritage (an Ellis Island clerk lopped the "ky" off the name of his arriving parents), Katims loved Russian music, and Tchaikovsky, Mussorgsky, and Rimsky-Korsakov colored the concert palette heavily during his tenure. As early as his second season at Seattle, though, he was serving up more adventurous fare—and meeting resistance. "Never play anything like that again!" harrumphed orchestra president Gordon Scott after Katims presented Ralph Vaughan Williams's jarring Fourth Symphony in his second season. The new conductor replied, "Gordon, if I *don't* play anything like that again, it will be your responsibility to fire me, because I will not have been doing my job." Scott knew he was licked (especially when he saw Ruth McCreery on the maestro's side), and in the sixties Katims aggressively pushed the boundaries with the likes of Edgar Varèse's *Deserts*, Alexander Scriabin's *Poeme d'Extase*, William Schuman's *Judith*, and Alan Rawsthorne's *Practical Cats*. "I try to aim over the audiences' heads," said the conductor, "but not so far that I lose them. I like to think that there has been a gradual change in Seattle's musical taste."[8]

Now, too, American composers got a hearing. Robert Parris's Concerto for Five Kettledrums, Paul Creston's Violin Concerto, and Frank Martin's Concerto for Seven Wind Instruments beckoned audiences into a new musical sensibility. Nor were Seattle composers—Gerald Kechley, Robert Suderburg, and even folk musician Earl Robinson—left out. Using first-chair players, Katims created the thirty-six-member Little Orchestra in 1958 to perform smaller-scale and avant-garde works, and its ten-season survival bore evidence of Seattle's growing receptivity to unfamiliar music. In the late sixties "multi-media" became an "in" thing, and Katims donned a blue velvet tuxedo and added light shows and specially choreographed dancing. For a performance of Bruckner's Seventh Symphony, he invited several painters to set up easels onstage and render their interpretations. The old guard was not amused: György Ligeti's *Atmospheres*, huffed one bejeweled society doyenne, should have been named *Air Pollution*, and, at the conclusion of *Judith*, a prominent businessman hissed at Virginia Katims, "Tell your maestro that if he ever subjects me to anything like this, I'll never come to another concert."[9]

The maestro stuck to his batons, adamant that the Seattle Symphony have its own "Katims sound": "I've achieved a musical attitude of my own, and it represents a fusion of influences—[Pablo] Casals, the Budapest String Quartet, Isaac Stern, and, above all, the Old Man [Toscanini]. . . . In all cases, I have only one goal in mind, and that is to be a prism for the composer's ideas by improving his score as I think he would do it, not by intruding my own personality." The personality, however, began to grate. Sporting a good-luck medallion given him by Toscanini, Katims emulated his master's habit of singing along with the orchestra, his sucking on hard candy during performances, even his speech ("Hit the notes, but go away, please. . . . Now, make nice"). He also screamed in rehearsal, berated players, and broke his baton angrily. Musicians objected to his rushed tempos and his "pre-editing" scores to fit his interpretations—more Toscanini traits. "He thinks he can predetermine everything," grumbled one, "without even doing us the courtesy of waiting to hear how a piece sounds when we play the composer's original version." Katims brushed off the criticism: Of course he pre-edited! This was essential, considering the evolution of musical instruments and the acoustics of different halls. How else was an orchestra to create its own sound? Aggravating relations between the maestro and the orchestra was the fact that symphony pay in Seattle, averaging $2,300 in 1964, continued to lag behind most other American orchestras. More hackles were raised when Katims imported new first chair cellist Raymond Davis, French horn Richard Bonnevie, and oboist Bernard Shapiro from New York. But the box office told another story: subscription levels soared to third-highest in the nation, hitting 6,000 by 1964, and attendance was matched by only a handful of American orchestras. *Seattle* magazine said of Katims, "This short, energetic, and extraordinarily young-looking man of 51 has come to symbolize the emergence of music as a major force in Seattle's cultural life."[10]

Howard Gilbert, symphony percussionist for twenty years, agreed:

> Milton Katims did an enormous amount for Seattle. He really took the symphony to a new level. He was very talented, and a nice man—offstage. Onstage, at rehearsal, he would bring people to tears, throw terrible temper tantrums, insult you personally. As a conductor, he could be difficult to follow. But *most* conductors, especially those who have been conducting awhile, are difficult to follow. The worst thing about playing in a symphony orchestra is the conductor's ego. Young conductors, who

haven't practiced their mannerisms in front of a mirror, are fine. But the older they get, the more egotistical they get, and the more unnatural in their direction. They adopt these weird mannerisms and spring all kinds of surprises on the orchestra, to show that they're in control. Some of the older ones will just leave you hanging in mid-air—you don't know what the hell to do.

Gilbert experienced the world of European art music at its best—and its worst—in a time of increasing pressure on musicians. "I joined the symphony right after the world's fair and stayed twenty-some years," Gilbert recounted.

The orchestra was a good living, and if you could stand the BS, it was fun. Some of the satisfaction you get in playing percussion in a symphony orchestra would be the same sort of satisfaction you'd get by knocking a ball out of the ballpark. But you get to the point you see the same material over and over again, and start to dread it: Ravel's *Bolero*—yecchh! Most contemporary music I can't stand; it sounds like the composer has taken a course at the university on how to write for percussion, because they throw in everything possible, usually things that don't work: embellishments and fancy stuff that's just pointless and impossible to play. And they always want crap like thirteen tom toms, two marimbas, five gongs, and you've got to be at rehearsal two hours early to help unload and set up the two marimbas and the five gongs and the thirteen tom toms! By the time rehearsal starts you're completely wasted.

Seattle Symphony musicians were working harder than ever, and the public was filling the Opera House. But big business kept its hands in its pockets. Corporate arts support remained among the nation's skimpiest, and in July 1965, Katims laid it on the line to businessmen and politicians: If the community did not step up and pay for a full-time, professional symphony orchestra, a forty-two-week season, more family concerts, and a youth outreach program, they were wasting their time and his. Young people, especially, stood to lose big if the arts continued to be starved. Things got better: The Ford Foundation advanced a whopping 1.75-million-dollar matching grant, and the federal government kicked in Title 3 moneys, allowing Katims to begin the transition toward a full-time orchestra. In 1967, though, corporate sponsorship was still anemic. "To date," said *Seattle* magazine, "business support for the arts in the North-west has been way below . . . contributions in other culturally ambitious cities like San Francisco and Minneapolis. . . . The leadership of one group was so incensed by a recent Boeing contribution that the donation was almost returned with a curt, 'Thanks, but no thanks.'" Weyerhaeuser spokesman John Hauberg Jr. (himself a generous arts backer) explained, "We're a generation behind the one running business back east, and it's usually the second generation, the one that's been brought up *with* cul-ture, that supports the arts in a big way." In Seattle, that generation was just graduating from high school.[11]

NEW DIMENSIONS

America has always been the land of I-know-what-I-like. Innovations in the arts, from abstract painting to Bauhaus buildings, face *New Yorker* car-toons at best and public ostracism at worst. In Seattle, as elsewhere, non-traditional, "new" music has been a tough sell. Periodic thaws in artistic conservatism are, even in the twenty-first century, followed by periods of aural reaction. When John Spargur, "with some misgivings," took a chance in 1920 and presented an evening of Debussy, the audience's enthusiasm came as a pleasant surprise. Thirteen years later, though, Paul Ashford lamented, "Years after Stravinsky has become commonplace as bread-and-butter in the centers of Europe and our own eastern metropolis, Brahms is still caviar to the general public in Seattle. The greatest trouble locally is the fact that Seattle audiences 'know nothing about music, but they know what they like.'"[12]

But the artistic impulse will not be stayed. In 1938 Los Angeles–born pianist John Cage was hired by the Cornish School to accompany Bonnie Bird's modern dance classes. Assigned to write incidental music for Syvilla Fort's short ballet, "Bacchanale," he responded with an African-flavored piece for gamelan orchestra. As there was no such thing as a gamelan within a thousand miles of Puget Sound (and even if there was, the stage had no room for anything larger than a piano), Cage had an inspiration. Remembering how his teacher, Henry Cowell, had produced interest-ing sounds by altering the inner works of the piano, Cage put screws and bolts between the strings of his rehearsal piano and made it *sound* like a gamelan. So was born the Cage "prepared piano." Cage invited other composers, among them Cowell, George McKay, and Ray Green, to contribute ideas for a longer work, *Imaginary Landscape*, and in 1940 the Cage Percussion Players and composer Lou Harrison took the new sound on a West Coast tour. If Cage's small revolution did not transform the conservative, Russian-émigré-dominated Cornish music department, it did stir up excitement among students and, as embraced by Bonnie Bird, her teacher Martha Graham, and fellow Cornish dancer Merce Cunningham, became a hallmark of modern American dance.[13]

In the sixties America was obsessed with modernity, and in the wake of Century 21, Seattle was the queen city of newness. The cultural imperative to be "with it" encouraged a new sonic movement, and Joan Franks Williams rode the wave with New Dimensions in Music. Born in Brooklyn and educated at the Eastman and Manhattan schools of music, Williams (1930–2003) was just starting out in New York when her engineer husband took a job at Boeing. The prospect of a move to the Pacific Northwest filled her with dread; how much of an audience for experimental music could there be in such a remote place? Arriving in May 1962, the apprehensive Williams was pleasantly surprised to find a sell-out crowd at a University of Washington festival honoring composer Anton Webern. Seattle Symphony oboist Bernard Shapiro, himself a newly transplanted New York friend, assured Williams that Seattle was happening, and encouraged her to start an experimental ensemble. Another eager acolyte was electrical engineer Glenn White Jr., the symphony's resident acoustician and a devotee of electronic music, who became Williams's indispensable technical adviser. When her 1963 debut concert drew more than 175 people to the Henry Art Gallery, Williams enthused that even in New York, audiences that big for new music were a rarity.

Williams introduced Seattle not only to Alban Berg, Karlheinz Stockhausen, Arnold Schoenberg, Luigi Dallapiccola, and other composers considered beyond the tolerance of the average symphony ticket buyer but also to unknowns such as Morton Subotnik, Vladimir Ussachevsky, and UW student Charles Carpenter. Audiences heard strange devices—oscilloscopes, square wave generators, and tape recorders—not normally considered musical instruments, and scratched their heads over Williams's own whimsically named pieces ("Humpty Dumpty Sat on a Waltz," "Frogs Revisited") that mixed instruments and voices in scurrying cross-rhythms, solo flights, and chattering call-and-response. Her piano sonata, *Homage to Louise Nevelson*, is a three-movement masterpiece that could just as well stand as a tribute to generations of Seattle keyboardists. In 1967 young music writer Patrick MacDonald declared that New Dimensions in Music afforded "without a doubt the most masterful, creative, and expressful journeys into the realm of music in Seattle today."[14]

Veteran Northwest radio personality Jim Wilke was an enthusiastic New Dimensions board member. "The sixties were such a great time for new music on the West Coast," Jim said to me, "and Seattle picked up some of that fever."

> But doing this stuff presented us with a lot of interesting challenges. For example, how do you present electronic music in concert? Do you just set up a couple of speakers and let people stare at them? One piece was nothing but filtered white noise: sound processed so it was constantly changing—*wheeoooshhh*. Somebody had the idea to put a parachute onstage, with some dancers underneath, and when the music started, this piece of cloth began moving like a living lava lamp. Then there were the hundred metronomes; a bunch of us walked onstage with trays carrying metronomes, and Joan directed us with her baton to set the metronomes on a table, then gave another cue to wind the metronomes, and then a cue to set them in motion. The whole idea was to hear the polyrhythms of all these metronomes beating against each other, and it worked great. And one person set their metronome on *largo*, so after all the others stopped, this one little metronome was still going *tick—tick—tick*.

Joan Franks Williams moved to Israel in 1971, where she led a new incarnation of New Directions and received growing international recognition. Seventeen years later, though, Williams succumbed to the lure of Puget Sound and returned to Seattle, where she resumed her distinguished role in the avant-garde music scene.

Williams was not alone in her innovations. A year after her arrival, William Bergsma assumed the chairmanship of the University of Washington School of Music and began his campaign to make it the "Juilliard of the West." Among Bergsma's first acts was to apply for a grant from the Rockefeller Foundation to hire a faculty new music ensemble. He would use the group and the money (and ace out Joan Franks Williams in the regional competition for the grant) to make the UW music program one of the most progressive in the country.

Seattle has Methodist minister Daniel Bagley to thank for the University of Washington, an institution that, in company with a broad industrial base, all but guaranteed the city's regional dominance and cultural development. Daily vocal training was part of the curriculum from the school's birth in 1861, and by 1889 the university was teaching piano, violin, mandolin, and guitar, and boasted a glee club and mandolin orchestra. Two years later, the first music major graduated. The UW moved to its permanent north Seattle site in 1893, and in 1908 history professor Edmond Meany and Reginald de Koven composed the official state song, "Washington Beloved." The university got its revered fight song, "Bow Down to Washington," in a 1915 contest—winner Lester Wilson got his name on the sheet music and twenty-five dollars. ("Bow Down" has forever overshadowed the university anthem, "The Old University," to the tune of "The Old Oaken Bucket," adopted in 1924.)

Pride of the School of Music during the mid-twentieth century was the "Dean of Northwest composers," tall, genial George Frederick McKay. Born in 1899 in the eastern Washington farm town of Harrington, McKay came from a musical family, studied at the University of Washington, and went on to the Eastman School of Music in Rochester, New York, to be its first composition graduate. Returning to the UW in 1927, McKay settled in for a forty-year term preaching the gospel of Americanism in modern art music. In his lectures (students included William Bolcom, John Cage, and Earl Robinson), McKay gleefully condemned as sterile and antihuman the European serialism and other avant-garde affectations popular in academic circles, and composed music that is harmonically lush yet transparent and lyrical. White rural tradition and Native American song inspired many of his works for orchestra, band, chamber ensemble, and organ. Many are Pacific Northwest evocations: The four-movement *From a Moonlit Ceremony* incorporates Muckleshoot Indian chants; *Harbor Narratives* is a tone poem to the waters and shores of Puget Sound; and *Symphony for Seattle* ("Evocation") is replete with hearty Seattle Spirit tempered with McKay's customary introspection. Performed and broadcast by many major orchestras during his lifetime, George Frederick McKay's music has been largely neglected since his death in 1970.

Presiding over UW music in the fifties was Dr. Stanley Chapple. A devotee of orchestral music and opera, Chapple had been a distinguished second-tier conductor in Europe, and when he took up his post in 1948 was shocked to find "a completely desolate place, artistically." In the absence of an opera company (the Civic Opera Association had folded in 1946), he formed the Seattle Opera Guild and presented the lyric repertoire under university auspices, using orchestra and choruses with mixed student and professional talent. Not only the standard repertoire was given but also new chamber works, such as resident composer John Verrall's *The Cowherd and the Sky Maiden*. Chapple invited the public to rehearsals, took performances into area high school auditoriums, and regaled musicians and listeners with his stories of working with his old friend Serge Koussevitsky and other classical music legends. At once Continental and down-to-earth, Stanley Chapple gave Seattle art music a significant boost.[15]

William Bergsma had bigger plans. A composer himself, Bergsma wrote string quartets, orchestral pieces—"Paul Bunyan" Suite, "Serenade to Await the Moon" (dedicated to Milton Katims)—and an opera, *The Murder of Comrade Sharik*. Now, though, he applied his pen to grant writing and with the forthcoming prize enlisted the front line in his campaign, the University of Washington Contemporary Group. Core members included Robert and Elizabeth Suderburg, violinist Irwin Eisenberg, clarinetist William O. Smith, and trombonist Stuart Dempster. Pianist Robert Suderburg was a craftsman of evocative vignettes: *Orchestra Music I*, "Solo Music I" for violin, and "Chamber Music III—Night-Set" for trombone and piano, which fused elements of jazz and film noir in a nostalgic tribute to his father, a dance band trombonist. Possessed of a crystalline voice, soprano Elizabeth Suderburg was praised by many, including the *Seattle Times*'s Wayne Johnson, as one of the Northwest's finest artists. "Bill Bergsma wanted to make the School of Music the 'Juilliard of the West,'" Stuart Dempster told me. "That was his phrase. He wanted to light a fire in the music scene and make it more reflective of the 'real world.' Some of the old guard resented us young whippersnappers at first, but a few became quite interested in what we were doing." The Contemporary Group flourished and, with Bergsma's equally groundbreaking ethnomusicology program, drew new attention and talent to the campus.

Purveyor of strange and joyful sounds since coming to Seattle in 1968, ex–Oakland Symphony principal trombonist Stuart Dempster brought puckish irreverence and much-needed humor to the School of Music. Dempster is a devotee of non-jazz improvisation and a pioneer in so-called therapeutic music, presaging the New Age and ambient idioms. Plumbing the nether depths (sometimes literally) of music's possibilities, he has taken a trombone and a didjeridoo to a medieval monastery and an underground cistern in his quest for new and often startling effects. His "Standing Waves" for solo trombone, "Sound Massage Parlor," and "In the

Great Abbey of Clement VI" are mind-expanding explorations of acoustics, resonance, and the limits of human breath. A Dempster performance features multiple tones, words spoken through the horn, flatulent gargles, and stentorian expostulations. "I like to offer a 'good, rich experience' to the audience," Dempster affirmed.

> That's Bob Suderburg's term, and it's what all performers should remind themselves before they go onstage. You're in a *dialogue* with your audience—exchanging brain waves. Never forget: they're *ready*! New music of all kinds in Seattle has really snowballed, and now it crosses over into jazz and rock, performance art, and world music, with groups like the Degenerate Art Ensemble. All the new stuff represents a *huge* plurality, something completely unheard-of thirty years ago.

Pride of the Bergsma blitz was the Philadelphia String Quartet. Fed up with being cogs in the Philadelphia Orchestra of autocratic conductor Eugene Ormandy, violinists Veda Reynolds and Irwin Eisenberg, violist Alan Iglitzin, and cellist Charles Brennand put out "at liberty" feelers. In 1966 they accepted Bergsma's offer and arrived in Seattle in a hail of headlines and litigation (Ormandy filed and lost three injunctions to stop them). For the first time since the demise of John Spargur's, Seattle had a professional string quartet, albeit one with another city's name, and the group packed decaying old Meany Hall. For more than twenty years the Philadelphia String Quartet was a jewel in Seattle's musical life; Roger Downey called it "one of the very few absolutely first-rate Northwest 'cultural assets' . . . which can stand comparison with the very finest anywhere in the world. . . . their performances consistently generate more pure musical excitement than any other local events, except for occasional Seattle Opera presentations." In 1989, as public funding dried up, the "Philly" disbanded, but it left a strong wake: Cellist Toby Saks, who played with the quartet in its latter days, spearheaded the creation of the Seattle Chamber Music Festival, while Alan Iglitzin established the prestigious Olympic Music Festival to further the cause of chamber music in the Pacific Northwest. Both attract audiences from around the world.[16]

The Contemporary Group and the Philadelphia String Quartet were sustained by a web of foundation grants and state and federal moneys, the latter an outgrowth of the Great Society programs of the Johnson administration that included the National Endowment for the Arts. That web was, and remains, fragile. "Bill Bergsma was a master at grantsmanship," said Stuart Dempster, "and getting the Rockefeller Grant was the key to his program."

> But the Rockefeller was structured so that it diminished each year in proportion to a theoretical increase in government matching funds: one hundred percent the first year, eighty percent the second. Well, when we got down to our last twenty percent in the early seventies, the state became a lot less interested in us. The Philadelphia String Quartet did not have a teaching contract, so the administration saw them as expendable; they folded, and a lot of talented people, Bob Suderburg among them, went to other states.

Nonetheless, William Bergsma wrought a campus music revolution, and when he stepped down as head of the department in 1971 he left behind a permanent Contemporary Group and a beautiful new Meany Hall.

JAZZ CHANGES

The early sixties were good times for jazz, especially in funky old Pioneer Square, where new clubs—the NoPlace, the House of Entertainment, and, most notably, the Penthouse—joined Pete's Poop Deck in offering live music, from Dixieland to bop, six nights a week. Opening just before the world's fair, Charlie Puzzo's Penthouse was the slickest of the lot, the first nightspot in town to regularly present national names. John Coltrane, Miles Davis, and Stan Getz were backed by a local house band of pianist Dick Palumbi, bassist Chuck Metcalf, and drummer Bill Richardson. Testimony to the high level of the group, they were hired by vocalist Anita O'Day for a 1962 tour, and Palumbi went on to work as accompanist for singer Buddy Greco. Cornets returned to the erstwhile tenderloin in 1960, when Jack Fecker and Jerry Kock opened the Blue Banjo just north of Yesler Way. Kenny Ball's raucous 1962 spin on "Midnight in Moscow" gave Dixieland a new, if short, revival, and in its five-year run the Blue Banjo took listeners back in time with Les Beigel's Dixie Dandies and Pep Peery's Firehouse Five Plus Three.

Cashing in on the world's fair boom, young pianist Overton Berry and four fellow musicians opened the House of Entertainment in Occidental

Park, then moved north up First Avenue. "We had a six-piece group," said Berry, "with guitarist Larry Coryell and Ken Murphy on trumpet."

We were totally nonalcoholic, just a coffee house, but still we packed the place. Lots of cats sat in, and after midnight we got the guys from the Penthouse. Miles Davis walked in one night, and Ken turned to me: "I'm not playin'!" "What are you talking about?" "Miles Davis just walked in—I can't play with him standing there!" "Well, if you walked into his job, he'd still be playing." "Yeah, but he *can!*"

Never one for barriers of any kind, Overton Berry delighted in connecting people musically:

We played the spectrum: blues to R&B to standards, even Dixie, and for dancing, too. But the jamming was *it*. One night a trumpet player from Stan Kenton's band came in, took out his horn, and called "Secret Love" at this absolutely *blistering* tempo. We usually all hung out together after work, but after this dude blew everybody away, the guys all said, "I gotta go." They all were in a panic to get home and practice, 'cause he said he'd be back the next night. He came back, and brought a friend with him, and by the time Saturday night rolled around there were ten guys from Kenton's band spread out through the entire room. We'd get going, and a trombone player would stand up and play a solo in one corner, then a trumpet player would stand up in the other corner, and we'd end up with a stereo jam session. That whole time was a fantastic scene—you could walk through downtown and hear live music just about every block.

Looming castlelike at the south end of the University Bridge was a curious jazz outpost, Jerry Heldman's Llahngaelhyn. In the mid-sixties the impossibly spelled hangout nurtured notable emerging talents, and Gary Peacock, Ralph Towner, Dave Friesen, and Larry Coryell were Llahngaelhyn regulars. Jerry Heldman himself was a bassist possessing formidable technique, lyrical tone, and some curious idiosyncrasies. "He had aluminum foil on the walls and ceiling because he was convinced the CIA was listening in on him," said drummer Howard Gilbert. "At one point he encased the piano with foil-covered wooden boards, to prevent FBI laser beams from penetrating. The piano players had to look out through a peephole." The Llahngaelhyn was emphatically about music, not money, a place where harmony and rhythm were stretched beyond familiar boundaries while most of Seattle slept. Pete Leinonen played bass there with guitarist John Day and drummer Jim Murray. "We played the early set," said Pete, "until the touring musicians came in, then we'd jam till five or six in the morning, go to sleep on the floor for a few hours, eat breakfast, then jam some more. We were all family."[17]

Then came the British Invasion and the Psychedelic Revolution, and jazz ran for cover. By 1968 the Llahngaelhyn, Black and Tan, Poop Deck, and Penthouse had closed, and *Seattle* magazine was giving the eulogy: "Jazz hereabouts is dead. The younger crowd—the unmortgaged swingers—are marching to a different drum." Dead? Not quite. "It's a misconception that jazz 'died,'" said trumpeter/saxophonist Jay Thomas.

> It wasn't that jazz was gone—it *changed*. Look, we got South American music, and rock, and pop, and bands like Weather Report. For somebody who was not adaptable, sure, it was bad; there's so many jazz players who don't know how to intersect. But lots of guys kept right on working, and jazz adapted itself to these gigs. I mean, I was out there improvising my face off on "Mister Magic!"[18]

Jay Thomas has been a Seattle jazz eminence since the 1980s. Twenty years before, though, he was just a green kid trumpet player. Not for long; following the footsteps of his father, trumpeter Marvin Thomas, he played his first professional jobs in 1964 and started hitting the jam sessions at the House of Entertainment and the Black and Tan. Then he graduated to the seminal jazz-rock band of organist Dave Lewis, who had started a new vogue with his crossover hit "Little Green Thing." "Dave Lewis was sort of a transitional figure," Jay told me.

> The influence of Ray Charles and Ramsay Lewis and Jimmy Smith was big all over, and Dave came out of that. He really could have jumped out of this pond and become a star. Not only could he play his rock stuff, but he could play standards. Seattle was a funky little backwater, with a strong bluesy influence in its music that came out of those clubs.

Versatile horn players had it good. "Around the Seattle music scene then," said Jay, "just about every dance band—the Counts, Jimmy Hanna's Dynamics, Jimmy Holden's Nightsounds—had sax-and-trumpet front line."

> Mark Doubleday played with a lot of these bands, a fantastic jazz trumpet player. He taught Larry Coryell and people like that how to relax and get a good feel. And Sarge West: he was *unbelievable*. My dad took me to one of the all-night jams at Chuck and Joni Metcalf's house; it was, like, four o'clock in the morning, and Sarge shows up—red hair and these little tiny sunglasses, looking like a dapper little mole—and he takes out his trumpet, and I go, "Oh, my God!" At that point, there were people telling Sarge, "Go to New York. Do not pass 'go. . . .'" But he never did. Doubleday did, and he ended up with Electric Flag, Janis Joplin, and many big-time bands in New York.

Jazz purists who disdained the new sounds created new ways to keep improvised music flowing. One was the Cornish School, which, as it had done for classical music in the twenties, now gave noncommercial jazz a place to renew and reinvent itself. "There was no jazz education in Seattle at all," said Stan Keen, who instituted jazz studies at Cornish in 1963. "The only one in the area was at Olympic College in Bremerton. I was never a jazz player myself, but I felt there ought to be a jazz program that you didn't have to take a ferry ride to get to." Keen enlisted as faculty pianists Jerome Gray and Peter Kok, bassist Chuck Metcalf, trumpeter Floyd Standifer, saxophonist Bob Winn, and drummer George Griffin, and as the Cornish Quintet the faculty group presented jazz as an academic discipline, presenting interpretive concerts and crafting distinctive arrangements to take jazz beyond jamming and to appeal to more structured tastes. The Cornish Quintet's was a two-way legacy: creation of a permanent jazz program that has spawned new talent and a new jazz audience, and a revitalization of one of the Northwest's major arts institutions.[19]

Jazz enthusiasts pitched in, among them disc jockey Jim Wilke, who in 1961 took a job at KING. The erudite public radio personality told me,

> Rock was really starting to push jazz out of the clubs, so about 1965 Irving Clark Jr., Sonny Buxton, Bob Gill, and I started the Seattle Jazz Society. We wanted both to create gigging opportunities for local musicians and to promote performances by them. We talked restaurants into letting us

put in jazz groups once a week; the musicians got the door, the venue got the food and drink receipts, and we'd bring them a crowd. It worked!

By 1970 a new jazz scene was beginning to stir, and with architect/bassist Chuck Metcalf the society opened the Jazz Gallery in the old Llahngaelhyn and inaugurated its popular jazz cruises in the waters around Seattle. Handy was help from high places. Wilke said,

> One of our board members was a promotions guy at Rainier Brewing Company, and bless 'em, they funded a lot of big jazz shows: outdoor concerts in Seward Park, and the Northwest Jazz Spectacular at the Seattle Center. We brought in the Herbie Hancock Quintet, Miles Davis, Cannonball Adderley, Bill Evans, and a young girl singer named Roberta Flack, who was just on her way up at that time. I look back and just shake my head—*wow*!

A jazz savior was Joe Brazil. Arriving from Detroit in 1962, the short, dignified alto saxophonist built a following at the Mardi Gras with fellow Detroiter and vocalist Don "Woody" Woodhouse and Yakima organist Mike Mandel. Recording at Puzzo's Penthouse with John Coltrane, Brazil was inspired to form a new group, the Joe Brazil Sextet, with trumpeter Ed Lee, pianist Lee Anderson, saxophonist Omar Brown, bassists Rufus Reid and Pete Leinonen, and drummer Bobby Tuggle. Brazil (1927–2008) fashioned his own interpretation of Coltrane's aggressively modern, Afrocentric sound and revived jazz as a music of consequence in the black community. With guitarist George Hurst, Brazil started the Brazil Academy of Music in 1967 to nurture young talent. From a church basement at 18th and Marion, Brazil and his faculty—trumpeter/saxophonist/vocalist Floyd Standifer, saxophonist Jabo Ward, and bassist Milt Garred—began passing along jazz techniques and traditions to young players. Brazil wrote music for Seattle's first African American theater group, Black Arts/West, and at the end of the decade began teaching at the University of Washington, which by this time had begun to take jazz seriously. Controversy erupted when Brazil's teaching methods were criticized (he claimed that Beethoven was black) and he was denied tenure. He sued twice and lost, and by the middle of the seventies had moved to Bellingham. Controversial Joe Brazil may have been, but he provided solid musical and life training to young musicians who may have otherwise gone without.

A veteran of jazz, blues, and early funk bands, trumpeter Ed Lee was band director at Garfield and Franklin high schools in the early seventies, helping keep money-starved music programs afloat. He learned much of his craft from Brazil. "Joe was *the* guy," Ed nodded.

> He was the guru! When I got out of the army in '64, I came to Seattle and went to a little club down on First Avenue, and that's where I met Joe. I had been playing in the army band, and so Joe took me right home with him. We played a little bit and listened to tapes, and from then on I was hangin' out with Joe and absorbing all his knowledge. Joe was a breath of fresh air in Seattle! There was a lot of jealousy from the established guys, and they put him down. But the thing was, Joe was connected with *everybody*. In Detroit, Coltrane and McCoy Tyner and all those guys hung out at his house. And Joe saved a whole bunch of guys on dope: got 'em down off the stuff, and then he brought them *up* just by having that place for them, where they could make *music*. We rehearsed there all day long, and as a result there are a lot of guys playing today because of his influence. When Joe started teaching at the UW, his methods were viewed as very nontraditional, which they were. And that was a *good* thing. I mean, he brought whole bands into his class—he brought Sun Ra to class! I was in Joe's group, and he'd bring us in and have us demonstrate playing different ideas on chord changes, and talk about the whole process of playing *jazz*. It was a tremendous inspiration for young musicians.

Elsewhere, jazz hung on by softening its edges, and in cocktail lounges across the city pianists, organists, and combos dispensed sophisticated sounds while keeping customers and cash registers happy. A master of the formula was Chuck Mahaffay, a suave, white-haired drummer/clarinetist/singer and lounge mainstay. Mahaffay came from Helena, Montana, in 1948 to study clarinet at the University of Washington, and at the school's Club Encore talent shows was discovered by Norm Bobrow, who hired him for Jazz at the Cirque concerts. (Mahaffay also produced his own Concerts in Miniature jazz shows during the fifties.) Playing bass with him was Tamara Burdette, who learned much of her trade from Mahaffay. "Chuck had no formal training," she told me in her Shoreline home—"no 'chops.'"

But he was very, very musical, and what he presented was strictly from himself. He would play clarinet riffs and drum things that no one else would play. He taught you things like looking good, not showing up drunk, knowing what you're going to play, knowing your tempos, your keys. Respect your audience: establish eye contact, keep the pace going. A lot of musicians forget these things, then wonder why they're not working.

The Mahaffay style required musicians to set aside their preconceptions. "Our repertoire," said Burdette, "was standards, Latin, and light jazz. Cocktail music: 'What Kind of Fool Am I?' 'Desafinado.'"

> We always kept it danceable, but we also stretched out and soloed. We were working at the Casa Villa, and Chuck called me: "You're going to start singing." I was very righteous about being a *bass player*, and I told him, "I don't *sing!*" He said, "If you want to keep working, you're sing-ing—*tonight*." Okay; that night I sang "Why Don't You Do Right?" I'm shaking in my boots, but it wasn't more than a couple of months before you couldn't keep me away from the microphone. The same went for Larry Coryell: "Larry, you're singing too." Larry, who of course went on to do great things, called Chuck his main mentor.

Mahaffay opened his young bassist's eyes to some harsh entertainment realities. Burdette said,

> The Casa Villa was a hip kind of scene, but being a woman, I'd get hassled. One night there were a couple of guys sitting at the bar and throwing lots of money around. They thought they were some kind of "rounders" and got fresh with me. I went to Chuck and said, "Tell them to knock it off!" He said, "I can do that. I can go to the owner and com-plain. But here's what will happen: We'll lose our job. So just go in the bathroom and wait till this guy leaves. I know it's not fair, but is this one jerk worth losing our gig over?" No, he wasn't.

Unfortunately, Mahaffay disregarded his own counsel on one high-profile gig. According to Burdette,

> A restaurant owner wanted to boost the nighttime business at his place on the waterfront, so he hired us. He demanded a three-month contract.

The less-than-glamorous venue of a Washington State ferry hosts the Chuck Mahaffay Quartet in the mid-sixties. Entertaining partygoers are pianist Danny Lowell, bassist Tammy Burdette, Mahaffay, and vibraphonist Bill Franklin. Courtesy of Tamara Burdette

Chuck preferred two weeks, but this guy insisted on three, so we went in there, and it took about a month for the word to get out, but after that we had the place jumping. The owner, a very well-known Seattle personality, came in one night and sat down at the bar, taking it all in. The place was packed—you could hardly move. At the end of the set he came over to us: "You're fired. Get out." Whaaa? We had made a success of his room, just like he said he wanted, right? No; he could not stand the fact that *he* wasn't the one who had made it a success. We still had half our contract to go, so Chuck took him to the union and we got paid for the three months. Great. Only, the guy badmouthed Chuck so much that he lost a lot of work after that. He should have taken his own advice. Sure, he was right, but the bottom line is, the price was too high. It wasn't fair, but who said this was gonna be fair?

To ears accustomed to plenty of low end, it's easy to forget that music was not always bass-heavy. Double bassists were few in early Seattle; compared with fiddle and cornet, the viol's bulk and grumpy personality discouraged intimacy, public transport was cramped or nonexistent, and long uphill walks would have further discouraged prospective bassists. Penny-pinching saloons and theaters were often content to leave the bottom end to the piano. Still, bassists are a determined breed, and their infectious bowing wormed its way steadily into Seattle's fabric. With the twentieth century came affluence, mobility, and syncopated dance music, bringing the cumbersome doghouse new importance.

When the Creole Orchestra came to town in 1914, bassist Bill Johnson dropped jaws with his percussive slapping technique. San Francisco bandleader Sid LeProtti exclaimed after hearing him, "We was kinda amazed out here in the West to see a man pick a bass!" (Amazed but also disgusted were bassists who, after hearing Johnson, realized that their job had just gotten a lot harder.) Because it recorded better on early equipment and was louder, the tuba displaced the string bass in dance bands of the twenties, but yielded again to the viol when swing and electrical recording came in after 1930. In the long line of Seattle bassists, some were mere tub-thumpers, but many—Percy Johnson, Adolphus Alsbrook, James Harnett, Gary Steele—were superb and versatile players. Al Larkins was known among black musicians for his fine bowing technique, and Gary Peacock, Freddy Schreiber, and Chuck Metcalf are legendary for taking the bass far beyond its presumed capabilities. For many Seattleites, the bass viol was synonymous with Leslie "Tiny" Martin, who as a neophyte played in the Gay Jones Orchestra, joined the symphony after the war, and with accordionist Frank Sugia and violinist Mori Simon formed the beloved Frederick and Nelson Christmas Minstrels. The latter spot assured that the portly virtuoso with the endearing grin would be the first bass fiddler many a Seattle toddler, myself included, would hear.[20]

Tamara Burdette's father, Vaughn Abbey, was a patriarch of Seattle bassists. Working with the symphony and dance bands from the thirties through the sixties, he bridged the eras from tuba to string bass to bass guitar. "Dad was *the* tuba player in Seattle for forty years," Tammy told me.

He was born on a farm in Waitsburg, Washington, and came to Seattle in the late thirties. Souders, Hoagy, Cloud—every band in town hired him. He took me along to his jobs, and I saw ice shows and circuses and the Aqua Follies sitting beside Dad, watching the action and following the music. The circus was the hardest—*oompah oompah oompah!*—and if you're not reading four bars ahead, you're dead. Dad used to be completely drained after a show. He wanted me to be a concert pianist, so I played piano in the school orchestra. There were already fifteen piano players, so I went to the music room locker and saw two instruments in there—an oboe and a bass. I took the bass. Dad yelled, "Nooooo!'

Father fell in line:

Once Dad knew my mind was made up, though, he was behind me all the way, and got me lessons with Tiny Martin. After a couple of years of study I was eager to start playing out, so Dad had me sub for him. He was working with the Esquires at the Washington Athletic Club every Friday and Saturday. These were the best guys in town—Ronald Phillips and Johnnie Jessen and Tubby Clark—and here I am, a fourteen-year-old kid. I couldn't even drive yet—someone had to take me to jobs. But I got to wear high heels and a cocktail dress and makeup! The first song I played was "Out of Nowhere"; when I first put the music up, I thought, "I am never gonna forget this." A few of the WAC board members' wives didn't like having a woman in the band, but the guys stuck by me.

Like Ed Gross, Burdette was early to amplify. "Amplifying the bass was getting to be a necessity," Tammy explained, "since bands were getting louder and you couldn't hear the bass except in the parking lot. I started using an amp about 1958, one of those classic Ampegs with the tubes on top. Dad made a wooden enclosure with a round speaker in it, and it had a nice, natural sound." By 1969 Tammy found that Seattle was running low on non-rock gigs, and headed for LA. She lucked into almost twenty years of work, but had some adjusting to do.

As soon as I got there I discovered I'd better learn electric bass, *fast*. I took lessons from Carol Kaye, a major studio player. All those TV shows from the sixties and seventies, that's Carol playing bass. Ray Charles used her a lot, and I mean *used*. I met Ray Brown, and he pointed me toward Howlett Smith, a piano player who had a steady gig at Sterling's in Santa Monica. I worked with Smitty for fifteen years, four nights a week. Smitty's was the perfect gig—it never got stale. We were constantly adding material: learn a new song every Tuesday, do it that night. Smitty was blind, and he figured that since he couldn't read, nobody else should read music on the job, either. Around 1988 LA got hit by an earthquake and a fire, so I came back to Seattle.

Burdette succeeded in a male-heavy profession through her own determination and some fatherly advice. "As a woman musician," she said, "you have to speak up for yourself—and carry your own gear.

Dad told me at the outset, "Carry your own instrument. They're not gonna take you seriously unless you do." Once you've gotten that out of the way and everybody knows you're serious, you can get help from anyone, because they know you're serious. The most uncomfortable I ever felt was with women singers who hated being upstaged by the bass player. *They* wanted to be the "star."

Tammy's father gave her another suggestion, which many other musicians would affirm:

Dad said, "Learn how to do something beside music. Just in case." So I went to business college and learned how to be a secretary. That has saved my hide more than once. I don't care how dedicated you are—give yourself a backup. Music makes the most wonderful *second* career. I raised my son on music. But you live on a two-week basis, and you have to realize that when you go into it. Music has been good to my soul. Not to my pocket. But very good to my soul.

SOUL SEARCHERS

In pre–World War II Seattle, the blues was a word occasionally glimpsed on a record label. Dee Dee Hackett and other cabaret singers sang blues at Doc Hamilton's, but more commercial pop songs were preferred in a time when many upwardly striving African Americans considered the blues an unwelcome reminder of a dark past. Three thousand miles from the Mississippi Delta, Seattle was simply not a blues town.

The arrival of thousands of southern blacks during the war changed that. Between 1940 and 1950 Seattle's black community jumped from not quite four thousand to over fifteen thousand residents and, in the words of historian Quintard Taylor, "acquired a decidedly southern ambience." The newcomers brought with them records of Meade Lux Lewis, Lionel Hampton, and Louis Jordan: artists revving the blues into a jumping dance music that would become a defining idiom of American pop. In the bottle clubs of Yesler Hill, swing gave way to a sound that by 1949 disc jockeys were calling "rhythm and blues." The sepia-toned tenor saxophone was the instrumental voice of African American blues, and in the fifties Billy Tolles was boss tenor. Blaring long and loud into the hot summer nights, the onetime Savoy Boy mixed bebop, blues, and standards for roistering biracial crowds.[21]

"Billy was an aggressive, funny, outgoing cat and an excellent entertainer," said trombonist Don Glenn, who in 1952 joined Tolles and trumpeter Floyd Standifer on the front line.

> We played the military bases and the social club dances downtown at the Chamber of Commerce. This was a very big deal then. The top five or six black social clubs—doctors, lawyers—would rent the Chamber ballroom every Saturday night and bring in big crowds. Billy knew how to please them; he could play bebop while folks were dancing, then shift into a blues, and then sing a ballad. People loved him.

As R&B took hold in the late fifties, Tolles went for a heavier style of backbeat blues and shuffle he'd picked up at college in the East and dug in at the taverns of East Yesler, Union, and Madison with drummer Tommy Adams and young Dave Holden, son of the legendary Oscar. Jazz purists dismissed the Tolles band as sellouts for playing "that funky butt stuff," but their gigs were packed with neighborhood steppers, and the college kids shrieked in delight when Tolles walked the bar, blasting "Shake, Rattle and Roll."

Tall, handsome, and eternally youthful, Dave Holden looked back happily telling me of his musical baptism:

> Our family home was up at 14th and Fir, where everything was happening. We had Ayers Café at 13th and Yesler, the Rocking Chair at 14th and Washington, and Washington Hall right across the street. I ran my paper route in the whole area, and I'd be deliverin' my papers and listenin' to Ray Charles inside the Rockin' Chair, singin' like Nat King Cole. Yeah! So I got bit by the music bug early on. Dad did not actually teach me, but when he sat down and played "Flight of the Bumblebee," the boogie woogie version, that was the first music I heard that really made me

want to play. Because we had a piano in the house, Dad's bands and the Bumps Blackwell Junior Band would rehearse right in the house, with Quincy Jones and Ernestine Anderson and all these others. Us kids'd get up on the piano and start bangin' around, so it was a case of us comin' by our music naturally.

Holden was fortunate, too, in belonging to a school district that continued to reflect the long, progressive legacy of former superintendent Frank B. Cooper, and in attending a school that offered young people of all backgrounds a quality education at a time when minority students elsewhere often got short shrift. "I went to Garfield High during 1956 to 1958," Dave affirmed, "and right away I found it to be a very special place. There were all kinds of kids going to Garfield at that time: Chinese, Japanese, Filipino, black, Jewish. We *all* got along, all the time. We didn't realize how good it was until we left there."

Dave's sister, Grace, also went to Garfield, and acknowledged the importance of its music program:

Dr. Parker Cook, just a little bitty white man, was the music teacher, and I tell you—there was none like him. He never looked down or talked down to anybody, and he had a music program that encouraged you to develop, musically, *in our own style*. Therefore, there came the *beginning* of jazz band at Garfield High School. I got my start playing piano there in the jazz band, and also was a singer in the Nonettes, which Dr. Cook directed. He was a wonderful inspiration.

Though she developed her own talents as a keyboardist and vocalist, Grace Holden stayed largely within her father's orbit, subbing for him on gigs and caring for him after his beloved Leala passed away in 1951. Grace echoed Dave in recounting how their talented parents coped in a restrictive society:

Mom and Pop both played *popular* music. That's what they got paid for. At home they played Tchaikovsky. They played *Rachmaninov*. But I never saw them express any frustration over things as they were, and over not having the opportunity to play classical music. If they did, they didn't let us know it. I think it began with my dad: His goal in life was to leave the South *in* the South. And, in his words, he told *me* that it was his intent to not marry until, when he had children, they would be born *free*. He even refused to play Dixieland music. Pop was always a very strong union man. He *believed* in union! Because unions had *laws*. And he had great respect for law—in *structure*. His attitude about anything and everything was that it had to have structure. For African Americans in those days, for him to have the mind to become a human being in a free society—that was vital to him.

Dave Holden took his father's talent and fortitude and fashioned a long and lucrative musical career.

While I was still in Garfield I started out playing little school gigs, and even worked some fraternity gigs at the University of Washington. Then, about 1958, I got my big break. I was walkin' home one night after attending class at Everett Community College, and I hear this music down the street. I thought, "Boy, that really sounds *good*." That music was comin' from Ayers Café, at 13th and Yesler, so I went and stood there outside the door listening to the music. The door flew open and a guy stumbled out, staggered over to his car, and drove away. I peeked my head in and I see Billy Tolles and Tommy Adams sittin' there all sad, like, "Man, what are we gonna do now?" Well, the guy stumblin' out the door, who I thought was some drunk, actually was the keyboard player, Mike Taylor, and he had just come down with the Asiatic Flu! So the band was minus a piano. I peeked my head in, and Billy Tolles looked right at me and said, "Ain't you one o' them Holden boys?" "Yes sir, I'm a Holden." "Well, don't you play the piano?" And I had been playin' around a little, so I said, "Yes sir, I can play a little." Billy says, "Well, come on in here and play!" I only knew three songs. Three songs and the blues. But I went in there and sat down and played one number, and Billy and Tommy got in on the beat and they made it *happen*. I didn't know what *I* was doin', but *they* made it happen! And people started *lookin'* at me and sayin', "Oh, that's that young Holden boy." Made me feel like I was somethin', even if I didn't know nothin'. And the club owner was over there smokin' his cigar and clappin'—"Yeah! Young Holden!"

After three weeks of Tolles's tutelage, young Holden absorbed the fine points of keyboard playing, singing, and engaging an audience. He was ready to work.

At this point, Holden was introduced to the instrument that would get him plenty of work, and set him apart from other Seattle keyboardists.

Ben Beasley, who owned the Mardi Gras Grill on 22nd and Madison, called my dad and said, "I hear you got a son who plays piano. Tell him I want him to come over here." So I went over there, and he says, "I want you to play this thing." What he had there was a Lowrey Organo: a keyboard that sets over the piano keys and makes it sound like an organ. And there was Vernon Brown and Jabo Ward, and they're sayin', "Come on, young boy, we'll help you." So I'm gettin' into the groove of the thing, and Jabo's playin' his butt off and smiling, and Vernon's playin' his butt off on the drums and smiling. And me, I was ecstatic—I had a gig! Now, at the time I'm only eighteen, nineteen years old. Not even drinking age! But the fact that I was not yet drinking age never caused any problems, because the club owners would talk to the beat cops. "We'll take care of him," they would say—"We won't let him drink." And so they let me, 'cause I'm a Holden. They know my dad, they know my mom.

At the swinging Mardi Gras, young Dave was in fast company:

Sam Cooke was in town with his big hit, "You Send Me," and he came in one night. They get him up on stage and he asks me, "Do you know 'You Send Me'? "No." I had not even *heard* it on the radio yet. Sam says, "It's just 'ice cream' changes: E-flat, C, F, B-flat." So, I played that, and it worked out—*bam*! But it was really that Lowrey Organo that gave me my advantage, 'cause there wasn't very many of 'em around, and I don't think anybody else in Seattle played it. And, the way I played, pretty soon I was workin' the bass in the left hand, and we were *rocking*! People used to come to hear me play the Organo from all over: up from San Francisco and Los Angeles and Portland, and all over the Northwest. Yeah!

Holden and Billy Tolles reunited to play Dave's Fifth Avenue during the world's fair, then headed south to become one of the top acts on the sixties West Coast lounge circuit. Along the way, the group developed an earthier sound. "That was when we started changing our thing," Holden related, "and we started playing the old kind of blues and rhythm stuff like Little Willie John, B. B. King, Arthur Prysock. More of the old funky-type things."

Holden at the Hammond: Dave Holden's trio holds a lounge crowd's attention in the late sixties. Singing is Virginia "V. J." Jackson, and at the drums is Pete Depoe, who went on to feature his unique "King Kong beat" in the band Redbone. Courtesy of Dave Holden

Billy Tolles was the greatest, and he played different things and changed things when nobody else would. Some folks got down on Billy for changing the way he played, and the reason he did it was because I was capable of it. I was younger and I wanted to play some of these other things. When I would rehearse with him, I'd say, "How 'bout this? How 'bout that?" And he'd say, "Yeah!" Tommy Adams was a wonderful drummer who also happened to sing beautifully, just like Billy Eckstein; he would put the little funky twist in it, and our *whole sound* changed."

Billy Tolles settled in Denver in the seventies and Holden went solo, pioneering the use of electronic keyboard racks later used by rock bands. "I was workin' the Hollywood Palladium and the Grove and the Name of the

Game, and I myself was considered the hottest act in L.A. I went right on, to Hawaii, Japan, England. And I know I was damn lucky to be one of the kids of Oscar and Leala Holden."

In the sixties Seattle's black community was energized by the widening struggle for civil rights. Declaring that "action by negroes is the word of the day," *The Facts* newspaper debuted in 1962 as a new forum for African American issues, and Gregory Huguley encouraged black artists and musicians to express themselves with pride, hosting showcases to rouse the "sleeping giant of Afro-American culture." Now, too, the black community could enjoy round-the-clock gospel, rhythm and blues, and jazz on its own radio stations KZAM and KYAC. Along East Yesler, Union, and Madison, the excitement poured from the clubs—Jolly Seven, Tiki, Red Rooster—as rhythm and blues slid into soul and "organ bands" of a pulsating Hammond B-3 and tenor sax throbbed into the wee hours.

The guitar was not left out. From his stand at the Soul Cellar, guitarist "Boss" George Hurst sent the blues wailing out onto First Avenue. "Playing with Boss George at the Soul Cellar was one of the great experiences of my career," smiled bassist Pete Leinonen.

> George was a fabulous player and all-round entertainer. He would kick off a funky blues vamp in his driving, southern style and work it for fifteen minutes, then move it up a half step, work that another fifteen minutes, then kick it up another step. That one song would constitute an hour's set.[22]

Taking the guitar into new grooves with Hurst was David "Guitar Shorty" Kearney, who arrived in 1960 full of Chicago blues. Kearney came of age inspired by B. B. King and T-Bone Walker, and was working Chicago's gritty south-side clubs when he was discovered by Willie Dixon. He recorded "Irma Lee" and "You Don't Treat Me Right," toured with Ray Charles and Guitar Slim, and developed a flamboyant and acrobatic presentation complete with somersaults and behind-the-head picking. "Shorty was *the* blues scene here in the sixties," said Gary Hammon, who backed Kearney on tenor.

> Jimi Hendrix and all those guys used to hang out with him up there at the Blue Post Tavern at 18th and Madison, and Hendrix took a lot of his style right from him. With Shorty, it was *shuffles* all the time. Whoever

David "Guitar Shorty" Kearney led a seminal blues band in the early
sixties. Left to right are John Keski, Kearney, Jordan Ruwe, James Adams,
and Ed Lee (top). Courtesy of Ed Lee

his drummer was, he had to be able to play a shuffle, because that's
where the energy was. A lot of the material was songs he had written, but
he had all kinds of standard blues and pop songs, too. Then Shorty would
do his show routine: go out and kick his feet up in the air, roll over, and
pick his guitar behind his back. Shorty was a *real* blues player.

Guitar Shorty was one of many taking rhythm and blues in a new direction. "We were playin' the crossover before it became popular," Ed Lee,

Kearney's trumpet player, said to me. "All the same kind of stuff that Miles Davis got into, we were doing here. We would play these funky blues, but then we'd put in these hip jazz lines." Gary Hammon chimed in with other innovators:

> When you look at R&B becoming funk, it was Big John Patton that led that. In the sixties, the organ players here all patterned themselves after Big John. He was from Kansas City, Kansas, and wrote "Personality," which Lloyd Price made a hit. You also got to remember Dave Lewis, who was a real pioneer with his organ sound, and you also had Ron Buford and International Love, and my own group, the Regents. Jimmy Hanna and the Dynamics were playin' funk out at Parker's Ballroom. They had a hit record, "New York Philly," with Lawrence Wilson as featured soloist. See, that sound was big with both black and white customers, and so we worked all over town: Blue Post Tavern, YMCA, out in West Seattle at the Embers, Birdland, the District Tavern. Man, there was so much music back then!

Grinding away night after night, year after year, Billy Tolles and Dave Holden and Ed Lee were transforming a white, northern European city. They had legions of cohorts across the land, and by 1960 the great African American music revolution was reaching critical mass, leading America into a new tonal sensibility: less major, more minor, deeper, earthier, richer. Black society itself was transformed by its music, growing stronger, more confident, proud. The power of the blues brought Seattle and all America to a better place. And for one underage white boy who had been weaned on Duke Ellington and Johnny Hodges, it was deeply satisfying to stand in an alcove across from the Soul Cellar on a rainy night and hear that sound at home on old First Avenue.

Far—yet not so far—from the world of nightclubs and funk is another world, one that has been of primary importance to the survival and ultimate triumph of black America: the church. The spirituals that Seattle heard from the Nashville Students in 1884 were taken up by the first black congregations—Mt. Zion Baptist, First A.M.E—of the East Madison neighborhood in the 1890s. In the thirties "Dwelling in Beulah Land" and "Brighten the Corner" were sung loud in charismatic storefront churches such as the Full Gospel Pentecostal Mission and Father Divine's Temple of Peace. The influx of southern African Americans in the forties brought gospel song into full cry, and by 1960 Mt. Zion, First A.M.E., Ebenezer A.M.E. Zion, and Immaculate Conception boasted superb gospel choirs. Radio stations KZAM and KYAC played gospel heavily, and choirs traveled up and down the West Coast in spirited competition. "Next to the Bible," Mt. Zion Baptist minister Reverend Samuel McKinney told me, "the hymn book has been the greatest repository of Christian faith in our church. In the late thirties, the Cleveland a cappella gospel choir Wings Over Jordan was an important inspiration for what you might call 'old school' gospel, and then in more recent times 'new school' has come up, influenced by non-church music. Seattle has been a crossroads for a lot of this activity."[23]

One who came to this crossroads was Patrinell Staten, who stepped off a bus in 1964, eager to sing the Lord's praise in her own way. The twenty-year-old did not find it easy: "I always had *attitude*," she told me in her East Cherry meeting hall, chuckling. "Like when I first got off the bus there at the Trailways station, my sister met me and I blurted out in this rather loud voice, 'Where are all the black folks?' She had to shut me up and get me *out* of there!" In the gray, northern city Staten found a well-established church music culture:

> When I came to Seattle, the person who was at the forefront of gospel was Mae Campbell. Mae was the president of Local number 8 of the Singers Association of America. Local 8 had chapters all over the West, and they put on annual conventions, with choirs from everyplace. The male gospel groups—a lot of them were called "quartets," but they might have six or eight members—were especially big then. Timothy Weatherly and Burl Garnett had extremely wonderful male quartets here in Seattle. But Mae Campbell, she had a *great* choir. Hoo-*wee*!

Chance and a little parental persuasion pushed Staten into music at an early age. "God gave me the gift of being musical," she nodded, "and I took that gift with gratitude."

> When I was a girl in Carthage, Texas, I would sit at our old piano and fool around. One day I was tinkling around on this hymn and my father heard me. Well, it so happened that there was to be a funeral reception in our home, and the piano player was late. So my father tells me, "*You* play until she gets here." I'm thinkin', "Me? I don't play!" But he had

heard me play this one little hymn with one finger, so I was trapped. Back then, you did *not* argue with your parents. So I played that one little hymn, with my one finger. Afterward, I taught myself to play that hymn with three fingers on the right hand, and by the end of the week I had picked up one finger on the left. By the end of two weeks, I was *playin'* the piano! I became my father's minister of music and played for two choirs in his church. The gospel music down south, when I was a girl, had that *waing* to it—that old-fashioned *waing*. In Texas we sang a lot of hymns, just as they were written. Nothin' fancy. You'd clap your hands every now and then, but not as part of the music. Up here, you're clappin' your hands and swayin', and they want to know what's wrong with you if you don't. But the old way was, "don't deviate." And that started gettin' me in trouble! Because I played what was in my head, and what was on that page didn't mean anything to me. My daddy did not go along with that—*no!*—but it got so people would come to our Pleasant Valley Missionary Church 'cause they knew they were gonna get a swinging choir. At last, my father gave up: "Okay, girl, go ahead and do what you got to do." I was not a pioneer; freestyle gospel was already being sung, I just didn't know about it. I had no idea that I was doing what the choirs on the East Coast were already doing. When I went back east later, to my surprise I saw that those folks were singing the same way *we* sang.

However talented, the new arrival got a chilly reception in Seattle.

The scene I found when I came into the black churches was kind of closed. Everybody had their own little set ways of doing things, and, if you didn't like it, too bad. Because I was fairly gifted, I had all this *confidence,* so if I was given the opportunity to do something, I did it with *mucho gusto.* In the black church, they ask if there's anyone in the congregation who has a talent they'd like to share. Well, when I got up and showed what I could do, I ran into a little thing called "jealousy." I started getting kicked out of churches, which was okay with me. I mean, you have to make your own way. But I'd go and do my thing, and after a while that would get me kicked out of one more church!

Unwelcome in churches, Staten started a band. Guiding her was another formidable talent:

It was Luvera Clark who created my rhythm and blues group, the Valentinos. She heard me sing in church and asked if I would sing with her company, Sepia Records. I thought, "Why the heck not? The churches are treatin' me bad, so I might as well try something else!" I signed with Luvera in 1968, and she sat me right down and said, "I'm gonna take care of you, and you're gonna take care of *me*." I told her, "I'm not a dive singer. I'm not singin' in taverns," so she did not book us in taverns. Luvera was a very *hard* woman, but she had been around enough to know how hard *Seattle* was, too. She had some very good artists who couldn't even sing in white clubs, and we're talkin' about the "liberal North." She had gone to these clubs and they had thrown her out on her face. So we had to do what black folks always do: We had to sing to each other. Luvera would say, "You're either gonna get it right, or you're gonna get it wrong. But I'm gonna *pay* you to get it right. If you get it *wrong*, then you're gone." Our band was strictly R&B: my gospel voice in front, organ, guitar, bass, and four background singers. We had a wonderful career, and I probably made more money then than I was making at the bank where I was working. All our music was completely original; Luvera wrote *eons* of songs, and she'd pull one out: "This will fit your voice." I'd say, "Okay, let's see what happens." Well, what happened was, Pat Staten and the Valentinos worked from Vancouver, BC, to LA. Not taverns— *clubs*. At that time we still had some pretty nice clubs here for black folks, like the Ebonee and the Cotton Club. We were very popular, which got me kicked out of church again: "Can't sing the devil's music and God's music at the same time!"

Pat Staten and the Valentinos enjoyed success and recognition. Unfortunately, they also encountered the all-too-prevalent venality of the recording industry.

In '69 Luvera Clark and I penned a little number called "I Let a Good Man Go," and the flip side is called "Little Love Affair." It recently resurfaced in Europe, where they'd been playing it for disco! Somebody from London e-mailed me: "Are you Patrinell Staten who does this 45?" "Yes, I am." "Well, I dance to it every night." She came all the way here from over there to see who I was, and brought me a copy of the disco CD. Some lawyers took my case *pro bono*—they couldn't believe that this was happening to somebody *right now*, like it doesn't matter that I'm still alive! Which happens to a lot of black artists from back in the day: Their music is stolen from them all the time. Not only did the lawyers stop it, they made 'em pay all the charges!

FOLK SCARE

When the Pacific Northwest Folklore Society was snubbed for engaging Pete Seeger in 1954, the folk scene entered a quiet period of house concerts and informal "hoots." The lull ended in 1958, when Bob Clark, owner of the Guild 45th Theater, opened Seattle's first espresso café, The Place Next Door, next door. Clark hired folk singers on weekends and was soon overrun by crowds in T-shirts, tuxedos, and evening gowns. By 1960 The Place Next Door was joined by the Pamir Espresso House on University Way and El Matador in the Eastlake neighborhood. Seattle had a new folk music community.

On certain evenings in 1961, a shy and waiflike girl fresh off the bus from Lake Chelan could be seen standing outside the Pamir House. Alice Stuart laughed as she remembered her scary start as an interpreter of folk songs and blues. "It took me a couple of days just to get the courage to go in," she told me in her Tumwater home.

> The whole place was painted black, even the windows. I was a small town girl—I had not been other places at all—and when you walked through the door, everyone turned around and *looked* at you. Finally, I got up the nerve and walked in with a baritone ukulele and about ten Burl Ives songs. I sat down and listened to the music, and after a while I asked, "Do you think I could play a couple of songs?" I sang one of my Burl Ives songs, probably "I Had a Little Dog, His Name Was Blue," and everybody was very gracious. There were no microphones, people sat on stools. Whoever was there, if it was *their* show they'd invite you up to do a couple of songs. Everybody had "their" songs—Don Firth had "Katie Moury," Mike Atwood had "Seven Daffodils"—and you did not do "their" song. I became a regular, five or six nights a week, and we'd play till about midnight, then go to somebody's house and play till four or five in the morning. The owner, John Timmons, paid us three or four bucks a night, so we lived on nineteen-cent hamburgers.

Alice Stuart, Dallas Williams, and Bill Sheldon at Pamir Espresso House, 1962. Courtesy of Alice Stuart

Alice Stuart was an early bird among the legions of young white musicians who would fall under the spell of southern blues during the 1960s.

One of the Pamir gang had an apartment filled with records, and he'd play Blind Willie McTell and Rabbit Brown and other old blues albums. And then Dallas Williams came to town and introduced me to the records of Bessie Smith. Hearing them was like a lightbulb going on: *"That's* what I want to do!" Outside of the black community, I was one of the only ones playing blues then. I started doing finger-picking stuff— "Statesboro Blues," "Stack 'o Lee"—and it went over great. Blues always has. I kept track of what got the most audience response, and every time I'd do something slightly bluesy, people liked it. After about a year at the Pamir House, Steve Lalor and Mike Hall and I put together a trio we called the Upper University District Folk Music Association, Mandolin Society, and Glee Club. We all sang, worked out arrangements, and practiced constantly. Steve Lalor was into the more gritty side of things, while Mike was more into the prettier side, and we also were getting into contemporary folk: things like "House in New Orleans," which the Animals made into "House of the Rising Sun." People would say, "Oh, that's that Animals song," but we did it first. Playing El Matador, which was a kind of upscale houseboat on Lake Union, and Stan James's Corroboree on 45th—the old Place Next Door—got us a lot of attention, and in 1963 we hosted the "Hootenanny" TV show at the Seattle Center.

All the acclaim prompted Stuart to strike out on her own, and she drove to Los Angeles, where she found a different vibe:

They liked my music, but down there they expected something a little more show-biz-y—"Hey, folks, for my next number. . . . " That was not me. I never *talked* to the audience; I figured they were there to hear me sing, not talk. But the director of the Berkeley Folk Festival heard me, and next thing I knew I was in the '64 festival, and scared to *death*. I mean, here I was with Mississippi John Hurt and Joan Baez! But I did all right, and after the festival, the director, Barry Olivier, decided he was gonna be my manager. That would've been great if he'd have known that being a manager means more than just booking gigs. But at the time I was an emotional nightmare, and he seemed to figure the more I worked, the more I'd overcome my shyness. So he sent me to New York and Philadelphia. I'd go into a deli—I was a country girl; I'd never been in a *deli* before! They'd yell: "C'man, lady, whaddya want?" I'd walk out in tears. I was living in fleabag hotels, paying my own expenses; I had no friends. None of the other musicians even invited me to their homes or to hang out—they were all getting into pot and drugs, and I didn't, so they shut me out. I found out later they thought I was a cop! I did get invited to be on Judy Collins's radio show, and I was on Dick Cavett. If I'd had confidence back then, I think I could've been huge. I have a lot of empathy for people who make it when they're young, before they know what's going on. People like Jim Morrison and Janis Joplin—they couldn't handle it. They hadn't developed the presence of mind, you know? I think I was spared, that I didn't become big fast. It would've killed me.

Back on the West Coast, Stuart dug in, honed her natural affinity for the blues, and after paying some dues was welcomed as the real thing.

I moved to the Bay Area and started working at some of the folk clubs and playing on Bill Graham's "Family Dog" shows. By then I was playing electric guitar, and I got signed with Fantasy Records. Their studio was manned by a lot of black engineers and producers, and I began hanging out with them at the black clubs in Richmond. I was the only white person in there, and sometimes the bands would invite me to come up and sit in with them. The customers would look at me playing the blues—"What's *she* doing here?" Finally they got used to me and were very accepting. I started writing my own songs in '68, and my first Fantasy album, *Full Time Woman*, was all my own stuff. Jerry Wexler, at Atlantic Records, called my song "Full Time Woman" an "icon," and he wanted Aretha Franklin to do it. It didn't appeal to her, unfortunately—we'd be living in a better house by now if it had!—but Irma Thomas and Jackie de Shannon covered it.

Stuart spent the next years touring, recording, and playing one-nighters, and all the while her Seattle friends begged her to come home. In 1989 she did: "I built myself back up, one gig at a time, and I've finally gotten to the point where I can say to myself, 'I'm not doing this just for money any-more.' I keep playing because I *have* to. It's why I get up in the morning."

The Century 21 Exposition did not overlook folk music. In a neglected corner of the fair, the staff of the United Nations Pavilion fretted over ways to attract visitors, and jumped at the suggestion of folk singers. "Us folk-ies would gather there about 2 o'clock on Sunday," said singer Don Firth, "and start singing in relays. We got bigger and bigger crowds, and suddenly a *lot* of us were getting offers. I got about half a dozen concert jobs from people who came and liked what they heard." The end of the fair did not end the music, and when the Seattle Center opened on the fairgrounds in the spring of 1963, management once again pondered ways to populate the site. With ABC's "Hootenanny" television show enjoying high ratings, promoter Len Hansen proposed doing a local knock-off, and the ensuing Wednesday evening telecasts from the Center grounds were the highlight of the summer. "I sang there one evening when police estimated the crowd at nearly six thousand," Firth told me. "Vivian Williams had just recently come back from winning a fiddling contest—the first woman ever to win. She and her husband, Phil, had a bluegrass band called the Turkey Pluck-ers, and their signature number was 'Orange Blossom Special.' It became well known later on, but it wasn't then, and when Vivian cut loose on the fiddle, the crowd went insane."[24]

Phil and Vivian Williams came to Seattle hot on the trail of American roots music. Multi-instrumentalists and singers, the Williamses played grange dances in Idaho and Oregon as teens in the early 1950s, then received further inspiration at Oregon's progressive Reed College. "Reed is a very open place that had, and continues to have, lots of folk music concerts," Phil told me.

> Pete Seeger rang a very responsive chord there, because everyone was into the social justice issues that he sang about. Odetta came and sang stuff from *her* background, blues and rural songs. When we first started coming to Seattle in 1957, the folkies would hang out at Gordon Tracie's Folklore Center, holding hoots in the back room and singing songs like "The Golden Vanity" and "Barbara Allen" in all ninety-seven verses. It was a very small group of academics and college kids, mostly playing for each other. There was no "authentic" folk talent here that we could see— all these folks were learning songs from *Child's Ballads* and *We Sing*. The people we were interested in did not learn their songs from books, but were carrying on an oral tradition from a family or community, and we had the feeling that, if Seattle and Puget Sound had any indigenous folk traditions, they were "underground" in church halls and homes.

In 1962 Phil and Vivian were Pamir House regulars as a guitar-auto-harp-vocal duo. By then they had discovered a true folk community. "There were a bunch of people living in the Darrington area," Vivian said—"'Tarheels.' These were folks from the Carolinas who had lost their logging work when the Great Smoky Mountain National Park was created. They came out here during the Second World War to log and work in the defense plants, and they brought their music with them." Gordon Tracie and his Seattle Folklore Center also had a hand in establishing bluegrass in Seattle. "The Darrington people found out they could get records of their music at Gordon's store," Vivian continued, "and they were some of his best customers. In fact, when he opened the Folklore Center in '56, Gordon got a flatbed truck and hired some of the Darrington folks like Fred McCalls to play."

When Appalachian musicians met Seattle enthusiasts, Northwest bluegrass was born. "Vivian and I went to Darrington in 1960 and met the Tarheels," Phil said, "and it changed our lives. In 1962 we put together a bluegrass band, the Turkey Pluckers, and did our first gig at The Place

Next Door." With Mike Nelson and Ron Ginther, the Turkey Pluckers began spreading the mountain music up and down Puget Sound. In 1966 the Turkey Pluckers became the Tall Timber String Band, for more than twenty years Seattle's definitive bluegrass and old-time ensemble.

Even as it peaked in the early sixties, folk music was heading for a fall. "There were hoots happening all around town," Phil declared, "in houses, the coffee houses, and in basements in Pioneer Square. But right around '62 groups like the Limelighters and the Kingston Trio started hitting big. And so the homegrown folk music scene became commercialized. We called it the 'folk scare.'" Don Firth also mourned folk's usurpation: "At The Place Next Door one night, somebody asked me if I knew 'Sloop John B.' 'Sure!' So I sang it, and the guy said, 'You didn't sing it right.' 'What do you mean?' 'You didn't sing it like the Kingston Trio.' Well, their record came out in 1958, and I had learned 'Sloop John B.' from Carl Sandburg's *American Songbook*, published in 1927!"[25]

As an antidote to commercialism, the Williamses helped form the Seattle Folklore Society in 1966. A crowded kickoff concert of Mance Lipscomb and Fred McDowell (and the group's subsequent endurance) proved that interest in folk music remained high. Phil Williams smiled as he recalled the society's early exclusivity:

> We started out as basically a fiefdom. We wanted to bring in really grass roots people—folks who would not even necessarily know the term "folk music"—so we adopted the policy of not presenting any local musicians. We wouldn't even have the Lost City Ramblers, 'cause they were too derivative! We finally gave in and brought them here, and of course they were fabulous. Later we opened it up to a general membership and brought in people like Doc Watson and Bill Monroe."

In 1965 Phil (by then an attorney) formed the Washington Old Time Fiddlers' Association, opening a new forum for a very old Seattle sound that had itself been "underground" for decades. Appalachian and midwestern fiddle tunes that had journeyed to Puget Sound in the 1860s found new life as a primary element in the emerging Pacific Northwest traditional music scene.

The Williamses' campaign to preserve folk music peaked in the Northwest Folklife Festival, which they inaugurated in 1971 with Mike Holmes and Charlie Gebler. (They also started their Voyager record label to capture folk artists on vinyl.) "We wanted to show people things they never got to see," Phil recounted, "things you don't get on commercial radio and TV. Folklife was formed as an outreach to the community, to give people a forum that didn't exist." Northwest Folklife had roots in the National Folk Festival, which dated from the thirties, as well as new urban outreach efforts backed by the National Parks Service and local arts commissions. Phil and Vivian planned a purely grass-roots festival, one that avoided the national festival's reliance on name artists: "We did not want the city importing 'stars'; we wanted to pull people in that otherwise would not have performed in public, and we wanted them to educate the public to what they were doing."

At a time of new appreciation of American heritage, the folk festival met with enthusiasm from the Democratic administration of Mayor Wes Uhlman. "The City of Seattle got right behind us," said Phil, "and gave us the Seattle Center for three days, and a budget of six thousand dollars."

> We in turn would give a stage to someone with a particular interest and let them run that stage. There were no auditions. Our philosophy was, "If you give somebody a stage, they *become* a star." And it happened, time and again. Our only requirement was that the musicians tell their audiences about where they came from and how they learned to play. Folklife's impact was *huge*. It created a great ripple into the community and pulled all kinds of talent out of the woodwork. This was a unique phenomenon in the country, where all the other "folk festivals" were dominated by professional artists. Mike Seeger said, "Only in Seattle do you see this."

Folklife generated a continuing "big bang" of American music of all styles, along with echoes of Central Europe, Russia, Latin America, Africa, and Asia—world music that has ever since been a vital part of the Seattle sound.

I asked Phil and Vivian, "What *is* 'folk music'?" "We used to sing 'The Old Settler's Song' around the campfire on Vashon Island," said Phil.

> We didn't consider it a "folk song"; it was just a song we sang. Of course, the music is *hatched* and made popular, and it may be the popular music of one period, but as time goes by it becomes the folk music of a later generation. We figure that folk music follows pop music by maybe thirty or forty years. "Oh, Susanna!" was a pop song in 1840; it's a folk song now.

Vivian echoed,

Stephen Foster is a good example; he wrote primarily for the minstrel stage, and "Home, Sweet Home" and "Oh, Dem Golden Slippers" were show tunes. They'd print the sheet music and circulate it, and after a while people lost track of where the songs actually came from. "Barbara Allen" was *composed* by somebody—these things don't just come magically out of the "soul of the folk." Now we have Beatles singalongs, and Elvis is a country star.

Out of the woodwork: Impromptu jam sessions are a Northwest Folklife Festival tradition. Photo by Kurt E. Armbruster

■ ■ ■

John Holte was a nut, but a he was a lovable nut. His gigs were suitably nutty, too, and for a neophyte musician with a new union card, they were an education. This one, for example. Only a few nights previous, Swing-land Express had played for a seething New Year's Eve crowd at the newly reopened Showbox in downtown Seattle. Now, however, John, a guitar-ist, and a green new bassist were playing a faded north-end roadhouse, the Jolly Roger, for one bartender, one elderly waiter, four friends, and the shade of Joe Darensbourg. John called "Stomping at the Savoy," and as the threesome pitched in to the old flag-waver, the young bass player closed his eyes and imagined playing those same notes at Roseland in 1939. In its day, the old Jolly Roger had been quite the hotspot itself. But now the Roger was far from jolly, and the eager young band was cranking out dead music on a dead Saturday night. Oh well, the bassist pondered; there'd be other gigs, and other music. And anyway, the white coat he'd just found in a second-hand store fit him like he'd worn it forever.

■   ■   ■

Chapter 9

Carrying the Torch

BY 1970 ROCK AND ROLL was definitely here to stay. Old nightclubs—the Seattle Town and Country Club, the Magic Inn—
closed, and new ones vibrated to the soft rock of Brownsmith and
Reilly and Maloney. But then something funny happened: Music that had
been written off as dead just a few years before came back stronger than
ever. Jazz was reborn, and symphony and opera advanced. Live dance
music was challenged by disco, but disco got kids interested in big band
dancing, and a new crop of orchestras—Rege Hudman, Percy Bronson,
the Fred Radke–Gina Funes Orchestra—filled the Olympic Hotel Grand
Ballroom and drew multigenerational crowds to the Seattle Center every
Saturday night. Threatened but far from silenced, live music flourished in
the seventies.

After hitting low tide in the late sixties, jazz surged back. New clubs—
the Pioneer Banque, Parnell's, the Bombay Bicycle Shop—brought Pioneer Square its second reawakening, this one longer and stronger. Behind
the revival were the new waves of Latin and fusion, and people such as Joe
Brazil, Jim Wilke, and William O. Smith. Gleefully dissolving boundaries,
Smith crossed over happily between classics and jazz, campus and cocktail
lounge. "Luck always seemed to be on my side," the impish clarinet wizard
averred.

In 1946 I studied with Darius Milhaud at Mills College, and that's where
I met Dave Brubeck. We formed The Eight, from the French group that

Milhaud belonged to, Les Six. We began democratically, but when Dave started to make a name for himself, the record companies suggested we call ourselves the Dave Brubeck Octet. That was my first recording; I was very proud of it and still am. One of my biggest breaks was being introduced to Les Koenig, who was starting Contemporary Records in LA. He opened all kinds of doors for me and recorded almost everything I wrote. Les had the idea of separating me into two different guys: "Bill Smith" on the jazz stuff, and "William O. Smith" for the classical albums. A real high point for me was when Gunther Schuller conducted my Concerto for Jazz Soloist and Orchestra with Orchestra USA. These were New York musicians of the so-called third stream—Ornette Coleman, Mel Lewis, Richard Davis—who could play jazz or classical.

In 1966 UW music head William Bergsma talked a wary Smith into joining the Contemporary Group. "I was living in Rome when Bill called," Smith told me, "and I had absolutely no interest in teaching. But Bill was very persuasive, so I came to have a look at Seattle one sunny day and I thought, 'Gee, this place is gorgeous!' I also like fishing—the Modern Jazz Quartet used to go out of their way to play in Seattle because they loved the fishing here. Bergsma told me, 'Do your thing with our kids. Shake things up a bit.'" Not content to stay on campus, Smith took new music into the heart of old Seattle, and with pianist Dan Dean, bassists Lee Humes and Pete Leinonen, and drummer Tom Collier, he became a prime mover in the awakening new Pioneer Square music scene. The group incorporated prerecorded sounds and an early synthesizer, and Smith compared the music—"Dialogue II," "Random Suite"—to eating snails: "The first time you try it," he told critic Ed Baker, "it may seem too exotic. But if you tried it several times, you wouldn't find it strange. You might even like it. . . . In other eras, audiences wanted what was new—the latest Haydn or Mozart." The public agreed, and the Merchants Café and Bombay Bicycle Shop buzzed with excited crowds.[1]

For fifty years Pete Leinonen has played bass and led bands in every musical genre, from Dixie to funk, and in every Seattle venue, from Rainier Avenue to Rainier Club. Along the way, he has experienced the music business in its soul-enrapturing glory, and at its soul-shriveling worst. As the wry Finnish American says, "I've played for arts commissions and I've played for gangsters. Gangsters are nicer." In the seventies Pete stood in the epicenter of the jazz renaissance, playing with William O. Smith

Clarinetist William O. Smith was in the front line of the seventies jazz resurgence. In 1976 the Bill Smith Jazz Ensemble plays to both sides of the wall at the Bombay Bicycle Shop, with drummer Pete Madsen, bassist Pete Leinonen, and pianist Eddie Creed. Courtesy of Pete Leinonen

and his own Mirage and New Seattle Three. The latter, with keyboardist Eddie Creed and drummer Candy Finch, enjoyed considerable success. "I worked a year at the Smuggler with that trio," Pete told me on a ski lift high above Steven Pass.

Candy Finch had become well known as house drummer for Blue Note Records and working five years with Dizzy Gillespie. Dizzy was Candy's mentor and admonished him that, when the time came, he expected him to pass on the training. Candy chose to share that legacy with me. His style was widely imitated, but few people were aware that he was drumming in Morse code, something he picked up while serving in Korea. Playing code patterns was his way of commenting on the music, life, or some pretty girl in the audience.

Leinonen has succeeded where many musicians fail, in taking care of the *business* of music. He has also found that success can backfire, and that the chemistry that makes a band popular is not easily replicated.

The so-called jazz crowd ignored us at the Smuggler, but I put flyers in the information racks in hotels and restaurants, and we filled the place with tourists, traveling musicians, test pilots, and everybody else. In other words, people that spent money, as opposed to sitting around nursing one beer all night and hating us for having the gig. It was a dream job, and we were on our third contract when the Cornish kids caught on and bugged the owner to hire them for less money. He wanted to keep us, but his bookkeeper won out, and so one Cornish band followed another, each time the crowds getting smaller and smaller, until the owner begged me to come back. He offered me fifty percent of the bar, but I had moved on to other gigs by then, so I had to say no.

Going back to the Jackson Street joints, the jam session has a long and distinguished history in Seattle. For years a session regular, Leinonen sadly watched the tradition die. "For a long time," he told me, "jam sessions were a friendly scene where nobody was out to 'cut' anybody or steal someone's gig."

But when clubs changed to rock, not all of them could afford live music on the slow weeknights, so they started having jam sessions to provide free music for the club owner. And, because rock and roll shifted the emphasis from individual players to bands, whole groups started showing up rather than musicians spontaneously interacting, the way it used to be. So jam sessions evolved into auditions, and if you wanted to get your foot in the door at a club, the owner'd say, "Come in on Monday night and show us what you got." And you know what? The owners seldom came in on Monday night, and the groups that did play on Mondays were seldom hired. At one point I was invited to lead jam sessions at Parnell's, and I got musicians on stage that didn't usually play together. We brought in lots of people, and the bartenders and waitresses were happy. Then the cliques started showing up—"I want to go on at nine fifteen and I want so-and-so on piano and so-and-so on bass"—and I became their slave. Nobody was buying drinks, the cash register wasn't ringing, and the joy was gone.

Even as he laments the decline of live music, Leinonen continues fronting working bands in 2011. He enjoys looking backward, even as he prefers to look ahead:

Alan Lomax said, "The greatest tragedy of the twentieth century is the corporatization of culture." People stopped going to hear their neighbors play at the local tavern, preferring to follow big "stars" or those who buy media favor. So eventually, the only reason to go to the neighborhood bar was to drink—and that's a pretty lousy reason! Still, the music business is crazy and wonderful, and I have great memories: playing with guys whose records I listened to as a kid, or the dance band I worked with in Oregon, playing high hat with my foot at the same time I was playing bass because there was no money for a drummer.

Giving jazz a huge push in the seventies was the Cornish School. In 1977 the venerable art school became the Cornish Institute, received full accreditation, and began offering a bachelor of fine arts degree. Coming from Chicago at the turn of the decade, trumpeter/composer James Knapp spearheaded the Cornish resurgence. "I came out in '71," said Knapp.

It was in the midst of the Boeing depression, and I applied for a job in a hardware store along with people with master's and doctoral degrees. But then the Cornish trumpet instructor, Floyd Standifer, left to teach at Olympic College, and I got the gig. I never thought I'd want to teach, but I got more and more into it, and the student body made it especially interesting. We had a lot of Vietnam vets and ex-cons on early release programs from the penitentiaries. Rock was really making itself felt; a lot of my students were interested in the Allman Brothers, Frank Zappa, and Chick Corea, the Mahavishnu Orchestra, and Weather Report were huge then, too. These were groups that were playing in roughly the same genre as rock, but doing it so much better, and they really stimulated interest in jazz studies.

By then, Knapp had been joined by reed player Denney Goodhew, pianist Art Lande, bassist Gary Peacock, guitarist Dave Peterson, and vocalist Joni Metcalf, stellar musicians around whom a constellation of new artists would emerge. A further innovation was the jazz vocal program, begun by Metcalf in 1975. "There was nobody teaching vocal jazz there," the vivacious and eternally young Joni told me, "so I created a program, and pretty quick we had a vocal jazz group, performance and music career development classes, and a four-semester repertoire class for singers: blues, pop, standards, jazz originals. We really got things going." At the same time, Knapp joined Matrix, an explorative chamber jazz ensemble begun by percussionist/composer Joe Field. "Joe Field had a jazz orchestra," said Knapp, "with woodwinds and strings in addition to horns, along with a rhythm section. I started writing for it, and when Joe moved back east, I slid into the leadership role." In 1977 Matrix became the Composers and Improvisers Orchestra, Cornish's group-in-residence for the next eight years. "We got good reviews," said Knapp, "and brought in guest artists like Gil Evans and Carla Bley. I liked to feature the people in the band and local composers like guitarist Milo Peterson and bassist Pete Leinonen. We created a lot of excitement."[2]

Even as Cornish revitalized jazz, jazz revitalized the venerable arts school. "Jazz brought it back from the brink," Knapp said.

> People don't like to admit it, but they were having a crisis and losing students who didn't want to go through all the classical stuff to get to learn how to play jazz. So they formed a separate track, and it caught on. There were some educators who thought we were too avant-garde—that's true! Art Lande, a great piano player, bandleader, and composer, moved in from Colorado, and a lot of people came to study with him. We got Julian Priester, Jerry Granelli, Jay Clayton: major, major artists. I think my big failing was in not working to establish a connection with secondary education teachers, but still, enrollment went up, so whatever we were doing worked.

In a West Seattle basement, a different kind of movement was stirring. Fresh out of the University of Washington, John Holte launched Seattle's swing revival in 1972 with the New Deal Rhythm Band. His timing was perfect; the late sixties vogue for nostalgia and "camp" was still fresh, and Holte gathered around him a gang of hirsute young players whose spirited delivery of Cab Calloway and Artie Shaw packed University District taverns. Holte was a goofy and frenetic reed player, and as a bandleader he lacked the drive and business sense essential for commercial success. In other words, he was a flake. (Holte was a staunch union member, but many of his jobs were under "business risk" contracts permitting playing for cover charges only.) He was also a starving artist (watching John and bandmate Ronnie Pierce demolish a buffet on break was not a sight for the weak of stomach) determined to keep the past alive, eschewing the jagged and cerebral latter-day big band idioms for the danceable jump style of the 1930s. In his tiny basement room he painstakingly crafted original pieces that made him unique among Seattle bandleaders. "At the Mummy's Ball," "New Delhi Stomp," and "Deco Rhythm" are classic swing romps full of joy and good humor.

I played bass with John for four years. His favored procedure was to dig in at an underused venue and once a week play fresh originals and moldy stocks from his extensive library for anyone who cared to show up (Holte had no head for promotion, and in any case his advertising budget was nil). The band itself was a felicitous mix of generations, novice players sitting beside swing-era veterans such as trumpeter Carle Rising, pianist Bob Evans, guitarist Al Turay, and drummers Murray Sennett and Mickey "Diamond Tooth" Martin. The old survivors eagerly shared their swing-era experiences, making us young bloods feel like torch bearers for a grand tradition and at the same time giving the band an authentic vibe. It was all an exercise in faith: the cast-iron young player's belief (none dare call it delusion) that making outré music every week for a few dollars in gas money was good practice or good "exposure," or would lead to discovery—even romance. For John Holte there was no doubt at all but unyielding faith that swing music could heal the ills of society. His belief in the power of the groove never faltered, and Holte and his equally faithful sidemen, many of whom stuck with him for years, continued to dig in every week and play for the love of it until his death from cancer in 2002.

Slipping from one era to the next with style and grace, from Frankie Roth to John Holte and beyond, is Ronnie Pierce. Good bands and bad, cherry gigs and bummers, Pierce has taken it as it comes, "laughing and scratching all the way." Ronnie is an at-liberty musician: Call him on the phone, give him a time and a price, and he'll show up (even better if food is being served). "I backed Billie Holiday twice and played 'Goofus' on a douche bag in Leon Plath's band," Ronnie told me at breakfast late one afternoon in his favorite Chinatown restaurant.

In the eighties I did three years of store openings with Ed Allenbach on accordion and Ed Gross on tuba—every Fred Meyer from Astoria to Nome. Play an hour in front of the meat department, freezing your butt off, then out to the parking lot. After that I went into Wild Waves at Federal Way seven days a week for four years. March to September, seven hours a day, two sets of rock, two sets of Dixie, two sets of country, two sets of standards. We starved to death on that damn job! We'd get twenty-minute breaks and food coupons, but the lines at the counters were always too long, and just about the time you'd get up to the front, the bandleader'd be back on the stand. We'd do endless medleys and try to stump each other; I finally nailed Kenny Olendorf on the bridge to "The Song Is You."

Making music is an intensely physical activity. Pianists and string players wrestle with carpal tunnel syndrome, wind players with respiratory issues, and years of gigging takes a heavy toll on the body in myriad unpredictable ways. A true survivor, Ronnie Pierce has paid some stiff dues:

I herniated myself twice on the job. First, I nailed my right side at this Chinese joint in Bellevue. I was borrowing a car, and it crapped out on the floating bridge a half-hour before downbeat, so I made it to the other side, got out my cases, and started hitchhiking. Finally, a bus stops, and I get a lift two blocks from the gig. I'm five minutes late, the owner is *screaming* at me. We start playing, I'm exhausted from hitchhiking and carrying my horns, so I sit down against the back of the stand. The owner comes over: "Stand up, Ronnie!" So, I stand up, and, RIP! There goes my right side. A couple years later, I was setting up my big band for a wedding reception; I went to lift a speaker from a wet grass lawn onto gravel, my feet sunk in, and RIP! There goes my left side. Two minutes till downbeat, I walk into this huge reception room, and there's 400 people. The groom was a police officer, and his parents requested us to play Nat Cole's "Too Young." Twenty minutes later a knock-down fight breaks out between the parents. They walk out—the whole *room* walks out! Nobody's left, just the bride, the groom, and the band. Then the bride says, "My husband doesn't know how to dance." Well, great. So we start in nice and easy, and I'm nursing this hernia—*They said we were too young, da da da da da.* Four hours, this police officer and his new bride stand there in the middle of that room, clinging to each other. At the end, he comes up: "I wanted to give you a three hundred dollar tip, but I've only got a hundred left. I hope that's okay." "Hey, that's *more* than okay!"

Survivor: In his sixtieth year on the stand, Ronnie Pierce stomps into a chorus at the Whisky Bar in 2006, backed by drummer Andre Thomas, bassist Chuck Kistler, and keyboardist Eric Verlinde. This now-typical one-night stand is closer to musical work of the 1870s than to the union-scale, six-night-a-week gigs of pro music's heyday; for drawing SRO crowds midweek, the musicians get fifty dollars each for four hours' work. Kitty takes up the slack. Photo by Kurt E. Armbruster

The pratfalls and unexpected weirdnesses of the musician's life have kept Pierce's sense of humor sharp and his joy in playing fresh:

All musicians have their instrument stories. One afternoon I had a job with Les Beigel playing Dixieland for the nurses on the lawn at Harbor-view Hospital. That morning I had a children's parade in Medina. That was a white pants gig, and Les's was a black pants gig, so I got to Harbor-view and got out of the car and put my horn on the roof of my car, and I'm changing pants there in the parking lot. All of a sudden, a helicopter comes in for a landing with some patient. The wash from the chopper hits, and my horn goes a hundred feet in the air. I'm standing there with my pants half-on, with my clarinet circling around and around. The pilot cut his motor, and my clarinet just floated down into my arms. You couldn't make something like that up! Now, I'm working the Muckle-shoot Casino with a guy who sings in five languages. I've had a lot of chicken, a lot of feathers.

As the musical landscape changed, good keyboard players have always had a gig. One of the best known of all Seattle pianists, Walt Wagner got his start in 1965 playing for weary businessmen at the posh Dublin House. "I lucked into my first steady job there," Wagner said, "and lasted five years! Owner Gene Clark was very supportive of local musicians, and he also put me into the Plaza 5 and the Windjammer." Unwilling to pigeonhole himself, Wagner sampled Oscar Peterson, Art Tatum, Peter Nero, André Previn, and Ahmad Jamal to forge his own sound. "I always preferred to play a mix of jazz and pop, which made some of the jazz types suspicious of me. It took me a while to decide it was okay to go with my own musical direction, and not try too hard to fit in to the tight-knit jazz scene. I decided just to get better at what I do, and let the categorizations fall where they might." The strategy paid off handsomely, but it couldn't have succeeded without Walt's strong empathy: "To me, music is sheer communication. When I perform, the audience is the other half of my conversation, and if it's not going both ways, it's a lousy conversation. So I bring my best game to the job, and make sure the people in my audience know I have their best interests at heart."[3]

An aura of timelessness surrounds Overton Berry, who has graced Northwest hotels and nightclubs since the early 1960s. Like many of his cohorts, he fuses core elements of American pop—blues, jazz, and standards—into his own warm, lyrical, and always captivating piano music. He, too, has preferred to shun categories, and I asked him if playing commercial music put him on the outs with "serious" jazz players:

No. It's as much as your imagination wants to make of it. I decided I could be content with my own development doing what I liked to do best, which was playing music that was across the board. I didn't have to be only a "bebop" artist or a "blues" artist. I love it all. When I was a kid I played classical music, and I have a love for that. I'm not a heavy blues player, but I am blues-*influenced*, and there's a little touch of it going through almost everything I do.

Like Ronnie Pierce, an innate gift of humor has served Overton well:

Overton Berry. Courtesy of Overton Berry

In 1969 I took a job as musical director for a guy, and he said, "We've got this job lined up with the Hollywood Overseas Committee." Well, that sounded pretty good—"Hollywood," "Overseas." Yeah, I'm with you! Next thing I know he says, "We got three weeks in Vietnam." I said, "Vietnam? Isn't that the place where they're having the war?" Okay! So we were signed on for a year, playing shows for the military, and it actually went great.

Overton laughs—in retrospect—at the patience required to make a living entertaining a public that doesn't know much about music but knows what it likes.

Somebody will ask, "Can you play the '1812' Overture?" I'm a piano player! "Does this *look* like a cannon?" I say, "No, I can't play that. But let me play something that's *close* to that, and see if you like it." And if they don't like it, that's part of the business you're in. Another thing: Sooner or later you will find yourself playing in some situation that is not right for you. One of the things you don't do is wind up blaming the venue or blaming yourself. You simply accept the fact: "You know what? I'm good at taking splinters out, but this calls for a heart surgeon!" If you're a musician or any kind of entertainer, you're basically saying, "Hey, see this bull's eye across my chest?" If you really love what you're doing, you will convey that love, and your experience will help you through.

African American pride blossomed in the seventies, and with it Patrinell Staten, who fought through racism in society and animosity in her own community to create one of Seattle's most enduring and uplifting musical groups. Though she enjoyed her time in rhythm and blues, Staten (pronounced "stayten," and who soon after married, taking the name Wright) never wavered in her love of sacred music. Across the country, women were prominent in a new gospel music revolution, and in 1973 Wright formed the Total Experience Gospel Choir. Total Experience (and few musical groups are more aptly named) creates sonic cathedrals that lift audiences from their seats. It has also brought generations of different racial, age, and economic groups together in joyful music making.

Pastor Wright has fought her way through many a barrier to create and maintain this Pacific Northwest treasure. "I was not too well-received when I came here," she smiled.

> No! Getting kicked out of all them churches led me to organize my own gospel group, the Inspiration Seven, in 1968. People started to pay us some attention, and in '73 I started the Total Experience Gospel Choir. I was working in the school system teaching gospel music to students, and after they kicked me out of the public schools for teaching what they hired me to teach, I took the choir to Mt. Zion Baptist Church. We eventually got kicked out of there, too, and so we went out on our own. We started out small and grew up to have as many as 130 members of all ages, black and white.

Wright and her choir hit a responsive chord with another congregation, one that made it possible for Total Experience to share its music with a wider audience. Wright said,

I tell parents that the best way for their kids to learn anything is to go see it. And thanks to Reverend Dale Turner and the University Congregational Church, we started going out on tour in '75, and we've never stopped. These kids, who had never been out of Seattle—never even been to Tacoma—have seen the South, East Coast, Disneyland, Nicaragua, El Salvador, Mexico. And when they heard us in those places—hoo-*wee!*

Through the seventies, clubs and restaurants along East Union, Madison, and Yesler kept a vibrant African American music scene jumping. Then came crack cocaine, recession, and new fashions. The clubs, and the musicians, vanished. Patrinell Wright pondered the decline:

> Seattle is not a place that caters to black folks at all. I've seen opportunities go downhill and many people leave. It was very, very disheartening to a lot of the black people who had started out at the same time that I did. A lot of them took the low road—drugs, alcohol. Why? There's nowhere for black musicians to perform. Most of what's left are dives, and so there are not a lot of bands and singers now. We had the Club Ebonee and the Cotton Club, which became the Heritage House, and they died for lack of support and lack of management skills.

How can this situation be changed? "We have to open up our perspective," Pastor Wright offered.

> I think that we shut ourselves down because we paint ourselves into corners. Well, I don't have any corners to paint myself into. Music is the thing that has brought me safe thus far, and music will carry me home. And perhaps this idiom of music that I teach will carry somebody else, too. The whole idea behind doing what I do is to help people see and feel our pain as African Americans in this country. 'Cause just talking about it, nobody listens. But when I sing about it, they seem to understand. So I'll keep singing for the rest of my life.

STURM UND DRANG

In 1970 Milton Katims and the Seattle Symphony stood at the summit of Seattle cultural life. The previous year his face graced the city telephone directory, and admirers proposed renaming Mercer Street bordering the

Opera House "Katims Street." (The *New York Times* called the relationship between Katims and Seattle one of America's great love affairs.) Like Henry Villard, who gave an anxious village a railroad connection with the outside world, the onetime radio fiddler gave an equally anxious metropolis a cultural connection to the international arts world far beyond that enjoyed in earlier years. On any short list of individuals who "made" modern Seattle, Milton Katims would have to be included.

The seventies began with customary Katims aplomb: Leontyne Price enthralled; eighty-four-year-old piano legend Arthur Rubenstein dazzled in his final U.S. appearance; and in 1972 Katims's Stars of the Future series featured sixteen-year-old Yo Yo Ma playing the Dvořák Cello Concerto. A frequent guest was the much-sung—yet purposely unsung—coloratura soprano Marni Nixon. The voice behind Natalie Wood in *West Side Story* and Audrey Hepburn in *My Fair Lady,* Nixon also distinguished herself with the symphony in Schoenberg's "Pierrot Lunaire" and Rossini's *Stabat Mater.* The fact that this intriguing "ghost" artist chose to live in Seattle gave locals the feeling of being let in on a musical secret. As always, Katims delighted in presenting new pieces by young unknowns, such as Luciano Berio's "Sinfonia," along with pops concerts where listeners could munch hot dogs to *The Pink Panther,* directed by Henry Mancini himself. In 1972 the orchestra made a triumphal (and exhausting) Alaska tour that added to its prestige as a truly regional orchestra, and the following seasons's ticket sales rose 20 percent. Milton Katims, it seemed, could do no wrong.

But Seattle in the early seventies was a city in depression. Century 21 was ancient history, swept aside by the Cuban Missile Crisis, the assassination of President Kennedy, and fire hoses spraying civil rights marchers. Seattle was shaken out of her long, insular complacency by the scandal of police payoffs, corruption in the county prosecutor's office, and revelations of racism and economic discrimination in what had long been thought an island of tolerance. As the political mood slumped, so did the economic; despite introducing the 747 at the end of the sixties, the Boeing Company fell into a tailspin that threw thousands of employees out of work and imploded the local economy. Columnist Emmett Watson mocked the old boosterism that had produced the world's fair, and campaigned for a "Lesser Seattle." And over all hung the tragedy of the Vietnam War. No one seemed to know a way out, except fleeing Boeing workers; at the city limits, the fabled billboard went up: *Will the Last Person Leaving Seattle Please Turn Out the Lights.*

Perhaps as an antidote to doldrums, amateur classical music flourished. Vilem Sokol took Francis Aranyi's legacy and made the thirty-year-old Seattle Youth Symphony one of the finest such orchestras in the country. Now, too, the Seattle Recorder Society (formed in 1965) and Early Music Guild (1975) were beginning to explore the long-neglected realms of the Middle Ages and Renaissance. "The late sixties and early seventies were an incredibly fertile time in Seattle for what became known as 'early music,'" reminisced composer/educator Peter Seibert, who with his wife, Ellen, has long been a mainstay of both groups. "The phrase 'doing your own thing' was popular then," Seibert told me, "and lots of folks did their thing by picking up period instruments like the viola da gamba and recorder. Ever since then, Seattle has been one of the most important American centers of early music."[4]

Making the classics fun and accessible was George Shangrow (1951–2010), an exuberant multi-instrumentalist and connoisseur of Baroque music who in 1969, at age seventeen, formed the Seattle Chamber Singers. "I met George in 1968, when he was still at Roosevelt High School," smiled Peter Seibert. "He asked me if I'd like to sing some Bach cantatas in his new group. 'Sure! When are the rehearsals?' Well, we had exactly one rehearsal, then sang *two* Bach cantatas!" The irrepressible maestro (also one of the nation's leading harpsichordists) created a lively forum for obscure early works as well as new music by local composers. Shangrow brought youthfulness, unabashed joy, and broader community participation (his annual *Messiah* singalong has become a revered holiday ritual) to art music. "George Shangrow was a big part of the early music movement here," said Seibert, "but his involvement extended far beyond that, and whether he was conducting the Chamber Singers, discussing composers on his popular radio show, or encouraging young musicians, he was for many the most beloved and influential musician of his time."

At the Seattle Symphony, joy was waning. "Eight years ago," said an orchestra board member at the end of 1969, "there was a feeling of tremendous excitement about the symphony . . . today that excitement has vanished." Critics puzzled over thin strings, flaccid woodwinds, and muddy brass, and musicians complained of inadequate preparation. String players were particularly vexed; "When he rehearses the music he knows well," said one, "Katims moves efficiently through the score, and the [string] bowings he has marked . . . are not questioned."

The problem comes when we get into the unfamiliar works. Here he does not come to the rehearsal knowing what he wants, so he does it by ear, fishing around for ideas. . . . In most orchestras, this problem . . . is worked out beforehand with the section leaders, and here we have asked that this be done. But instead, we have very slow and inefficient rehearsals that tax everybody's patience.

With time consumed trying to figure out bowings, other details like tempos and dynamics suffered. Last-minute changes resulted in limp, tentative performances, and string bowings went unresolved. In the spring of 1968 a musicians' committee informed the board that the Seattle Symphony Orchestra was in trouble; Katims must change his approach, or the ensemble's already perceptible decline in quality would become more and more apparent. Sighed one player, "I fear for a very rough winter."[5]

Ron Simon stood in the bass section from 1960 to 2007 (for twenty-two of those years beside his father, Mori). He had high praise for the increasingly controversial director:

Katims was absolutely the right guy at the right time. He took us from a regional orchestra to much more a *major* orchestra. He did an awful lot for the city. Eventually, I think we felt we outgrew him. He sometimes had a bombastic style and approached the orchestra that way, which doesn't go over very well. But then, if any conductor's been with an orchestra a long time, people get tired of them. It should be remembered, though, that this orchestra got great reviews when Rainer Meidel took us to Europe in 1980. Well, that was the *Katims* orchestra.

Simon enjoyed making music with principal bassist James Harnett and section mates Dave Postetter, Ed Shoemaker, Don Snow, Marion West, and Barney Wood. "I played violin in school," Ron told me, "but switched to bass because Dad said, 'You're gonna learn how to play the bass.' Oh. Okay! Well, eventually I got to like it. In the Katims orchestra we had a good, solid bass section." It took Simon the younger some time to get his footing:

It was absolutely the most wonderful and frightening experience to be part of an orchestra that had that much horsepower. It took me five years to learn how to be an orchestra player. You can play an instrument, but it's quite another thing to play with others, and it takes a *long time* to become a seasoned orchestra musician. When I finally got it, the group felt really good to me.

It wasn't the money. It took years of hard work off the podium for Milton Katims to make the Seattle Symphony a full-time, salaried orchestra. "When I joined in 1960," Simon continued, "we got $12 a service—about $3,100 a year. We got fifty cents more each year, and we fought a long time for that, and to increase the number of guaranteed services, and for a lot of benefits that we take for granted now. In 1967 Title 3 money—the cultural enrichment program—came in and we were finally able to get a weekly wage of $175." Even then, it wasn't enough, and symphony musicians had to moonlight to take up the slack. "I did a lot of playing outside the orchestra," Ron added, "took up electric bass for rock gigs, played tuba in the world's fair band, and taught anywhere from twenty to thirty students a week. That's how I was able to get by."

For years, Ron Simon served as the orchestra's personnel director. He enjoyed the post, but it was a minefield he learned to tread lightly over.

The most important thing is, don't arm the mines! I saw myself as a facilitator, there to help everybody do the best job they could. Sometimes you have to say no, and tell someone that what they're doing is not quite correct. People get angry, but you have to understand *why*. Basically, musicians are like nervous thoroughbreds. It's very easy for people to get *slighted*, and you're already in a subservient position, anyway. You have big tensions between colleagues. There are a lot of egos that easily get hurt, or offended, and sometimes rightfully so.

Those egos were chafing badly under Katims, who waved away the growing complaints: "There are always those in any orchestra who are unhappy within themselves as people and who would be unhappy in any situation." The maestro was a string player himself, after all, and was widely regarded as an expert on bowing. He referred his critics to testimonial letters by Rubenstein, Stravinsky, and Toscanini that praised his skill as a musical director. In any case, Katims declared, the Seattle Symphony was *his* orchestra, and it was up to the musicians to follow orders. Such remarks were not calculated to smooth things over; early in 1971 forty symphony string players handed the symphony board and the Musicians' Association a petition requesting that all bowing indications, so essential for a full and unified string sound, be marked in parts before rehearsal. It was ignored.[6]

The lid blew off in April 1972, when the fledgling alternative newspaper *Seattle Flag* ran a jaw-dropping expose, "Milton Katims: The Man and the Mess." Freshman arts writer Roger Downey roused passions on both sides with horror stories of an out-of-control "maestro complex" that had brought the orchestra to the brink of implosion. Katims, said Downey, was nervous on the podium; he yelled; he rushed tempos; he threw tantrums. He conducted from memory and got lost. He couldn't even get the orchestra in tune. "We see the man for four days every two weeks," growled one player.

> He's never made any secret of his lack of respect for his own orchestra. . . . When we go onstage for a concert we are underrehearsed, out of tune, nervous. I wish the audience could see it from our side just once: we charge into something and someone makes a mistake. . . . Katims will just seem to forget about the concert and *glare* at the offender. I mean, he actually shows his *teeth!*[7]

Longtime arts writer Maxine Cushing Gray chided the "impatient young people" at the *Flag*, but got down to cases on Katims: Instead of letting music "breathe and develop and draw the listener into it," Katims "propelled" music . . . he liked overblown "George M. Cohan" finales . . . he hired green guest conductors who didn't threaten his position. For all his faults, though, Gray saw the Katims conundrum as a symptom of a larger problem: "We're a provincial capital, not one of the great cities of the world, and we should set our sights accordingly—unless the city and county and state really want to put big money into the arts as a tourist draw." In other words, you get what you pay for. And Seattle was not paying for the arts. Gray rounded on the symphony board of trustees for not exercising closer control on programming and choice of soloists and guest conductors, and Seattleites in general, who "find it difficult to separate the artists from the social being. . . . The criterion of acceptance here is to be 'nice.'" For Seattle to become a truly cosmopolitan arts center, Gray lectured, newspapers must give more space to concert reviews, arts commissions must be more inventive, and the Seattle Symphony needed more young faces on its board. Above all else, the city, the state, and local business must recognize that a strong arts scene was vital to Seattle's well-being. And pay for it.[8]

All agreed that Milton Katims had done much for Seattle. But he had led the symphony for almost two decades, and even his wife Virginia said that was long enough. The stress of being not only a symphony conductor but a pitchman, a glad hand, and a diplomat undoubtedly fueled the Katims temper. As symphony board meetings degenerated into shouting matches, the musicians fumed. Among them was principal flutist Scott Goff, who had joined the orchestra in 1969. "Milton Katims was not a good conductor," Goff told me.

He hired me, so I probably should have treated him better. But he had the idea that throwing tantrums was a proper way to conduct rehearsals, and he would berate and insult players to a degree that nobody would tolerate now. The repertoire we did was pretty standard, and we did a decent job. But on the fine points that make for a top-level orchestra— ensemble and dynamics and subtlety—Milton just wasn't there most of the time. The real tragedy is that, with his considerable musical gifts, there was something there that would have let him be a good conductor. But he was never able to get away from the spell of Toscanini, so he tried to turn himself into something he wasn't. Because of that, there were a lot of frustrations, and it didn't get any better.

Scott Goff grew up in Tacoma to join a distinguished line of Seattle flutists that included Glauco Meriggioli, Sid Zeitlin, Felix Skowronek, and Frank Horsfall. He took to the flute at an early age:

I came up in a time of fabulous music programs in the public schools. My school music director, Renwick Taylor, had been a horn player with the symphony and was a great inspiration. When I showed some talent on the flute, he hooked me up with all the right people, and it wasn't too long before I was doing Mozart concertos. Oh sure, I took some ribbing on the flute being a "girl's instrument," but I stuck with it. I figured I'd work as a school band director or maybe join the Seattle Symphony.

Goff went on to the University of Washington, where he played under Stanley Chapple, then attended Juilliard.

Stanley ran the University Symphony like a professional orchestra, and for operas he would hire the first chairs from the symphony to play with the students. The upshot of this was, at Juilliard I was *way* ahead of the other students. When it came time to sit down in the orchestra and play like a pro, I really knew how to lay it down. Nowadays, kids are lucky if they find a job, and even if they do, they're hanging on by their thumbs for the first few years.

Leaving Juilliard, Goff spent a year in the Pittsburgh Symphony before returning to the Northwest. "When I got here," he told me, "I found a pretty good orchestra."

> It was a very insular and provincial orchestra, just like the city was very insular and provincial. It was also a divided orchestra. Seattle was probably more isolated than any mainland city in the country. Because of that, Seattle developed a remarkable number of institutions for a city its size. That was the good news. The bad news was, the isolation tended to have a negative effect on the quality of those institutions. You had amateurism, provincialism, and a lot of bickering. Katims had already aroused a lot of bitterness by importing Bernie Shapiro, Raymond Davis, and Richard Bonnevie from New York. These were players who would have been first-rate anywhere. I was one of his imports, too, and I felt the hostility, even though I was originally from Tacoma.

By the spring of 1974, board members and musicians were pressing for a new conductor. Katims's relationship to the orchestra, said one player, was "like a marriage gone stale. He had no more surprises or inspiration to bring us." Rumors flew that the trustees were poised to "kick out Katims." No, sighed symphony president Dr. Ellsworth Alvord; no one was going to "kick out" Katims. He had done great things and given Seattle a "pretty good" orchestra. Now, however, it was time for something better than pretty good.[9]

At the *Seattle Post-Intelligencer*, Milton Katims's old friend Lou Guzzo suffered the *Flag* impudence and rumors in silence. But Dr. Alvord's statement was the last straw. For years, the daily press had blown hot and cold on the arts, reflecting the short symphony and social seasons. Befitting a fish and timber town, occasional reviews by Everhardt Armstrong, Richard Hays, J. Willis Sayre, and James Wood alternated with long periods of silence. By 1952, though, the arts had become recognized as an integral part of the social fabric, and the *Seattle Times* promoted Louis R. Guzzo (whom it had hired in 1945) to full-time reviewer. Born into a musical family, Guzzo had played violin in the Cleveland Summer Symphony and he took all music, including jazz, seriously. From the time of Katims's arrival, the conservative, bespectacled journalist was among his stoutest supporters ("Guzzo," said Roger Downey, "is one of the half-dozen Seattleites responsible for the fact that there is a Seattle Symphony at all"), and for fifteen years his "Words and Music" column promoted broader music appreciation across the region. The *Post-Intelligencer* met the challenge with John Voorhees, and for the first time Seattle enjoyed daily, year-round arts coverage. In the sixties, the *PI*'s Rolf Stromberg and the *Times*'s Wayne Johnson (late in the decade Guzzo moved to the *PI* as managing editor) did their expected share of Katims boosting, but they also did not hesitate to call him out on lackluster performances.[10]

As the Katims ship took on water, Guzzo bailed frantically, calling in markers and buoying drifting allies. Breaking his two-year silence, he railed in a prominent editorial against Alvord and orchestra manager Lanham Deal. The pair, he thundered, were leading a "power play" to oust Katims for "a younger conductor who would bow to the musical and administrative demands of the present regime." The long-festering complaints of the musicians were common to all such ensembles, he explained, and they were being addressed. And, he reminded Seattle, Milton Katims was responsible for some of the best attendance in the country. His popularity was proved by the fact that ticket sales fell dramatically whenever a guest conductor replaced him. The issue, Guzzo insisted, came down to who was really in charge: the music director, or the well-meaning but wrong-headed contributors and board members. And if it was the latter, he warned, Seattle "can kiss its orchestra goodbye."[11]

As Guzzo fumed and the orchestra fretted, Katims's old friends begged him to step down gracefully. He was, after all, sixty-five; wouldn't he care to move on to new fields, or take things a little easier? No, he would not. "Hell," Katims told the *New York Times*, "when I think of Stokowski at the age of ninety-three signing a three-year record contract in London, I'm just a babe!" Katims swatted away generous offers to ease him out as director-emeritus but at last accepted the inevitable. "Perhaps the orchestra did need a new face after 22 years," one board member lamented, "but the way Milton was pushed out was just lousy. They lowered the boom on him! There was all kinds of rotten talk behind his back, and a lot of lying." Milton Katims gave his last concert as the Seattle Symphony's conductor on April 15, 1976, then he and Virginia began packing boxes for the move to his new position as artistic director at the University of Houston, the city he had rejected twenty-three years earlier. Old nemesis Roger Downey paid tribute to the departing maestro: "Thanks in large part to Milton Katims . . . only a very good conductor indeed will be good enough for the orchestra we now have."[12]

Scott Goff agreed:

> Milton Katims's big legacy was reorganizing the orchestra so that it had a board, and getting it organized along business lines so that it could really go after community support. This included much more than just fund-raising, but it organized and focused the orchestra. Katims provided the political framework in which the orchestra could grow according to the wishes of the community, and he transformed the Seattle Symphony from a mediocre provincial orchestra into good regional one.

The Katims legacy is hard to overstate. He not only remade the symphony but was largely responsible for giving Seattle a concert hall, grand opera, and ballet. Simply, he and his wife transformed the cultural life of the Pacific Northwest. When Milton Katims died in 2006, one of the brightest lights in Seattle history was extinguished.

On July 1, 1976, Rainer Miedel took charge of the Seattle Symphony. The thirty-eight-year-old German had been principal cellist with the Stockholm Symphony, conductor of the Gavleborgs, Sweden, symphony, and associate conductor of the Baltimore Symphony before winning the Seattle contest over Eduardo Mata, Guido Ajmone-Marsan, and Varoujan Kodjian. Miedel drew mixed feelings from his musicians. "He was mean," barked Howard Gilbert—"arrogant."

> He didn't like women in the orchestra. He wanted all of the overweight people out of the orchestra. And all the old people. He wanted young musicians—young male musicians—but some of the best musicians in the symphony were elderly women who'd been there forever. And he tried to fire them. One of them demanded an audition, and she played so beautifully Miedel had to rehire her.

Scott Goff differed:

Miedel was a very good conductor and a very good musician. He had a fine sense of *sound*. The sonority and warmth he wanted was European. Katims never fired anybody—and there were a lot of people in his orchestra who *should* have been fired. It was left to Rainer to do the dirty work. He didn't like it; he was not an unkind man, but at the same time, he didn't cut any slack.

Unfortunately, the audience didn't cut Miedel any, either. A little of the Katims flamboyance might have stood the new maestro in good stead, but he was no Toscanini, and attendance sagged. It was also Miedel's misfortune join the symphony as many of its principals were aging. He made no secret of his wish to bring in young faces—the orchestra needed them. "I was on Miedel's firing list," admitted Ken Cloud, whose once-imperious lead trombone was faltering. "I'd had asthma since the army, and as time went on, the medication made me play with a ripple. I couldn't always get a straight tone or an accurate attack—not so good for a trombone player in an orchestra. I only had a couple of years to go, so I appealed and the board let me finish out my time." Then there was Ronald Phillips, who had played in the clarinet section since 1927, most of that time as principal. His party piece, the Mozart Clarinet Concerto in A Major, had been performed dozens of times since Beecham's day and was a guaranteed house-packer. Beginning in the thirties, Phillips was also a fixture in a string of chamber wind ensembles that further burnished his and the symphony's reputation, and he served as music director for the Seattle Art Museum for over twenty years. For many, Ronald Phillips *was* classical music—the soul of the orchestra. In the seventies his accuracy and phrasing were as brilliant as ever, and his solo work continued to earn the admiration of critics. But his crystalline French tone was fading, and when Miedel proposed hiring a "co-principal" to back him up, his outraged colleagues threatened to walk out. The matter was deferred, but the young maestro persevered on other fronts; longtime concertmaster Henry Siegl was eased out, and new string players and first trumpet began the transition to a Miedel orchestra. Miedel would, he told reviewer Melinda Bargreen, institute sectional rehearsals, engage exciting young guest artists, and expand the repertoire with new music. "In three years," he declared, "I think the Seattle Symphony can be on a par with—or perhaps even better than—the orchestras of San Francisco, Minneapolis, and Atlanta."[13]

But no. In January 1979 the musicians walked out over pay and stayed out ten debilitating weeks, costing Miedel several ambitious programs and pushing the year's deficit to $575,000. By this time a web of local arts commissions—Seattle, King County, *and* Washington—provided a safety net only dreamed of by Miedel's predecessors, but even this stretched only so far. The Seattle Symphony was pinching every penny it could, said orchestra president William Bain Jr.; administrative costs were below the national average, and it earned a higher percentage of its annual budget than many orchestras. But, he warned, community support continued to fall far short of the necessary sustaining funds. It was only thanks to matching grants from the National Endowment for the Arts and—shockingly—personal loans from the trustees that the orchestra kept going at all. "Volunteer board members," said Bain, "have contributed nearly as much money as the entire amount raised . . . by local business through the Corporate Council of the Arts." If Seattle really wanted a symphony orchestra, he warned, there must be "a change in attitude." The orchestra embarked the following year on a European tour, winning good reviews, and things began looking up. Then, in 1983, forty-five-year-old Rainer Miedel died of cancer. He had only begun to make his mark on the Seattle Symphony.[14]

"Rainer Miedel had a vision of the Seattle Symphony as an internationally acclaimed orchestra," said timpanist Michael Crusoe. "Sadly, he didn't get to realize it. But I liked him as a conductor." St. Louis-born Crusoe never dreamed he'd play in a symphony orchestra, let alone live in Seattle. But employment options for timpanists are scarce, and when Meyer Slivka's chair in the Seattle Symphony came open, Crusoe's wife encouraged him to audition. Soon after, the Crusoes were Puget Sound–bound. "Living in St. Louis," Michael told me, "I loved the Motown sound."

> I was fascinated by the strings and horns that backed so many of the R&B
> singers. The St. Louis Symphony came and played at our school, and
> hearing the percussion section and seeing all the instruments really got
> me. When I got my first drum set, I would play records by the Temptations and the Supremes as loud as I could get, and play along with 'em.
> Guys'd sit outside on the curb and call down requests—"Hey, how 'bout
> some Smokey Robinson!" I never thought I would be good enough to
> get into a symphony orchestra. That kind of thing was just way up on the
> pedestal. But at college I became adept at all the percussion, and timpani
> became my strongest instrument, and I decided to hit the audition circuit.

The cumbersome kettledrums present a huge challenge to the most dedicated students. "Practicing timpani *is* a problem," Crusoe nodded.

> If you're a flute student, you just put it in your case and carry it home, right? But most parents aren't often likely to go buy their kid a set of timpani. If you aspire to something like that, most kids have to rely on the school they're attending. I would go over to campus at ten on Saturday morning, my band director would meet me there and unlock the door, and I'd be there until two in the afternoon, practicing and playing along with recordings, developing my techniques.

Orchestral percussionists read more rests than notes, a feat that demands plenty of internal fortitude. "It takes a lot of patience," Mike said, "standing there for measure after measure and not playing anything."

> I like to approach the score and mentally prepare myself as though I'm actually conducting the piece. I think about all the entrances I have to pick up and who is coming in, when. Being a drum of musical pitch, you're influencing both the rhythmic and the tonal aspect of the ensemble. Conductors rely on you very heavily, and of course, once you get out on stage Murphy's Law is all *over* the place! I like the old Nelson Mandela quote: "It's not how you fall, it's how you get up." When you make a mistake, you just keep goin'. I had a spot once where I didn't come in—I missed one little *boom*, and there was perfect silence. The conductor looked at me—"'Oh, okay"—I hit the note, and afterward, some of my colleagues who are amateur comedians would say things like, "I notice you tend to play behind the beat a little bit." Rainer Miedel used to say that timpani are the "king of the orchestra," and a lot of musicians tell me that, when things get wobbly, they latch on to me. That's a big responsibility.

In all the history of the Seattle Symphony, Michael Crusoe and bassist Bruce Lawrence (who retired in 2006 after thirty-eight years) have been its only African American members. In 1968 the orchestra adopted a resolution repudiating discrimination after the protests of one man: Douglas Q. Barnett, dramatist, founder of Black Arts/West, and son of black musicians' union founder Powell S. Barnett. "I was friends with a lot of jazz musicians in those days," Barnett told me, "and we had many discussions about the music scene."

I filed suit against the Seattle Rep in 1966, resulting in the hiring of three minority actors, and my musician friends started talking about doing the same with the symphony, which was taking public money from the National Endowment for the Arts but not hiring any African American musicians. In October 1967 a group of us decided to go down to the Opera House and picket the symphony on opening night. Well, I was the only one who showed up! But I walked around there with my sign, and Howard Hall, the KING TV commentator and a good friend of mine, came in his tuxedo and interviewed me. I was glad to see him 'cause I was getting some dirty looks! I told Howard how the symphony discriminated against minorities and that some of us hoped to change the situation. A couple of weeks later a woman called, saying she was from the symphony. She told me that picketing was bad for their image. I said, "Okay. What are you going to do about it?" She said that she would use her influence to get Katims to examine his hiring policies. And for almost a year this lady, who never told me her name, worked at it. I had the impression she was lobbying hard, but that there were forces aligned against her. Then, in the summer of '68, she called me and said, "Maestro has seen the light!" Katims and the board signed a resolution that there would be no more racial discrimination, and later that year Bruce Lawrence was hired.[15]

Forty years later, Mike Crusoe's remains the only black face in the orchestra. Nationally, the Sphinx Organization is helping young African American and Latino musicians prepare for orchestra careers. The Seattle Symphony, however, remains virtually all white. I asked Mike if he saw any chance of improving things:

I think more African Americans are showing up in orchestras around the country, but unfortunately not here in Seattle. I don't see any promising young kids coming up, either. The best hope for getting minorities interested in playing symphonic music is through education. I know that sounds cliché, but that's really where it starts. I went to a conference on this several years ago, and that was the consensus. When you look at what kids are dealing with today, I'm afraid there is a certain value that's been lost, in terms of who we are and what we represent. It seems to me that there are fewer kids getting an instrument put in their hands. Beyond just being an important cultural institution, we need to keep symphony orchestras strong in order to reach our youth and instill positive values.

BRAVO OPERA!

Out of the void, three thousand pairs of eyes stared. Suspended twenty feet above the stage, a young woman pretended to swim the gossamer green waters of the Rhine. *Swimming while flying,* she mused: *only in opera!* But she dared not let her concentration waver from the music emanating from far below. Six thousand eyes were watching, six thousand ears listening, millions of dollars had been spent, reputations were at stake, and careers were hanging—like hers was, literally, right now. Banishing all extraneous thoughts, the young woman focused her mind on one thing: counting. And as the music soared and the trumpets called out, she opened her mouth.

That hot summer of 1975, Glynn Ross and the Seattle Opera Association took an enormous gamble and staged a spectacle that few opera companies had the resources or the nerve to bring off: Richard Wagner's epic cycle, *The Ring of the Nibelungs.* Ross had done well in his eleven years. But this was orders of magnitude bigger than anything the young company had attempted—the biggest musical undertaking ever seen in Seattle. Would it succeed? As the curtain rang down on *Das Rheingold,* a storm of applause said yes.

It had been a long journey. The Sprottes's Standard Opera of 1914 survived only a year, and even after fourteen successful seasons, Seattle Civic Opera folded in 1946. Struggling under postwar recession and lack of corporate commitment, the symphony itself faced a dubious future. Who would dare consider starting another *opera* company under such circumstances? Cecilia Schultz, for one. She'd had a good run with Civic Opera, after all, and was confident that Seattle had the resources and talent to do it again once the dull times were past. In 1950 Schultz joined forces with conductor Eugene Linden (still smarting from losing out to Manuel Rosenthal in the battle for control of the symphony), Hans and Thelma Lehmann, Sasha Schneider, and Olympia Brewing Company owners Peter and Clara Schmidt, and founded the Northwest Grand Opera Association.

A daring artistic model was formulated: Linden would premiere works in Seattle, then tour them around the Northwest. It was an expensive proposition; "No one was vaguely concerned with establishing a realistic budget," marveled Hans Lehmann. Nonetheless, the company survived for seven seasons, playing not only Seattle but Tacoma, Olympia, Portland, Vancouver, and (for its last term) Spokane. Nationally known principals such as Francis Yeend, Tomiko Kanazawa, and Walter Cassel led local talent—Alvin Elyn, Pat Farwell, Charles Gonzales—through the standard repertoire, drawing big houses and good reviews. Keeping things on track was the company's manager, a young ex-GI named Glynn Ross. It couldn't last. As the deficit neared $50,000, Linden wilted under the pressure and sought refuge in alcohol. Early in 1957, inebriation, divorce, and mental collapse brought down Eugene Linden, and with him Northwest Grand Opera. Thereafter, lyric drama was in the capable hands of University of Washington School of Music director Stanley Chapple. Chapple did good work, but the Metropolitan, it wasn't. Then came Century 21, and how better to christen the grand new Opera House than with an equally grand production of *Aida*? Initiated by Milton Katims and paid out of the symphony treasury, the Verdi warhorse proved as effective a stalking horse as it had in 1927, and Seattle (Cecilia Schultz had by this time eased into a long-deserved semiretirement) launched yet another try for permanent grand opera.[16]

There was one small hurdle: Symphony president Gordon Scott foresaw certain financial calamity and adamantly opposed the gamble, and his prediction came true as various production interests demanded nothing but the best, driving costs through the roof. The show lost $35,000, which Scott demanded be repaid immediately. Seattle stood at a crossroads: She could cut her losses and think small, or think big. Among the think-biggers was Hans Lehmann, who stated, "Without *Aida* we would have been hard put to organize our own opera company in 1964. Instead, we would likely have imported the San Francisco Opera Company for brief seasons, as was the wish of several . . . musical potentates." Stepping up was a man who, by his own admission, seldom attended a concert or play. But jeweler Paul Friedlander did believe Seattle needed fine arts, and had tart words for the cultural establishment: Stop stewing over nickels and dimes and pull together. They started pulling and formed Patrons of Northwest Cultural and Historical Organizations (PONCHO), which raised money enough to pay off the *Aida* debt and then some. For big thinking, the timing could not have been better; over the next decade PONCHO would get assistance from the National Endowment for the Arts, Seattle and King County arts commissions, and hefty support from private backers such as the Lehmanns and Louis and Charlotte Brechemin. With real money at hand, Seattle arts entered an age of unprecedented growth.[17]

First, however, there was more sorting out to do. With the arts community's customary Byzantine intrigue, two rival opera companies vied for primacy during 1962–63: the Seattle Symphony's fledgling Seattle Opera Association, which staged *Carmen* and *La Traviata* that season, and a group of independents known as the Western Opera Company, which put on its own shows and quickly found itself swimming in red ink. Rival cabals spat and hissed: the Opera Association, backed by symphony management and musicians, versus Western Opera, which possessed verve aplenty, along with scruffy costumes, tatty scenery, and green leadership. To counter Western's objections to the opera being tied too closely to the symphony, Milton Katims proposed setting up an independent, self-governing organization. The groups merged, and at the end of 1963 the Seattle Opera Association hired its first director.

As an opera-loving soldier in Italy during World War II, Glynn Ross directed for the San Carlo and Goldoni Theater companies, married into a leading Neapolitan family, and in the early fifties directed Eugene Linden's Northwest Grand Opera. Ross (1914–2005) went on to assist Gaetano Merola at the San Francisco Opera, by the late fifties considered by many to be the nation's top company. When Seattle again turned to him in 1963, the eager impresario was ready to make his mark. Ross and Seattle were a perfect fit, and from the outset the Seattle Opera Association enjoyed full houses and full treasuries. A fall 1964 staging of *Lucia di Lammermoor*, featuring American superstar Roberta Peters, was a sensation, and there were few missteps thereafter.

Booming "Nothing succeeds like excess!" Ross delighted in flexing his larger-than-life personality in a city in the midst of reinventing itself. Against some objections, he vigorously promoted the star system, adamant that the "merchandising value" of a Joan Sutherland or Franco Corelli would guarantee attendance and provide the revenues necessary to build a permanent company. As Milton Katims was friends with Isaac Stern and Arthur Rubenstein, Ross knew most of the stars of the opera world and was a genius at creating roles for them that would advance their careers *and* fill the Opera House. Ross wanted young faces in his seats, and alongside his premium-priced, star-vehicle International series he vigorously promoted a bargain-priced National series (the only regular opera-in-English anywhere) featuring coming young talent. He ran ads, ballyhooed on rock radio stations (*Opera is* NOW!), and his operatives handed out fliers at summer teen spectaculars. Ross knew how to exercise iron will in a velvet glove; behind him was a battalion of assistants and work-study students who jumped at his every command. "He's so friendly and mild-mannered all the time," said one, "that you never feel he's pushing you, but that's exactly what he's doing—*all* the time." Some dismissed Ross as a huckster, but the public—9,000 subscribers by 1966—loved him. As *Bravo Opera!* bumper stickers appeared on the streets, *Seattle Times* arts editor Wayne Johnson credited the association's "extraordinary box office achievements" to Ross's "insistence on operating with flair, with style, with the little added touches that make opera-going not a cultural duty but an event."[18]

Arts critic and future novelist Tom Robbins tried to fathom opera's peculiar popularity on Puget Sound—perhaps it was its "hot, florid old-fashionedness" that hit a chord in a "cool" electronic age, and that its "unabashed hedonism" and colorful ostentation were an antidote to "a society of mass-produced plastic dreariness." And, of course, its snob appeal was a natural for "a city as self-conscious as Seattle." In the end, though, Robbins admitted that it was the *music* which kept opera alive and well in the sixties: "It is this banquet of sound that brings people back to the same operas again and again, even though the all-too-familiar plots are usually as inane as the sentiments in a high school year book." Asking Glynn Ross when Seattle audiences might expect something fresher than *Carmen* and *Turandot*, the director responded, "We'll get to contemporary opera, but before we can *break* the rules, we must *know* the rules. Why, we haven't even done Mozart or Strauss yet. The Northwest should have a solid background in traditional opera before it is exposed to the offbeat." Then he went ahead and put on Gounod's rarely staged *Romeo and Juliet*, Robert Ward's adaptation of *The Crucible*, and Beethoven's *Fidelio* (with sets made from junk). Ninety-four percent of subscription seats sold before the 1967 season began.[19]

It was a composer once considered radical who blasted Seattle Opera into international acclaim. Glynn Ross had always loved the music of Richard Wagner, and so had Seattle. Touring pianist August Seurat raised the curtain in 1877 with a performance of the grand march from *Tannhauser*, Innes's Royal Italian Band featured Wagner every Friday night at the Alaska-Yukon-Pacific Exposition, and during the mid-twentieth century the symphony was virtually Wagner-obsessed, performing his works more than any other composer's. Even in the depths of the Second World War,

Sir Thomas Beecham served up liberal doses of the *meister.* To Glynn Ross, Seattle, ringed by forests and mountains, was made for Wagner—"a new Bayreuth." Here, too, was a golden opportunity. Wagner, especially his epic, four-opera cycle, *The Ring of the Nibelungs,* had long been out of favor among American companies; only the Metropolitan was doing any of the *Ring* at all, and that without much enthusiasm. Ross was convinced that a fresh yet traditional *Ring,* with all its nineteenth-century trappings, would lure hordes of opera-lovers to Seattle, especially since his production would do the cycle in both English and German. Impossible, muttered doubters, who dismissed Wagner as old-hat and feared that the expense would bankrupt the company.

Ross proved them wrong. Opera lovers from around the world sold out both English and German cycles, and as the final notes of *Gotterdammerung* faded the Opera House exploded in a torrent of *bravos,* and ecstatic spectators rushed the stage. Reviewers at both daily newspapers were reduced to blubbering incoherence, stunned that Seattle had pulled off such a feat. In two weeks Glynn Ross created a new Northwest music tradition, made Seattle's one of the nation's leading opera companies, and made the city a world music Mecca. At a time of continuing civic self-doubt and economic malaise, it was a transforming moment in the city's history. The *New York Times* proclaimed Seattle "the cultural center of the West."[20]

Seattle Opera was blessed in the head office, but equally so in the orchestra pit and onstage. Wayne Johnson lavished praise on conductor Henry Holt ("The Seattle Opera is lucky to have Henry Holt. The music world is lucky to have Henry Holt!"), and so did six-season chorus member Chai Ahrenius: "I *loved* Henry Holt for one reason: You could always count on him for entrances. He would look over at you just before you were supposed to come in and mouth the opening lines. You could always tell where his beat was, whereas with a lot of other conductors, it would get flaky." Chorus master Hans Wolf succeeded in making solid walls of sound from young neophytes. Ahrenius credited the Hamburg-born Wolf with implanting in Seattle Opera a superb choral tradition: "Hans was fun— fun but demanding. He wanted strict attention to line and the musicality of every phrase. When we did things in German, they had to be just right; like this line in *Die Rosenkavalier: 'ein schuligen eugenant.'* We'd try it and Hans would yell, 'Nein, nein! You got to do it vid a country accent—*ein schuligen eugen*aaaant!'"[21]

Lord and legend of the Opera House stage was baritone Archie Drake. The courtly Englishman had been a merchant seaman when his love of song compelled him to join a Vancouver, B.C., choir in 1950. Drake (1925–2006) was encouraged to develop his vocal talent, and made his operatic debut with the San Francisco Opera in 1968. Glynn Ross heard about the big-voiced baritone and lured him north that same year for a production of *Fidelio*. Drake delighted Seattle audiences in one thousand performances over thirty-nine seasons (sometimes in two languages in one day), including the role of Gunther in *Gotterdammerung* from 1975 to 1983. Ross's successor, Speight Jenkins, called Drake the soul of Seattle Opera, and soprano Pamela Casella agreed: "Archie Drake was a dear soul and a gentleman. He helped you in your role and made everything seem easy. And *what* a voice! But you learned not to chew gum around him."

There can be no opera without advertising, sharp pencils, and lots of money. But when the curtain goes up, it's the artist who matters. And on July 15, 1975, Pam Casella sang the first note in the Seattle *Ring*. "I was the lead Rhinemaiden in *Das Rheingold*," she told me.

The opera begins with the famous water music swirling around and around. Seven pages of that stuff. It's very amorphous and hard to find the beat in, and at the end of it the lead Rhine Maiden starts singing—meaning *me*. So here I am, swimming around with the other two Rhine Maidens, knowing that if I don't make my entrance *perfectly* I'll throw the whole first scene off. Henry Holt was conducting for dear life, waving his arms with his head buried in the score, so I knew I couldn't count on any help from him. Luckily, my coaches told me, "You MUST count from the very first beat. Keep the beat in your head!" So I'm swimming and counting furiously to myself, "One-two-three-four, one-two-three-four," and when my spot came, I *nailed* it—right on the money. When I hit my note, Henry's head jerked up like he'd been electrocuted, and he mouthed, "Thank you." Well, *somebody* had to do it!

"The *Ring* was a huge challenge," said Pamela's husband, Craig Nim, who escaped singing the Wagner marathon but essayed numerous baritone roles in his seven years with the company. "I think Seattle Opera may have bitten off more a little bit more than they realized," Nim continued. "A lot of the European singers coming over for the *Ring* were not used to such huge houses. They were used to singing in 800-seat houses. Well, our

Archie Drake's powerful baritone helped make the Seattle Opera *Ring* cycle an international sensation. In 1975 he played the role of Gunter in *Gotterdammerung.* Des Gates photo, courtesy of Seattle Opera

Opera House was 3,200. They'd take one look—'Aacckk!' A lot of singers learn how to sing in small studios, and suddenly they're standing onstage before three thousand people and having to compete with a seventy-piece orchestra." Pam Casella echoed, "That's one thing we went away with from Seattle Opera: how to sing in a huge house without hurting yourself. We noticed that a lot of our colleagues hadn't had that experience. It really makes a difference in how you use your voice, as opposed to just blasting."

Though she died in 1971, the long arm of Cecilia Schultz has continued to bring new talent, such as Casella and Nim, to Seattle Opera through the Cecilia Schultz Singers' Fund. Casella said,

I graduated from the Curtis Institute of Music in Philadelphia, came back to Seattle, and got into the Cecilia Schultz program. That gave me the kind of experience you can't pay for. My first part was probably the high priestess in *Aida*. Then, with Mary Costa, I was Posette in *Manon*,

and I did the *Ring*. Glynn Ross knew his stuff, and he gave me the
chance to achieve things. They were very respectful of new singers here.

Craig Nim nodded emphatically:

> Cecilia Schultz attracted a *lot* of talent. It's a hard thing for singers, espe-
> cially just out of college, to get out and do their craft. It was beneficial
> to Seattle Opera, too, because they could put us to work fund-raising—
> going to homes and singing soirees, drumming up interest in opera.
> Making music on this scale takes a *bunch* of selling, and who better
> than young, fresh faces? In show business they teach you a lot about the
> "show," but very little about the "business!"

Cissy Schultz would be most pleased.

As a successful working couple in a notoriously treacherous field,
Casella and Nim were a rare phenomenon. "Most couples would never
survive," laughed Casella. "We only know two other couples that did.
Craig and I never had an ego thing; we were always happy for the other
one if they got a job, because as a couple it benefits the family, and you
want to see them doing well." Casella, too, reminds would-be opera singers
that they have selling to do: "You have to create opportunities just as we
did, working up and down the coast. You keep your name out there and
contact people—'I'm gonna be in your town. Would you have an opportunity for me to sing?' The glue is the music, and if you love what you're
doing, you'll find a way to survive."

■ ■ ■

Afterword

ITTING IN THE BOARD ROOM of the Musicians' Association of Seattle, one is surrounded by ghosts. The faces of past union presidents—Theodore Wagner, Harry Pelletier, Chet Ramage—smile out on a changed world. Looking at those faces, one is impressed by how long so many of Seattle's musicians were active in a business that has become synonymous with youth. Rock and roll may be the longest-lived genre of modern popular music, but how many of rock's practitioners, hoary legends such as the Rolling Stones aside, play for even five years, let alone forty? In its naïve innocence, rock and roll remains shackled to the cruel imperatives of youth and novelty. Not so, the music of Seattle's first hundred years. Dad Wagner was a beloved figure for half a century, Jackie Souders worked school proms from the twenties to the fifties, and Ronald Phillips played in the symphony for almost sixty years. They were not considered anomalies, and their music had no age limit.

What is now an anomaly is music for money. Essential to live music's survival over the decades was its role as adjunct to other activity: gambling, liquor sales, prostitution, world's fairs. In that capacity, music was the advance guard of Seattle's coveted cosmopolitanism, a stalking horse for all other arts, even team athletics. At first in service to the "subterranean" economy of saloon and theater, by the late nineteenth century music was an adjunct of the solid, middle-class mercantilism that has always been at the core of the city's personality. The early rise and long success of the Musicians' Association of Seattle reflected the importance and status of

Two generations of bass players: Vaughn Abbey initiates daughter Tamara into the mysteries of professional music-making at a park concert in 1942. Courtesy of Tamara Burdette

music *as a business*, in a business-obsessed age, and the union vigorously defended music as such. Bill Douglas and his associates were businessmen, and so were the rank and file who, despite occasional outward manifestations of Bohemian or jazzbo eccentricity, bought houses, raised families, and built community ties.

Art music, which in other communities was identified with the social elite, was a much less rarefied phenomenon in Seattle. While some continued to believe that the classics were effete, many more felt that "good music" should be part of the urban fabric. Seattle's wealthy elite was, after all, much smaller than its eastern counterparts, much less bound by old money and class prejudice, and closer in professional interests, economic concerns, and regional identity (fish and timber) to the middle class. Wagner's Band, the Alaska-Yukon-Pacific Exposition, school orchestras, and radio took classical music across class lines while enlisting it as a tool in the building of a greater Seattle. Musicians shared in the general prosperity, and their profession grew hand-in-hand with the city.

But who would have guessed that the symphony would become a rare enclave of paid musicians, and that in the years since 1980 work for players of other genres would become virtually extinct? In forms far beyond John Philip Sousa's imaginings, canned music has triumphed, and music itself has passed from discreet event presented by performers to all-pervasive *commodity*, controlled by no one and everyone. The musicians' union succeeded in keeping music a remunerative profession only as long as it represented a relatively small number of skilled artists/craftspeople offering something a large number of nonskilled nonmembers wanted. It couldn't stay that way, not with records, radio, and the baby boom. Music did indeed become ubiquitous and less "special." "The Beatles changed everything," said bassist/bandleader Pete Leinonen. "Now any guy with a guitar could be a musician." In the eighties the decline of live music was hastened by crack cocaine, which drove many nightspots out of business; new forms of mass-media entertainment and personal music reproduction, which kept people at home; the continuing flight to the suburbs, which emptied downtown venues; recession; and, simply, changing tastes. And so the working blues bands of Pioneer Square, the funk groups of the Central District, the downtown restaurant trios, the cocktail keyboards, even the cover rock bands of West Seattle taverns have all but disappeared. After a brief heyday, professional music stands revealed as a century-long anomaly lost in more centuries of hat passing and amateurism.

Nonetheless, dedicated pros eke out opportunity. "All through the nineties," Leinonen told me, "my groups had an excellent run in the society and corporate markets. We made it a point to learn every request, booked as many as 300 dates some years, and generated over a million dollars in earnings for the jazz community." He affirms that there remains a market for live traditional music: "The dot-com bust and 9/11 really slowed things down, but I have no doubt that someone will do the same thing again when the economy picks up." Pete offers sage advice for would-be pros:

> To most Americans, music is an abstraction—something like the weather
> or insects. They have no concept of it actually being labor, or a craft. And
> neither do most young musicians, so they are easy marks for exploitation.
> They let themselves get suckered into the "good exposure" dodge. "Come
> play our benefit. We can't pay you, but it'll be good exposure." For a long

time, my band did every benefit in town. And after a while, I noticed that all the paying gigs were going to other bands. Why? We had gotten the reputation as amateurs, and were dismissed as a "real" band. If you hire yourself cheap, or free, that's how you will be perceived. And someone else will get the gigs. If you're good enough to command an audience, then you're good enough to be *paid*. There are plenty of wealthy clients backing most foundations, and they'll benefit you to death if you let them. We still play the occasional benefit and when a colleague has medical expenses to pay. But if I want "exposure," I'll go fishing in Alaska.

As a union bandleader, though, Leinonen is a rarity, and for most Seattle musicians Local 76–493 has become an irrelevancy. To legislators and a large segment of the public in the forties and fifties, the blustering of American Federation of Musicians president Petrillo and his recording bans seemed of a piece with teamster violence and dockyard corruption. Long despised by theater and club owners, things like house minimums appeared as just one more case of "featherbedding," like the fireman in the cab of a diesel locomotive. When Uday Shankar and the Indian Ballet played the Civic Auditorium in February 1952, they were nonplussed to find that the union required seven local musicians to provide "accompaniment." Shankar did wangle a concession: As the western musicians had no experience with Indian music, they were allowed to play in the lobby.

The legislation of the forties was a shot across unionism's bow, and it found its mark. "The union lost a lot of its strength when Taft-Hartley came in," longtime Local 76 official Carl Challstedt told me, "and it caused a division between the leader and the sidemen."

> The union represented only the sideman and not the leader. If the sideman wasn't paid, then the union would have to go against the leader. But say these guys were playing a tavern someplace: You couldn't picket the place if the men weren't getting paid because that would be a secondary boycott on the owner of the tavern. That's really when the teeth were pulled on the union. Before Taft-Hartley, you could picket and get the guys paid.

By the sixties, many viewed the union as good for nothing but levying fines and feeding jobs to a shrinking coterie of insiders. "Some of the guys would use the union hall to catch gigs," Floyd Standifer chuckled.

They'd sit there, and the jobs would come in, and the business agent or whoever who took the call would say, "Hey, got a gig just came in." Now, to be equitable, they should have put that gig up on the board. Give everybody a crack. But it didn't always work that way. People would call in—"Is Terry Cruise available?"—and the business agent would say, "I'll see." He'd give his buddy sittin' there a wink and tell the party no, even though Terry *was* available, and give the job to a crony. Terry would never know somebody'd been askin' about him!

Symphony bassist and long-serving Local 76 official Mori Simon responded to charges of cronyism. "It has been rumored that your Association is being run by a CLIQUE," he wrote in the union paper. "Upon investigation it was found that this rumor is true. Furthermore we find the clique is composed of faithful members who are present at every meeting, who accept appointments to committees, who give willingly of their time . . . and who sincerely believe that the more one puts into his Association, the more he will get out of it." In other words: Get involved.[1]

Percussionist Howard Gilbert got involved, and took on the struggle to obtain pensions for working musicians. He found clique-ism in spades: "A lot of the 'old guard' had good day jobs," Howard told me, "and had pensions wherever they were working, so they did everything they could to keep us 'peons' from getting our pensions."

So a bunch of us organized, and the membership put through the pension. Then, when we turned our backs, the old boys reversed us! We never did get the full package. It was only for musicians working full-time, six nights a week. The casual musician couldn't get it. I live well now, and that's because I got the pension.

Pete Leinonen got involved, as business agent, vice president, board member, and *Musicland* editor, and bucked the tide of cronyism and hostility to innovation:

In the sixties there was so much work they had to make a rule against playing seven nights. You could not audition for a job and you could not solicit a job if there was already a band under contract. The musicians respected that and they made a living. If a place wanted to audition you, they had to hire you. If you were lame, you'd probably have to change your name before you'd get another shot. Then the Beatles hit, and the union coasted about ten years on momentum. It was finally destroyed from within by a handful of old cronies who turned the union into their personal plaything. Ken Shirk and I tried to salvage things; we got the referral system going, and the video program, and we actually gained a lot of new members. But that only freaked out the old guard. In election after election I ran against the entrenched guys; I didn't owe anybody and I said some strong stuff. It was a losing battle—my life was actually threatened.

Still, the musicians' union survives. Why? "As long as there are arts organizations requiring the services of highly trained musicians," Local 76–493 secretary/treasurer Warren Johnson told me, "there will be a need for collective bargaining and for a union." Johnson enumerated innovations that have kept the Musicians' Association relevant: health insurance at group rates; a new AFM contract that makes it easier for free-lance musicians to vest in the pension fund; a possible endowment fund to support lower-budget professional and semiprofessional arts organizations that act as "feeders" to the symphony, opera, and theaters. Said Johnson, "It's these kinds of working partnerships that will keep the musicians' union relevant." In an overwhelming buyer's market, though, the odds remain daunting. "Everybody wants music," says union office secretary Monica Schley, "but nobody wants to pay for it. This big, famous coffee company calls, wanting a duo for a Friday evening. They say, 'We can't pay anything.' Why not? They're a billion-dollar company! We don't ask for free coffee, do we?"[2]

Oblivious to such quibbles are the thousands of eager young trumpeters, violinists, and singers who flood the market every year. People have debated this conundrum for decades. "The world is . . . not equipped to make use of so much highly-trained musical ability," said Jacques Barzun in 1956. "It therefore becomes a question whether encouraging the young [to study music] is not perhaps risky to the point of immorality. . . . It may be that we should revise our idea of the musical life, redefine amateur and professional in keeping with the facts . . . and reorient education accordingly."[3]

Mentor of many promising young musicians over the last twenty years, Jay Thomas is a major factor behind the acclaim enjoyed by the Garfield

High School jazz program. Only a handful of graduates find opportunity to employ their musical talents, however, so I asked Jay what it was it was all for. "It's not 'for' anything," he replied.

> That's a "subject-object" way of looking at it, and the universe doesn't work that way. There's no "reason" for music education at all, other than it's enlightening to be involved in something that is larger than the individual. They learn what it's like to work as a team on something that they *can't master*, ever. They can get *better* at it, but there's no end in sight. They learn a different way to react with one another that's not dependent on language, and they learn to cooperate with the *common* goal to create something great, or beautiful. So, it's really not *"for"* anything. It is what it is.

Nevertheless, a few fry make it downstream. "I've had a couple of really good students," Jay smiled—"better than me. They got good *real* fast, did everything I told them, and now they're in New York makin' hay." Clarinetist/educator William O. Smith offered this:

> Music is like a lottery. I think the only answer is to love it for itself, and to develop your musicianship out of a love for the craft and not be overly concerned about making a fortune. When you're teaching a young student, and they have one foot in computers and one foot in music, and they ask, "Should I go into music, or computers?" what are you going to tell them? "Follow your inner voice." Okay. But our society has built itself on the star system, so unless you're a star, forget it.

Despite all the discouragements society arrays against those who sustain one of its core needs, live, professional music will survive. There will be casualties, for those discouragements terminate many a promising musical career—or worse, rob music-making of its one essential ingredient: joy. How to keep the joy in music is a question all practitioners must ask themselves. For many of the musicians I interviewed, the answer was simple: Do it part-time. One of the hardest-working violinists in Seattle, Nick Potebnya fiddled through fifty years of bored Elks clubbers and inebriated St. Patrick's Day revelers, and never burned out. "Spread joy!" Nick told me.

That's what it's all about. But what has kept music fresh for me is the fact that I've always made a living in something *other* than music. I was a general contractor for years, and I can't begin to count all the feast-or-famine musicians I've known. They refuse to take a day job—they think it's beneath them. And they're miserable. I used to go around and around with my drummer, one of the top guys. "I'm a *professional* musician," he'd say. He was starving!

In over forty years with the Seattle Symphony, flutist Scott Goff has witnessed the worst of orchestra politics, but never grew jaded:

If you let the bitterness of the business get to you, you're a goner. I've seen it happen with symphony players; they retire and say, "As soon as I got out of the orchestra, I discovered my joy for music." I listen to this and think, "Too bad you couldn't separate the two things." One of those things is human folly. Well, come on—you get that anywhere. That's why I stay away from the politics. Who wants to listen to the nut cases shooting their mouths off, then come back onstage all inflamed? If you don't think it affects your playing and your whole existence, you haven't lived very long. But the other thing, the thing that matters, is *the music*. We're doing *Don Giovanni* now; I've probably played it fifty times, and I *still* love it!

Bonnie Guitar has taken plenty of knocks, but has never stopped loving music in all its aspects:

There are so many things I could say about the music business that would shock you: payola . . . the things you have to do to get a record out . . . how many hit records were lost because someone along the chain of distribution dropped the ball. Still, I look upon it all as a blessing. If you raised a bunch of crystal spires, the one that says "musicians" would be the tallest and the brightest. We are so *blessed* to be musicians!

And Seattle was blessed that they were. For, weaving like a golden thread through the social fabric, music was an essential catalyst in the city's development. Hymns stiffened the resolve of early settlers, brass bands bucked up mill hands, and women were emboldened by song to stride boldly into a man's world. Music was among the city's first connections to the outside world, and it has been its most durable.

Was there anything uniquely "Seattle" about the city's music in the pre–rock and roll age? After all, artists Mark Tobey and Kenneth Callahan, architects Paul Kirk and Victor Steinbrueck, and poets Theodore Roethke and Richard Hugo have long been acclaimed as eminences in a "Pacific Northwest school" of their chosen fields. The music of the Duwamish people is a truly indigenous expression of place, developed over centuries and central to the group's identity. What of other strains?

People have pondered this since the thirties, when H. G. Merriam looked at the Pacific Northwest and lamented that "the regional temperament . . . was too tame, too tied to ideas and customs alien to the area" to create its own musical idiom. Seventy years later, Seattle Symphony director Gerard Schwarz told me flatly, "I don't believe that there is such a thing as a Northwest sound. I think our orchestra has a very distinctive sound, but I don't think it has much to do with our region." Ever since white settlers arrived in Elliott Bay bearing ready-made music, Seattle has looked outward for inspiration and affirmation. Our hunger for connection made us all the more disdainful of regionalism; in a "world city," after all, parochialism is anathema, and as a diverse population grows and cross-pollinates, so do the centripetal forces of commonality and universality. Even the "Seattle songs" of the early twentieth century had generic counterparts in hundreds of other striving cities, and our continuing deference to European masters has meant that, so far, Seattle has failed to create a canon of down-home art music that is both recognized as regional expression and performed regularly.[4]

Mary Carr Moore, George Frederick McKay, and Earl Robinson wrote music that might have started something, but no "school" coalesced around them, and their Northwest evocations, once so highly praised, languish in obscurity. Seattle's most prolific and eminent art music composer, Alan Hovhaness, closed the circle in 1963 when he came to Puget Sound from New York and settled in as the Seattle Symphony's first composer in residence. Hovhaness (1911–2000) loved nature, and at least three of his sixty-seven symphonies pay tribute to the mountains and rivers of Washington. One of his most popular works, the suite *And God Created Great Whales*, carries salt-chuck connotations, not least because some of the "musicians" were recorded in the waters off Washington and British Columbia. But Hovhaness's musical language owes at least as much to his ancestral Armenia and to Asia, and he is known not as a regional but a world composer. In any case, where music is concerned, one man's Rainier is another's Ararat. As composer and educator Peter Seibert told me, "It's very hard to say that a succession of notes from E-flat to G to A means 'the Northwest.' I believe that notes are about notes."

The Seattle-ness of the city's colorful jazz heritage is perhaps more complex and, given the evanescent nature of the medium, more subjective. "Seattle [jazz] has not had a bonafide tradition, the way the East Coast does," declared jazz writer Paul de Barros—"there is no significant Seattle style." Others disagree. "I have always heard a subtle Northwest quality in our most innovative recording artists," Pete Leinonen insists, "and I've noticed that the best Seattle arrangers, though influenced by bebop, used a less dissonant approach." Jim Wilke offers,

> I think there is a Northwest sound, but it's very hard to define. In many cases, it's *not* what's going on someplace *else*. People really look for their own thing, and *not* being in an East Coast urban center, we're less influenced by what's going on there. We're makin' our own fun out here! To me, a group like Oregon is very organic—a uniquely Northwest group. Their sound really comes from the soil and I can't imagine them developing anyplace else.

Consider, too, that the very *persistence* of Seattle jazz through many phases, down at times but never out, seems to indicate a natural, harmonic empathy with the city's restless, improvising spirit: a vocalization of the city's constant search for new ways to define itself.[5]

Anyone daring to venture into musical regionalism must deal with regional self-loathing. Gazing eastward for validation, we have always found a million reasons why local talent is never quite good enough. The "regional prejudice" that may have kept Moore's *Narcissa* off the New York stage goes both ways, and the assumption that "if they were any good, they wouldn't be *here*" has been the despair of generations of culture commentators. "Everybody has to get away from Seattle," lamented Rolf Stromberg. "When you return, if you've been to New York, everybody looks at you with respect. It's also true [that] all outsiders who come here are experts in their field, or we regard them as such." Phil and Vivian Williams see this phenomenon in folk music, too: "If you're from Kentucky," Phil said, "you're real. If you're from Seattle, you're dissed. We knew an Oregon fiddler who was ignored for years by the folk community, so he moved to Kentucky and within a short time was 'discovered' by those same arbiters, who now considered him 'real.'" Outside rock and roll, Pat Suzuki and Seattle

Opera stand virtually alone in hitting it big while staying at home. Still, a century and a half is only an eyeblink, after all, and the water, mountains, and animals of the Pacific Northwest continue to work their magic on those who live among them. In finding her voice, maybe Seattle has just been warming up.[6]

The question of Seattle's musical identity will hang, subject to countless interpretations, for a long time to come. In the end, perhaps "The Old Settler's Song"—an Irish tune seasoned with acres of clams—will remain the one piece of music closest to the city's soul. One thing is certain: In any future discussion of Seattle's essential character, music will not be overlooked. From brass band to symphony, opera to grunge, Seattle has used music as a primary tool with which to maintain an identity and a place in the world. And as every generation has harkened to variations of music handed down from people before, that music will persist even as new sounds burst forth. We hold tight to the music of our fathers and find in it, as Seattleites always have, connection with the past and a bridge to the future. In a Pioneer Square restaurant, a cornet carries forth echoes of Tom Brown, while on the banks of the Duwamish, a young fisherman sings softly to the night.

■ ■ ■

Notes

INTRODUCTION

1   *That job paid an actual, honest-to-goodness living wage:* Don Smith interview, 2005.

2   *Be assured that if:* Davis, *History of Music,* vol. 1, 5. *I would rather see you in a hearse:* Handy, *Father of the Blues,* 11. *There was a general feeling:* Jack Hungerford interview, 2004.

3   *ninety-nine percent:* Speidel, *Doc Maynard,* 262. Firsthand records of everyday life in early Seattle are scarce. Historian Clarence Bagley declared, "The printed and written record of the first twenty years of Seattle's existence are scanty almost beyond belief. Few, if any, pioneers kept diaries." Bagley, *History of Seattle,* preface.

1   SONG OF THE DUWAMISH

1   *The entire city is a palimpsest:* Thrush, *Native Seattle,* 14–15.

2   *One day, North Wind blew hard:* ibid., 102, 242.

3   *more Indian than white, the frogs:* ibid., 77–79. *For days at a time:* Bagley, *History of Seattle,* 96.

4   *twenty-two Native American residents:* Berner, *Seattle in the Twentieth Century,* vol. 1, 60.

5   *After long contact with Europeans:* Crawford, *America's Musical Life,* 14. *All the spiritually powerful songs:* Haines, "Singers, Dancers, Dreamers, Travelers," in *Spirit of the First People,* 13.

2   GASLIGHT SERANADE

1   *happy hours, jolly nights:* Denny, *Blazing the Way,* 89. *a dance that kept all the pioneers busy:* Sayre, *This City of Ours,* 78. *Ezra Meeker walked the dusty streets:* Seattle *Post-Intelligencer,* June 16, 1901, 35.

2   *had a powerful imaginative effect*: P. Thomas, *Songs of the Pacific Northwest*, 61. Thomas states that there are at least two versions of "Seattle Illahee" and calls it "the oldest song yet found orally in the Pacific Northwest." It is unknown exactly when the song first appeared and whether it inspired, or was inspired by, Pennell's bawdy house.

3   *There are enough good singers here*: Rev. David Blaine and Catherine Blaine, Letters. Seattle's first pipe organ was a $1,500 instrument built by John Bergstrom of San Francisco and dedicated at the Trinity Episcopal Church on August 22, 1882.

4   *Almost every couple that sets up housekeeping*: Mussulman, *Music in the Cultured Generation*, 170.

5   *extremely backward condition*: Bagley, *History of Seattle*, 140–41. *Plummer built Plummer's Hall*: Speidel, *Doc Maynard*, 145–46. Though well researched, Speidel's delightful popular histories contain liberal amounts of conjecture.

6   *The improvement of the band*: *Seattle Press-Times*, July 8, 1893, 9.

7   *What fine times were had*: ibid.

8   *consolidate the musical talent of Seattle*: Sayre, *This City of Ours*, 118.

9   *music of very superior quality*: *Puget Sound Dispatch*, December 9, 1876, 3.

10   *It would be safe to wager*: Jewell, "Performances," 116. *The progress which the American people show*: Mussulman, *Music in the Cultured Generation*, 74.

11   *generational discontinuity*: Riddle, *Flying Dragons, Flowing Streams*, xxii. Of Chinese music, Riddle states that, before 1983, "there has been little or no scholarly study of this interesting sector of Chinese-American culture." See ibid., x.

12   Curiously, the *Post-Intelligencer* of July 1, 1907 (8) found that Seattle had fewer *human* whistlers than most American cities.

13   *It is surprising how many really fine musicians*: Jewell, "Performances," 118.

14   *Those who followed music as a profession*: *Seattle Press-Times*, July 8, 1893, 2.

15   *paid a very respectable ten dollars apiece*: Eaton, *Musical U.S.A.*, 201. *playing all night for a keg of beer*: Greer, "Seattle's Local Musicians," 3.

16   *competitive encroachments*: Musicians' Association of Seattle, Local 76, AFM, meeting minutes, March 15, 1892. Bandleader Pete Leinonen told me that, in the 1970s, his band "had to compete with military rock bands that came with forty-foot semi-trailers full of equipment, like major touring acts—and played for free."

17   *the profession of musician in the face of the times*: ibid., February 13, 1894, 1. *it was a hard problem*: *Musicland*, November 20, 1921, 7. *Often in the afternoons*: *Musicland*, December 5, 1921, 1.

18   *It is at about 8 o'clock in the evening*: *Seattle Post-Intelligencer*, July 30, 1899, 10.

19   *Since the main requirement*: Crawford, *America's Musical Life*, 75. *remarkable taste*: ibid., 425.

3 MUSIC ON THE MAKE

1   "The Old Settler's Song" exists in numerous permutations, among them "Rosin the Bow," "Lay of the Old Settler," and "Acres of Clams." In 1955 Seattle singer Walt Robertson recorded the song on the Folkways label (FA2046) as "Puget Sound," and

a year later Earl Robinson adapted it for his tone poem "A Country They Call Puget Sound."

2 *but it made another story in the papers: Seattle Times* magazine, April 22, 1962, 7.

3 A 1916 law abolishing unregulated taverns would join World War I austerities and Prohibition in finishing off Seattle's wide-open saloon culture.

4 80 percent: Greer, "Seattle's Local Musicians," 2.

5 *I notice that the union:* Leiter, *Musicians and Petrillo*, 24.

6 *cannot maintain his ability: Musicland*, August 22, 1922, 1.

7 Between 1890 and 1910 federal census records show 22,681 persons of German origin settling in Seattle. The next largest group, the English, totaled 16,480. *German and German-Jewish businessmen: Town Crier*, October 1936, 22. Census records reveal 65,089 Swedes and Norwegians arriving in Seattle between 1910 and 1930, and 27,736 English émigrés. *The first two things:* Knudsen, "Norwegian Male Chorus," 51.

8 Some historians claim that the Dream Theater was first in the nation, if not the world, to employ organ accompaniment. Historian John Landon, however, said that "no one knows for sure when or where" the first theater organ was installed, and suggested that it may have been at Thomas Talley's Los Angeles Theater, which opened in 1905. See Landon, *Behold the Mighty Wurlitzer*, 4.

9 *You are breaking up my home life: Seattle Times*, September 5, 1909, 72. *The Ellery band has become a live influence:* ibid., October 16, 1909, 3. It is interesting to speculate why John Philip Sousa, whose band had appeared at many other world's fairs, did not play the Alaska-Yukon-Pacific Exposition. Before and after the exposition, beginning in 1896, Sousa was a fairly regular Seattle visitor. By 1909, though, the March King had settled into the pattern he would maintain for the rest of his performing career: January through July for rest, family, and composition, then a season-opening month at Philadelphia's Willow Grove Park. Only in September did the band embark on its grueling annual tour, which in 1909 did not reach the West Coast until late October. Existing AYPE files at the University of Washington reveal no correspondence with Sousa.

10 The *Seattle Post-Intelligencer* of August 23 and October 10, 1909, declared the Hawaiian Glee Club and quartet among the most popular performing groups at the fair.

11 *The whole fraternity held his fist: Seattle Times*, September 7, 1909, 4. *a fresh middle class:* Berner, *Seattle in the Twentieth Century*, vol. 1, 54.

12 *It was a grand old trip: Seattle Post-Intelligencer*, April 27, 1914, 10. *"Dad" Wagner is a man: Musicland*, December 27, 1926, 2. The phrase "poor in worldly goods" is sobering testimony to the precarious economic stature of even a musician as popular as Wagner. In 1909 a journalist complained that Wagner "has better men than the support Seattle has given his band entitles them to hear." *Argus*, October 30, 1909, 1.

13 *of low economic standing:* Mumford, *Seattle's Black Victorians*, 94. *From the early nineties:* ibid., 51. Mumford offers no further documentation on African American musicians. In 1900 five African American musicians were recorded by the census taker; in 1910, twenty-three. U.S. Bureau of the Census, *Occupations, 1900*, 13, 730–32, and U.S. Bureau of the Census, *Occupations, 1910*, vol. 4, 1234–35.

14 Another component of the African American string band tradition, rural black fiddle playing, appears to have remained largely east of the Mississippi, and during the twenties faded to virtual extinction.

15 *I've got to have that music:* Gushee, *Pioneers of Jazz,* 95. *This orchestra plays ragtime music:* ibid., 111. *The music of contemporary savages: Cayton's Weekly,* September 1, 1917, 4.

16 *They don't want you:* Powell S. Barnett interview, 19. *It doesn't make any difference:* ibid.

17 *We had a colored band here, they wouldn't have any part:* ibid., 20. *waive the social rights:* Local 76 minutes, May 28, 1913, 353. *color question:* ibid., 354.

18 *Why does Mr. Thomas play:* Davis, *History of Music in American Life,* vol. 2, 14. *With this word Culture:* Baur, "Music, Morals, and Social Management," 67. *The musical activity of this country:* Mussulman, *Music in the Cultured Generation,* 103.

19 *The annual expenditure of the American public:* Whitesitt, "Role of Women Impresarios," 170. In 2011 the Ladies Musical Club continues to present distinguished soloists, sponsor school concerts, and provide a forum for promising young artists.

20 *The great audience was charmed:* Campbell, *Bagpipes in the Woodwind Section,* 1. Christensen's Hall was located in the old Arcade Building on Second Avenue, directly across from today's Benaroya Hall.

21 *Symphony orchestras are expensive luxuries: Seattle Times,* September 1, 1907, 30.

22 *plethora of attractions: Town Crier,* March 7, 1914, 11.

23 *exceedingly interesting:* ibid., February 21, 1920, 14. Always a partisan of American composers, Henry Hadley went on to establish the National Association of American Composers and Conductors and to lead many of the world's top orchestras, and in 1934 founded the Berkshire Music Festival.

24 *New York managers looked: Town Crier,* April 13, 1912, 11. *America now has a grand opera:* ibid. *Cries of "Bravo!":* ibid., April 27, 1912, 10. The *New Grove Dictionary of American Music* has praised *Narcissa's* "naïve but often persuasive expressionism" and has echoed the *Town Crier* in noting that "both regional prejudice and sex discrimination prevented Moore from receiving the recognition that the achievement of *Narcissa* warranted and probably slowed her artistic development." *New Grove Dictionary of American Music,* vol. 3 (Macmillan Press, New York, 1986), 268.

25 *an extraordinary achievement: Town Crier,* May 9, 1914, 11.

26 *The "Seattle Spirit": Town Crier,* January 6, 1912, 1. *create an artistic atmosphere:* ibid., January 24, 1914, 10. Resident musician population: U.S. Bureau of the Census. *Occupations,* 1900, vol. 13, 730–32; and U.S. Bureau of the Census. *Occupations,* 1910, vol. 4, 1234–35.

27 *Let us have payrolls:* Sale, *Seattle, Past to Present,* 101.

28 *We believe that Seattle: Music and Musicians,* February 1915, 1. *The menace of the popular song: Town Crier,* May 2, 1914, 1. *Musicians may deride ragtime: Music and Musicians,* May 27, 1916, 6.

29 *give us some: Town Crier,* July 22, 1916, 11.

30 *danger zone of hate: Town Crier,* December 15, 1917, 22–23. *I want no German music:* ibid., December 8, 1917, 7.

31 *Music in Seattle: Seattle Post-Intelligencer,* March 3, 1918, 6.

4 MUSICIAN'S DREAM

1   *Let us make* HARMONY *our keynote: Musicland*, September 1, 1921, 1.

2   *King Choy better come around: Musicland*, October 15, 1921, 3. *jazz a little*: ibid., September 21, 1921, 4. *average union membership of 75 percent*: Greer, "Seattle's Local Musicians," 4.

3   *a menace to the community: Music and Musicians*, July 1921, 12. *It is not much of a trick: Musicland*, January 5, 1922, 1. *From the slums of New Orleans: Seattle Post-Intelligencer*, July 13, 1921, 18.

4   *Dad was one of the greatest*: Interview with Dave Holden, 2009.

5   Of Jelly Roll Morton, Oscar Holden's daughter Grace told me in 2009 that, "Some writers have said that our father worked for Jelly Roll, when it was really the other way around. *Dad* hired Jelly."

6   *a slug of complaints*: see Powell S. Barnett interview. The Musicians' Association of Seattle, Local 76, meeting minutes reveal little discussion of Local 458.

7   *interfere in any way with: Musicland*, March 10, 1925, 4; *Mister Average American citizen*: ibid., June 15, 1922, 6.

8   *This leaky, wind-driven instrument*: ibid., March 5, 1927, 3.

9   *We wouldn't see the picture first*: Klos, "Life and Times of Gaylord Carter," *Theater Organ/Bombarde* 9, no. 5 (October 1967): 5. *Small audiences on off-days*: Muri, "Playing the Film," *Theater Organ/Bombarde* 16, no. 3 (June 1974): 28–29. One of the most influential sources of silent-movie music was the *Remick Folio of Moving Picture Music*, first published in 1914. This compendium of stock melodies, including J. Bodewalt Lampe's creepy classic "Mysterioso Pizzicato" (Remick no. 89), became part of America's musical subconscious.

10 *I like and respect Mr. Kay*: Musicians' Association of Seattle, meeting minutes, April 1921, 498.

11 *Gobby was a wonderful old-time vaudeville musician*: Dick Rose interview, 2004.

12 *I started school*: Ronald Phillips interview, 1992.

13 *a hustling, bustling, materialistic city*: Haarsager, *Bertha Knight Landes*, 158. *I do not like*: Ammer, *Unsung*, 250.

14 *sometimes compared to the sound: Time*, January 24, 1949, 37–39. *a 50-year jump: Seattle Post-Intelligencer*, October 20, 1965, 7.

15 *one of the most interesting figures: Town Crier*, June 17, 1916, 16. *factionalism, financial losses*: Campbell, *Bagpipes in the Woodwind Section*, 14.

16 *artists, musicians, businessmen*: Cornish, *Miss Aunt Nellie*, 59. *It's a wonderful school*: ibid., 73.

17 *There was little recognition*: Sale, *Seattle, Past to Present*, 161.

18 *We have an orchestra of sixty-five artists: Seattle Times*, January 8, 1933, 15. *The situation is unique*: ibid. The reborn Seattle Symphony faced one encumbrance: former conductor John Spargur, who claimed that he was owed $6,000 in back wages. The Philharmonic Society graciously paid the arrears.

19 *Krueger was a very good conductor*: Ronald Phillips interview, 1992.

20 *What decided strides forward: Town Crier*, November 3, 1928, 17.

21 *I have never seen anything superior:* Seattle Post-Intelligencer, August 12, 1927, 1.

22 In 1946 Norm Bobrow and Adolph Linden produced a 78 rpm record of the Gay Jones Orchestra performing "The Darktown Strutters' Ball" and "Alexander's Ragtime Band." In one of our many conversations, Bobrow told me, "That was the first commercial recording made by a Seattle record label."

23 *Contrary to all pessimistic predictions:* Town Crier, October 1936, 14.

24 *My friends among the music teachers:* Seattle Post-Intelligencer, May 4, 1930, 6E.

25 *The Seattle musician holds an enviable position:* Musicland, December 30, 1928, 2; *We do not feel that the police:* ibid., April 25, 1928, 1.

26 *With such competition:* Musicland, April 15, 1928, 2.

27 *In many of our eastern and Pacific Coast cities:* Musicland, December 30, 1928, 2. *Sound has been our nightmare:* ibid., December 25, 1929, 1, 31.

5 EASING DEPRESSION

1 *I was a pretty average musician:* Andy Piatt interview, 2004.

2 *by 1929 only 5,000:* Leiter, Musicians and Petrillo, 56.

3 *It is hard to do this:* Seattle Post-Intelligencer, May 15, 1931, 17.

4 *Be alive!:* Seattle Times magazine, September 15, 1963, 4–5; *Oeconomacos had great phrasing:* Ronald Phillips interview, 1992.

5 *Seattle union lost as much as one third:* Greer, "Seattle's Local Musicians," 8.

6 *El's was a good, solid dance band:* Hugh Bruen interview, 2005.

7 *I won't tell any lies:* Seattle Times, May 29, 1991, E12. To be fair, Meyers was far from being the only bandleader who sometimes failed to pay his sidemen!

8 *We were playing stuff:* Darensbourg, Jazz Odyssey, 74.

9 *Old-time ethnic music:* Greene, Passion for Polka, 77.

10 In a 2008 interview, musicologist Vivian Williams told me that traditional Scandinavian fiddling persisted in lodge and grange dances throughout the early twentieth century, becoming a key component of "Northwest style" old-time fiddling as it is now recognized.

11 *Families brought picnic lunches:* Pete Leinonen interview, 2007.

12 *Center Case was a real nice guy:* Ed Gross interview, 2005. *The Madhatters came out of Ballard High:* Mitchell Taylor Bowie interview, 1991.

13 *I would like to see swing music:* de Barros, Jackson Street after Hours, 54. Norm Bobrow was another fan of the great Jimmie Lunceford, and his enthusiasm may well have rubbed off on the Jones band. "That Lunceford rhythm section just knocked me flat," Norm told me. "I used to get into arguments at the U by saying that Duke Ellington couldn't carry Lunceford's shoes. I ran into Duke years later and told him that. He laughed and said, 'Norm, I always thought the Lunceford band was the best, too'!" The Bobrow-Lunceford connection went beyond hero worship; in the late thirties Bobrow wrote a tune and sent it to Lunceford, who liked it well enough to feature in his band as "Slot Machine Blues." Norm Bobrow interview, 2004–7.

14 *Tiny Martin and I:* Milt Kleeb interview, 2004.

15 *A lively jazz scene:* Segell, Devil's Horn, 33.

16 *Jimmy was a marvelous jazz player:* Norm Bobrow interview, 2004.
17 *Winfield was a real, entertainer-type piano player:* Floyd Standifer interview, 2004.
18 *Black Seattleites had long prided themselves:* Taylor, *Forging of a Black Community*, 155. *One time the city of Seattle: Northwest Enterprise*, March 31, 1938, 4.
19 *a musician whose individual achievement: Seattle Times*, December 22, 1931, 9. Krueger stated in his resignation that he felt that Seattle was "unwilling to give the orchestra the kind of financial support it required." See *Argus*, September 4, 1948, 4.
20 *Had a similar occasion: Town Crier*, April 3, 1933, 6.
21 *At the beginning of radio popularity: Town Crier*, October 1936, 22. *Basil Cameron has literally made:* ibid., December 1936, 23.
22 *I practiced it constantly:* Ronald Phillips interview, 1992. *Gershwin's music may be: Seattle Post-Intelligencer*, December 16, 1936, 9. As if the Gershwin weren't enough, the December 15 concert also included Chabrier's *Espana* and Schubert's "Unfinished" Symphony. *suppressed genius: Seattle Times*, July 12, 1937, 6.
23 *A very small minority:* Campbell, *Bagpipes in the Woodwind Section*, 24. *too much fish and timber: Town Crier*, April 1, 1933, 6. *A five-cent glass of beer:* Campbell, *Bagpipes in the Woodwind Section*, 24.
24 *It is . . . no secret: Town Crier*, February 10, 1934, 5. *The dullest stretch:* Campbell, *Bagpipes in the Woodwind Section*, 32.
25 *a new high for local grand opera performances: Seattle Times*, May 12, 1938, 23.
26 *good enough to be copied: Seattle Post-Intelligencer*, November 1, 1938, 22. *The Seattle Times* ignored the event completely. The *Northwest Enterprise* also sponsored the weekly KEEN Radio "All-Negro Hour," providing a forum for non-jazz African American music. Church choirs and orchestras, the black community band, and soloists were featured on the Thursday night show.
27 *These big business tycoons: Time*, January 24, 1949, 37–39. *By April nothing was happening:* Maxine Cushing Gray interview by Jill Severn.

6 WARTIME WHOOPIE

1 Gay Jones returned to Seattle after the war and worked with combos for the next four decades. His many compositions include "I Nearly Lost My Mind," a theme song that he sold to Lionel Hampton, who in turn featured it with vocalist Evelyn Williamson, herself a Seattle native. Jones's "Riffette" became a minor hit for boogie-woogie pianist Freddie Slack. *Curt's checks weren't always good:* Dick Giger interview, 2005.
2 *Al had that old, slick style:* Floyd Standifer interview, 2005.
3 John Barbirolli and Edwin McArthur conducted the winter slots during the Beecham regime.
4 *You can go home now:* Gilmour, *Sir Thomas Beecham*, 18. *Will someone kindly introduce:* ibid., 10.
5 Sandra Haarsager noted, "Gains women made in the 1920s disappeared in the 1930s, as movements to keep women out of the workplace grew under the guise of protecting jobs and self-respect for family breadwinners." Haarsager, *Bertha Knight Landes*, 239.

6 *Set your shoulder to the task: Seattle Star* and *Seattle Post-Intelligencer*, November 15, 1941, 5. Reporters from the two dailies transcribed Beecham's remarks identically. Even Seattle Symphony historian Esther W. Campbell perpetuates the "put-down" interpretation; see Campbell, *Bagpipes in the Woodwind Section*, 44.

7 *pompous little Britisher: Seattle Post-Intelligencer*, November 17, 1942, 26. *If this action continues: Seattle Star*, October 15, 1943, 1. Symphony trustee and Beecham intimate Hans Lehmann claimed that it was Arthur French's opening night ejection that launched the *PI*'s "ugly newspaper vendetta" against the conductor; see Lehmann and Lehmann, *Out of the Cultural Dustbin*, 22–23.

8 Hans Lehmann said that Beecham may have been at least partly motivated to take the Seattle job in order to "share his life in the Elysian fields of Seattle" with Miss Humby, as far away as possible from his wife. Lehmann and Lehmann, *Out of the Cultural Dustbin*, 21. *Great break: Seattle Post-Intelligencer*, November 6, 1943, 4.

9 *an offense to the ear: Seattle Post-Intelligencer*, September 11, 1966, 4.

10 *Oh, it just makes me sick:* Campbell, *Bagpipes in the Woodwind Section*, 53.

11 *Schneider acted as a catalyst:* Lehmann and Lehmann, *Out of the Cultural Dustbin*, 30–31.

12 *musical mobsters: Time*, January 24, 1949, 37–39. *She has always wanted:* ibid. *when there was so much caterwauling: Time*, August 23, 1948, 51–52. *All those board members have been pretty good about this:* ibid.

13 *a beautiful body without a brain:* Campbell, *Bagpipes in the Woodwind Section*, 62.

14 *We had some excellent jazz players:* Don Glenn interview, 2004.

15 *Bumps couldn't play anything:* Floyd Standifer interview, 2004.

16 *We elected a president, he had a taxicab business:* Jones, *Autobiography of Quincy Jones*, 46.

17 *Music made me full:* ibid., 49.

18 *Sometimes we'd start in playing:* de Barros, *Jackson Street after Hours*, 143.

19 *We recorded fourteen sides:* Ronnie Pierce interview, 2004.

7 DIZZY DECADE

1 *Music has become for many people:* Barzun, *Music in American Life*, 15.

2 *Can't you play something:* Tamara Burdette interview, 2005.

3 In its November 26, 1959, review of the Mastersounds, *Down Beat* magazine credited San Francisco, not Seattle, with launching the group to prominence.

4 *Jazz was the popular music:* Jim Wilke interview, 2008.

5 *Doc Exner loved New Orleans–type jazz:* Johnny Wittwer interview by Pete Leinonen, 1989.

6 *patriotic project in musical archaeology: Down Beat*, March 24, 1948, 14.

7 *Ernie was more of a swing player than bebop:* Floyd Standifer interview, 2004. *the nearest thing to an Art Tatum:* Norm Bobrow interview, 2004.

8 *Gerry was a wizard:* Norm Bobrow interview, 2004.

9 *You'd be surprised:* de Barros, *Jackson Street after Hours*, 174.

10 *Frank Sugia was the classic bandleader:* Floyd Standifer interview, 2004.

11 *I blew about $300: Seattle Times*, April 12, 1972, C8. Paul Tutmarc was tinkering with the steel guitar concurrently with several others across the country, most notably Alvino Rey, but Bonnie Guitar was adamant in telling me, "I believe Paul built the first steel guitar. Some people talk about Alvino Rey, but Paul came before Alvino Rey." In a less successful venture, Tutmarc also created what some consider the world's first electric bass, the Audiovox 736, in 1936.

12 *I took some heat*: Norm Bobrow interview, 2004.

13 Firth elaborated to me the spread of the hootenanny phenomenon after the 1941 Seattle concert of Pete Seeger and Woody Guthrie: "Seeger's *Complete Folksinger* describes how he and Woody, calling themselves the Almanac Singers, had come out to Seattle to do some singing at a fund-raising for old union organizations. After the concert they were invited to the group's hootenanny, and when they got back to New York, they had Friday afternoon concerts to raise rent money. They started calling them 'hootenannies,' and the word spread from there."

14 *Urban migrants often grew nostalgic*: Davis, *History of Music in American Life*, vol. 2, 364.

15 In the 1970s Joe Venuti himself became one of the few authentic music legends to reside in Seattle, playing circles around musicians half his eighty years and mentoring young fan Paul Anastasio into one of the country's top jazz violinists.

16 *It is so ghastly*: Campbell, *Bagpipes in the Woodwind Section*, 69.

17 *almost in one luncheon*: ibid., 64, 69. *There is nothing new: Seattle Post-Intelligencer*, August 30, 1951, 14.

18 *some people who didn't like me*: Campbell, *Bagpipes in the Woodwind Section*, 76. *he is a great artist*: ibid. Symphony board member Hans Lehmann later denied that anyone was out to get Rosenthal, including his old rival, Eugene Linden, who "possessed no knowledge of Rosenthal's double life." Lehmann thought the most likely whistle blower was Madame Traoussier herself. See Lehmann and Lehmann, *Out of the Cultural Dustbin*, 35. Stanley Chapple was himself considered for the symphony directorship, with considerable agonizing. "As much as I admired him," said Hans Lehmann, "I was . . . instrumental in blocking his appointment. My motivations were based on the notion that the symphony, in order to grow, should not have to share the services of its conductor with a teaching institution. Furthermore, the musicians . . . were annoyed by the distracting grimaces of his face." Ibid., 37.

19 *Milton, you must come: Seattle* magazine, November 1964, 35. *He's like a Greek God!*: Lehmann and Lehmann, *Out of the Cultural Dustbin*, 39. *held the most potential*: Katims and Katims, *Pleasure Was Ours*, 86.

20 *These days an orchestra conductor*: Di Biase, "Culture at the 'End of the Line,'" 87. *I would make no concessions*: Katims and Katims, *Pleasure Was Ours*, 91. *Just sitting around*: Milton Katims interview by Louis Guzzo, part 1. Katims worked hard to conceal his strong desire to remain in Seattle; in the same interview he told Guzzo that Houston offered more money, but he did not want to raise his children in the South: "There was something about the Texans at the time that just went against my grain. They thought they could buy and sell anybody."

21 *The financial problems*: Campbell, *Bagpipes in the Woodwind Section*, 112.

22 *We owe our contemporary knowledge:* Barzun, *Music in American Life,* 75–77. The city "amusement tax" on admissions particularly incensed Milton Katims, who, like many, considered it an obtuse barrier to the city's artistic development. In the fall of 1953 he buttonholed city councilman David Levine and extracted an "under-the-table" agreement: the city would rebate $7,000 of the orchestra's annual $7,500 admissions tax, in return for free grade-school concerts. The arrangement carried forward, in increasing amounts. See Milton Katims interview by Louis R. Guzzo, part 1.

23 *I would like to talk:* Katims and Katims, *Pleasure Was Ours,* 103.

24 *The music profession: Musicland,* July 1955, 1. *We seem to have taxpayers' money:* ibid., November 1953, 1.

25 *no fixed policy: Musicland,* April 1955, 4. "When I had a gig at the New York Pizza Place in the seventies," bandleader Pete Leinonen told me, "the liquor board told the management that children couldn't come in when we were playing, even with their parents, because live music created a 'tavern-like' atmosphere."

26 *American musicians have suffered: Musicland,* August 1955, 2.

27 *Musicians in general have become lazy:* ibid., August 1958, 8.

28 *The musicians of Seattle:* ibid., February 1958, 2.

29 *When we went into Local 76:* de Barros, *Jackson Street after Hours,* 177.

8   GROOVIN' HIGH

1 *I've got a whole trunkful of tunes: Musicland,* April 1961, 1.

2 *I got $52 a week: Seattle Post-Intelligencer,* May 2, 1964, 11.

3 *Jackie was eternal youth: Seattle Times,* February 16, 1968, 9.

4 *The big bands did so much:* Stan Keen interview, 2006. *Cupid's favorite weapon: Seattle Post-Intelligencer,* February 16, 1968, 17.

5 *Max worshipped Guy Lombardo:* Dick Rose interview, 2004. *Max had the smoothest band:* Harley Brumbaugh interview, 2005.

6 Cecilia and Gustav Schultz also donated the Opera House chandeliers and a rehearsal room off the main lobby, which in 1965 was named in her honor. Surviving Opera House fixtures may be enjoyed at the Rendezvous Restaurant and Lounge. *If Washington State carpenters: Argus,* September 21, 1962, 5. *half a million dollars: Seattle Post-Intelligencer,* November 9, 1962, 5.

7 *I live every phase: Seattle Times,* August 8, 1960, section 5.

8 *Gordon, if I don't play:* Milton Katims interview by Louis R. Guzzo, part 3. *I try to aim: Seattle* magazine, November 1964, 37.

9 *Tell your maestro:* Katims and Katims, *Pleasure Was Ours,* 338.

10 *I've achieved a musical attitude: Seattle* magazine, November 1964, 38. *He thinks he can:* ibid. *This short, energetic, and extraordinarily young-looking man:* ibid., 34.

11 *To date, business support: Seattle* magazine, August 1967, 18–19. *We're a generation behind:* ibid., 56.

12 *Years after Stravinsky: Town Crier,* April 22, 1933, 6.

13 *gamelan orchestra:* Bell-Kanner, *Frontiers,* 10. Nellie Cornish said in her autobiogra-

phy only that Cage had "taught percussion instruments [and] started his percussion instrument orchestra." See Cornish, *Miss Aunt Nellie Cornish*, 260.

14 *without a doubt the most masterful: Seattle Post-Intelligencer*, February 10, 1967, 28.

15 *a completely desolate place:* Seattle Opera, *Encore, Magazine of the Arts*, vol. 1, no. 3 (November 1976): 6.

16 *one of the very few: Argus*, April 20, 1973, 6.

17 *He had aluminum foil on the walls:* Howard Gilbert interview, 2004. *We played the early set:* Pete Leinonen interview, 2004.

18 *Jazz hereabouts is dead: Seattle* magazine, March 1968, 60.

19 *There was no jazz education:* Stan Keen interview, 2006.

20 *We was kinda amazed:* Gushee, *Pioneers of Jazz*, 102.

21 *acquired a decidedly southern ambience:* Taylor, *Forging of a Black Community*, 187.

22 *Playing with Boss George:* Pete Leinonen interview, 2004.

23 *Next to the Bible:* Rev. Samuel McKinney interview, 2005.

24 *Us folkies would gather:* Don Firth interview, 2008.

25 *At The Place Next Door one night:* Don Firth interview, 2008.

9   CARRYING THE TORCH

1 *The first time you try it: Seattle Times*, January 28, 1968, 2D.

2 *There was nobody teaching vocal jazz:* Joni Metcalf interview, 2009.

3 *I lucked into my first steady job:* Walt Wagner interview, 2009.

4 *The late sixties and early seventies were an incredibly fertile time:* Peter Seibert interview, 2010.

5 *Eight years ago: Seattle* magazine, October 1969, 28. *I fear for a very rough winter:* ibid., 29.

6 *There are always those: Seattle* magazine, October 1969.

7 *We see the man: Seattle Flag*, April 12, 1972, 17.

8 *Breathe and develop: Argus*, March 17, 1972, 6. *We're a provincial capital:* ibid., April 7, 1972, 6. In a 2007 e-mail, Roger Downey told me that he felt Maxine Cushing Gray had "little or no" impact on the growth of corporate arts funding after the 1960s; rather, "the change is due more to the growing power and shamelessness of arts marketing departments."

9 *like a marriage gone stale: Seattle Post-Intelligencer*, June 27, 1974, C1. *kick out Katims: Seattle Times*, June 26, 1974, C7.

10 *Guzzo is one of the half-dozen Seattleites: Argus*, December 20, 1974, 8. In the April 1972 *Flag* article, Roger Downey claimed that Katims had the *Post-Intelligencer* replace the "overly critical" Rolf Stromberg. Throughout the sixties, Stromberg had in fact been generally favorable toward Katims' performances, and in his final review of March 31, 1970, he praised a "superlative" season. Nevertheless, when the season resumed in October, Stromberg had been replaced as symphony reviewer by Stephanie Miller and Patrick MacDonald. Two years later, though, Stromberg was again critiquing symphony performances. In a 2007 e-mail, Downey told me, "Guzzo was particularly important to Katims not only because of his control over his newspaper's

arts policy, but because he was a prominent Gentile, and the bulk of Katims's long-term support was within the Jewish community, which continued fiercely to back Katims when a new general manager began trying to engineer a timely succession, and which withdrew a great deal of support from the symphony when he succeeded in doing so."

11   *power play: Seattle Post-Intelligencer,* June 27, 1974, A-10.

12   *Hell, when I think: Seattle Times Magazine,* August 8, 1976, 4. In the same article, Katims told Wayne Johnson, "Throughout this whole thing I never made a public comment, and I never will." *Perhaps the orchestra did need: New York Times,* August 15, 1977, C-32. *Thanks in large part: Argus,* December 20, 1974, 11.

13   Ronald Phillips retired in March 1983 under Miedel's successor, Gerard Schwarz. *In three years: Seattle Times,* April 10, 1977, Q6.

14   *Volunteer board members: Seattle Post-Intelligencer,* March 15, 1979, B3.

15   The identity of the woman who contacted Barnett remains unknown. "I think she was Virginia Katims, but I'm not sure," Barnett told me. Another likely possibility is orchestra manager Ruth McCreery.

16   *No one was vaguely concerned:* Lehmann and Lehmann, *Out of the Cultural Dust-bin,* 32.

17   *Without Aida:* ibid., 46.

18   *He's so friendly: Seattle* magazine, October 1967, 50. *extraordinary box office achieve-ments: Seattle Times,* November 3, 1967, 26.

19   *hot, florid old-fashionedness: Seattle* magazine, November 1966, 22. *We'll get to con-temporary opera:* ibid.

20   *the cultural center of the West: New York Times,* August 15, 1977, C32.

21   *I loved Henry Holt:* Chai Ahrenius interview, 2008.

AFTERWORD

1   *It has been rumored: Musicland,* March 1963, 1.

2   *Everybody wants music:* conversation with Monica Schley, 2008.

3   *The world is not equipped:* Barzun, *Music in American Life,* 47.

4   *I don't believe that:* Gastil, "Pacific Northwest as a Cultural Region," 158.

5   *new ways to define itself:* de Barros, *Jackson Street after Hours,* 202.

6   *Everybody has to get away: Seattle Post-Intelligencer,* October 14, 1967, 18. *If you're from Kentucky:* Phil Williams interview, 2008.

Bibliography

Ahrenius, Chai. Interviewed in Seattle, 2008.

Alaska-Yukon-Pacific Exposition. Scrapbooks. Special Collections, University of Washington Libraries.

Allen, Linda. *Washington Songs and Lore*. Ed. Barbara Chamberlain, John Shideler, and Chrystle Snider. Sponsored by the Washington Centennial Commission. Spokane, WA: Melior Publishing, 1988.

Ammer, Christine. *Unsung: A History of Women in American Music*. Portland, OR: Amadeus Press, 2001.

Bagley, Clarence. *History of Seattle from the Earliest Settlement to the Present Time*. Vol. 1. Chicago: S. J. Clarke, 1916.

Ballard, Arthur C.: *Mythology of Southern Puget Sound*. Seattle: University of Washington Press, 1929.

Barnett, Douglas Q. Interviewed in Seattle, 2009.

Barnett, Powell S. Interview by Richard C. Berner, March 31, 1967. Special Collections, University of Washington Libraries.

Barzun, Jacques. *Music in American Life*. Garden City, NY: Doubleday and Company, 1956.

Bass, Sophie Frye. *Pig-Tail Days in Old Seattle*. Portland, OR: Binfords and Mort, 1937.

Baur, Steven. "Music, Morals, and Social Management: Mendelssohn in Post–Civil War America." *American Music* 19, no. 1 (Spring 2000): 64–130.

Bell-Kanner, Karen. *Frontiers: The Life and Times of Bonnie Bird, American Modern Dancer and Dance Educator*. Amsterdam: Overseas Publishers' Association, Hammond Academic Publishing, 1998.

Berner, Richard C. *Seattle in the Twentieth Century*. Vol. 1, *From Boomtown, Urban Turbulence, to Restoration, 1900–1920*. Seattle: Charles Press, 1999.

———. *Seattle in the Twentieth Century*. Vol. 2, *From Boom to Bust, 1921–1940*. Seattle: Charles Press, 1999.

―――. *Seattle in the Twentieth Century*. Vol. 3, *Seattle Transformed, From World War II to the Cold War*. Seattle: Charles Press, 1999.

Berry, Overton. Interviewed in Seattle, 2007.

Bierley, Paul E. *The Incredible Band of John Philip Sousa*. Chicago: University of Illinois Press, 2006.

Binns, Archie. *Northwest Gateway: The Story of the Port of Seattle*. Garden City, NJ: Doubleday, Doran, 1941.

Blaine, Rev. David, and Catherine Blaine. Letters. Special Collections, University of Washington Libraries.

Blecha, Peter. "Country Music in the Pacific Northwest." HistoryLink.Org, http://www.historylink.org/index.cfm?DisplayPage=output.cfm&file_id=7441. Accessed 2005.

―――. "Lewis, 'Texas' Jim (1909–1990): Seattle's Pioneering 1950s Kiddie-TV Show Host." HistoryLink.Org, http://www.historylink.org/index.cfm?DisplayPage=output.cfm&file_id=8657. Accessed 2009.

Blesh, Rudi, and Harriet Janis. *They All Played Ragtime*. New York: Oak Publications, 1966.

Bobrow, Norm. Interviewed in Seattle, 2004–7.

Boreson, Stan. Interviewed in Seattle, 2005.

Bowie, Mitchell Taylor. Interviewed in Seattle, 1991.

Broderick, Henry. *Seattle's Old Saloons*. Seattle: Dogwood Press, 1966.

Bruen, Hugh. Interviewed in Seattle, 2005.

Brumbaugh, Harley. Interviewed in North Bend, Washington, 2005.

Buerge, David. *Seattle in the 1880s*. Ed. Stuart R. Grover. Seattle: Historical Society of Seattle and King County, 1986.

Burdette, Tamara. Interviewed in Seattle, 2005.

Burnett, Charles "Tiny." Papers. Special Collections, University of Washington Libraries.

Campbell, Esther W. *Bagpipes in the Woodwind Section: A History of the Seattle Symphony Orchestra and Its Women's Association*. Seattle: Esther W. Campbell, 1978.

Casella, Pamella. Interviewed in Seattle, 2008.

Challstedt, Carl. Interviewed in Seattle, 1991.

Chew, Ronald, ed. *Reflections of Seattle's Chinese-Americans: The First 100 Years*. Seattle: University of Washington Press; Seattle: Wing Luke Asian Museum, 1994.

Cloud, Ken. Interviewed in Seattle, 1991.

Collier, James Lincoln. *The Reception of Jazz in America: A New View*. New York: Institute for Studies in American Music, Brooklyn College Conservatory of Music, City University of New York, 1988.

Cornish, Nellie. *Miss Aunt Nellie Cornish: The Autobiography of Nellie C. Cornish*. Seattle: University of Washington Press, 1964.

Coryell, Larry. *Improvising: My Life in Music*. New York: Backbeat Books, 2007.

Crawford, Richard. *America's Musical Life: A History*. New York: W. W. Norton, 2001.

Crusoe, Michael. Interviewed in Seattle, 2008.

Cumming, William. *Sketchbook: A Memoir of the 30s and the Northwest School*. Seattle: University of Washington Press, 1984.

Dahlgren, Martin "Marty." Interviewed in Seattle, 2006.

Darensbourg, Joseph. *Jazz Odyssey: The Autobiography of Joe Darensbourg as told to Peter Vacher*. Supplementary Material Compiled by Peter Vacher. Baton Rouge: Louisiana State University Press, 1987.

Davis, Ronald L. *A History of Music in American Life*. Vol. 1, *The Formative Years, 1862–1865*. Malabar, FL.: Robert Krieger Publishing, 1982.

———. *A History of Music in American Life*. Vol. 2, *The Gilded Years, 1865–1920*. Malabar, FL.: Robert Krieger Publishing, 1982.

———. *A History of Music in American Life*. Vol. 3, *The Modern Era, 1920-Present*. Malabar, FL.: Robert Krieger Publishing, 1982.

de Barros, Paul. *Jackson Street after Hours: The Roots of Jazz in Seattle*. Seattle: Sasquatch Books, 1993.

Dempster, Stuart. Interviewed in Seattle, 2007.

Denny, Emily Inez. *Blazing the Way, or, True Stories, Songs, and Sketches of Puget Sound and Other Pioneers*. Seattle: Rainier Printing, 1909.

Di Biase, Linda Popp. "Culture at the 'End of the Line': The Arts in Seattle, 1914–1983." Master's thesis, California State University, 1984.

Downey, Roger. Interviewed via e-mail, 2007.

Eaton, Quaintance, ed. *Musical U.S.A.: How Music Developed in Major American Cities*. New York: Allen, Towne and Heath, 1949.

Elliott, Eugene Clinton. *A History of Variety-Vaudeville in Seattle: From the Beginning to 1914*. Seattle: University of Washington Press, 1944.

The Fashion Group. *The Heritage of Seattle Hotels: 1853–1970*. Seattle: The Fashion Group, 1971.

Firth, Don. Interviewed in Seattle, 2008.

Flom, Eric L. "The Theatrical History of Seattle to 1930." In *More Voices, New Stories: King County, Washington's First 150 Years*, ed. Mary C. Wright, 1–40. Seattle: Pacific Northwest Historians Guild, 2002.

Garrett, Burke. Interviewed at Federal Way, Washington, 2004.

Gastil, Raymond D. "The Pacific Northwest as a Cultural Region: A Symposium." *Pacific Northwest Quarterly* 64, no. 4 (October 1973): 147–62.

Giger, Dick. Interviewed at Seattle, 2005.

Gilbert, Howard. Interviewed at Quilcene, Washington, 2004.

Gilmour, J. D. *Sir Thomas Beecham: The Seattle Years, 1941–1943: A Documentary Presentation of News Media Articles*. Compiled and Edited by J. D. Gilmour. Aberdeen, WA: World Press, 1978.

Glenn, Don. Interviewed in Seattle, 2004.

Goff, Scott. Interviewed in Seattle, 2007.

Goleeke, John Wallace. "A History of the Male Chorus Singing Movement in Seattle." Ph.D. diss., University of Washington, 1969.

Grant, Howard F. *The Story of Seattle's Early Theaters*. Seattle: University Bookstore, 1934.

Gray, Maxine Cushing. Interviewed by Jill Severn. Radio KING-FM, June 15, 1977. Special Collections, University of Washington Libraries.

Greene, Victor. *A Passion for Polka: Old-Time Ethnic Music in America*. Berkeley: University of California Press, 1992.

Greer, Ian. "Seattle's Local Musicians: One Hundred Years with the AFM." Master's thesis, Bard College, 1968.

Gross, Ed. Interviewed in Seattle, 2005.

Guitar, Bonnie. Interviewed in Soap Lake, Washington, 2007.

Gushee, Lawrence. *Pioneers of Jazz: The Story of the Creole Band.* London: Oxford University Press, 2005.

Haarsager, Sandra. *Bertha Knight Landes of Seattle: Big-City Mayor.* Norman: University of Oklahoma Press, 1994.

Haines, Roberta. "Singers, Dancers, Dreamers, Travelers. Native-American Song Traditions, Musical Instruments, and Dance Regalia in Washington State." In *Spirit of the First People: Native-American Musical Traditions in Washington State*, ed. Esme Ryan and Willie Smith, 6–24. Seattle: University of Washington Press, 1999.

Hammon, Gary. Interviewed in Seattle, 2008.

Handy, William C. *Father of the Blues: An Autobiography.* New York: Da Capo Press, 1991.

Harich-Schneider, Eta. "The Relations of Foreign and Native Elements in the Development of Japanese Music." Master's thesis, University of Washington, 1954.

Hazen, Margaret Hindle, and Robert Hazen. *The Music Men: An Illustrated History of Brass Bands in America, 1800–1921.* Washington, DC: Smithsonian Press, 1987.

Hill, Bob. Interviewed in Edmonds, Washington, 2005.

Hobi, Mike. Interviewed in Renton, Washington, 2007.

Holden, Dave. Interviewed in Kent, Washington, 2009.

Holden, Grace. Interviewed in Seattle, 2009.

Howard, Wyatt. Interviewed in Seattle, 1991.

Hungerford, Jack. Interviewed in Union, Washington, 2004.

Jessen, Johnnie. *It's All in the Tone: The Life and Music of Johnnie Jessen. As told to Kim Pearson.* Seattle: Jessen Music Foundation, 2001.

Jewell, E. Harvey. "Performances of Contemporary and American Music in Seattle, 1853–1912." Ph.D. diss., University of Washington, 1977.

Jones, Quincy. *Q: The Autobiography of Quincy Jones.* New York: Doubleday, 2001.

Katims, Milton. Video interview by Louis R. Guzzo, May 10, 1986. Seattle Collection, Seattle Public Library.

Katims, Milton, and Virginia Katims. *The Pleasure Was Ours: Personal Encounters with the Greats, the Near-Greats and the Ingrates.* Mill Valley, CA: Vision Books International, 2004.

Keen, Stan. Interviewed in Sequim, Washington, 2006.

Keller, David. "Seattle's Black Musicians." Master's thesis, Western Washington University, 1996.

———. "Sweethearts of Jazz: The Women of Seattle's Black Musicians' Union." *Columbia* 23, no. 4 (Winter 2009–10): 6–12.

King, Sally. Interviewed in Edmonds, Washington, 2004–5.

Kleeb, Milt. Interviewed in Bellingham, Washington, 2004.

Klos, Lloyd E. "The Life and Times of Gaylord Carter." *Theater Organ/Bombarde* 9, no. 5 (October 1967): 5, 36–40.

Knapp, James. Interviewed in Seattle, 2010.

Knudsen, Alf Lunder. "The Norwegian Male Chorus Movement in America: A Study." Ph.D. diss., University of Washington, 1989.

Kraft, James P. *Stage to Studio: Musicians and the Sound Revolution, 1890–1950.* Baltimore: Johns Hopkins University Press, 1996.

Landon, John W. *Behold the Mighty Wurlitzer: The History of the Theater Pipe Organ.* Westport, CT: Greenwood Press, 1983.

Lee, Ed. Interviewed in Seattle, 2008.

Lehmann, Hans, and Thelma Lehmann. *Out of the Cultural Dustbin: Sentimental Musings on the Arts and Music in Seattle from 1936 to 1992.* Seattle: Crowley Associates, 1992.

Leinonen, Pete. Interviewed in Seattle, 2004–7.

Leiter, Robert D. *The Musicians and Petrillo.* New York: Bookman Associates, 1953.

Lilienthal, Meta Stren. *From Fireside to Factory.* New York: Rand School of Social Science, 1916.

Locke, Ralph P., and Cyrilla Barr, eds. *Cultivating Music in America: Women Patrons and Activists since 1860.* Berkeley: University of California Press, 1997.

Loesser, Arthur. *Men, Women, and Pianos: A Social History.* New York: Simon and Schuster, 1954.

Lomax, Alan. *Mister Jelly Roll: The Fortunes of Jelly Roll Morton, New Orleans Creole and "Inventor of Jazz."* Berkeley: University of California Press, 1950.

MacDonald, Wally. "A Forty-Nine-Year Musical History of the Northwest." Unpublished manuscript. Musicians' Association of Seattle, Local 76–493, n.d.

McKay, Frederick Leslie. *McKay's Music: The Composer Chronicles: George Frederick McKay's Musical Trek through the Landscape of 20th Century America.* Seattle: Frederick Leslie McKay, 2007.

McKinney, Rev. Samuel. Interviewed in Seattle, 2005.

Metcalf, Joni. Interviewed in Seattle, 2010.

Miller, Jay. *Lushootseed Culture and the Shamanic Odyssey: An Anchored Radiance.* Lincoln: University of Nebraska Press, 1999.

Mitchell, Lucy. Interviewed in Seattle and Belfair, Washington, 2004–5.

Morgan, Murray. *Skid Road: An Informal Portrait of Seattle.* Seattle: University of Washington Press, 1951.

Moton, Johnny. Interviewed in Seattle, 2005.

Mumford, Esther. *Seattle's Black Victorians, 1852–1901.* Seattle: Ananse Press, 1980.

Muri, John. "Playing the Film." *Theater Organ* 16, no. 3 (June 1974): 28–29.

Musicians' Association of Seattle, Local 76–493, American Federation of Musicians. Meeting minutes, 1889–1964.

Musicland. Musicians' Association of Seattle, Local 76–493, American Federation of Musicians, 1922–1964.

Mussulman, Joseph A. *Music in the Cultured Generation: A Social History of Music in America, 1870–1900.* Evanston, IL: Northwestern University Press, 1971.

Nelson, Gerald B. *Seattle: The Life and Times of an American City.* New York: Alfred A. Knopf, 1977.

Newell, Gordon. *Westward to Alki: The Story of David and Louisa Denny.* Seattle: Superior Publishing, 1977.

New Grove Dictionary of American Music, vol. 3. New York: Macmillan Press, 1986.

Nim, Craig. Interviewed in Seattle, 2008.

Noonan, Jeffrey J. *The Guitar in America: Victorian Era to Jazz Age.* Jackson: University Press of Mississippi, 2008.

Nordal, Marius. "Floyd Standifer Jr., 1929–2007." *All About Jazz Seattle* 24 (April 2007).

Nusbaum, Philip. "Norwegian Traditional Music in Minnesota." In *American Musical Traditions.* Vol. 4, *European-American Music.* Ed. Jeff Todd Titon and Bob Carlin, 112–14. New York: Smithsonian Folkways, 2002.

Pacific Northwest Sheet Music Collection. Special Collections, University of Washington Libraries.

Phillips, Ronald. Interviewed in Seattle, 1992.

Phillips, Ronald. Papers. Special Collections, University of Washington Libraries.

Piatt, Andy. Interviewed in Seattle, 2004.

Pierce, J. Kingston. *Eccentric Seattle: Pillars and Pariahs Who Made the City Not Such a Boring Place after All.* Pullman: Washington State University Press, 2003.

Pierce, Ronnie. Interviewed in Seattle, 2003–10.

Potebnya, Nick. Interviewed in Seattle, 2004.

Prosch, Thomas W. "A Chronological History of Seattle from 1850 to 1897." Seattle: Thomas W. Prosch, 1901.

Puget Sound Theater Organ Society. "Puget Sound Pipeline." 2006. http://www.pstos.org. Accessed 2007.

Rasmussen, James. Interviewed in Seattle, 2007.

Rege, Karen. "Ticklers' Secrets. Ragtime Performance Practices, 1900–1920: A Bibliographic Essay." In *Perspectives on American Music, 1900–1950,* ed. Michael Saffle, 19–49. New York: Garland Publications, 2000.

Richardson, David. *Puget Sounds:. A Nostalgic Review of Radio and TV in the Great Northwest.* Seattle: Superior Publishers, 1981.

Riddle, Ronald. *Flying Dragons, Flowing Streams: Music in the Life of San Francisco's Chinese.* Westport, CT: Greenwood Press, 1983.

Roberts, Jack. Interviewed in Kenmore, Washington, 2006.

Roberts, Jim. *How the Fender Bass Changed the World.* San Francisco: Backbeat Books, 2001.

Rose, Dick. Interviewed in Seattle, 2004.

Rublowsky, John. *Music in America.* New York: Crowell-Collier Press, 1967.

Ryan, Esme, and Willie Smyth, eds. *Spirit of the First People: Native American Music Traditions of Washington State.* Seattle: University of Washington Press, 1999.

Sablosky, Irving L. *American Music.* Chicago: University of Chicago Press, 1969.

———. *What They Heard: Music in America, 1852–1881, from the Pages of Dwight's Journal of Music.* Baton Rouge: Louisiana State University Press, 1986.

Sale, Roger. *Seattle, Past to Present.* Seattle: University of Washington Press, 1976.

Sanderson, Richard "Sandy." Interviewed in Edmonds, Washington, 2006.

Sayre, J. Willis. Scrapbook. Special Collections, University of Washington Libraries.

———. *This City of Ours*. Seattle: J. Willis Sayre, 1936.

Schultz, Cecilia Augspurger. Papers. Special Collections, University of Washington Libraries.

Seattle Civic Opera Company. Scrapbook. Special Collections, University of Washington Libraries.

Segell, Michael. *The Devil's Horn: The Story of the Saxophone, from Noisy Novelty to King of Cool*. New York: Picador, 2005.

Seibert, Peter. Interviewed in Seattle, 2010.

Seltzer, George. *Music Matters: The Performer and the American Federation of Musicians*. Metuchen, NJ: The Scarecrow Press, 1989.

Simon, Ron. Interviewed in Seattle, 2007.

Smith, Catherine Parsons. *Making Music in Los Angeles: Transforming the Popular*. Berkeley: University of California Press, 2007.

Smith, Catherine Parsons, and Cynthia S. Richardson. *Mary Carr Moore: American Composer*. Ann Arbor: University of Michigan Press, 1987.

Smith, Cecil "Cec." Scrapbook. Special Collections, University of Washington Libraries.

Smith, Don. Interviewed in 2005.

Smith, Merle Irene. *Seattle Had a Tin Pan Alley, Too!* Seattle: Merle Irene Smith, 1989.

Smith, William O. Interviewed in Seattle, 2006.

Speidel, Bill. *Doc Maynard: The Man Who Invented Seattle*. Seattle: Nettle Creek Publishing, 1978.

Standifer, Floyd Jr. Interviewed in Seattle, 2004.

Stephens, Doug. *Ivar: The Life and Times of Ivar Haglund*. Seattle: Dunhill Publications, 1988.

Stuart, Alice. Interviewed in Tumwater, Washington, 2008.

Sudhalter, Richard M. *Lost Chords: White Musicians and Their Contribution to Jazz, 1915–1945*. Oxford: Oxford University Press, 1999.

Takami, David A. *Divided Destiny: A History of Japanese-Americans in Seattle*. Seattle: University of Washington Press; Seattle: Wing Luke Asian Museum, 1998.

Tawa, Nicholas E. *Sweet Songs for Gentle Americans: The Parlor Song in America, 1790–1860*. Bowling Green, OH: Bowling Green University Popular Press, 1980.

Taylor, Quintard. *The Forging of a Black Community: Seattle's Central District from 1870 through the Civil Rights Era*. Seattle: University of Washington Press, 1994.

Thomas, Jay. Interviewed in Seattle, 2010.

Thomas, Phillip J. *Songs of the Pacific Northwest*. Saanichton, BC: Hancock House Publishers, 1979.

Thrush, Coll. *Native Seattle: Histories from the Crossing-Over Place*. Seattle: University of Washington Press, 2007.

U.S. Bureau of the Census. *Occupations, 1900*. Washington, DC: Bureau of the Census, 1900.

———. *Occupations, 1910*. Washington, DC: Bureau of the Census, 1910.

———. *Occupations, 1920*. Washington, DC: Bureau of the Census, 1920.

———. *Occupations, 1930*. Washington, DC: Bureau of the Census, 1930.

Wagner, Walt. Interviewed via e-mail, 2009.

Watson, Emmett. *Digressions of a Native Son*. Seattle: Pacific Institute, 1982.

Whitesitt, Linda. "The Role of Women Impresarios in American Concert Life, 1871–1933." *American Music* 7, no. 2 (Summer 1989): 159–80.

Wilke, Jim. Interviewed in Seattle, 2008.

Williams, Phil. Interviewed in Seattle, 2008.

Williams, Vivian. Interviewed in Seattle, 2008.

———. "Old-Time Dance Fiddling in the Northwest." In *American Musical Traditions*. Vol. 3, *British Isles Music*, ed. Jeff Todd Titon and Bob Carlin, 160–61. New York: Smithsonian Folkways, 2002.

Wittwer, Johnny. Interviewed in Seattle by Pete Leinonen, 1989.

Wright, Rev. Patrinell Staten. Interviewed in Seattle, 2007.

Index

electric bass, 182, 269, 277, 307, 345n11
electronic music, 240, 255–56, 292
Elks Club: "black," 187, 197; Everett, 201, 226; Lake City, 212
Ellery, Channing, 59–61, 64, 66
Ellington, Edward Kennedy "Duke," 136, 149, 164, 183, 184, 196, 206
El Matador, 282, 284
Engberg, Madame Mary Davenport, 109, 142
English Grand and Comique Opera Company, 30, 80
Entertainers Club, 90, 92
erhu, 130
The Esquires, 269
ethnic music: Chinese, 32–33, 62, 130, 241; French, 62; German, 53, 241, 243; Hawaiian, 62, 116, 207; Italian, 116, 200; Japanese, 62, 131, 132; Latin, 168–69, 262; Mexican, 241; Norwegian, 53–54, 62, 129, 201, 202–3; Philippine, 63; Scottish, 62; Spanish, 62; Swedish, 53, 54, 61, 129, 201, 202–3; Turkish, 62–63
Evans, Bill, 264
Evans, Gil, 296
Evergreen Drifters, 224–26
Excelsior Minstrels, 68
Exner, Dr. Frederick, 190–91, 192

Fabor Records, 208
The Facts, 276
Fantasy Records, 285
Farwell, Arthur, 61, 81
Feather, Leonard, 190
Federal Music Project. See Works Progress Administration (WPA) Federal Music Project
female impersonators, 128
Fengler, Gretchen, 106
Fengler, Julie, 106
Fiedler, Arthur, 229
Field, Joe, 296
Fifth Avenue Theater, 98, 118, 123, 206

Finch, Otis "Candy," 293
Fiorito, Ted, 126
Firth, Don, 215, 216, 219, 282, 285, 287
Fisher, Orin, 115
Fitzgerald, Ella, 210, 211
Flame Tavern, 183
Flotow, Friedrich von, 30
flute, 20, 35, 40, 52, 60, 110, 113, 125, 131, 132, 135, 154, 161, 183, 201, 277
folk music, 213–14, 215, 216, 217, 218–19, 241, 251, 282, 283, 284–89
Foo Hsing Theater, 241
Foosness, Martha, 98, 105
Ford, Bruce, 176, 242
Ford, Viva, 105, 115
Ford Foundation, 253
Fort, Syvilla, 254
The Four Freshmen, 210
Fowler, David, 218
Fox Theater, 96, 123, 206. See also Music Hall Theater
Franck, Cesar, 76
Frederick and Nelson, 94, 102, 200–201, 228, 268
Freeman, Miller, 82, 83
French horn, 60, 77, 80, 157, 252
Friedlander, Paul, 318
Friesen, Dave, 261
Frye, George, 24–26, 31
Frye's Opera House, 33, 68

gamelan, 254
Gandy, Joseph, 155
Garber, Jan, 147
Garden of Allah, 128
Garred, Milton, 183, 197, 264
Garrett, Burke, 244–46
Gavrilowitsch, Ossip, 108
Gershwin, George, 96, 102, 139–40
Getz, Stan, 168, 188, 260
Gibson, Earl, 114
Gilbert, Howard, 241–43, 244, 252, 261, 312, 329
Gill, Elmer, 169, 182, 199, 205, 236

Mardi Gras Grill, 169, 264, 274

marimba, 103, 199, 253

Martin, Leslie "Tiny," 134, 232, 234, 236, 268, 269

Martin, Suzanne, 152–53

Martin, Vic, 221, 226

The Mastersounds, 182, 344n3

Mata, Eduardo, 312

McClelland, William R. "Bus," 128

McCreery, Ruth Allen, 250–51

McCune, Don, 215

McDowell, Fred, 287

McGlothern, Harriet, 200

McKay, George Frederick, 139, 214, 254, 257, 333

McKee, Garcia, 197

McKinney, Rev. Samuel, 279

Meany, Edmond, 257

Meany Hall. *See* University of Washington

Meeker, Ezra, 20

Meier, Ernest A. R., 66

Melchior, Lauritz, 139

The Melo-Dears, 152

Melody Shop, 45, 47

Mendelssohn, Felix, 138, 150

Menuhin, Yehudi, 229

Mercer, Sarah, 20

Mercer, Tom, 20

Merchants Café, 292

Meremblum, Peter, 110

Meriggioli, Glauco, 110, 113, 125, 309

Merola, Gaetano, 319

Merriam, H. G., 333

Metcalf, Chuck, 193, 260, 263, 268

Metcalf, Joni, 210, 263, 295–96

Metropolitan Opera Co., 80, 113, 150, 321

Metropolitan Theater, 78, 79, 110, 138, 142, 167

Meyerbeer, Giacomo, 35

Meyers, Victor A. "Vic," 103, 105, 114, 126, 127, 140, 147, 174, 242

Miedel, Rainer, 306, 312–14

Milhaud, Darius, 291

Miller, Glenn, 146, 175, 245

Miller, Ned, 207

Mills Brothers, 160

Modern Jazz Quartet, 292

The Modernaires, 210, 212

Monroe, Bill, 287

Montgomery, Buddy, 182

Montgomery, Monk, 182

Montgomery, Wes, 182

Moore, Donovan, 98, 99

Moore, Mary Carr, 61, 81, 139, 333, 334, 340n24

Moore Theater, 67, 76, 77, 78, 80, 81, 101, 143, 156, 167, 179, 219

Morehouse, Roland "Rollie," 161, 192

Mormon Tabernacle Choir, 61, 64

Morton, Ferdinand "Jelly Roll," 68–69, 90, 92, 341n5

Moten, Benny, 195

Moton, Johnny, 195, 196, 197–99, 237

Mount Zion Baptist Church, 73, 278–79, 302

movie music, 57, 58, 59, 97–98, 99, 100–101, 117–19, 122–23, 304, 339n8, 341n9

Mowrey, Dent, 80, 110

Mozart, Wolfgang Amadeus, 113, 150, 151, 229, 313, 320

Mumford, Esther, 68, 339n13

Murtagh, Henry, 57

Music and Musicians, 83, 91

Music Box Theater, 101

Music Conservatory of the Northwest, 66

Music Hall Theater, 150. *See also* Fox Theater

Music Performance Trust Fund (MPTF), 171, 174, 234, 246

Musical Courier, 91

Musical Guild Association, 235

Musical Protection League, 118

Musicians' Association of Seattle Local 458, AFM, 72, 96

Musicians' Association of Seattle Local 493, AFM, 96, 134–35, 148, 164, 236–37

organ: electric, 199–200, 245, 262, 264,
    274, 275, 276, 278; pipe, 57, 58, 59,
    97–98, 99, 123, 128, 129, 200, 257,
    338n3, 339n8, 341n9; reed, 20, 21
Original Dixieland Jazz Band, 71
Ormandy, Eugene, 259
Orpheum Theater (first), 78, 93, 97, 100
Orpheum Theater (second), 100, 123
Ory, Edward "Kid," 190–91
Our House Saloon, 37–38

Pacific Cornet Band, 29
Pacific Northwest Folklore Society, 219, 282
Pacific Northwest Symphony Orchestra,
    154
Palace Hip Theater, 97, 101, 117
Palladium Ballroom, 157, 174
Palomar Theater, 101, 123, 159
Pamir Espresso House, 282, 283, 286
Pantages, Alexander, 56, 70
Pantages Theater (first), 51, 56, 70, 83, 97
Pantages Theater (second), 105, 118, 123.
    See also Palomar Theater
Paramount Theater, 99, 123
Parker, Charlie, 167, 168, 185, 188
Parker's Ballroom, 5, 174, 175, 241, 246,
    248, 278
Parris, Robert, 251
The Pastels, 210
Patchen, Kenneth, 191
Patrons of Northwest Cultural and Histori-
    cal Organizations (PONCHO), 318
Patton, "Big" John, 278
Patty, Stanton, 159
Pavlova, Anna, 110
Payne, John C., 62
Peabody, Zoe, 52, 205, 212, 213
Peacock, Gary, 261, 268, 295
Pelletier, Harry, 66, 110, 119
Pennell, John, 21
Penthouse, 260–62
People's Theater, 34, 47
Pepper, Jim, 13–14
Peralta, Frances, 113

Perboner, H. Bernhard, 52
Peters, Roberta, 319
Peterson, Dave, 295
Peterson, Milo, 296
Peterson, Virginia. See Katims, Virginia
Pete's Poop Deck, 182–83, 260, 262
Petrillo, James C., 169–71, 235, 236, 237,
    328
Philadelphia String Quartet, 259–60
Philharmonic and Choral Society of
    Seattle, 27, 53, 74
Phillips, Ronald, 101–2, 112, 125, 140, 145,
    150, 151, 152, 155, 176, 245, 269, 313
phonograph records, 87, 114–16, 121, 122,
    151, 170, 173, 180, 190–91, 197, 207–9,
    210–11, 219, 220–21, 226, 232, 233, 234,
    249, 264, 270, 276, 281, 283, 285, 286,
    292, 342n22
piano: 22–24, 27, 29, 31, 38–39, 41, 45,
    47–48, 49, 51, 52, 57, 68, 69, 71, 77, 80,
    92, 93, 94, 95, 101, 104, 105–10, 114, 123,
    127, 128, 133, 135–36, 140, 146, 147, 149,
    153, 161, 165, 169, 174, 176, 177, 178, 182,
    183, 189, 190, 191, 192, 195, 196, 197,
    199, 210, 214, 222, 226, 229, 236, 241,
    247, 249, 254, 255, 257, 258, 260, 261,
    263, 267, 268, 271–72, 273–74, 292, 293,
    295, 296, 297, 299, 300, 301, 302, 304
Pierre, Al, 149, 165
Pierce, Ronnie, 94, 147, 157–63, 170, 174,
    240, 297–98, 299, 300
Pigford, Major, 149, 165, 166
Pillar, Max, 177, 247–48
Pioneer Square, 36, 102, 182–83, 188, 193,
    200, 287, 291, 292, 327
Pixley Sisters, 30, 51
The Place Next Door, 282, 284, 286–87
Plath, Leon, 160, 297
Playland Amusement Park, 132
Poindexter, Pony, 168
Poore, Hugh "Cowboy Joe," 116, 220
Potebnya, Nick, 236, 331–32
Powell, Bud, 194
Powell, Maude, 79

154, 308, 310–11, 314, 347n10; venues, 77, 78, 108, 113, 139–40, 150, 154, 156, 227, 229, 232, 249, 250; wages, 141, 231–32, 252, 307; women in, 107, 151, 249, 312

Seattle Tennis Club, 93, 166, 194

Seattle Theater (first), 52, 66*

Seattle Theater (second). *See* Paramount Theater

Seattle Times, 59, 77, 79, 80, 140, 155, 231, 258, 310–11, 320

Seattle Town and Country Club, 3, 180–82, 212, 291

Seattle World's Fair, Century 21 Exposition: creation of, 239; marching band, 240–41; music at, 240, 241, 285, 318; venues, 241, 249, 285, 318

Seattle Youth Symphony, 156

Seeger, Mike, 288

Seeger, Pete, 214, 216, 219, 282, 286

Seibert, Ellen and Peter, 305, 333–34

Seig, Lee Paul, 134

Sennett, Murray, 177, 190, 297

Sepia Records, 281

Setterberg, Doug, 204, 215

Seven Cedars Ballroom, 203

Seward Park, 264

shamisen, *131*, 132

Shangrow, George, 305

Shankar, Uday, 328

Shapiro, Bernard, 252, 255, 310

sheet music, 20, 22, 29, 39, 44–45, *46*, 47, 65

Sheriff Tex. *See* Lewis, "Texas" Jim

Shevenko, Jimmy, 160–61

Sibelius, Jan, 79, 112, 151

Siegl, Henry, 250, 313

The Signatures, 210–11

Silver Slipper, 128

Simon, Morris "Mori," *178*, 268, 306, 329

Simon, Ron, 306–7

Sing Verein Arion/Germania, 53

Singers' Association of America, 279

Singleterry, Preston, 14

Skowronek, Felix, 309

Smith, Cecil "Cec," 104, 132

Smith, E. Russell "Noodles," 68, 90, 91, 92, 135

Smith, Harry, 216

Smith, Jimmy, 262

Smith, Lillian, 71

Smith, William O., 258, 291–92, 293, 331

Sokol, Vilem, 305

Sokoloff, Nikolai, 141–42, 149

Songs of the Workers, 213, 219

Sonora Records, 170

Souders, John R. "Jackie," 104, 105, 114, 164, 174, *176*, 177, 200, 210, 211, 240, 241–42, 245, 246–47

Soul Cellar, 276

Sousa, John Philip, 35, 113, 170, 327, 339n9

Spanish Castle, 126, 161, 163, 174, 224, 234, 243

Spargur, John, 79–80, 82, 84, 101, 108, *111*, 123, 125, 142, 254

Speidel, William, 6

Sphinx Organization, 316

Spikes, Benjamin "Reb," 90, 135

Spinning Wheel, 128, 169, 199

Sprotte, Mr. and Mrs. Berthold, 81–82

Squire, Watson C., 31

Squire's Opera House, 23, 31, 80

Standard Grand Opera Co., 81–82, 317

Standard Oil Co. of California, 116, 139

Standifer, Floyd Jr., 137, 149, 165–67, 183–88, 189, 191, 194, 201, 236, 237, 244, 263, 264, 271, 295, 328–29

Staten, Patrinell. *See* Wright, Rev. Patrinell Staten

steel guitar (lap/pedal), 62, 206, 207, 345n11

Steinbrueck, Victor, 333

Stern, Isaac, 229, 233

Stettler, Dave, *178*, 183

Stimson, Harriet Overton, 110–11, 124

Stockhausen, Karlheinz, 255

Stokowsky, Leopold, 229

Storm, Anson "Bud," 147, 164